KT-177-711

LANDOWNERSHIP AND POWER IN MODERN EUROPE

Edited by

RALPH GIBSON & MARTIN BLINKHORN

HarperCollins*Academic*
An imprint of HarperCollins*Publishers*

Published by
HarperCollins*Academic*
77–85 Fulham Palace Road
Hammersmith
London W6 8JB
UK

10 East 53rd Street
New York, NY 10022
USA

First published in 1991

ISBN 0-04-940091-6

British Library Cataloguing in Publication Data

A catalogue record for this book is available
from the British Library

Library of Congress Cataloging in Publication Data

A catalog record for this book is available on request

Typeset in 10 on 12 point Garamond by Fotographics (Bedford) Ltd
and printed in Great Britain by The University Press, Cambridge

Contents

Acknowledgements

We wish to thank the Economic and Social Research Council for funding in 1987 the seminar at Lancaster of which this book is the final fruit. Our thanks are also due to those academic colleagues who, as guests at the seminar and without contributing directly to this volume, nevertheless influenced it through their participation, comment, criticism and support: John Beckett, Paul Corner, John Davis, Dick Geary, Peter Jones, Yvon Lamy, Roger Magraw, Roger Price, Keith Tribe, Bill Vaughan, John Walton and Michael Winstanley. Finally, we should like to express our gratitude to Jane Harris-Matthews, who took the project on, nursed it and chivvied us through some difficult times thereafer, and to our great regret left Unwin Hyman just two weeks before the final typescript was delivered.

Ralph Gibson and Martin Blinkhorn

Introduction

Ralph Gibson and Martin Blinkhorn

This book is about the exercise of power. As André-Jean Tudesq remarked in his monumental study of French elites in the first half of the nineteenth century:

> Social power, the influence exerted by one man over other men, presents one of the most universal – and also the most complex – problems in the study of human relations. . . . The whole history of humanity could be written, or re-written, in the perspective of the subordination of men to a minority.[1]

It is that control of minorities by elites which interests us here. While the phenomenon is universal, this study is inevitably limited in both time and space. Obviously, we are concerned here only with rural society. The scene is exclusively western and central European: three of the studies in this collection are set in France, three in Germany, two in Italy, two in Spain, one in England and one in Ireland. Any generalizations made in this introduction are therefore limited to Europe – and to those parts of it covered by our contributors. This study is also limited in time, to the period from the late eighteenth century to the mid-twentieth. We are thus looking, for the most part, at European rural society after Emancipation (though the German case studies include periods before Emancipation was complete) and before the utter transformation of rural society in Europe after the Second World War.

The case studies to which the body of this book is devoted are mostly of a very local or regional kind. All our contributors have been asked to address themselves to the exercise of power in the particular rural society with which they are concerned. The purpose of this introduction is to try to bring together their material, along with material from elsewhere, in the form of some synthetic generalizations about the way power has been exercised within European rural society in modern times, and what factors affected the success of those who were trying to exercise it.

There already exists a massive literature on *conflict* in rural society – on movements which contested existing power structures, and on what determined their success or failure.[2] We shall evidently be much concerned with such phenomena – particularly where Italy, Spain and Ireland are concerned. One of the purposes of this book, however, is to reverse the perspective, to look in the first instance at the actual exercise of power, rather than at the ways in which such power was contested. This does not imply any ideological preference for stable power situations – in fact, quite the contrary (at least as far as the editors are concerned). But it does mean that our contributors, and we ourselves in this introduction, are preoccupied with the mechanisms of the successful exercise of power as much as with its failure. We hope that this perspective, less common in historical studies, will help in the study of stable power structures and of how and in what conditions they may be contested.

The dramatis personae of this book are 'landowners' and 'peasants'. This involves some unavoidably loose definitions. In the first place, those who exercised power in rural society were not always land*owners*. The chronic absenteeism of landowners in certain societies could effectively abandon power into the hands of their representatives. As Tim Rees emphasizes for the Spanish province of Badajoz, *labradores* (large tenants) and estate managers were often the real power elite in the countryside. In Spain more generally, the phenomenon of *caciquismo* often meant that effective power lay in the hands of local bosses whose ability to control others, while not necessarily resting on legal ownership of large quantities of land, might be enormous: in an inquiry into *caciquismo* around 1900, a respondent from Córdoba province reported that 'when a drought scorches the fields, the local people say: Tolico does not want it to rain'.[3] In western Sicily, during the eighteenth and nineteenth centuries, the *gabellotti* – usually 'ambitious and ruthless men' – who rented the latifundia of absentee Palermitan landowners took control of the countryside (except in so far as they shared it with the Mafia).[4] In the twentieth century, the Crotonese district of Calabria saw the rise of *industrianti*, who rented land in large quantities and by the 1940s controlled half the latifundia of the area, savagely exploiting both the land and the people.[5] In this volume, Frank Snowden shows the power of the Apulian *massari* (an even harder-nosed Italian equivalent of the *labradores* of Badajoz) and Anthony Cardoza describes how the large leaseholders of the province of Bologna steadily – though incompletely – elbowed the old landed elite out of positions of power.[6]

The concept 'landowners' as used in this introduction may thus be a rather imprecise one. It is, however, a term which has led to the spilling of much less ink – and academic blood – than has the term 'peasant'. Anthropologists in particular can, as Roland Sarti remarks, 'be very touchy about who gets to be called a peasant'.[7] There is often a determination to exclude landless labourers entirely from the category of 'peasant'. Peasants are seen as being necessarily landowning, family-based, part of a state system creaming off their surplus, and having various other characteristics which students of peasant society seem to add or subtract at will.[8] No doubt the anthropologists have compelling reasons for doing this, for the purposes of their own analyses. But where *power* in rural society is the issue, we need a term which includes not only those who in one way or another 'hold' land, but also those at the bottom of the social pile, usually with nothing to sell but their labour. We shall therefore here follow the lead of Henry Landsberger in using the term indiscriminately to refer to all cultivators who occupy relatively low positions in rural society.[9] A study of *power* in rural society could scarcely do otherwise.

The rest of this introduction will be devoted to our attempt to develop a framework of analysis for studying the exercise of power by landowners in modern European history. What we propose is merely a tentative typology, and one which has modest ambitions. It is not intended to be anything more than classificatory; it has no claim to the explanatory value of (say) Weber's typology of legitimate authority, or Gramsci's concept of hegemony. (Both Weber's and Gramsci's concepts might very well be applied to the analysis of power relations in rural society, but we have found them, for various reasons, insufficiently comprehensive.)[10] Our typology is scarcely even a 'model', but rather a simple check-list of elements that one might consider when attempting to analyse landowners' power. If there is an advantage to the modesty of this ambition, it is that such a check-list is capable of almost indefinite expansion and emendation. It would almost certainly be necessary to modify it for looking at non-European or pre-modern societies. We are fully aware that the same is probably true even within the limited time and space that this volume involves.

Our suggested typology has two major sections. The first deals with the ways in which landowners exercised power, the second with the factors affecting their ability to do so.

I THE WAYS IN WHICH LANDOWNERS EXERCISED POWER

1 Force

This category comprises the use or menace of direct physical violence. It is this element that Weber consciously excluded from his analysis, either regarding it as outside the domain of 'meaningful action', or because of his belief that authority structures could not in the long run endure through coercion alone.[11] In most relationships between landowners and peasants in modern Europe, however, crude physical force has often been either directly present or not very far beneath the surface.

1.1 'Private' force

At the simplest level, landowners provided their own force, as described by Tim Rees in the case of Badajoz before the First World War.[12] Italian examples of recourse to private violence abound. Field guards were a characteristic sight in many parts of the Italian and Sicilian countryside: a typical Sicilian latifundium before the First World War employed five *campieri* on a regular basis to keep control over about a hundred share-croppers (and, during the harvest, about sixty day labourers).[13] Frank Snowden's contribution to this book paints a frightening picture of the naked violence increasingly used to keep the agricultural labour force of Cerignola, in Apulia, under control. Some, at least, of the origins of the Sicilian Mafia lay in the landowners' need for private violence to repress their turbulent peasants, when the state refused to do the job for them – a tradition which resurfaced in murderous form after the Second World War, when some forty left-wing leaders of agricultural unions lost their lives to Mafia violence.[14] The classic example of private violence at the service of a beleaguered landowning class, however, is surely the fascist squads of rural Italy in the aftermath of the First World War, described here by Anthony Cardoza. Tuscany was perhaps the ultimate case, where the fascists' inability to raise any significant support among the peasants themselves meant that Tuscan fascism was singularly marked by violence, the function of which was very clearly to destroy a rampant agrarian revolution.[15]

1.2 'State' force

On the whole, however, landowners seem to have provided their own physical force only when the more efficient – and no doubt for them cheaper – force of the state was for some reason not available (for example, when the Bourbon government of the Two Sicilies, in the first half of the nineteenth century, tried to create a yeoman peasantry, or when Giolitti's prewar governments adopted a policy of neutrality in social conflict, at least in northern Italy).[16] Private violence itself usually required at least the connivance of the state to be effective; otherwise it was all too likely to be met by effective counter-violence. The success of fascist *squadrismo* in destroying the agrarian leagues of the Po Valley, Tuscany, or Apulia thus depended upon the massive collusion of the state apparatus; as one syndicalist leader from Apulia remarked bitterly, 'We were defeated not by the fascists but by the *carabinieri*.'[17] In Badajoz province in the 1930s, as elsewhere in southern Spain, landowners were able to mobilize a fair amount of private violence, but as it threatened to prove inadequate they, together with the larger landowners of the rest of Spain, turned in 1936 to the army and to an ultimately more friendly state.

Most of these examples come from Spain and Italy, where the threat of agrarian revolution in the early twentieth century was manifest. Landowners' recourse to state force has been common, however, even in apparently more peaceful societies. Silesia saw extensive peasant unrest in the eighteenth century (in protest against economic exploitation by Junkers), which was in the last resort put down by 'military execution'.[18] In southeastern France, in

1851, Louis-Napoleon's army was needed against those peasants who fought to preserve a republic which would be 'democratic and social', that is, which would threaten large-scale property.[19] More commonly still, the implicit threat of state violence backed up landowner domination. Even in eighteenth-century England, the prevalence of rick-burning, poaching, threatening letters and other forms of anonymous protest suggests that it was at least in part the armed force of the British state standing in the shadows that kept the English peasant in subjection.[20] In twentieth-century Italy, even though (as Cardoza here points out) the Fascist state was never entirely at the beck and call of landowners, and even if some small substance was given to fascist rhetoric about 'the land to the tiller', it was the implicit violence of the Fascist state that kept the lid on peasant discontent in many parts of the countryside. Thus the fall of Mussolini in 1943 spelled the end of latifundism; as Pino Arlacchi has pointed out in the case of the Crotonese, the end of the Fascist regime 'struck the political prop of baronial power and knocked it from beneath the system'.[21] A Demo-Christian state interested in developing a yeoman peasantry would allow enough rein to postwar peasant mobilization to transform the rural structures of much of Italy.

2 The state as a guarantor of landowner power

The examples given above concern the reliance of landowners on state force, or at least the implicit threat thereof, to bolster their power. More generally, of course, landowner power has often depended on their control of the state, which might well have acquired a legitimacy going beyond the simple resort to physical violence, explicit or implicit.[22] The classic example is no doubt eighteenth-century England, where the state might fairly be described as the executive arm of the landowning class. Landowner grasp of state power may have been slowly eroded during the course of the nineteenth century, but – as Eric Evans points out in his chapter – the process was a slow one; even in the world's first industrial nation, landowners held on to many aspects of state power until at least the First World War. They were, however, less strikingly successful in this respect than the Junkers examined here by Hanna Schissler. The eighteenth century had seen the culmination of a more or less explicit deal between the Prussian Crown and the Junker aristocracy, whereby (in crude terms) the Junkers accepted the national taxation and compulsory military service against which they had previously struggled, in return for their domination of the officer corps and bureaucracy, and above all for royal acceptance of their continued complete seigneurial control of their estates.[23] F. L. Carsten sums up the situation:

> Until the end of the eighteenth century the Prussian nobility retained its domination of state and society. But it was only able to do so because the state preserved its privileges and accorded it massive help: subsidies after

> the long wars, exemptions from many customs and taxes, great efforts to prevent the acquisition of knights' estates by commoners, preference in filling the most important offices, sinecures in cathedral chapters and pious foundations, and last but not least the use of the army against rebellious peasants.[24]

The hiccup of the Reform era was fairly easily surmounted: the liberation of the serfs led in practice to 'an enormous expansion of the large estates' (Franz Schnabel)[25] and one calculation suggests that the period 1811–90 saw the land occupied by great estates in East Elbia grow by two thirds.[26] These estates did not always remain in noble hands, but a very effective process of 'feudalization of the bourgeoisie' ensured that new recruits to the landowning class were rapidly assimilated to the cultural and political world of the Junker aristocracy.[27] Most crucially, the Junkers (to a considerable extent because of Bismarck's political skill) retained their most-favoured-class status with the Prusso-German state, even through the period of Germany's spectacularly successful industrialization. Thus they were able to withstand (for example) the late nineteenth-century crash in agricultural prices, which would mark the beginning of the end for the British landowning class, and which would also see off the rural bourgeoisie in France (see the contributions by Eric Evans and Ralph Gibson). The tariff protection and tax privileges offered to Junker grain producers by the German state helped them to remain more or less economically viable.[28] It was not surprising that Junkers found the new state of the Weimar Republic less to their liking – to the degree that they preferred the rule of even a Bohemian corporal, with ultimately disastrous results not only for Europe but also for themselves.

The Junkers were thus the great success story where the use of the state to back up landowner power was concerned. Other nobilities were less successful. In Hesse-Cassel, studied here by Gregory Pedlow, a nobility which had utterly dominated both landowning and state decision-making in the eighteenth century saw state backing decline sharply in the nineteenth. In France (as the chapters by Pierre Lévêque and Ralph Gibson show) a landowning class threatened by the spectacular spread of democratic socialism in the countryside turned to Napoleon III's Second Empire to save it. This provided a respite for only two decades, however, before universal suffrage (with responsible government) combined with agricultural crisis to produce something like a peasant democracy by 1914. Yet perhaps the most interesting case of a landowning class which suffered from an unsympathetic state is provided by Ireland. Theo Hoppen's contribution shows how Irish landowners, after the 1840s, never had total and unconditional state support. The British state did back their economic demands on tenants – but only within limits; there were few mass evictions.[29] Furthermore, the development of a state police force and civil service, and a professional magistracy, actually weakened landlord power, since government was increasingly conducted in accordance with bureaucratic principle (even if the personnel were from landlord families). The state, Hoppen concludes, 'was more and more establishing itself as an alternative centre of influence and power and as such was not always prepared to dance to the landlords' tune'. In the long run, the inadequate sympathy of the British government for Irish landlords would mean that the land war in Ireland was won by the tenants, who finally came into possession of the land.

Some groups of landowners, when faced with a less than sympathetic state, have been so worried about losing such an essential prop of their power that they have associated themselves with the creation of a new and more favourable state, usually through the use of force. Spain in the 1930s is the paradigmatic example. Martin Blinkhorn's chapter shows how large landowners in Navarre reacted to the advent of a Second Republic which was dedicated, at least in principle, to the redistribution of rural wealth and power. Systematic obstruction limited effective reform in the period 1931–3, after which the *bienio negro* saw a series of more landowner-friendly governments in office. But the electoral victory of the Popular Front in February 1936 unleased such a threat to landowner power (as in the peasant occupations of unused or usurped land) that landowners rapidly involved themselves in conspiracies aimed at overthrowing the regime. The rising of July 1936 was followed by vicious repression of those who had threatened the bases of landowner power. As Tim Rees's account of Badajoz illustrates, much the same story, often in even starker terms, could be told for the rest of Spain.[30]

The experience of parts of Italy in the first quarter of the twentieth century was slightly less violent, but the process was essentially similar. Those who controlled the land in, for example, Bologna, Ferrara, Tuscany and Apulia were under open threat from peasant mobilization. The Giolittian state, with its at least partially applied policy of evenhandedness, and the weak governments of postwar Italy seemed to provide inadequate protection. Landowners (and leasers) thus financed and promoted fascist violence and welcomed the advent of the Fascist state (a process described in the chapters by Anthony Cardoza and Frank Snowden). Mussolini's rise to power should not of course be seen as *merely* a kind of landowner coup, any more than should the Spanish rising of July 1936; the former was an immensely complex process, while the Spanish Civil War involved many issues, notably that of religion, besides the simple defence of landowner power. Yet both are examples of a landowning class's reaction in the face of a state which had ceased, whether via rapid political transformation (as in Spain in 1931) or via a mere shift of policy (as in early twentieth-century Italy), to provide the necessary physical support for, and broader legitimation of, landowner control over rural populations. In these situations, landowners turned once again to force – though of a rather different kind from that discussed in the previous section. For the function of violence in the Italy of the early 1920s and the Spain of 1936–9 went beyond mere repression of rural unrest, to encompass the creation of new states which also would, and for a time did, provide landowner power with a restored legitimacy.

The cases of Hesse-Cassel and Ireland, and perhaps also of the French Third Republic, make it clear that European states – even fairly conservative ones – have not always been wholly sympathetic to large landowners.[31] In many cases, however, the power of landowners has depended upon the backing of state power – whether by brute force, or because the mass of the population accepted the authority of that state as in some way legitimate (as in the case of the peasants of the Périgord who, after having been massively committed to 'democratic socialism', willingly supported the regime of Napoleon III). Where the backing of state power has faltered, as in the Spanish and Italian cases just discussed, landowners have played an active role in organizing the overthrow of the state concerned and its replacement by another, more congenial, one.

Access to state power was thus often crucial in maintaining or, through the creation of a 'new state', reasserting landowner power. Most European landowning classes, however, have hoped in some way to base their control over rural populations on willing acceptance by the latter of the landowners' economic privilege and social authority. It is to this phenomenon that we now turn.

3 Aspects of authority

3.1 Deference

> There is a good deal of historical evidence [writes Howard Newby] to suggest that farmers and landowners have recognized that a labour force that *identified* with the system that subordinated it was in the long run more reliable and more efficient than a group of workers who gave their grudging consent under the threat of sanctions. Employers often therefore set about cultivating this identification.[32]

This is not, of course, always true, as the cases of Badajoz, Bologna and Cerignola in this volume show; many rural elites have relied on naked force, wielded either by themselves or by a sympathetic state. Others, however, liked to think that they were respected and even loved by their peasants. Prussian Junkers on the whole chose to see themselves as patriarchal rulers on their estates; their psychic satisfactions came overwhelmingly from the sense of legitimate authority that they experienced. Some Junkers nevertheless had their doubts. Baron von Bassewitz, in his 1847 memoirs, recalled that in the pre-Reform era the much-talked-of patriarchal relation between landlord and peasant was an exception; most peasants were hostile.[33] More typical perhaps was Elard von Oldenburg-Januschau, who claimed in his memoirs under the Weimar Republic that he had been able to establish a good relationship with his labourers – while admitting that he had been forced 'to confront many a rebellious and disobedient man personally and enforce order and obedience with his fist'. When he returned to his estates at the end of 1918 he was told that one of his workmen considered himself the new master. He took the man by the ear and asked, 'Who rules in Januschau?' and when he got no reply declared, 'I'll hit you in the snout until you stand on your head.' The man lost courage and acknowledged von Oldenburg-Januschau as his master, and 'the mutual confidence was restored'.[34] English landowners in the eighteenth and nineteenth centuries, or *châtelains* in the West of France (see Donald Sutherland's contribution), certainly liked to imagine that they were looked up to with respect and affection by the peasants of their area – a self-image recently brought vividly alive on screen by James Mason in Alan Bridges's *The Shooting Party*.

Were they deluding themselves? It is a very thorny historical problem to decide what subject peoples really thought of those set in authority over them. Were the outward signs of deference (the forelock-tugging in England, the greeting 'I kiss your hand' in Sicily, and so on) merely what John Davis has recently called 'part of the peasants' strategy for survival?'[35] Or were they the outward and visible signs of a genuinely internalized respect? It is desperately hard to tell. Many historians have taken the former view. Frank Snowden has suggested that the ideology of class hegemony which apparently dominated the Tuscan countryside before the First World War was denied by the prevalence of theft, fraud, poaching and even murder that marked relations between sharecroppers and their proprietors.[36] Howard Newby has similarly suggested that the poaching, rick-burning and cattle-maiming of traditional English rural society implies a less than universal internalization of deference.[37] Josef Mooser quotes the *Novelle* writer Annette von Droste-Hulshoff's impression that the peasant saw his lord as

> an arch-enemy and usurper of the property which really belonged to *him*. It was only out of cunning and self-interest that a true son of the land would flatter [the landowner]; in every other way he would do him harm wherever possible.[38]

Roger Price derides the way in which conservative landowners in nineteenth-century France fondly imagined that in the past labourers had freely chosen to accept relationships which were in fact forced on them by links of dependence which were inescapable.[39]

There is thus widespread support for the 'cynical' view of deferential behaviour. Other historians, however, are more prepared to believe that deference could in some circumstances be internalized and genuine. Martin Blinkhorn, in his contribution to this volume, considers that in at least some districts of Navarre 'acceptance of the situation seems to have been relatively deep-rooted and deference genuine', while Donald Sutherland judges that the power of traditional authority in western France was naturally accepted and even actively sought out (as Tocqueville found in 1848). Peter Jones has suggested elsewhere that this was also true of the southern Massif Central, where 'voluntary social subordination made coercion unnecessary'.[40] Since the form, degree and genuineness of deference were in all likelihood dictated by local conditions, this seems to be a matter for judgement by historians deeply familiar with a particular rural society. Perhaps, as James Scott suggests, language provides a clue:

> The role labels that tenants attach to landlords are a good indication of whether they view the relationship as generally fair and collaborative or unjust and speculative.[41]

One might then judge that the Angevin peasants who, as late as the interwar period, would say 'Je suis dans la sujétion de Monsieur X', or the Poitevin peasants who, even under the Fourth Republic, still referred to 'Not' Maître', were not simply being deferential out of calculation and weakness.[42] But the problem of knowing what poor country people really thought about their superiors will remain a difficult one.

3.2 'Traditional' authority

To the degree that landowners managed to attract, or even create, genuine deference, how did they do it? To a considerable extent, by simply being there for a long time. This was Weber's 'traditional' authority, 'resting on an established belief in the sanctity of immemorial traditions and the legitimacy of the status of those exercising authority over them'.[43] Authority resting on this basis is often also referred to as 'paternalist'.[44] It can of course only exist where large-scale property has remained in the hands of more or less the same families for generations. One of the reasons why Silesia was the most troubled part of rural East Elbia in the eighteenth century was the rapid turnover of estate ownership; one Silesian *Landrat* remarked that a nobleman would sell

> an estate as quickly as a garment from his wardrobe, and with the estate unfortunately also his poor subjects who within a year often get several new lords, who demand more from them than their original master

– and thus the bond between lord and peasant 'disintegrates completely'.[45] This kind of thing appears to have happened frequently in the nineteenth century where commercial agriculture took over from older-established and probably less rapacious noble families. As Marx remarked in another context,

> The bourgeoisie, wherever it has got the upper hand, has put an end to all feudal, patriarchal idyllic relations. It has pitilessly torn asunder the motley feudal ties that bound man to his 'natural superiors', and has left remaining no other nexus between man and man than naked self-interest, than callous 'cash payment'.[46]

Several of our contributors point to situations where Marx's analysis was rigorously appropriate: it was a wave of greedy new leaseholders whose drive for capitalist agriculture upset traditional paternalism in the Bolognese countryside, while in Navarre the power of *corraliceros* (mainly bourgeois, or occasionally erstwhile 'rich peasants') was bitterly resented and contested by a peasantry which had largely swallowed the authority of older noble proprietors – at any rate where these were resident.[47] In cases where the old elites remained, however, they continued to exercise 'social power of a traditional kind' (see Pierre Lévêque's chapter on Burgundy) and to derive their authority (or at the very least their security) from 'the simple legitimacy bestowed by time and continuity' (Blinkhorn).

3.3 Patronage and clientelism

'Immemorial custom' would thus sometimes do the trick. Usually, however, it required something more concrete to get subordinates in rural society willingly to accept the authority of the wealthy. Landowners had to show themselves materially *useful* if they did not want their authority – and even their wealth – to be contested. The rendering of such services by landowners has usually been known as 'patronage' and the system whereby the poor are thus tied to the wealthy is often called 'clientelism'.

Patronage in European rural society could take very diverse forms. In the case of Spain, Raymond Carr has pointed out how *caciquismo* was in part, at least, based upon the 'grand *cacique*'s . . . general services to, and interest in, his "country" ', whose enfranchised small farmers' interests he would seek to defend in Madrid, and towards which, if successful, he might channel railways, schools, or even a university.[48] In central and southern Italy it might involve giving cheap loans, employment, dowries for tenants' daughters, free medicine, or finance for parish festivities.[49] It might also take the form of technical assistance with agriculture (though Theo Hoppen here suggests that improving landlords in Ireland were merely likely to make themselves unpopular).[50] In this volume, Pierre Lévêque has catalogued the activities of Burgundian nobles who set out to attach the rural poor to their person, as has Gregory Pedlow for the nobles of Hesse-Cassel. One major form of patronage was simple *charity*. In France at least, noble charity in the nineteenth century was real. One château in the Eure, for example, was said to succour up to 200 poor a week (and as many as 1,600 a week in the 1817 famine); David Higgs is led to refer to 'highly deserving efforts to alleviate human misery at a time when the state had not taken up its responsibilities in this regard'.[51] The royalists of the Mayenne studied by Michel Denis not only had a paternalistic vision of themselves, but were genuinely charitable.[52] Some historians have been dubious as to whether such charity actually amounted to much,[53] but there is in fact a lot of evidence that the French nobility took its charitable self-image seriously and gave away large sums (if not in cash) to the poor.[54] Nor was it just the nobility who were capable of being good *patrons*.

Louis Charles, for example, a typical representative of the rural bourgeoisie in the Var in the early nineteenth century, had distributed large amounts of free grain in time of famine, paid the taxes of a number of hard-up families, kept 30 workers on during winter in his olive oil plant, given clothing and money to conscripts, donated a village fountain costing 10,000 francs, got the prefect to exempt his commune from a decree prohibiting the grazing of goats in the woods, and so on; no wonder that by the time of his death in 1829 he had stamped his moderate republican politics on the commune.[55]

Patronage was of course often used by landlords as a very explicit and calculating means of social control. On the Medici estates of the Altopascio in the eighteenth century, the estate manager often considered petitions from tenants and was perfectly willing to accept their genuineness – but if the behaviour of the tenant was unsatisfactory he was likely to conclude: 'Under these circumstances it does not seem to me that the demeanour of the petitioner is of the sort that merits the charitable subsidy required.'[56] Theo Hoppen has described in this volume how rent arrears were tolerated by certain Irish landlords – but only for those who voted as required. A most striking example of patronage for political purposes comes from Corsica in 1887, when one large landowner told a journalist:

> One of my brothers manages our properties; as the eldest, I'm in charge of the political side. I've devoted my life, and I could almost say our whole fortune, to our clients, and our clients give us their votes. . . . Our properties are let to about fifty sharecroppers on fairly generous conditions which we don't always rigorously enforce anyway. These fifty households live alongside us, and are wholly devoted to us. That's nearly two hundred votes already. . . . In some villages, our land is so mixed up with that of the rest of the inhabitants that if we didn't allow their animals free passage, everyone would find it impossible to pasture them. The soil lies fallow for two years out of three; during that time, we let them run their animals freely. Our woods are similarly left in a state of neglect: any of our friends can pick up firewood there as they please. This tolerance, indispensable for their way of life, attaches to us another three hundred electors. Along with the first lot, they form the nucleus of our followers, those that we can count on. In former times, they would have followed us to war; nowadays they follow us to the ballot box.[57]

The exercise of patronage in such circumstances was scarcely disinterested. In other circumstances, however, it probably was. Pierre Lévêque has described how Édouard Carrelet de Loisy, a wealthy Burgundian landowner, regarded wealth as 'a public duty', imposing very real obligations; there is no reason to doubt his sincerity, or that of others like him. Perhaps, as Michael Thompson argues, most nineteenth-century English landowners regarded the function of the countryside as to provide good sport and neglected their social responsibilities towards the majority of the people living on their estates.[58] If so, and if much the same was true of (for example) many southern Spanish landowners, there were plenty in France, and probably in Germany, who were not like them.

By and large, patronage systems seem to have worked. Peter Jones has argued that the peasants of the southern Massif Central, in the eighteenth and nineteenth centuries, nursed a trans-generational sense of gratitude for services rendered, and that this was the key reason for the durable power of notables in that area; that power was only effectively undermined when the Third Republic established itself as a much wealthier source of patronage, able to attach peasants to the regime not out of republican conviction, but out of a conviction that the Republic was the most munificent source of concrete rewards (particularly state employment) for political loyalty.[59] Henry Landsberger has even argued that among the possible causes of peasant revolution is the failure of landowners to perform such patronage functions.[60] The picture painted by several of our contributors would seem to bear this out: peasant revolution, or a level of unrest that appeared to threaten it, in the province of Badajoz, in the Navarrese Ribera, in Bologna province, or in Apulia does seem to have been directed against a landowning class who were pure creamers-off of surplus, not engaged in any function useful to the peasant.[61]

3.4 Mediation

One form of patronage which has particularly attracted the attention of anthropologists is best referred to as 'mediation'. In any society where village horizons are still very localized, but where villagers are engaged in relations with an outside market or with state authority, *mediators* will be necessary to link peasants to the wider world. Such mediators have been variously referred to in the anthropological literature as (for example) 'brokers' (Wolf), 'hinges' (Redfield), or 'gatekeepers' (Kenny); we adopt here the term used by Sydel Silverman.[62] Silverman suggests, on the basis of the central Italian experience, that mediation became the key form of patronage after national unification in 1860 (that is, when relations with the outside world became more problematic); mediators – still usually landlords – would help their tenants with filling out papers, speaking to bureaucrats, obtaining government benefits (when they later became available), intervening with the *carabinieri* and the courts, providing recommendations for government jobs, and so on.[63] This kind of mediating service could be so crucial in the lives of peasants episodically engaged in national markets or with a national state that it could be very important in conferring legitimacy on the wider authority of those that were able to render it. It may be, of course, that such services were sometimes largely fraudulent. Landed elites may well have been merely returning with one hand what they had first taken away with the other. Douglas Hay has described dramatically how the ability of eighteenth-century English landowners to intervene with the law, and thus to save their clients from the noose, looks a lot less generous when one considers that it was a landowners' state that had legislated capital punishment for such a wide range of offences in the first place; landowners were merely saving peasants from a menace created by landowners themselves.[64] Caroline White has argued, with reference to mid-twentieth-century Italy, that the ability of patrons to render services like the speeding up of pension payments depends on a system that deliberately slows them down in the first place.[65] Nevertheless, there is enough evidence of the mediating function of landowners in European society in modern times to make possible the conclusion that it played an important part in legitimizing landowner authority in the eyes of many peasants. Along with the wider patronage functions of landowners, it was often a key element in enabling them to exercise power.

4 Ideology

It is clear that there was usually a limit to how long landowner domination could be maintained by simple force. Frank Snowden's study of the Apulian town of Cerignola is an excellent case in point.[66] The power of immemorial custom, and practical patronage of various kinds seem to have been more effective. However, the most effective weapons of all for the maintenance of landowner power were probably ideological. A wide variety of ideologies have had at least the objective function of reconciling rural populations with their subordinate lot.

The commonest such ideology in the European context has without doubt been the Christian religion. Catholicism in the west of France, as Donald Sutherland shows, was the key to royalism, and crucial for the continued dominance of traditional landowners. Martin Blinkhorn describes how in Navarre, despite the presence of genuinely social-Catholic impulses, Catholicism over time fulfilled an undeniably conservative role. In Italy, the most socially quiescent regions were precisely those where a conservative Catholicism was strongest (for example, Lombardy and Venetia); in Apulia, or in the reclaimed lands of the Po Valley, where the church's roots were weak, peasant protest in the early twentieth century was at its sharpest.[67] As Tim Rees demonstrates in the case of Badajoz, the same was true in southern Spain. Protestantism could possess a similar function. Eric Evans reminds us of how the established Anglican Church was a linchpin of landowner power in England. Lutheranism in Germany, with its long tradition of acceptance of the established social order, showed itself what Otto Hintze called 'a useful instrument for the domination of the peasant'.[68]

It is thus not surprising that Christianity in its various forms was often seen as a bastion of the social order – so much so that it does need emphasizing that there was nothing *intrinsically* conservative about the Christian religion; everything depended on the circumstances. 'Social'-Catholicism could, in the early twentieth century, be remarkably radical. In parts of northern Spain where the church was deeply entrenched, such as in Navarre, early social-Catholicism displayed a critical attitude towards large landowners, who at the time were mainly identified with 'liberalism'.[69] Italian social-Catholicism, especially in parts of central Italy, possessed a radical wing that was both more genuine and more resistant to conservative erosion than its Spanish counterpart, as evident in the work of Murri and the Catholic peasant leagues – and the leagues' fate at the hands of fascism.

There have been many other ideologies which have fulfilled similar conservative functions in European rural society. One of the commonest has been royalism, in the form of the myth of the benevolent sovereign who is really on the side of the peasants but whose good intentions are thwarted by wicked ministers and landowners. The most famous case, although it falls outside the geographical scope of this volume, is the devotion of many (not all) Russian peasants to the tsar, which meant that even if they were often prepared violently to contest the power of landowners at a local level, they would not strike against the linchpin of the system, the tsar himself – unless it was in the name of someone they believed to be the 'true' tsar.[70] A similar royalist mythology could operate elsewhere, with similar effects.[71] Here again, however, it was not so much the intrinsic content of the ideology that mattered, as the way it operated in the particular local circumstances. Ralph Gibson's study of the Périgord suggests that *anti*-royalism, and *anti*clericalism, served as 'deflecting' ideologies, inasmuch as they deflected the antagonisms of peasants away from bourgeois landowners, onto the largely imaginary menace of royalist restoration and clerical domination. In Navarre, as Martin Blinkhorn shows, the 'alternative royalism' of Carlism played a somewhat similar role in the 1930s, despite its earlier history as a more or less authentic movement of the peasants against the 'liberal' rich. Nationalism, similarly, could cut both ways. In Wilhelmine Germany it may have helped to rally rural producers behind Junker leadership, but in Ireland it was a mobilizing ideology against landlord domination.

5 Hegemony

The list of ideologies that have helped to underpin landowner power could be almost indefinitely prolonged (anti-Semitism is an obvious candidate). It will not do, however, to have an overly simple picture of ideological manipulation. There is an increasing consensus that rural (or urban) populations could not be brought to believe just anything; there had to be something in it for them. In other terms, the development of an ideological hegemony usually involved an ongoing and complex process of interaction, of consensus, of the *negotiation* of consent. This aspect of Gramsci's theorizing about hegemony has recently been much in vogue.[72] It may be noted in passing that those who emphasize this element tend to rely unduly on a now notorious passage in the

Prison Notebooks, which will not perhaps carry the weight of interpretation that is so often placed upon it.[73] But it will certainly help us to avoid a crude manipulative model when looking at relations between landowners and peasants. Peasants who joined right-wing organizations in Wilhelmine Germany were not simply being manipulated, deflected from their true interests by the appeal of nationalism and anti-Semitism; they were also protesting spontaneously against the old *Honoratiorenpolitik* which had ignored their interests since unification.[74] Nor could they be mobilized without offering them something concrete in exchange. The peasant mass membership of the Agrarian League, which campaigned for the tariff protection that was crucial for Junkers, was not in fact having its interests ignored, since German peasants on the whole benefited from agricultural protection.[75] The general lesson of recent work on German rural society before the First World War is that peasants *could* be mobilized by ideologies which united them behind their class enemies, but that for such mobilization to be successful it had to offer the mobilized some concrete benefits.

What is clear is that ideological hegemony, however acquired, was usually crucial to the durable exercise of power by landowners. Irish landlords lost the battle against their tenants, in the long run, because they did not possess that hegemony – unlike their English counterparts, who, in Theo Hoppen's words, 'remained able to contain English farmers within a species of broad cultural hegemony according to which the latter continued to accept landlordism as a "natural reality" '. Such hegemony was never acquired by force, or by appeal to the state; it was more likely to be the product of immemorial tradition and the long-term exercise of patronage by landowners. Without it, they were unlikely to exercise power in the countryside for very long.

II FACTORS AFFECTING THE EXERCISE OF LANDOWNER POWER

1 The structure of landownership

The power that landowners were able to exercise was evidently correlated with the amount of land they owned. The power of the nineteenth-century British landed elite, of whom under 7,000 owned in 1873 about 80 per cent of the surface area of Britain, was almost inevitably greater than that exercised by the landed elite of France, where in 1882 the richest 100,000 proprietors owned only some 40 per cent of the land.[76] The possession of broad acres seems to have been particularly likely to confer power in localities where such ownership was concentrated in one or very few pairs of hands. The 'Captain Swing' riots in the south of England in the 1830s appear to have been much less likely to affect villages where ownership of the land rested with one man or with a small oligarchy.[77] The Limousin area of France provided the proof *a contrario*: it was an area with few large landowners, even by French standards, and Alain Corbin believes that this was one of the major reasons why it became in the nineteenth century (and remains) perhaps the most radical part of rural France.[78]

In a sense, power must have been proportional to landownership, inasmuch as a population containing a solid phalanx of landowning peasants was evidently harder to push around than one composed of tenants or labourers who depended utterly on major landowners for land or employment. Yet several of our contributors have observed that the relationship between landownership, as such, and power is far from straightforward. Pierre Lévêque has noted that the power of Burgundian landowners did not simply depend on the ownership of land. Donald Sutherland notes of the West of France that 'land brought power, but only after certain intervening factors are taken into account . . . there was no lock-step simple relationship between land and power'. The largest, mainly noble, landowners in Navarre, Martin Blinkhorn points out, may before 1931 have dominated the lives of the peasants in their own former *señoríos*, yet they possessed little or no wider social or political power within the 'kingdom'. Ralph Gibson, finally, argues that the ownership of considerable tracts of land conferred on Périgord nobles almost no ability to control the peasantry at all. This less than one-to-one relationship between the actual ownership of land and the exercise of power is of course scarcely a new discovery. It is nearly thirty years since Paul Bois exploded André Siegfried's belief that the power of conservative landowners in the West of France depended on the ownership of land, demonstrating 'the total failure of any attempt to explain political attitudes by the structure of landed property'.[79] There are in fact some good reasons why a great concentration of landed property, at least when it is farmed by wage labour, should on many occasions have failed to confer power – indeed the reverse. Frank Snowden shows how Apulian latifundism, involving 'the immediate juxtaposition of social extremes', was tailor-made to generate social hatreds, and how the shared experience of the desperately impoverished *braccianti* led to collective solidarities, such that agrarian revolution was kept in check only by naked force. Very similar circumstances are described by Anthony Cardoza in respect of the province of Bologna (and elsewhere by Paul Corner for Ferrara) and by Tim Rees with regard to the *jornaleros* of Badajoz.

2 Tenurial arrangements

Large landed property evidently did not always directly confer social power; there were simply too many intervening variables. One of these, as the preceding paragraph has already suggested, was the way in which such property was actually farmed. The direct employment of wage labour in large gangs, as on Apulian latifundia or on the reclaimed lands of the Po Valley, was likely to prove a very risky business. Other 'tenurial' arrangements were less risk-laden, if not exactly risk-free. The latifundia of western Sicily were usually leased to *gabellotti*, who then sublet them to impoverished sharecroppers in widely dispersed plots. The result was that Sicilian sharecroppers had little contact with each other during their work (unlike the *braccianti*) and were often in competition with each other for the best plots. They do not appear to have been best pleased with the system, but at least it discouraged the growth of proletarian solidarity.[80] The classic sharecropping of central and northern Italy, the *mezzadria* system, however, was very much more effective at ensuring peasant quiescence. Anthony Cardoza's contribution describes how the sharecropping system which dominated parts of the province of Bologna led to dispersed habitat and landlord control.[81] The real heartland of classic *mezzadria*, however, was nineteenth-century Tuscany. It was characterized by relatively large sharecropping farms, often operated by extended families who resided on the property and practically never left it; isolation from the outside world, and the active patronage practised by many Tuscan landowners, ensured a docile peasantry. The *reggitore*, designated by the landowner from among the adult males of the extended family, was vested with considerable authority in the day-to-day running of the farm. He served as something of a bridge between the owner and the family workforce, and his patriarchal authority nipped any youthful dissidence in the bud.[82] These structures proved for a long time remarkably successful in ensuring the uncontested exercise of landowner power, with the result that the Tuscan section of the 1860s Jacini inquiry concluded that 'the system of *mezzadria* in Tuscany fully achieved the solution of the most difficult problem of our age and removes all antagonism between capital and labour'.[83] The system began to break down, however, in the late nineteenth and early twentieth centuries under the pressures of commercial agriculture, but Tuscany remained until after the First World War a region where landowner power was, at least on the face of things, uncontested.

The Spanish equivalent of *mezzadria*, *aparcería*, appears to have generated a wide variety of relations between landowners and subletting leaseholders on the one side and *aparceros* (sharecroppers) on the other. Although, given the inadequacies of research into this aspect of Spanish rural society, the generalization can be only tentative, it seems fair to suggest that throughout much of northern and central Spain, and in those districts of the south (more numerous than is often supposed) where *aparcería* existed, sharecroppers, rarely as large as those of Tuscany, remained more often than not docile and amenable to mobilization by landowner-dominated interest groups and political parties. This may well have been in part because, in contrast to parts of France and Italy, *aparcería* was seldom the dominant system of an entire district or province, *aparceros* more commonly existing, as in central and southern Navarre, intermingled with small tenant farmers and lesser proprietors. It was chiefly in regions where highly distinctive forms of sharecropping existed that sharecroppers showed a readier susceptibility to social and political radicalism: in, for example, Galicia and, more particularly, Catalonia – two regions, each of which also possessed a distinctive and, in Catalonia's case, a relatively 'modern' political culture. The *yunteros* of Extremadura, described here by Tim Rees, constituted another, highly idiosyncratic, case. That *aparcería* tended in the main to benefit landowners and that by them, at least, it was believed to engender rural stability are clear from the vehemence and oratorical passion with which they and their political spokesmen defended it.[84]

Sharecropping in France could have different consequences again. Whether landowners found the *métayage* system satisfactory or not seems to have depended on their political conviction, and even more on whether they lived in an area where social conservatism was deep-rooted in the peasantry for other reasons. The secretary of the agricultural society of Mayenne (in the conservative West) waxed lyrical about *métayage*, in words which could have been uttered by defenders of sharecropping anywhere in Europe:

> Establishing between the peasant and the proprietor a very great solidarity, it must necessarily lead to union. The cultivator, seeing that no opportunity to improve his situation is let slip, ends by developing a trust in his master and by believing him devoted to his interests. Regular contact between proprietor and peasant gives rise to a genuine friendliness between them.

Michel Denis seems to think that, at least in the 1840s, there was something in this beatific vision.[85] Perhaps there was. It certainly did not apply in the radical Limousin, however, where a large landowner opined in 1862 that

> the sharecropper is, whatever way you look at him, lazy; he is dirty, disorderly, unintelligent, hidebound, obstinate, suspicious, crawling and fawning before his master, whom he cordially detests, almost always a thief, careless, given to frequenting fairs, sometimes alcoholic. He is a brutish and brutalizing being. When one examines him closely, one observes that civilization in his case is no more than skin-deep. . . . He is the enemy of property, and above all of the proprietor.[86]

It is not surprising that one of the major landowners of the Limousin should think this about the sharecroppers of his region, whose peasantry were always (from the mid-nineteenth century) on the extreme political left, and whose descendants are today the one secure electoral bastion of the French Communist Party.[87]

There was an almost infinite variety of tenurial systems in nineteenth- and early twentieth-century European rural society, not all of which can be considered here. It is nevertheless clear that one important factor affecting the ability of landowners to exercise power was the tenurial arrangements that prevailed in their area. There were 'high-risk' systems, such as those in Apulia and the reclaimed lands of the Po Valley (not strictly 'tenurial' arrangements at all, to be accurate), and 'low-risk' systems such as those of Tuscan *mezzadria*; most of the others, where their effect on landowner power was concerned, probably fell somewhere in between.

3 Absenteeism

One of the more obvious generalizations about the power of landowners is that it depended heavily upon whether they were resident on their estates. As Pierre Lévêque observes, absenteeism 'tended to nullify the social power of landowners, by all too often transforming a patriarchal-type system into one of pure economic exploitation without any appreciable services in return'.[88] Most large landowners were in fact non-resident for at least some of the time; the French and English nobilities were 'amphibious', in that they lived on their properties during the summer and in town during the winter season.[89] The classic examples of absentee landownership are western Sicily, parts of southern Italy such as Apulia, and southern Spain. Western Sicilian landowners lived in Palermo or abroad, some never setting eyes on their estates.[90] They had absolutely no interest in what went on on their properties; Denis Mack Smith remarks that 'no landowner except the most eccentric would stoop to be an active farmer, let alone live in the countryside'.[91]Owners of Sicilian latifundia merely collected the rents from the *gabellotti* to whom they were leased; evidently their influence over the peasants who worked their land was correspondingly nil, and the Sicilian countryside was abandoned to the power of the grasping *gabellotti* and to that of the Mafia. The situation in the south of Spain was very similar. Of 262 grandees who owned 355,000 hectares of arable land in southern Spain in 1933, only 14 had been born there, and all of them in the large cities of the region; all 262 lived in Madrid or abroad.[92] Tim Rees describes how the *labradores* of Badajoz fulfilled a role similar to that of the *gabellotti*, renting latifundia and exploiting them to the hilt. The result in both cases was similar: a landless peasantry, ruthlessly exploited both by leaseholders and by absentee owners, almost untouched by any benefit of patronage, was kept under control by more or less naked force. These cases were perhaps extreme; the noble landowners of Hesse-Cassel seem to have been able to get away with absenteeism and renting out their estates without seriously eroding the legitimacy of their authority – perhaps because of their paternalistic practices even when non-resident. But as a general rule, effective landowner power depended on residence for at least a part of the year.

4 Divisions

4.1 Divisions among elites

The ability of landowners to exercise power also clearly depended on their own unity as a class. Perhaps the best example of a unified landowning class were the landed notables of Tuscany, mostly of similar wealth, economic function and ideology; here was yet another reason for the quiescence of the Tuscan *mezzadri*.[93] Most landowning classes were internally riven, however, as our contributors have shown. The rift might be largely economic, as between stockbreeders and cereal interests in Badajoz, or between grape and wheat interests in Cerignola. In Bologna province it was between an old guard of largely aristocratic agrarian notables with paternalist ideas, and a newer group of commercial farmers and leaseholders who sought higher profits through the intensified exploitation of labour – a division of interest and ideology which it took the threat of a full-fledged rural revolution to overcome.[94] In Burgundy, the rift was essentially ideological; landowning society was riven by

> a deep fault-line . . . on one side the victims and the enemies of the French Revolution, very numerous in the old nobility . . . on the other the supporters and beneficiaries of the new social order, a majority among the bourgeoisie, basing themselves on the principles of 1789.

The same division was evident in the Périgord, where the fault-line of the French Revolution was almost exactly that between nobles and the rural bourgeoisie; here, though, the result was a curious one, inasmuch as it enabled the rural bourgeoisie to mobilize the Périgord peasantry under the banner of anti-nobleism, anti-monarchism and anticlericalism, that is, to exploit the division in the elite in such a way as to ensure that their own economic position was not contested. A not dissimilar phenomenon was observed by Christian Marcilhacy in the Orléanais, where the rural bourgeoisie exploited above all the ideology of anticlericalism to rally the peasantry behind them and to deflect any possible antagonism away from themselves.[95] In some cases, finally, the internal division of the landowning elite reached a point where 'a small section of the ruling class cuts itself adrift and joins the revolutionary class'. Maurice Agulhon has underlined the crucial role of bourgeois sympathizers in the development of peasant radicalism in the 'red Var' – in particular that of sons of the rural bourgeoisie, often with legal training, not very rich, but resident and in touch with local artisans.[96]

4.2 Divisions among peasants

Just as an agrarian elite divided against itself had difficulty in standing united against peasant discontent, so a peasantry split by internal differences was less of a threat to landowner power. As Henry Landsberger remarks, 'one of the greatest inhibitors to the build-up of strong organized pressure for rural change are antagonisms within the peasantry itself'.[97] Hence perceptive traditionalists often implement a divide-and-conquer strategy, as did Stolypin with his 'wager on the strong' after the 1905 revolution in Russia. Italian Christian Democrats employed a not dissimilar strategy after the Second World War, encouraging the growth of a landed peasantry to counter the upsurge of communism in the countryside. They had predecessors in the fascists, who made a certain (if limited) attempt to encourage peasant proprietorship.[98] This was not surprising, since rural fascism in areas like the Po Valley had found much of its popular support among peasant proprietors and sharecroppers. Sharecroppers were often employers of labour and their attitude to the post-1918 mobilization of the *braccianti* in the socialist leagues was more often than not hostile. Together with small proprietors, they gave fascism a mass base in the countryside, without which its simple violence might have been inadequate.[99] A broadly similar situation arose in many parts of Spain during the early twentieth century, and in particular under the Second Republic of 1931–6. Whatever possibility existed of unity among the rural lower classes was obstructed by internal divisions, particularly between labour-employing smallholders (whether proprietors, tenants, or *aparceros*) and rural labourers. Especially in such culturally conservative regions as Navarre, this division was aggravated by religious passions; the skilful and costly propaganda of Catholic landowners' organizations, by deliberately confusing anticlericalism with 'Bolshevism', successfully bound large numbers of Catholic smallholders to the political right.[100]

German rural history in the nineteenth and twentieth centuries appears to have been particularly marked by class divisions within the peasantry. This may indeed be one reason why the modern German peasantry has so very rarely presented a radical face. Jonathan Osmond's contribution describes the usually conservative role in the Bavarian Palatinate of a group of owner-farmers whose sympathy with anything proletarian was very slight. Other recent studies have made class divisions within the peasantry something of a theme. Josef Mooser has described, for a part of Westphalia, the extreme tensions that existed between the *Heuerlinge* (renting land, day-labouring, spinning and weaving, and so on) and the often prosperous middling and large peasants.[101] Hainer Plaul's study of the Magdeburg black-earth region shows how the penetration of agricultural capitalism in the nineteenth century led to clashes not only between lords and labourers but also between labourers and landed peasants; the latter increasingly sided with the great landowners against the agricultural proletariat, which they thus succeeded in isolating.[102] These internal divisions of the German peasantry need much further investigation; they may be quite as important as Junker control of the state, or ideological manipulation of the rural masses, in explaining the absence of any real threat of rural revolution in the post-Emancipation German countryside.

The picture in France is a rather complex one. Class distinctions within the

French peasantry there certainly were – though the existence in most areas of a series of almost infinite gradations made class formation difficult.[103] As the nineteenth century saw the steady expansion of peasant proprietorship, at least one knowledgeable (if biased) observer thought that 'the noble is no longer the object of hatred on the part of the *roturier*, it is the peasant proprietor who is the object of hatred on the part of those who have no land'.[104] Certainly French peasants were strongly aware of social distinctions among themselves: the wife of an independent proprietor would not associate with the wife of a day labourer, and the independent proprietor would not normally let his daughter marry a man without land.[105] On the other hand, French village life could often create a sense of community which overrode the potential for conflict between economically differentiated elements – and this appears to have been true of both radical and conservative areas. Alain Corbin has shown how the radicalization of the Limousin was based on an intense hamlet-level solidarity, which rendered the peasant community impermeable to notable influence.[106] This communal solidarity in the Limousin was due in part to the absence of any major economic divisions within the peasantry. In the conservative heartland of the southern Massif Central,

> a gulf separated the humble *colon* or plotholder from the *ménager* or *laboureur*. Yet that gulf was bridged by a common relationship to the soil and an archaic mentality which overrode objective inequalities of condition. . . . Despite internal differences and rifts, rural communities had a clear sense of their existence, and members were often loyal to community rather than class.[107]

We shall take up this point about community solidarity again in the section on habitat. The point here is that the social and political behaviour of French peasants – whether radical or conservative – does not seem to have been much influenced by internal economic and social differences. In this they differed considerably from the peasantry of Germany, where internal class division appears to have been an important element in enabling large landowners to continue to exercise not only economic but also social and political power.

5 Wealth

5.1 *The wealth of landowners*

It is more or less self-evident that the ability of landowners to exercise power depended upon their economic situation. In particular, many of the landowning classes of Europe were badly hit by the fall in agricultural prices in the last quarter of the nineteenth century. Theo Hoppen points out, apropos of Irish landlords, that 'their own vulnerability to agricultural depression seriously weakened their capacity to ride out the storm'. Eric Evans concludes for the English case that 'the primacy of land, and the power that went with it . . . was ended by the collapse of prices and not by direct bourgeois challenge'. The rural bourgeoisie of the Périgord was similarly undermined by the increasing unprofitability of agricultural capital under the Third Republic. Only the Junkers, via their control of the state and thus of its tariffs, managed largely to insulate themselves from price decline.

The problem of estates becoming unprofitable, so that their traditional owners were relieved to sell them off to tenants, landowning peasants, or parvenus, is obvious enough. But the power of large landowners also depended on their resources in a slightly less obvious sense. The exercise of patronage – which we have argued was often crucial to the long-term exercise of landowner power – naturally depended upon having disposable resources.[108] Any ideological hegemony, moreover – as we have also argued – hinged on the capacity to make certain sacrifices. Landowners who were unable to make such sacrifices were unlikely to be able to legitimize their power, and more likely to have to resort to public or private force. Traditional Italian landlords had rarely pressed tenants for full payment; debt was a system of control and encouraged deference (debts were often commuted in wills). But the speculative contractors who leased old properties had often incurred heavy debts themselves and could not or would not wait. Their authority in rural society thus rested on a much more tenuous base than that of the old landed nobility.[109]

5.2 The wealth of peasants

How prepared peasants were to accept landowner authority naturally depended in part upon how poor they were. Peasant restlessness was likely to be stimulated by objective decline in their condition – but also by relative deprivation, or by expectations that were rising faster than reality.[110] James Scott has produced a very interesting analysis of what general circumstances might lead peasant tenants to regard themselves as unjustly exploited and thus to feel rebellious. What mattered crucially, he argues, was not the actual level of exploitation, not the rate of extraction of surplus value, but whether the system of tenancy guaranteed subsistence for the peasant and his family even in crisis years:

> The stability and security of subsistence income are more critical to the tenant's evaluation of the relationship than either his average return or the proportion of the crop taken by the landlord as rent. . . . Arrangements which honour this central need are likely to retain a modicum of legitimacy. Arrangements which abrogate this right . . . are justifiably seen as unfair and exploitative.[111]

6 Labour supply

Landowners' ability to exercise power depended very much on whether there was a superabundance of available labour; when peasants were in competition for tenancies or employment, it was obviously the landowner who set the terms. Both Frank Snowden and Tim Rees have emphasized in their contributions how the 'terrible imbalance between supply and demand in the labour market' enabled landowners or their representatives ruthlessly to exploit an agricultural proletariat. The rural exodus that affected much of Europe in the second half of the nineteenth century was thus a major threat to landowner power. In Italy, mass migration to North and South America was the key. Those who remained understood this very well: when the tenants of one western Sicilian estate organized a strike in 1901, they used the rallying cry 'Fair contracts or all to America!' – knowing no doubt that the decrease in the labour force had already increased the wages of day labourers by a third.[112] Prussian Junkers faced the same problems as Sicilian latifundists, except that the rise of German industry meant that the surplus agricultural population could go to German cities rather than to the Americas. Between 1885 and 1905, 1,904,000 people – mostly rural labourers – left the provinces of East and West Prussia, Pomerania, Poznan and Silesia (that is, the East Elbian countryside).[113] Junkers were not, however, the kind of people to suffer a reversal of their bargaining position in silence and they ensured themselves a continued docile workforce by organizing massive immigration of Polish agricultural workers; by the eve of the First World War, almost one third of German agricultural employees were foreign migrants.[114] French landowners had less entrepreneurial spirit – or perhaps less easy geographical access to a pool of labour; at any rate, when faced with the *exode rural* of the second half of the nineteenth century, what they mostly did was moan (though they also turned to a certain extent to mechanization[115]). They found themselves faced with *métayers* who used the threat of departure to get better contracts,[116] with tenants who used the declining number of candidates for tenancies to get more favourable leases[117] and with the need to pay higher wages to a depleted pool of agricultural labourers.[118] The result was an endlessly repeated complaint from the landowning class about '*le manque de bras*'. In reality, as Jean Pitié remarks,

> this phrase always articulated the same concern: that of property owners faced with the reduction of the reserve agricultural army formed by the rural proletariat. They hankered after the time when the presence of a superabundant labour force had put at their permanent disposition workers prepared to accept almost any employment, at whatever wage was offered. The diminution of that proletariat threatened to provoke a rise in salaries and to bring in its wake either a reduction in profit margins or an agonizing transformation of the economic structure.[119]

In the light of the foregoing, it is important and curious to note that latifundism does not seem normally to have provoked emigration. This appears, at any rate, to have been true of both Italy and Spain. Perhaps this was because, as Bernaldo de Quirós wrote in 1920, 'a general prostration of the human being [caused] a pessimistic renunciation of the hope for betterment in any part of the world whatever'. Or perhaps, as Edward Malefakis suggests, it was because the victim of latifundism 'preferred to combat the injustice of his situation rather than flee from it'.[120] If the latter is the case, then the argument of the preceding paragraph may need to be modified: a superabundance of labour may well give landowners great bargaining power, but it also makes them the object of profound – and, in some cases at least, potentially dangerous – resentment.

It remains true, however, that a 'reserve agricultural army' was a crucial element of landowner power. Before industrialization the permanent population surplus of European rural society had enabled the landed elite to rule the roost; for such power to continue, some replacement needed rapidly to be found for those who left for industrial employment or for the New World. A reduction of labour requirements via mechanization, and the recruitment of migrant labour from the less developed parts of Europe, were palliatives but not cures. For landowner power to last, it needed a lot of people to rule over.

7 Habitat

7.1 Agglomeration and dispersion

One of the oldest observations about landowner power is that it flourished best in societies with an isolated habitat structure. In a sense, all peasant communities are likely to have a more scattered habitat than that of the industrial working class, which is surely one reason why the latter has been rather better at organization – if not at protest – in modern European history.[121] Marx, of course, used this as one explanation of why the French peasantry supported Napoleon III:

> The smallholding peasants form a vast mass, the members of which live in similar conditions but without entering into manifold relations with one another. Their mode of production isolates them from one another instead of bringing them into mutual intercourse . . . the great mass of the French nation is formed by simple addition of homologous magnitudes, much as potatoes in a sack form a sack of potatoes.[122]

Peasants were consequently unable to develop a consciousness of their class interests and thus to mobilize as a class; they could only look to a dictator.

Italian *braccianti* often seem to be proof of this *a contrario*. They, like the southern Spanish *braceros*, were usually huddled together in agro-towns, which stimulated a shared sense of exploitation and facilitated the organization of protest. Cerignola was perhaps the extreme example, surrounded by a countryside which, in Frank Snowden's words, 'presented a vista of utter and unbroken desolation'. The agro-towns of the Po Valley, including the shanty towns which sprang up on reclaimed land, were similar hotbeds of peasant radicalism in the early twentieth century.[123] It does need noting that agglomeration in agro-towns in Sicily did not have quite the same radicalizing effect. The sharecropping peasantry who inhabited them were divided by competition for access to the land, and by the diversity of their productive activities; moreover such towns had no trading contacts with each other (only with the coast and Palermo), so that the roads between them were poor and communications infrequent.[124] Nevertheless, the Italian example does mostly suggest that an agglomerated habitat was likely to radicalize and that a dispersed habitat favoured the exercise of landowner power. The *locus classicus* of the latter situation was Tuscany, where *mezzadria* isolated families in their *podere* in a way that actually corresponded much better to Marx's analysis than did the situation in France. The English economist Bowring noted in 1836

> the universal isolation of the peasants which is a necessary consequence of the *mezzadria* system. Where there is no association, there is necessarily extreme ignorance. Every peasant's family in Tuscany stands as it were alone: this is indeed a great gain for public security; but it is a tranquillity purchased at a terrible price – at the price of a stationary and backward civilization.[125]

The same correlation between dispersed habitat and landowner power seems to apply in Spain and France. Martin Blinkhorn's analysis of Navarre shows a sharp contrast between the fragmented habitat of the north and the far more agglomerated south, with a closely corresponding contrast in peasant militancy. Other northern Spanish provinces (for example, León, Alava, Huesca and Lérida), and even some in the south, show comparable, if geographically less neat, divisions. As for France, Maurice Agulhon has described the 'urban villages' of lower Provence, which he sees as playing a central role in the rural radicalization which surfaced in that area in the mid-nineteenth century; *démocrate-socialiste* successes in the department of the Var under the Second Republic were clearly correlated with agglomeration.[126] The *bocage* countryside of the West, by contrast, with very low levels of agglomeration, enabled landowners to exercise considerable social and political power even if they did not own a very large proportion of the land (see Donald Sutherland's contribution). The southern Massif Central did have a number of considerable *bourgs*, but the extremely dispersed habitat of the rest of the area meant that the radicalism of the *bourgs* was unable to penetrate the countryside.[127] The only exception (a major one) to the correlation between peasant discontent and agglomerated habitat was the Limousin, where the closed community of the *hameau* was the seed-bed of radicalism; Alain Corbin concludes that 'isolation can absolutely not, in this case, be considered as a factor of conservatism'.[129]

7.2 Isolation

In most cases, however, in most countries, 'isolation was a major component of lordly power' (Snowden). Communities which were what Lewis Coser has called 'greedy institutions'[129] – that is, closed local societies where access to sources of legitimacy other than those offered by the local landowner(s) was difficult to obtain – have, like the monopoly or oligarchic villages of East Anglia in which the 'Captain Swing' agitation awoke little echo,[130] been fertile ground for landowner power. Landowners have been perfectly well aware of this and have fought to preserve such isolation wherever possible. In Italy, for example, during the rule of the democrats in 1849, the correspondence of a future prime minister, Baron Ricasoli, stresses that it is both vital and possible to keep the peasants in complete ignorance of current events.[131]

Subversive ideas were usually perceived as coming from the towns; typically, the landowner-dominated general council of the French department of the Loiret complained in 1870 that 'due to the ease of contact with the towns, ideas of independence are developing'.[132] Urban influence probably depended, however, on the nature of economic links between town and hinterland. The department of the Sarthe, ever since the Revolution, has been divided between a conservative west and a more radical east. Paul Bois' classic analysis of this dichotomy suggests that in the 1790s the peasantry of the western part became rapidly very hostile to a Revolutionary ideology spreading from the towns, because they were well enough off to be selling a grain surplus for urban consumption (leading to a clash of interests over prices), and also rich enough to compete with – and lose out to – the urban bourgeoisie over the sale of church lands. The eastern Sarthe, where agricultural poverty meant that rural weaving was important, had closer and non-conflictual contact with the urban bourgeois in the textile trade and was thus more permeable to an ideology of urban origin.[133] Ted Margadant has used a similar argument to explain the geography of the rural insurrection against Louis-Napoleon's *coup d'état* in 1851: areas dominated by cereal production were in natural conflict with towns over grain prices, and were thus uninfluenced by the *démocrate-socialiste* ideology spreading from the towns; areas producing goods for a wider market (wine, olive oil, madder, wood, and so on) had shared economic interests with the towns of their region and were thus prepared to listen.[134] Neither of these analyses is beyond criticism. Nevertheless they are supported by evidence from outside France – that, for example, provided in Spain by the case of the radical wine-growing *rabassaires* of Catalonia[135] – and do strongly suggest that the capacity of subversive ideas of urban origin to undermine landowner power depended in large part upon the nature of market relationships between town and hinterland.[136]

It is now possible to offer a summary of the framework which we tentatively propose for the analysis of power in rural society:

I *The ways in which landowners exercised power*

1 Force
1.1 'Private' force
1.2 'State' force

2 The state as a guarantor of landowner power

3 Aspects of authority
3.1 Deference
3.2 'Traditional' authority
3.3 Patronage/clientelism
3.4 Mediation

4 Ideology

5 Hegemony

II *Factors affecting the exercise of landowner power*

1 The structure of landownership

2 Tenurial arrangements

3 Absenteeism

4 Divisions
4.1 Divisions among elites
4.2 Divisions among peasants

5 Wealth
5.1 The wealth of landowners
5.2 The wealth of peasants

6 Labour supply

7 Habitat
7.1 Agglomeration and dispersion
7.2 Isolation

We wish to stress once again that the pretensions of this framework are modest. It is not designed to be applicable outside western and central Europe in the modern period. In itself, it has no explanatory power. We offer it as a simple check-list of elements that any analysis of power relations in the countryside, in that place and time, might fruitfully examine. It is no doubt capable of almost indefinite expansion and possibly also of contraction. We hope that it will, with all its limitations, be useful to historians of rural Europe in modern times.

For the purposes of this volume, such a framework may help to tie together the case studies offered by our contributors. These studies deal with vastly different societies, from the conservative West of France to the turbulent rural societies of parts of Italy and southern Spain, from highly successful landed elites in nineteenth-century Prussia and England to a frankly disastrous one in Apulia, and so on. All of them, in their different ways, are, however, concerned with a problem fundamental to all study of human society: who could tell whom what to do, and how were they able to get away with it? In other words, they are about power.

NOTES

1 A.-J. Tudesq, *Les grands notables en France (1840–1849): Étude historique d'une psychologie sociale*, 2 vols (Paris: 1964), Vol. I, p. 87 (see also Vol. II, p. 1237).

2 For classic general treatments, see: H. A. Landsberger (ed.), *Rural Protest: Peasant Movements and Social Change* (London: 1974); E. R. Wolf, *Peasant Wars of the Twentieth Century* (London: 1971); Barrington Moore, Jnr, *Social Origins of Dictatorship and Democracy: Lord and Peasant in the Modern World* (Harmondsworth: 1967), ch. IX; and J. Blum, *The End of the Old Order in Rural Europe* (Princeton, NJ: 1978), ch. 15.

3 Quoted in Richard Herr, in D. Spring (ed.), *European Landed Elites in the Nineteenth Century* (Baltimore, Md: 1977), p. 113. The classic contemporary study (and indictment) of *caciquismo* is Joaquín Costa, *Oligarquía y caciquismo como la forma actual de gobierno en España: urgencia y modo de cambiarla* (Madrid: 1902). Valuable recent studies include Javier Tusell, *Oligarquía y caciquismo en Andalucía, 1890–1923* (Barcelona: 1976); José Varela Ortega, *Los amigos políticos. Partidos, elecciones y caciques en la Restauración (1875–1900)* (Madrid: 1977); and Robert Kern, *Liberals, Reformers and Caciques in Restoration Spain (1875–1900)* (Albuquerque, N. Mex.: 1974). *Caciques* could, of course, also be landowners, but they did not need to be great ones (though some were). Even where large estates were not important, relatively small differences in the distribution of property could still create *caciques* out of those families who had, or determinedly acquired, the edge over the rest. Navarre and other parts of northern Spain provide plenty of examples: see Martin Blinkhorn's contribution to this volume, and C. Lison-Tolosana, *Belmonte de los Caballeros. Anthropology and History in an Aragonese Community* (Princeton, NJ: 1966), esp. pp. 15–54.

4 A. Blok, *The Mafia of a Sicilian Village, 1860–1960. A Study of Violent Peasant Entrepreneurs* (Oxford: 1974), pp. 32–3; J. Schneider and P. Schneider, *Culture and Political Economy in Western Sicily* (New York: 1976), p. 69.

5 P. Arlacchi, *Mafia, Peasants and Great Estates: Society in Traditional Calabria* (Cambridge: 1983), pp. 160–2.
6 See also A. L. Cardoza, *Agrarian Elites and Italian Fascism: the Province of Bologna, 1901–1926* (Princeton, NJ: 1982), pp. 49–52.
7 R. Sarti, *Long Live the Strong. A History of Rural Society in the Apennine Mountains* (Amherst, Mass.: 1985), p. 13.
8 For such approaches see (*inter alia*): E. Wolf, *Peasants* (Englewood Cliffs, NJ: 1966), pp. 2–4; G. M. Foster, 'What is a peasant?', in J. M. Potter, M. N. Diaz and G. M. Foster (eds), *Peasant Society: a Reader* (Boston, Mass.: 1967), pp. 2–14 (esp. p. 6); T. Shanin, 'Peasantry as a concept', in T. Shanin (ed.), *Peasants and Peasant Societies: Selected Readings* (Oxford: 1987 [first pub. 1971]), pp. 1–11.
9 Landsberger, *Rural Protest*, pp. 6–18.
10 Many modern sociologists have offered frameworks for the analysis of power in general. We have not found any of them ideally suited to our purpose, but of those we have considered the two that come closest are: J. R. P. French and B. Raven, 'The bases of social power', in D. Cartwright (ed.), *Studies in Social Power* (Ann Arbor, Mich.: 1959), pp. 150–67, and A. Etzioni, *A Comparative Analysis of Complex Organizations* (New York: 1975), pt I ('Towards an analytical typology'). For a good general discussion, see R. Martin, *The Sociology of Power* (London: 1977).
11 See Max Weber, *Economy and Society: an Outline of Interpretative Sociology*, ed. G. Roth and C. Wittich, 3 vols (Berkeley, Calif.: 1968), Vol. I, ch. 3 ('The types of legitimate domination'), or Max Weber, *The Theory of Social and Economic Organization*, tr. Talcott Parsons (New York: 1947, 1964), esp. pt III ('The types of authority and imperative control'). For critical commentary, see (*inter alia*): P. M. Blau, 'Critical remarks on Weber's theory of authority', in D. Wrong (ed.), *Max Weber* (Englewood Cliffs, NJ: 1970), pp. 147–65; R. Grafstein, 'The failure of Weber's concept of legitimacy: its causes and implications', *Journal of Politics*, 43, 2 (May 1981), pp. 456–72; F. Parkin, *Max Weber* (Chichester: 1982), ch. 3; and A. T. Kronman, *Max Weber* (London: 1983), ch. 3.
12 See also P. Preston, 'The agrarian war in the south', in P. Preston (ed.), *Revolution and War in Spain, 1931–1939* (London: 1984), pp. 159–81.
13 A. Blok, 'Mafia and peasant rebellion as contrasting factors in Sicilian latifundism', *European Journal of Sociology*, x, 1 (1969), pp. 95–116 (p. 99). See also Arlacchi, *Mafia, Peasants and Great Estates*, pp. 155–6 and F. Snowden, *Violence and Great Estates in the South of Italy: Apulia, 1900–1922* (Cambridge: 1986), pp. 145–7 (and the illustration on p. 36).
14 Blok, 'Mafia and peasant rebellion', p. 112; see also Schneider and Schneider, *Culture and Political Economy in Western Sicily*, ch. 9 and Blok, *Mafia of a Sicilian Village*, pp. 11, 141 and *passim*.
15 F. Snowden, *The Fascist Revolution in Tuscany, 1919–1922* (Cambridge: 1989), esp. pp. 286–7; F. Snowden, 'On the social origins of agrarian fascism in Italy', *Archives Européennes de sociologie*, xiii (1972), pp. 286–95; Snowden, *Violence and Great Estates*; Cardoza, *Agrarian Elites*; and P. Corner, *Fascism in Ferrara, 1915–1925* (Oxford: 1975).
16 See Anthony Cardoza's contribution; also Cardoza, *Agrarian Elites*, pp. 70–6 and Snowden, *Violence and Great Estates*, pp. 172–3.
17 Snowden, *Violence and Great Estates*, p. 196 (also pp. 134–5); Snowden, *Fascist Revolution in Tuscany*, pp. 198 ff.; Cardoza, *Agrarian Elites*, pp. 214–16; and Corner, *Fascism in Ferrara*, pp. 140–1, 179–80, 205–6. It is important to note that the success of fascist violence depended partly on the refusal of the Socialist leadership to encourage counter-violence.
18 F. L. Carsten, *A History of the Prussian Junkers* (Aldershot: 1989), pp. 58–64, 106–7.
19 See T. W. Margadant, *French Peasants in Revolt: the Insurrection of 1851* (Princeton, NJ: 1979).
20 See E. P. Thompson, *Whigs and Hunters: the Origins of the Black Act* (Harmondsworth: 1975).
21 Arlacchi, *Mafia, Peasants and Great Estates*, p. 196.
22 The already classic analysis of the durability of such power in Europe is A. J. Mayer, *The Persistence of the Old Regime: Europe to the Great War* (London: 1981).
23 H. Schissler, 'The Junkers: notes on the social and historical significance of the agrarian elite in Prussia', in R. G. Moeller (ed.), *Peasants and Lords in Modern Germany: Recent Studies in Agricultural History* (Boston, Mass.: 1986), pp. 24–51 (esp. pp. 26–7); Carsten, *Prussian Junkers*, pp. 36, 193.

24 ibid., p. 70.

25 Quoted in ibid., p. 88.

26 H.-U. Wehler, *Das deutsche Kaiserreich, 1871–1918* (Göttingen: 1973), p. 21.

27 H. Rosenberg, 'Die Pseudodemokratisierung der Rittergutsbesitzerklasse', in H. Rosenberg (ed.), *Machteliten und Wirtschaftskonjunkturen: Studien zur neueren deutschen Sozial- und Wirtschaftsgeschichte* (Göttingen: 1978), pp. 83–101 (esp. pp. 91–2); Wehler, *Das deutsche Kaiserreich*, pp. 129–31; L. W. Muncy, *The Junker in the Prussian Administration under Wilhelm II, 1888–1914* (New York: 1970), esp. pp. 192–6; Spring, *European Landed Elites*, pp. 4–5.

28 Wehler, *Das deutsche Kaiserreich*, pp. 46–7, 53–6.

29 See also (*inter alia*) W. E. Vaughan, 'Landlord and tenant relations in Ireland between the Famine and the Land War, 1850–1878', in L. M. Cullen and T. C. Smout (eds), *Comparative Aspects of Scottish and Irish Social and Economic History, 1600–1900* (Edinburgh: n.d.), pp. 216–26.

30 On landowners and the Spanish Second Republic of 1931–6, see Preston, 'Agrarian war in the south'; A. López López, *El boicot de las derechas a las reformas de la Segunda República* (Madrid: 1984); E. Malefakis, *Agrarian Reform and Peasant Revolution in Spain. Origins of the Civil War* (New Haven, Conn.: 1970), pp. 131–400 *passim*; M. Pérez Yruela, *La conflictividad campesina en la provincia de Córdoba, 1931–1936* (Madrid: 1979); G. A. Collier, *Socialists of Rural Andalusia. Unacknowledged Revolutionaries of the Second Republic* (Stanford, Calif.: 1987), esp. pp. 119–30; F. Pascual Cevallos, *Luchas agrarias en Sevilla durante la Segunda República* (Seville: 1983), pp. 47–66.

31 Even the Prussian state liked on occasion to protect peasants from excessive exactions on the part of their lords. See Carsten, *Prussian Junkers*, p. 51 and W. W. Hagen, 'The Junkers' faithless servants: peasant insubordination and the breakdown of serfdom in Brandenburg-Prussia, 1763–1811', in R. J. Evans and W. R. Lee (eds), *The German Peasantry: Conflict and Community in Rural Society from the Eighteenth to the Twentieth Centuries* (London: 1986), pp. 71–101 (esp. pp. 83–4).

32 H. Newby *et al.*, *Property and Power: Class and Control in Rural England* (London: 1978), pp. 26–7.

33 H. Harnisch, 'Peasants and markets: the background to the agrarian reforms in feudal Prussia east of the Elbe', in Evans and Lee, *The German Peasantry*, pp. 37–70, 94 (p. 63).

34 Carsten, *Prussian Junkers*, pp. 142, 159.

35 J. A. Davis, *Conflict and Control: Law and Order in Nineteenth-Century Italy* (London: 1988), p. 277. Even Max Weber was aware that submission to authority might be merely the consequence of 'individual weakness and helplessness because there is no acceptable alternative' (*Economy and Society*, Vol. I, p. 214).

36 F. Snowden, 'From sharecropper to proletarian: the background to fascism in rural Tuscany', in J. A. Davis (ed.), *Gramsci and Italy's Passive Revolution* (London: 1979), pp. 136–71 (p. 142).

37 H. Newby, 'The deferential dialectic', *Comparative Studies in Society and History*, 17 (1975), pp. 139–64 (pp. 142–3) – though see also Newby, *Property and Power*, p. 279 and H. Newby, 'Agricultural workers in the class structure', *Sociological Review*, 20, 3 (1972), pp. 413–39 (esp. pp. 414, 431–2), where the author suggests that deference may well be internalized.

38 J. Mooser, 'Property and wood theft. Agrarian capitalism and social conflict in rural society, 1800–50: a Westphalian case study', in Moeller, *Peasants and Lords in Modern Germany*, pp. 52–80 (p. 62). See also Ivan Turgenev's *Fathers and Sons* (Harmondsworth: 1965), pp. 217–18.

39 R. Price, 'Labour supply and social relationships in the French countryside during the Second Empire', unpublished paper, kindly made available by the author.

40 P. Jones, *Politics and Rural Society: the Southern Massif Central, c. 1750–1880* (Cambridge: 1985), pp. 70, 77. See also J. Merley, *La Haute-Loire de la fin de l'Ancien Régime aux débuts de la Troisième République (1776–1886)*, 2 vols (Le Puy: 1974), Vol. I, pp. 424–5.

41 J. Scott, 'Exploitation in rural relations: a victim's perspective', *Comparative Politics*, vii, 4 (July 1975), pp. 489–532 (pp. 526, 531).

42 Y. Lequin *et al.*, *Histoire des Français, XIXe–XXe siècles*, Vol. II, *La Société* (Paris: 1983), pp. 46–7.

43 Weber, *Economy and Society*, Vol. I, pp. 226–41.
44 Newby, 'The deferential dialectic', p. 151.
45 Carsten, *Prussian Junkers*, p. 67.
46 K. Marx and F. Engels, *Collected Works* (London: 1976), Vol. 6, pp. 486–7.
47 When the Medici estate of Altopascio was leased in 1740, 'all genuine concern disappeared along with the lease' – and it was only thereafter that signs of peasant resentment began to show. See F. McArdle, *Altopascio: a Study in Tuscan Rural Society, 1587–1784* (Cambridge: 1978), pp. 171, 203–5.
48 R. Carr, *Spain 1808–1975*, 2nd edn (Oxford: 1982), pp. 366–79.
49 S. Silverman, 'Patronage and community-nation relationships in Central Italy', *Ethnology*, 4, 2 (1965), pp. 172–89 (p. 180); Snowden, *Fascist Revolution in Tuscany*, p. 15.
50 Marshal Bugeaud, when not engaged in conquering Algeria, was a progressive *agronome* on his Périgord property; the attempt by some peasants to put it to the sack in 1848 suggests that his genuine contributions to agriculture had done him little good in the eyes of the local population. See G. Rocal, *1848 en Dordogne* (Paris: 1934), pp. 105–6.
51 D. Higgs, *Nobles in Nineteenth-Century France: the Practice of Inegalitarianism* (Baltimore, Md: 1987), pp. 150–2.
52 M. Denis, *Les Royalistes de la Mayenne et le monde moderne (XIXe–XXe siècles)* (Paris: 1977), pp. 177, 347–9.
53 R. Price, *The Modernization of Rural France: Communications Networks and Agricultural Market Structures in Nineteenth-Century France* (London: 1983), p. 124.
54 See R. Gibson, 'Les notables et l'Église dans le diocèse de Périgueux, 1821–1905', doctorat de IIIe cycle, université de Lyon III, 1979, 2 vols, Vol. I, pp. 297–318.
55 M. Agulhon, *La vie sociale en Provence intérieure au lendemain de la Révolution* (Paris: 1970), pp. 279–83.
56 McArdle, *Altopascio*, pp. 146, 176.
57 Lequin *et al.*, *Histoire des Français, XIXe–XXe siècles*, Vol. II, pp. 44–5.
58 F. M. L. Thompson, 'Landowners and the rural community', in G. E. Mingay (ed.), *The Victorian Countryside* (London: 1981), pp. 457–74.
59 Jones, *Southern Massif Central*, pp. 85, 262, 295–6, 299–303.
60 Landsberger, *Rural Protest*, pp. 29–30; see also Barrington Moore, *Social Origins of Dictatorship and Democracy*, p. 471.
61 On patronage in general, see also J. D. Powell, 'Peasant society and clientelist politics', *American Political Science Review*, LXIV, 2 (June 1970), pp. 411–25 (reprinted in J. L. Finkl and R. W. Gable [eds], *Political Development and Social Change* [New York: 1971], pp. 519–37), and H. Mendras, 'Un schéma d'analyse de la paysannerie occidentale', *Peasant Studies Newsletter* (1972). For a contemporary French example, see A. Morel, 'Pouvoir et idéologies au sein du village picard hier et aujourd'hui', *Annales E.S.C.*, a. 30, 1 (janvier–février 1975), pp. 161–76.
62 Silverman, 'Patronage and community-nation relationships'; E. Wolf, 'Aspects of group relations in a complex society: Mexico', *American Anthropologist*, 58, 6 (1956), pp. 1065–78 (pp. 1075–6), reprinted in Shanin, *Peasants and Peasant Societies*, pp. 50–68 (pp. 65–6); R. Redfield, *Peasant Society and Culture* (Chicago: 1956), pp. 43–4; M. Kenny, 'Patterns of patronage in Spain', *Anthropological Quarterly*, 33 (1960), pp. 14–23 (pp. 17–18); C. Tilly, *The Vendée* (London: 1964), p. 80.
63 Silverman, 'Patronage and community-nation relationships', p. 180. See also P. L.-R. Higonnet, *Pont-de-Montvert: Social Structure and Politics in a French Village, 1700–1914* (Cambridge, Mass.: 1971), p. 17; A. Lyttelton, 'Landlords, peasants and the limits of liberalism', in Davis, *Gramsci and Italy's Passive Revolution*, pp. 104–35 (pp. 117–18); Spring, *European Landed Elites*, p. 117; J. A. Pitt-Rivers, *The People of the Sierra* (London: 1954), pp. 137–59.
64 D. Hay, 'Property, authority and the criminal law', in D. Hay *et al.*, *Albion's Fatal Tree: Crime and Society in Eighteenth-Century England* (Harmondsworth: 1977), pp. 17–63.
65 C. White, *Patrons and Partisans: a Study of Politics in Two Southern Italian Comuni* (Cambridge: 1980), pt IV (conclusion). For an alternative view, see Schneider and Schneider, *Culture and Political Economy in Western Sicily*, ch. 8 and Blok, *Mafia of a Sicilian Village*, pp. 223–4.

66 See also Arlacchi, *Mafia, Peasants and Great Estates*, p. 158 (suggesting that force will not work against skilled labour), and Tudesq, *Les grands notables*, Vol. II, p. 1238.

67 Davis, *Conflict and Control*, pp. 142–3, 278; Snowden, *Violence and Great Estates*, pp. 79–86.

68 Quoted by Blum, *End of the Old Order*, p. 335. See also Higonnet, *Pont-de-Montvert*, pp. 75–81 (for the conservative functions of French Protestantism).

69 Spanish social-Catholicism is dealt with in J. J. Castillo, 'Notas sobre los orígenes y primeros años de la Confederación Nacional Católico-Agraria', in J. L. García Delgado (ed.), *La cuestión agraria en la España contemporánea* (Madrid: 1976), pp. 204–48; J. J. Castillo, *Propietarios muy pobres. Sobre la subordinación política de pequeño campesino* (Madrid: 1979); and J. Cuesta, *Sindicalismo católico-agrario en España (1917–1919)* (Madrid: 1978).

70 D. Field, *Rebels in the Name of the Tsar* (Boston, Mass.: 1976).

71 Blum, *End of the Old Order*, p. 335 and ch. 15 *passim*.

72 J. Femia, 'Hegemony and consciousness in the thought of Antonio Gramsci', *Political Studies*, xxii, 1 (1975), pp. 29–48; T. R. Bates, 'Gramsci and the theory of hegemony', *Journal of the History of Ideas*, xxxvi, 2 (April–June 1975), pp. 351–66; A. S. Sassoon, 'Hegemony, war of position and political intervention', in A. S. Sassoon (ed.), *Approaches to Gramsci* (London: 1982); G. Eley, 'Reading Gramsci in English', *European History Quarterly*, 14, 4 (October 1984), pp. 441–78; S. Hall, B. Lumley and G. McLennan, 'Politics and ideology', *Working Papers in Cultural Studies*, 10 (1977), pp. 45–76; R. Bocock, *Hegemony* (London: 1986); and many more besides.

73 *Selections from the Prison Notebooks of Antonio Gramsci*, ed. and tr. Q. Hoare and G. Nowell Smith (London: 1971), p. 161.

74 G. Eley, *Reshaping the German Right: Radical Nationalism and Political Change After Bismarck* (New Haven, Conn.: 1980), esp. ch. 5; Moeller, *Peasants and Lords in Modern Germany* (chapters by I. Farr, J. Osmond, L. Jones and H.-J. Puhle); Evans and Lee, *The German Peasantry* (chapter by I. Farr); R. J. Evans (ed.), *Society and Politics in Wilhelmine Germany* (London: 1978) (chapters by G. Eley and I. Farr); D. Blackbourn, 'Peasants and politics in Germany, 1871–1914', *European History Quarterly*, 14, 1 (January 1984), pp. 47–75; R. G. Moeller, 'The Kaiserreich recast? Continuity and change in modern German historiography', *Journal of Social History*, 17, 4 (1984), pp. 655–83; G. Eley, 'Some thoughts on nationalist pressure groups in Imperial Germany', in P. Kennedy and A. J. Nicholls (eds), *Nationalist and Racialist Movements in Britain and Germany before 1914* (London: 1981), pp. 40–67; J. C. Hunt, 'The "egalitarianism" of the right: the Agrarian League in south-west Germany, 1893–1914', *Journal of Contemporary History*, 10, 3 (July 1975), pp. 513–30.

75 I. Farr, 'Populism in the countryside: the peasant leagues in Bavaria in the 1890s', in Evans, *Society and Politics*, pp. 136–59 (p. 147); Moeller, *Peasants and Lords in Modern Germany*, pp. 100–2 (Puhle), p. 129 (Farr) and p. 145 (Moeller).

76 F. M. L. Thompson, *English Landed Society in the Nineteenth Century* (London: 1963), p. 27; Ministère de l'Agriculture, *Statistique Agricole de la France publiée par le Ministère de l'Agriculture. Résultats généraux de l'enquête décennale de 1882* (Nancy: 1887), p. 278 (this calculation involves making some assumptions about *cotes multiples*).

77 E. J. Hobsbawm and G. Rudé, *Captain Swing* (Harmondsworth: 1973), pp. 151–3.

78 A. Corbin, *Archaïsme et Modernité en Limousin au XIXe siècle*, 2 vols (Paris: 1975), Vol. I, pp. 226–61 and *passim*.

79 P. Bois, *Paysans de l'Ouest: des structures économiques et sociales aux options politiques depuis l'époque révolutionnaire dans la Sarthe* (Le Mans: 1960), p. 96; A. Siegfried, *Tableau politique de la France de l'Ouest sous la Troisième République* (Paris: 1913), pt 2.

80 Blok, *Mafia of a Sicilian Village*, pp. 43–4, 63–7; Schneider and Schneider, *Culture and Political Economy in Western Sicily*, pp. 59–61; F. Sabetti, *Political Authority in a Sicilian Village* (New Brunswick, NJ: 1984), pp. 53–4.

81 See also D. I. Kertzer, *Family Life in Central Italy, 1880–1910: Sharecroppers, Wage Labor and Co-residence* (New Brunswick, NJ: 1984), pp. 26–32; S. Silverman, *Three Bells of Civilization: the Life of an Italian Hill Town* (New York: 1975), ch. 3; C. Poni, 'Family and "Podere" in Emilia Romagna', *Journal of Italian History*, i, 2 (Autumn 1978), pp. 210–34.

82 Snowden, *Fascist Revolution in Tuscany*, pt I (esp. pp. 17–18); Snowden, 'From sharecropper to proletarian', pp. 136–71 (esp. p. 147).
83 Lyttelton, 'Landlords, peasants and the limits of liberalism', p. 112.
84 M. Blinkhorn, *Carlism and Crisis in Spain, 1931–1939* (Cambridge: 1975), pp. 79–80. On *aparcería*, see Malefakis, *Agrarian Reform and Peasant Revolution in Spain*, pp. 93, 117–18, 122–3, 125–9; Pitt-Rivers, *People of the Sierra*, pp. 43–7; R. Behar, *Santa María del Monte. The Presence of the Past in a Spanish Village* (Princeton, NJ: 1986) (on León), pp. 107–8; and, on Spanish small farmers generally, see especially Castillo, *Propietarios muy pobres*.
85 Denis, *Les Royalistes de la Mayenne*, pp. 247 (for the quotation), 248, 268, 345.
86 Corbin, *Archaïsme et Modernité en Limousin*, Vol. I, p. 274 (see pp. 267–77 on *métayage*).
87 See L. S. Boswell, 'Rural communism in France: the example of the Limousin and the Dordogne', PhD dissertation, University of California, Berkeley, Calif., 1988. For the radicalism of sharecroppers in the Allier, see S. Sokoloff, 'Land tenure and political tendency in rural France: the case of sharecropping', *European Studies Review*, 10, 3 (July 1980), pp. 357–82, and P. Amann, 'French sharecropping revisited: the case of the Laurageais', *European History Quarterly*, 20, 3 (July 1990), pp. 341–68.
88 See also C. Marcilhacy, *Le diocèse d'Orléans au milieu du XIXe siècle: les hommes et leurs mentalités* (Paris: 1964), pp. 51, 183, and Newby, 'The deferential dialectic', esp. pp. 155–7.
89 Tudesq, *Les grands notables*, Vol. I, p. 196; Marcilhacy, *Le diocèse d'Orléans*, pp. 72–3, 109–10. We do not share the doubts expressed by David Spring in his introduction to *European Landed Elites* (pp. 10–12).
90 Schneider and Schneider, *Culture and Political Economy in Western Sicily*, p. 71; Lyttelton, 'Landlords, peasants and the limits of liberalism', p. 120.
91 D. Mack Smith, 'The latifundia in modern Sicilian history', *Proceedings of the British Academy*, 51 (1965), pp. 85–124 (p. 87).
92 Malefakis, *Agrarian Reform and Peasant Revolution in Spain*, pp. 83–6, 425–6.
93 Snowden, *Fascist Revolution in Tuscany*, p. 59.
94 Cardoza, *Agrarian Elites*, pp. 8, 79–81; Snowden, *Violence and Great Estates*, pp. 97–8, 174.
95 Marcilhacy, *Le diocèse d'Orléans*, pp. 138–40, 202–17 and *passim*.
96 M. Agulhon, *La République au village: les populations du Var de la Révolution à la Seconde République* (Paris: 1970), pp. 255, 476–8 and *passim*. For a somewhat different perception, see Margadant, *French Peasants in Revolt*, ch. 8.
97 Landsberger, *Rural Protest*, p. 50.
98 P. Corner, 'Fascist agrarian policy and the Italian economy in the inter-war years', in Davis, *Gramsci and Italy's Passive Revolution*, pp. 239–74. Corner emphasizes the severe limits of any such policy.
99 Cardoza, *Agrarian Elites*, pp. 22, 118–19; Snowden, *Violence and Great Estates*, pp. 128–30, 179–81; Snowden, *Fascist Revolution in Tuscany*, pp. 95–9; Corner, *Fascism in Ferrara*, pp. 15, 160; Kertzer, *Family Life in Central Italy*, pp. 47–8; Snowden, 'On the social origins of agrarian fascism in Italy', pp. 276 ff.
100 See M. Blinkhorn, 'War on two fronts: politics and society in Navarre, 1931–6', in Preston, *Revolution and War in Spain*, pp. 59–84.
101 J. Mooser, 'Property and wood theft', in Moeller, *Peasants and Lords in Modern Germany*, pp. 52–80.
102 H. Plaul, 'The rural proletariat: the everyday life of rural labourers in the Magdeburg region, 1830–1880', in Evans and Lee, *The German Peasantry*, pp. 102–28. See also the articles by Harnisch, Schulte and Wilke in the same collection.
103 P. Vigier, *La Seconde République dans la Région Alpine: étude politique et sociale*, 2 vols (Paris: 1963), Vol. II, p. 73.
104 Mme Romieu (Marie Sincère), *Des paysans et de l'agriculture en France au XIXe siècle. Intérêts – Moeurs – Institutions* (Paris: 1865), p. 419. (We have translated '*cultivateur*' as 'peasant proprietor', which would not always be correct but which is clearly meant here.)
105 ibid., pp. 319–20. Status divisions concerning marriage within the French peasantry are well evoked in the television film *Jacquou le Croquant*, and in the first French film to be shot in patois, *Histoire d'Adrien*.
106 Corbin, *Archaïsme et Modernité en Limousin*, Vol. II, p. 825 and *passim*.
107 Jones, *Southern Massif Central*, pp. 93–4.

108 Newby, 'The deferential dialectic', pp. 150–1.
109 Davis, *Conflict and Control*, p. 69.
110 Landsberger, *Rural Protest*, pp. 17–18, 33.
111 Scott, 'Exploitation in rural relations', pp. 493, 515.
112 Sabetti, *Political Authority in a Sicilian Village*, p. 99; see also Mack Smith, 'The latifundia in modern Sicilian history', p. 118.
113 Carsten, *Prussian Junkers*, p. 143.
114 J. A. Perkins, 'The German agricultural worker, 1815–1914', *Journal of Peasant Studies*, xi, 3 (April 1984), pp. 3–27 (p. 24); Carsten, *Prussian Junkers*, pp. 143–4.
115 J. Pitié, *Exode rural et migrations intérieures en France. L'exemple de la Vienne et du Poitou-Charentes* (Poitiers: 1971), p. 323 (and bk 2, ch. III in general).
116 Lequin *et al.*, *Histoire des Français, XIXe–XXe siècles*, Vol. II, p. 43.
117 P. Simoni, 'Agricultural change and landlord-tenant relations in nineteenth-century France: the canton of Apt (Vaucluse)', *Journal of Social History*, xiii, 1 (Fall 1979), pp. 115–35.
118 Price, 'Labour supply and social relationships in the French countryside during the Second Empire', esp. p. 8.
119 Pitié, *Exode rural*, p. 459. See also P. Pinchemel, *Structures sociales et dépopulation rurale dans les campagnes picardes de 1836 à 1936* (Paris: 1957), p. 95; Vigier, *La Seconde République dans la Région Alpine*, Vol. I, pp. 42–3; A. Armengaud, *Les populations de l'Est-Aquitain au début de l'époque contemporaine: recherches sur une région moins développée (vers 1845–vers 1871)* (Paris and The Hague: 1961), p. 267; Romieu, *Des paysans et de l'agriculture*, pp. 413–21.
120 See Malefakis, *Agrarian Reform and Peasant Revolution in Spain*, pp. 104–6, and J. S. MacDonald, 'Agricultural organization, migration and labour militancy in rural Italy', *Economic History Review*, 2nd series, 16, 1 (August 1963), pp. 61–75.
121 Landsberger, *Rural Protest*, pp. 46–7.
122 Marx and Engels, *Collected Works*, Vol. 11, p. 187.
123 Corner, *Fascism in Ferrara*, p. 4; Cardoza, *Agrarian Elites*, pp. 26–7.
124 Blok, *Mafia of a Sicilian Village*, pp. 25–6; A. Blok, 'South Italian agro-towns', *Comparative Studies in Society and History*, 11 (1969), pp. 121–35; Blok, 'Mafia and peasant rebellion', pp. 95–116 (p. 102).
125 Davis, *Gramsci and Italy's Passive Revolution*, pp. 112, 147. See also Snowden, *Fascist Revolution in Tuscany*, pp. 18–20.
126 M. Agulhon, 'La notion de village en Basse-Provence vers la fin de l'Ancien Régime', *Actes du 90e Congrès national des Sociétés Savantes* (Nice: 1965), Section d'Histoire Moderne et Contemporaine (Paris: 1966), Vol. I, pp. 277–301; see also the same author's *La vie sociale en Provence intérieure*, pp. 59–61 and his *République au village*, p. 299.
127 Jones, *Southern Massif Central*, p. 25.
128 Corbin, *Archaïsme et Modernité en Limousin*, Vol. II, p. 991.
129 L. Coser, *Greedy Institutions* (New York: 1974).
130 Hobsbawm and Rudé, *Captain Swing*, pp. 152–3.
131 Lyttelton, 'Landlords, peasants and the limits of liberalism', p. 113.
132 Price, 'Labour supply and social relationships in the French countryside during the Second Empire', p. 11.
133 See Bois, *Paysans de l'Ouest*.
134 See Margadant, *French Peasants in Revolt*.
135 On the *rabassaires*, see A. Balcells, *El problema agrario en Cataluña. La cuestión Rabassaire (1890–1936)* (Madrid: 1980).
136 Landsberger, *Rural Protest*, p. 52. In this context, rural literacy was clearly also a factor. Landsberger has observed, for example, that better-educated groups of peasants have usually been more likely to participate in protest movements (ibid., p. 52). Frank Snowden notes, however, that in the case of Cerignola the *braccianti* were all the more unmanageable because they had not known the 'civilizing' influence of primary education. It might also be argued that the peasants of the French Third Republic accepted the existing order – as their *démocrate-socialiste* forebears had not – at least in part because they had passed through the Republic's schools.

FRANCE

1

Land and power in the West of France, 1750–1914

Donald Sutherland

Everyone is familiar with the story Tocqueville tells of leading his peasants to vote on 23 April 1848.[1] A little parade with Tocqueville at the head, everyone else in alphabetical order, made its way to the *chef-lieu de canton* to vote the son of their former seigneurs into the Constituent Assembly. Tocqueville himself had conducted a restrained campaign in the Manche and on voting day limited himself to a little warning to his people not to be diverted into the taverns before casting their ballots. Earlier, he referred to the family seat as 'the natural centre of my influence'. Tocqueville, then, took his election entirely for granted, and was clearly uncomfortable when earlier he had to solicit votes from the masses. So was the Comte de Falloux. He stood in the elections of 1863 in Maine-et-Loire and campaigned by going around to the great houses. He referred to the influence of a neighbour, the Marquise de Maillé, who 'conquered a popularity which extended far by her virtue and charity alone'.[2] That those at the top of the social heap should consider their authority natural and legitimate is entirely to be expected, but there are plenty of indications that those lower down the scale shared the same view. During the counter-revolutionary wars of the West in the 1790s, ordinary people not only accepted the leadership of their erstwhile seigneurs, they actively sought it out. After a time, they developed notions of deference and hierarchy to which individual nobles had to conform or else face a kind of popular derogation.[3] A bitter deception that some nobles accepted the compromises demanded by the Napoleonic settlement even surfaced in the risings of 1815 and 1832.[4].

In normal times, ordinary people appear to have accepted notions of hierarchy and deference imposed by the elite. This was not necessarily always accomplished without coercion. One disgruntled notary from Ernée in the Mayenne blamed the estate stewards who 'held in their hands the direction of agriculture and the recruitment of the near totality of sharecroppers of the region. . . . No one dared challenge them, so feared was their vengeance which they used without pity . . .' This may well have been so, yet the landlords hardly monopolized the land and so the basis of the elite's power is elusive.[5] As the inquiry of 1884 showed, the West of France was hardly an area of large estates (in this case, those exceeding 100 hectares); quite the contrary.[6] Nor was the hierarchy of wealth a formidable misshapen hourglass which allowed the regional elite to abuse its wealth to gain authority. Nor, contrary to a persistent myth, was the region notable for the heavy hand of an ancient feudalism. Nor, finally, do we have to descend into an eerie historical mysticism attributing popular respect for social hierarchy to timeless habits of mind.[7] In fact, the uniqueness of the West – that is, the region comprising the three departments of Lower Normandy, the five Breton, the two of Maine and the four from the Vendée militaire – can be explained in concrete terms. Land brought power but only after certain intermediary factors are taken into account.

Evaluating the continued importance of the great estate over the period is not possible in any strict sense. Agricultural inquiries from the nineteenth century rarely used the same categories of analysis over more than two periods. Comparisons are therefore difficult. Nonetheless, a rough comparison of the figures demonstrates that the West remained an area of infinite small holdings, great inequality and significant landed estates. The maldistribution of private wealth, for instance, was quite remarkable. In 1910, roughly 3 per cent of the successions were worth 50,000 francs and more, representing just over 50 per cent of the value of all successions. That is, a tiny minority held half the wealth. At the other end of the scale, just over half the successions were worth less than 2,000 francs yet they comprised less than 5 per cent of all successions.[8] Of course this distribution of private wealth on the eve of the First World War contained income not only from agricultural sources but also from domestic and foreign stocks and bonds, bank accounts, insurance policies, businesses, urban real estate, and so on, but the land still contributed enormously to the region's portfolio. In 1898, roughly half of the successions for 48 per cent of the overall value had landed income, while real estate and debts owed comprised 75 per cent of the overall volume.[9] Landed wealth alone therefore must have reflected similar gaps between the very rich and the very poor.

There was also a significant variation in the distribution of wealth between departments. In both the Morbihan and Finistère 60 per cent of the successions accounted for only 1 per cent of the private wealth. At the other end of the scale, in the Calvados roughly 4 per cent of the successions accounted for nearly two thirds of all the wealth while the same proportion took in over 60 per cent in the Loire-Inférieure.

There is no earlier source which represents the pyramid of wealth in such lush detail but some manipulation of the land-tax figures for 1858 shows some intriguing continuities.[10] In the middle years of the Second Empire just under 5 per cent of the population paid over 100 francs in land tax but this tiny minority accounted for 48 per cent of that tax's overall yield. Poverty was also widespread. Just over 60 per cent of the population paid less than 10 francs but they accounted for only 9 per cent of the yield. Broadly speaking then the hierarchy of land-tax assessments in 1858 was not much different from the hierarchy of private wealth recorded in the testaments of 1910. It therefore seems reasonable to suppose that the distribution of wealth did not change dramatically in this period. Indeed, as we shall soon see, it had not changed very much since 1835. It is very likely, therefore, that these sources reveal the broad post-revolutionary land and wealth settlement, a settlement that assured personal equality before the law without the formal privileges of the *ancien régime* but a property settlement which nonetheless reserved an impressive share of society's resources to a very few.

There was some fluidity within this pattern both in space and in time. An examination of the regional distribution of the land tax in 1858 shows that Finistère and Morbihan were not yet the poorest departments that the records of 1910 revealed them to be. Instead the land-poor departments were the Côtes-du-Nord and Deux-Sèvres while the fairly well off were once again Calvados, joined by the Maine-et-Loire and Mayenne. Such shifts in the regional distribution of land and wealth may be due to an illusion, in that the land-tax and succession records are not strictly speaking comparable, but interlocking shifts in the pattern of population, land use and local industry were also undoubtedly responsible.

The figures also suggest that the concentration of poverty was increasing over time, albeit slowly. Thus between 1862 and 1882, the proportion of tiny holdings of less than 5 hectares increased from 48 per cent of all holdings to 65 per cent. Small holdings of between 5 and 40 hectares declined from 48 per cent to 33 per cent while medium and large holdings fell from 4 per cent to 2 per cent.[11] In other words, the pyramid of landholding was broadening at the base while becoming more sharply defined at the top. Moreover, it is likely that much of the broadening occurred between the middle years of the Second Empire and the early years of the twentieth century. A comparison of the hierarchy of tax assessments by category shows almost no change between 1835 and 1858.[12] The increase in the percentage of those paying less than 10 francs and the decrease in those paying less than 300 was only slight. Those above remained unchanged.

Taken by itself, large property held its own for much of the century. It increased its share of the surface from 23 per cent to 28 per cent between the Restoration and the 1890s in the Calvados. In the Mayenne, the proportion of land taken up by holdings of over 50 hectares scarcely changed between 1830 and 1884. Afterwards, there was a rearrangement of property among the elite. Estates of over 200 hectares, never very numerous anyway, were half as common in 1914 as in 1830 while those in the 100–200 hectare range doubled their share of the surface. In the Sarthe, between the 1820s and 1913 the experience of large property varied greatly. In some cantons there was almost no change, while in others the decline was of the order of from 25 to 50 per cent, the beneficiaries being small and medium holders.[13]

What these rather abstract figures could mean in personal terms can be illustrated with a few examples taken from various parts of the West. In 1846, the Comtesse de Pontavice Boishenry died in Fougères leaving 78 hectares in the commune of St-Etienne-en-Coglès in Ille-et-Vilaine. Her son and heir, Louis-Marie, who was descended on both sides from illustrious noble families with service in the royal armies of the *ancien régime* and the conspiracies, emigration and *chouannerie* (counter-revolutionary guerrilla war) of the Revolution, added property from other sources to bring the total to 141 hectares. Indeed the Comte de Pontavice proved himself to be quite adept in the land market. He bought two sizeable farms in St-Sauveur-des-Landes from his cousins, the De la Haye Saint-Hilaires, in 1859 and 1865, farms which raised his holdings in the commune to over 100 hectares and which remained in his family throughout the period. When he died, his daughter, Marie-Thérèse, inherited in 1876 and, aside from selling a few outbuildings and some small pieces of land in 1911, she held on to the property intact.[14] Property could be enlarged too. In 1838, the Vicomte de Bouteiller added to his already impressive estates by acquiring 260 hectares in the commune of Fleurigné in the Ille-et-Vilaine from a *rentier* in Laval. Aside from the sale of 25 hectares over the years, the purchase was still in the family's hands in 1906.[15] Indeed, estates could continue more or less intact longer than many of the families who owned them. One of the clearest examples of this began in 1735 when Jean-Baptiste Berset, a rich banker in Laval, bought a noble title. His son, also Jean-Baptiste, bought the substantial estate of Hauterive in the parish of Argentré in Lower Maine two years later and spent the rest of the century adding more land to it. Aside from being arrested as suspects, the family survived the Revolution little the worse for wear. The owner for most of the next century, Sébastien-Charles Berset d'Hauterive, managed the estate, now covering 416 hectares, with few changes – he sold off a few isolated fields in 1834, added a new farm the next year, sold a mill in 1845, experimented with marling in the 1820s and brought in new cattle breeds. He was a meticulous manager but he died childless in 1882. The estate then passed through a number of collateral branches of the family until it settled on Maurice Fitzgerald in 1898. In 1935 the estate was split among his three grandchildren, two of whom lived in Paris and the other in Le Mans. Aside from the sale of 30 hectares in 1925, the estate was practically the same size under Léon Blum as it had been under Napoleon III, or probably as it had been under Louis XVI for that matter.[16]

So long a continuity in the structure of an estate, irrespective of who owned it, was by no means unique. The 102 hectares of farmland in the commune of Louvigny in the Calvados, for example, passed in 1844 from a *rentier* in Paris to a nun in Caen and in 1877 to the Comtesse de Bourmont. As army and navy officers for the next half-century, the Bourmont men were rarely resident and the women lived elsewhere with their husbands; even so, in 1935, Henri Ghaine de Bourmont still held 80 hectares of the original holding while his aunt Marguerite owned the remaining 20-odd.[17]

Estates also declined, sometimes quite dramatically. The Hay de Nétumières family sold off their entire estate in Erbrée and Balazé in Ille-et-Vilaine in two waves in the 1840s and the 1890s. The origin of the family's troubles is not clear but when the son emigrated to Canada in 1893, only his widowed mother stayed behind to liquidate the remnants of an estate which at one time was close to 1,000 hectares. The château was acquired by another nobleman in 1910 but the purchasers of the rest of the domain represent a fair cross-section of the 'couches nouvelles': a deputy, a 'directeur du crédit foncier de France, à Rennes, rue de la monnaie', a miller, a 'juge suppléant à Fougères' and a 'docteur-médecin à Argentré'. None of these people was a peasant, none was a resident.[18] This example and others like it show that the shattering of the great estate at the *fin de siècle*, where it took place, benefited a diverse, largely urban bourgeoisie, not the resident peasantry.

The dramatically varying histories of these families, some amassing land in one generation, others divesting themselves over several, still others investing and improving on their inheritance, show how diverse the experiences of large landed families could be. But whatever the combination of good sense and private misfortune which governed a family's destiny, all of those cited above started the 'bourgeois century' rather well placed. Indeed, by far most of them were prominent regional families in the *ancien régime*. Unfortunately, it is simply not possible to describe in anything like the same detail the place of the large estate in the landholding structure of the pre-revolutionary period, so that any estimate of the effect of the Revolution on the land is problematic. A few educated guesses are all that can be offered.

In the *ancien régime*, almost all large estates were owned by nobles, and nobles commanded a greatly disproportionate share of landed revenues. Although comprising only 2 per cent of the population the nobility of the diocese of Rennes owned between one fifth and one third of the land and as the exclusive lay owners of seigneuries, which were far from moribund in Upper Brittany, they were easily the wealthiest single class in the region.[19] Indeed, nowhere, except perhaps the sugar and slave fortunes at Nantes, could *roturier* wealth generally match that of the blue-bloods. In the diocese of Vannes nobles owned about 70 per cent of the land, a situation which was characteristic of the rest of Lower Brittany as well.[20] In the region of Anjou south of the Loire, nobles comprised less than 10 per cent of the proprietors but owned nearly 60 per cent of the land.[21] Two seigneurs alone owned over two thirds of the parish of Mouliherne in Anjou in the mid-eighteenth century.[22] Examples could be multiplied but they would all show how much of a grip the local nobility had on landed resources.

The Revolution shook this authority considerably but it did not overturn it. The Sarthe may have been exceptional in that by 1830 the nobility had recovered the one fifth of the property it had owned before the Revolution. Elsewhere the losses were more permanent, although hardly startling. In the Mayenne, the loss of land was just 6 per cent and fewer than one in ten of the nobility's châteaux were sold. In the *bocage* region of the Calvados around Vire, 'nobles and privileged' could account for anywhere between 15 per cent and 40 per cent of the land, but by the early part of the nineteenth century they held less than 10 per cent. In one representative commune, Coulances, less than one fifth of the land was ever recuperated and, taking *biens nationaux* and other land sales into account, the privileged had lost one third of their holdings by 1830. In the southern part of the Loire-Inférieure, the nobility lost about 20 per cent of their holdings.[23]

Just as the extent of losses of land varied from place to place, so also did the effects of the loss of fiscal privilege and feudal dues. Indeed the effects of the loss of seigneurial dues varied practically from one family to another. With the exception of the huge château de Vitré and a few piles of rocks which were the ruins of ancient dungeons, the fortunes of the Ducs de la Trémoille consisted almost entirely of dues, tolls, private taxes and transfer fees. A stroke of the legislator's pen and peasant intransigence willed them away. Elsewhere in Upper Brittany, dues contributed half the annual revenues of the wealthy, exclusive and haughty *parlementaires* of Rennes. The duchy of Mayenne was worth close to 1.5 million *livres* in 1779 and was the overlord of dozens of inferior fiefs and sub-fiefs, yet its domain was insubstantial. On the other hand, the feudal portion of a lord's revenue could also be minimal. The barony of Neuvy in Upper Maine drew 641 *livres* from farms in 1708 but only 13 *livres* and 51 bushels of oats from its fiefs. In the reign of Louis XVI, the Comte de Tessé, one of the most important seigneurs around Le Mans, drew less than 3 per cent of his estate income from feudal dues. In short the impact of the abolition of seigneurialism on family fortunes varied greatly.[24]

Although the law of 1825 known as the *milliard des émigrés*, partially indemnifying *émigrés* for their losses, did not apply to feudal dues, another law aided landlords immeasurably. On 1 December 1790 the Constituent Assembly allowed landlords to add the equivalent of the former tithe to the lease. For erstwhile seigneurs like the Comte de Tessé with relatively large domains, this was a trade-off well worth making. Even for others whose fief income was more important, the loss was less severe than it looked. With a rising population and rising demand for land, landlords were in a position to fix higher rents. The extent to which this actually happened is difficult to determine but the experience of the tenants on the estates of the Duc de Cossé-Brissac in the Deux-Sèvres is instructive. Because they no longer paid the *taille*, taxes, salt tax and indirect taxes, their rents rose by 25 per cent in 1791 alone.[25] Berset d'Hauterive, by contrast, held most of his farms in the Mayenne on a sharecropping basis so it was impossible to raise the rent.

Indeed his share of taxes on his newly acquired *métairie* of La Bourianière tripled but since he took all of the tithe for himself (which he described as 'my indemnity'), the net effect was that he paid a mere 20 *livres* more in 1792 than he had in 1790.[26] Arrangements like these certainly made paying equitable taxes much easier to bear.

The Revolution shook the position of nobles as estate owners but no one displaced them. Indeed a broader view suggests a *longue durée* of remarkable stability. Marc Bloch argued that the history of the great estate in the early modern period is the history of trying to recapture the domain and with it the position of dominance over rural society it had once had.[27] The reconstitution of the domain in the sixteenth century in Poitou and no doubt elsewhere was largely a process in which the local nobility revoked the *censives* and regrouped them into larger holdings, trampling over common rights and enclosing fields at the same time. The result was the *métairie*, a farm of about 30 hectares which practised a balanced polyculture.[28]

In fact, the *métairie* defined the agriculture, the settlement patterns and the social arrangements of the West for long after the demise of the *ancien régime*. Unlike the northern plains whose agrarian system is so well known to students of the *ancien régime*, the West practised an enclosed agriculture and what common rights there were existed only on the extensive wastelands. The interminably complex disputes over gleaning, grazing, passage and other rights were largely absent in the West. Property rights were thus more strongly defined. Settlement patterns were different too. Instead of the nuclear or linear villages of classic *ancien régime* agriculture, people lived in isolated family farms or tiny hamlets of no more than a dozen households each. High hedgerows surrounded the tiny fields, there were clumps of forest everywhere and the trees arched over the deep-rutted roads so that travellers invariably described the region as lonely and forbidding. Finally, strong property rights and scattered settlement went hand in hand with a fairly equitable distribution of wealth within peasant communities. Exceptionally wealthy peasant families existed, but they were rare. Instead, landowners divided their estates into moderate-sized farms.

These farms were rented under any one of three forms of lease: the *domaine congéable*, which dominated western Brittany and was a system of shared ownership in which tenants owned the buildings, crops and fruit trees and rented the land from the landlord;[29] *fermage*, which was the most common form of leaseholding in the West, whereby landlord–tenant relations were increasingly governed by a cash rent, with minor payments in labour services gradually being eliminated; and finally *métayage* or sharecropping, which was centred on the Mayenne and in patches around its neighbouring departments.[30]

Whatever the form of leasehold, agriculture in the West has proved itself to be adaptive and resilient. By the eighteenth century in the West, the reconstitution of the estate had generally gone as far as it would go. The estates stabilized, rarely acquiring land and not even bothering with anything which could be called a 'seigneurial reaction'. Instead landlords doubly benefited. They were the passive beneficiaries of rising rents which climbed faster than prices. They were also successful opportunists as the terms of trade between them and the urban grain merchants tilted in their favour.[31] By the nineteenth century they were well poised to lead the agricultural revolution. Since land was already enclosed, improvement meant the steady exploitation of waste-land and an increasing emphasis on dairying, a phenomenon which began as early as the seventeenth century in parts of Normandy. By the early years of the twentieth century, the western departments were almost invariably near the top of the national league table depicting the rental value of both pasture and arable land – an undoubted reflection of the heavy investment in agricultural renewal.[32] Given the structure of wealth, proprietors led this movement, seizing the opportunity presented by rising cattle prices and stagnant grain prices down to the 1870s to finance the conversion to pasture and then, with the onset of the Great Depression, reducing their farmers' rents. This was too much for some and the major theme of rural history in the past hundred years is the gradual decline of large absentee-owned property and the emergence of medium-sized peasant property.[33] But it has been a very slow process. Around Nantes, it has been imperceptible. In the canton of Cambremer in the Calvados, noble property declined by only 4 per cent between 1880 and 1935, and while the average size of holding doubled to 10 hectares, peasant cultivators increased by only 10 per cent. In Brittany as a whole, leaseholding declined by only 20 per cent between 1882 and 1970 and there are even cantons in the interior of the Ille-et-Vilaine and throughout Lower Normandy where *fermage* has increased substantially since 1929.[34]

Although it is a subject which cries out for further research, one of the reasons for this resilience has been the reliance on tenant families and the manner in which they in turn have organized their labour. In the larger estates at any rate, tenants were remarkably secure. In the *domaine congéable* regions of Lower Brittany, this uninterrupted tenure could last several generations, while in the *fermage* and *métayage* regions, a single generation appears to have been the norm, although there are examples of sharecroppers passing tenancies from father to son.[35] Whatever the arrangement these were ways of masking labour costs, or rather of absorbing them within tenant families. Neighbourly and occasional help always supplemented family labour and, depending on the size of the farm, it was also common to retain a hand for years at a time. Young men and women were also taken on for a few years but this was a temporary service usually undertaken when the tenant's own children were still too young and while the quasi-permanent employees were building up their own nest-eggs.[36] One example among hundreds available shows this pattern well. Louis Jolivet of Bourgneuf in the Mayenne presided over a household which in 1881 consisted of his wife, four daughters, two young sons, his father-in-law and a farmhand. Five years later, his wife's father had died and since his own sons were now in their mid-teens, a hand was no longer necessary. Over the years, the children gradually moved away, all except one son, also named Louis, who inherited the lease in 1901 after his parents' death. By 1910, this Louis had two children, his mother-in-law was living in and he employed his brother-in-law as a labourer. The Jolivets were still there in 1936. In fact, they were by then the only inhabitants of the hamlet.[37]

Because a system based on moderately sized family farms forced tenants to absorb labour costs, there were invariably periods of tension over rents and, once the rural exodus began in the 1840s, over wage rates and terms of payment. Yet agriculture did not require a huge pool of cheap and easily available rural workers, so that the explosive tensions detailed elsewhere in this volume were absent. Nor did owners regard their estates as merely temporary sources of income to be exploited for all they were worth. Instead, as the massive landowner apologia of the period reiterated, estates were patrimonies to be preserved, the essential underpinnings of a family's continuity and status.

Enough has been said so far to indicate that the relationship between the large estate and the rural community has varied greatly over time; aggressive in the sixteenth century until it found a quasi-benign commercial vocation in the seventeenth and eighteenth, then mutating once again into an agent of progress in the nineteenth. Certainly, too, owners of large estates were always powerful men. Wealthy proprietors dominated the general councils down to at least 1870 while nobles were especially prominent and wealthy within this group. Given the nature of wealth and electoral restrictions, wealthy proprietors were prominent among the deputations to all the legislatures between 1800 and 1848, but even the advent of universal suffrage did not impair their representation in the legislatures of the Second and Third Republics. The descendants of some *parlementaires* of Rennes even managed to find a career in the judiciary for themselves in the nineteenth century. Nobles were even prominent mayors; they rarely provided less than 20 per cent of mayors in the Sarthe in the nineteenth century, and as late as the 1950s the West in general was remarkable for the proportion of noble mayors.[38]

Disproportionate command of resources as well as prominence in public life certainly represented power and brought with them the ability to influence others. But there was no lock-step simple relationship between land and power. There is a multitude of ways of demonstrating this but the most concise is to try to correlate electoral results with the various measures of landholding. Unfortunately, for the 14 departments of the West as a whole there was no significant correlation between what contemporaries called the 'reactionary' vote in 1885 and the percentage of *cotes foncières* over 40 hectares in the tax survey of 1884. Nor is there a relationship with the percentage of exploitations of over 40 hectares counted in the agricultural survey of 1882.[39]

A global approach by department is not always advantageous. The sample of 14 is rather small and a unit as large as a department might eclipse several types of economic geography. It is possible to break departments down in some cases. Fairly complete results of the tax inquiry of 1884 survive for the entire Mayenne and the *arrondissement* of Vannes in the Morbihan.[40] The sample sizes are certainly large enough but perhaps because of its unique landholding arrangements there is still no relationship between royalism and large property in the Morbihan. There is for Mayenne, however. A significant correlation exists between monarchist votes in 1877 and the proportion of estates over 100 hectares ($r = 0.22$, $p = 0.01$, $n = 114$ communes) but the explanatory value of this relationship is rather low. This is not to say that wealth had no bearing on the incidence of royalism. When the size of the urban population is controlled for, there is a highly significant negative correlation with the relative amount left in successions ($r = 0.58$, $p = 0.02$) of between 10,000 and 50,000 francs. That is, a fairly preponderant role for this type of middle-ranking wealth, which accounted for 14 per cent of the successions and 29 per cent of the wealth, tended to depress the royalist appeal. It appears as if the rural 'middle class' of independent, owner-occupying peasants and liberal professionals was hostile to royalism. On the other hand, still taking urban effects into account, there was a highly positive correlation ($r = 0.50$, $p = 0.05$) with areas where the proportions of successions leaving less than 500 francs was high.[41] Royalism did not, however, appeal to the poor as such but its appeal was certainly popular. Nor did it particularly depend, contrary to a thesis André Siegfried made famous, on the presence of large property.[42] The châtelains had influence, but for other reasons.

Siegfried was right, however, to stress the importance of the church. In the Ille-et-Vilaine, Mayenne and Sarthe, the correlation between royalist voting in the legislative elections of 1849 and the percentage of men performing their Easter duties is particularly strong. Moreover, this influence was more or less significant, no matter what critical election is considered, those of 1849 and 1877 where the existence of the Republic was at issue or that of 1906 which amounted to a referendum on the separation of church and state, and the subsequent controversial and often violent inventories of church property.[43] This was even related to the past in that in both the Mayenne and the Ille-et-Vilaine, there was a strong relation between church-going and the intensity of *chouannerie*, the Catholic and royalist guerrilla war which devastated the West during the First Republic.[44] Whether it expressed itself with guns or with ballots, religion thus appears to be the key to royalism.

Certainly contemporaries thought so. Indeed, legitimists knew it. In 1849, the militant bishop of Rennes, Brossais Saint-Marc, vetoed the original list of the Party of Order and imposed his own.[45] In the Mayenne, one legitimist worried about the danger of letting 'the clergy produce a strictly Catholic candidate and wean the electorate from accepting the candidate proposed by the legitimists . . . the influence of the [Catholic newspaper] *L'Univers* will replace our own'.[46] For the most part, however, the clergy acted in the legitimist interest, and right across the century there was an incessant barrage of criticism or solicitation of the clerical role in politics. As early as 1824, Mgr de la Myre, bishop of Le Mans, issued a *mandement* which claimed: 'We cannot tell you how to vote but only remind you that you only ought to choose virtuous men, friends of order, of the legitimate monarchy and of religion.'[47] The victory of moderates in the elections of April 1848 in Finistère was attributed to the 'incomparable organization of the clergy put to the service of the legitimists'.[48] In the Vendée, there was a similar appreciation from an outraged republican: 'The clergy is the winner. The Grand Elector of the Vendée is the bishop of Luçon. He made a list of candidates, distributed it through the *curés*, imposed it in the confessional and spent the whole of Lent in these manoeuvres.'[49]

The clergy was as partisan in the Third Republic. Priests at Gorron in the Mayenne in February 1871 toured the markets shouting, 'Do you want peace? Take these ballots.'[50] In 1880, the *vicaire* of Nort in the Loire-Inférieure referred to the tricolour as 'this muck'; the *recteur* of Plouganveur in the Côtes-du-Nord denied calling Republican voters 'servants of Satan'; the *curé* of Maure in the Ille-et-Vilaine was accused of preaching that 'the church is persecuted, they want to close the churches, chase the priests out, take Christ out of the schools'; and the *recteur* of Brice near Redon was so transported by his own oratory as to claim that 'two armies were doing battle, the army of the devil and that of God, the Republic was the devil's and the conservatives were God's'.[51] Finally the *desservant* of Chamie in the Ille-et-Vilaine in 1889 was supposed to have preached, 'I firmly hope that you will not vote for the thieves and scoundrels, partisans of the godless school', and, in a direct appeal to women, said that 'women ought to blush with shame to know that their husbands vote for men like that'.[52]

Such inflammatory remarks usually resulted in a reprimand from the bishop or, in the most blatant cases, a steep 100-franc fine. But there were ways of delivering the same message which provoked no reprisals. As convoluted as it was, everyone knew what the *Semaine du fidèle* of Le Mans meant when it declared in 1875: 'Catholics . . . have decided to go from sanctuary to sanctuary to implore . . . the Sovereign Master of empires and kingdoms to obtain the triumph of the two causes which their prayers do not separate any more than their love.'[53] Language did not always have to be euphemistic. According to the *Semaine religieuse* of Rennes in 1893, women should implore their men to choose 'honest representatives and to expel in the process the abominable sectarians who are oppressing us'.[54] Even the most inflammatory talk did not always provoke official reprisal. In 1902, the *recteur* of Plénée-Jugon in the Côtes-du-Nord got away with claiming, 'We imagine the horrors of the Terror could not be reproduced and yet here in our own day we see monks and nuns in exile.'[55] Amid a growing torrent of denunciations of freemasons and a shameful, demagogic anti-Semitism in religious journals and from candidates, the bishop of Vannes in 1902 exhorted prayers from the faithful 'to obtain representatives who are friends of the church and of all the liberties which Jesus Christ brought to men'.[56]

These are extreme cases but they grew out of the clergy's conception of its pastoral role. Contrary to a persistent myth, the clergy of the West did not live in an affable bonhomie with its flock. Instead, the nineteenth century witnessed the apogee of an *ancien régime* conception of pastoral obligation first enunciated at the Council of Trent. The total failure of the constitutional church and the restoration to the parishes of what amounted to the refractory in the Concordat of 1801 was also a victory for those who believed the clergy should live as a separate estate. An ordinance on ecclesiastical discipline issued in 1828 by the bishop of Rennes reminded the clergy that 'Placed in an order apart, raised by his estate above all that surrounds him, the priest . . . is like a mirror where the simple believer finds a model which he will always imitate in all things'.[57] Later in the century, a priest in the Finistère wrote that 'the priest ought to be above all a mysterious being who lives between the vestibule and the altar'.[58] For the most part these men followed a life of unadorned austerity, believing in the necessity of reducing the body to elevate the soul. Obituaries may not be the best source for evaluating everyday conduct, and those of priests are especially suspect since the descriptions of their lives and the manner of their dying were so obviously meant to inspire their colleagues to emulation. But beyond the standard fare emphasizing the deceased's charity, his dedication to devotional institutions, his ability to get the parish church rebuilt, his serene, courageous and pious death, and so on, on occasion a real individual pops through. Thus the Abbé Martineau, *curé* of Saint-Denis-du-Maine, was a man who 'joining to the firmness of character a great goodness of soul, of an exemplary regularity right to the end, pious and charitable, was a model for all'. Or another: 'this clarity of decision and firmness in the execution of his thoughts . . . incapable of compromising his duty or betraying his conscience'. Or still another: 'the gravity of his conduct, the wisdom of his advice and direction'. Lay friendships outside the family were evidently rare. Thus the Abbé Morin of Cossé-le-Vivieu near Laval: 'he found his happiness in gathering about him the members of his family, his colleagues from around the region, his old *vicaires* and the *abbés* of the parish.'[59] Probably few were so self-disciplined as the Abbé Doussin of Teillé in the Loire-Inférieure, who said his breviary while fishing in the local pond, but many led the austere life they preached to the laity.[60] Bishops and priests together stressed the importance of duty to God, to the state and to parents. Questioning the status quo was equivalent to disobeying God.[61] Self-discipline was critical too. There was an incessant criticism of drunkenness and cabarets as irreligious and of dancing as promiscuous. 'The most monstrous obscenities,' one shocked *vicaire* wrote of dancing, 'impure gestures, infamous looks, shameful actions, each demon finds his faithful servants in the middle of dancing.'[62]

A self-denying clergy preaching a strict morality of family and civic duty generally had an appeal. Yet there were occasions when the clergy went too far and were consequently ignored. People always danced at the harvest and at weddings. The arrogance of some priests could provoke their removal, as with the Abbé Keraudren in the Finistère who vainly tried to impose a railway halt on his parishioners in 1899 and got himself displaced for his trouble.[63] Indeed, whether clerical intervention always brought success for the right is problematic. In the Calvados, for example, people in some communes so resented their *curés*' attempts to lead them by the nose that they voted Republican more solidly than they ever had before. Moreover, clerical hostility to the Republic was not a constant. In the Calvados in the 1880s, a period of acute tension over ecclesiastical and educational issues, about half the parish clergy were classed as enemies of the regime. In the next decade the majority of clerics were classed as apolitical. Yet the Calvados remained a bastion of anti-republicanism.[64] In other words, clerical influence on the laity mattered but, ultimately, the religious and political mentalities of the West grew out of the social situation in which people found themselves.

Intense loyalty to the church and to right-wing causes was associated with distinct social phenomena. If the Mayenne was at all typical, attendance at Easter Mass was highest in cantons where small property in the 4 to 9 hectare range had weight (average $r = 0.46$), where literacy was low ($r = -0.64$, $p = 0.03$), where sharecroppers were common ($r = 0.75$, $p = 0.01$), and where farmers who also owned property were rare ($r = -0.51$, $p = 0.003$). That is, religious practices were associated with certain social phenomena, in this case small holdings and relative cultural isolation. This was also largely the profile of a royalist commune, with some important differences: illiteracy was less important, property holdings were slightly larger, but the relationship with tenancy remained significant (Mayenne $r = 0.27$, $p = 0.004$, $n = 93$ sections in 1849 elections; Morbihan $r = 0.30$, $p = 0.04$, $n = 34$ sections; Ille-et-Vilaine $r = 0.73$, $p = 0.01$, $n = 17$ sections). Royalism and Catholicism thus had similar constituencies.[65] Large landowners, the local nobility and others had influence in the region because they had the confidence of more humble men.

Siegfried, of course, had a ready answer to explain this: cleric and châtelain used their spiritual authority and economic power to influence the humble. While they certainly tried, the power of the great operated in a social milieu. Thus, popular legitimism and religious practice depended not only on landholding but possibly also on certain traits of family organization. According to the census of 1901, the West was remarkable for a number of demographic characteristics: a high male and female celibacy rate, a fairly late marriage age, a longer than usual interval before the birth of the first child, a fairly high number of families with no children at all and others with many children and a low life expectancy.[66] Whatever the relation to the structure of work among the medium-sized tenants and sharecroppers and their management of family resources, such a pattern must have created tensions, especially among those deprived of the chance of marriage at all or among those who had to wait out much of their youth until they could get established. A clergy which practised self-abnegation and which preached self-discipline performed a useful role in such circumstances.

But this is almost entirely pure speculation. Certainly the elements which gave Tocqueville such authority were very complex. He would have wished it otherwise. Surely it is both odd and significant at the same time that he crossed out a sentence which included the clergy in his little parade?

NOTES

1 A. de Tocqueville, *Recollections* (Cleveland, Ohio: 1959), pp. 103–4, 95.
2 Comte de Falloux, *Mémoires d'un royaliste*, 2 vols (Paris: 1888), Vol. I, p. 407 and the highly romanticized view in *Mémoires de Mme la Marquise de la Rochejacquelin* (Paris: 1823), pp. 32–3.
3 D. M. G. Sutherland, *The Chouans. The Social Origins of Popular Counter-Revolution in Upper Brittany, 1770–1796* (Oxford: 1982), pp. 166–78.
4 E. Queruau-Lamerie, 'Les dernières convulsions de la chouannerie mayennaise (1815 et 1832)', *Bulletin de la commission historique et archéologique de la Mayenne* (1923), p. 213 and (the title speaks volumes) A. Billard de Veaux, *Mémoires . . . pour servir à . . . détourner les habitants de l'Ouest de toute tentative d'insurrection*, 3 vols (Paris: 1832).
5 Cited in M. Denis, *L'Église et la république en Mayenne, 1896–1906* (Paris: 1967), pp. 38–9.
6 See the map in *Bulletin de législation et de Statistique comparée*, xvi (1884), pp. 389–91.
7 But see M. Lagrée and R. Gildea, 'The historical geography of the West of France: the evidence of Ille-et-Vilaine', *English Historical Review*, xciv (1979), p. 879.
8 Figures in *Bulletin de législation et de Statistique comparée*, lxx (1911), pp. 678–85.
9 ibid., xlv (1899), pp. 434–41.
10 Ministère de l'Agriculture, Statistique de la France, *Agriculture: Résultats généraux de l'enquête décennale de 1862* (Strasbourg: 1870).
11 ibid., and Ministère de l'Agriculture, Statistique agricole de la France, *Résultats généraux de l'enquête décennale de 1882* (Nancy: 1887).
12 See note 9.
13 G. Désert, *Une société rurale au XIXe siècle. Les Paysans du Calvados, 1815–1895* (New York: 1977), pp. 104, 669–70. M. Denis, *Les Royalistes de la Mayenne et le monde moderne* (n.p.: 1977), p. 451; G. Macé, *Un Département rural de l'Ouest. La Mayenne*, 2 vols (Mayenne: 1982), Vol. I, p. 17; P. Bois, *Paysans de l'Ouest. Des structures économiques et sociales aux options politiques depuis l'époque révolutionnaire dans la Sarthe* (Le Mans: 1960), p. 81.
14 The story can be reconstructed from the *matrice cadastrale* of St-Sauveur-des-Landes in Archives Départementales d'Ille-et-Vilaine [hereafter AD, IV], 3P 2812 and that of St-Etienne-en-Coglès in AD, IV, 3P 2459. Genealogical points can be clarified in H. Froter de la Messélière, *Filiations bretonnes, 1650–1912*, 5 vols (St-Brieuc: 1914), Vol. IV, p. 418.
15 AD, IV, 3P 985, *matrice cadastrale* of Fleurigné.
16 AD, Mayenne [hereafter AD, M], 3P 16, *matrice cadastrale* of Argentré, 1825; AD, M, 3P 1055, *matrice cadastrale* of Argentré, 1911. There is also an important collection of account books and estate papers in AD, M, 179J 27, 62, 64–5. AD, M, L1593, registre du comité de surveillance, 15 germinal An II. Biographical information in A. Angot, *Dictionnaire historique, topographique et biographique de la Mayenne*, 4 vols (Mayenne: 1982), Vol. I, pp. 235–6.
17 AD, Calvados, 3P 4956–7, 4958, *matrice cadastrale* de Louvigny, 1823, 1913.

18 AD, IV, 3P 218, 928, *matrices cadastrales*, Balazé, Erbrée; Froter de la Messélière, *Filiations bretonnes*, Vol. III, pp. 45, 286.
19 Sutherland, *The Chouans*, p. 77.
20 T. J. A. Le Goff, *Vannes and Its Region. A Study of Town and Country in Eighteenth-Century France* (Oxford: 1981), p. 154.
21 R. H. Andrews, *Les paysans des Mauges au 18e siècle. Étude sur la vie rurale dans une région de l'Anjou* (Tours: 1935), pp. 11–15.
22 R. Plessix, 'Une paroisse angevine au XIXe siècle, Mouliherne', *Revue du Bas-Poitou* (1969), p. 57.
23 Bois, *Paysans de l'Ouest*, p. 323; Macé, *La Mayenne*, Vol. I, p. 38; Désert, *Paysans du Calvados*, p. 108; P. Nicolle, *La Vente des biens nationaux à Vire et dans les communes voisines* (Vire: 1923), pp. 73–155; D. C. Higgs, *Nobles in Nineteenth-Century France: the Practice of Inegalitarianism* (Baltimore, Md and London: 1987), p. 54.
24 J.-F. Labourdette, 'Fortune et administration des biens de La Trémoille au XVIIIe siècle', *Annales de Bretagne*, lxxxii (1975), pp. 163–77; Sutherland, *The Chouans*, p. 181; J. Mayer, *La Noblesse bretonne au XVIIIe siècle* (Paris: 1966), pp. 14–17; Bois, *Paysans de l'Ouest*, p. 383.
25 D. M. G. Sutherland, *France, 1789–1815. Revolution and Counter-Revolution* (London: 1985), p. 105.
26 AD, M, 179J 64, accounts for *métairie* of La Bourianière.
27 For a striking confirmation of this hypothesis, see Jon Dewald, *Pont-St-Pierre, 1398–1789. Lordship, Community and Capitalism in Early Modern France* (Berkeley, Los Angeles, Calif. and London: 1987), esp. pp. 224–38.
28 L. Merle, *La Métairie et l'évolution de la gâtine poitevine de la fin du Moyen Age à la Révolution* (Paris: 1958), *passim*.
29 Le Goff, *Vannes and Its Region*, p. 158.
30 Comte de Tourdonnet, *Situation du métayage en France* (Paris: 1879–80), pp. 91–8.
31 Le Goff, *Vannes and Its Region*, pp. 299–302.
32 Ministère des Finances, Direction générale des contributions directes, *Évaluation des propriétés non bâties prescrite par la loi du 31 décembre 1907*, 2 vols (Paris: 1913).
33 M. Lévy-Leboyer, *Le Revenu agricole et la rente foncière en Basse-Normandie. Étude de croissance régionale* (Paris: 1972), pp. 86–90, 112–14.
34 G. Dallas, *The Imperfect Peasant Economy: The Loire Country, 1800–1914* (Cambridge: 1982), p. 205; G. Rollinger, 'La propriété foncière dans le canton de Cambremer (1880–1935)', Mémoire de maîtrise, Caen, 1975, pp. 41, 49, 75, 81; Ministère d'Agriculture, Service régional de statistique agricole, *Les Agriculteurs et la propriété. L'évolution des modes de faire valoir en Bretagne* (Rennes: 1976), pp. 20–2; Lévy-Leboyer, *Revenu agricole en Basse-Normandie*, p. 19.
35 T. J. A. Le Goff and D. M. G. Sutherland, 'The social origins of counter-revolution in western France', *Past and Present*, 99 (1983), p. 70.
36 R. de Montecler, *Un Domaine dans une région d'élevage (Bas-Maine)* (n.p.: 1922), p. 27.
37 AD, M, série M, dénombrements de la population, Bourgneuf.
38 L. Girard, A. Prost and R. Gossez, *Les Conseillers généraux en 1870. Étude Statistique d'un personnel politique* (Paris: 1967), pp. 110–20; Higgs, *Nobles in Nineteenth-Century France*, pp. 134–47; G. Désert, 'Les Paysans Bas-Normands et la politique', *Annales de Normandie*, xxvi (1976), p. 197; T. Zeldin, *France, 1848–1945*, 2 vols (Oxford: 1973), Vol. I, p. 411.
39 Election results from *Le Temps*, 18 October 1885; Ministère des Finances, Direction générale des contributions directes, *Nouvelle évaluation du revenu foncier des propriétés non bâties . . . Résultats généraux* (Paris: 1883); Statistique agricole de la France, *Enquête décennale de 1882*.
40 Election results, Mayenne: AD, M, 3M 478; Morbihan: AD, Morbihan, 3M 264. Land: Cadastre. Relevé des totaux de la contenance imposable par article de la matrice cadastrale des propriétés non-bâties, 1884 in ibid., P 1024–6 and AD, M, P 360–2.
41 See notes 7 and 8 for sources.
42 A. Siegfried, *Tableau politique de la France de l'Ouest sous la troisième république* (Paris: 1913), *passim*.
43 Figures by canton in P. Fourcault, 'Aspects de la vie chrétienne dans un grand diocèse de l'Ouest de la France au XIXe siècle. La diocèse du Mans de 1830 à 1854', doctorat de III

cycle, Caen, 1980, pp. 510–12; for Ille-et-Vilaine, index constructed from map in H. Goallou, 'Pratique religieuse et opinion politique en Ille-et-Vilaine à la fin du XIXe siècle', *Annales de Bretagne*, lxxii (1965), p. 307. Election results as in note 38 plus Archives Nationales [hereafter AN], C1510, 1530, 1558; AD, Sarthe, M supp. 13, 367/39; AD, M, 3M 138, 482; *Journal de Rennes*, October 1877, May 1906.

44 Index of *chouannerie* constructed from AD, IV, 5R 1–6, 17–22; AD, M, R 978.

45 H. Goallou, 'Les élections à l'Assemblée législative en Ille-et-Vilaine (13 mai 1849)', *Annales de Bretagne*, lxxx (1973), pp. 360–71.

46 Cited in Denis, *Royalistes de la Mayenne*, pp. 322–3.

47 Cited in Chanoine Sifflet, *Les Évêques concordataires du Mans*, 6 vols (Le Mans: 1914–27), Vol. II, p. 56.

48 Cited in M.-T. Cloitre, 'Aspects de la vie politique dans le département du Finistère de 1848 à 1870', *Bulletin de la société archéologique du Finistère*, xcix (1972), p. 749.

49 Cited in L. Monnier, 'La Révolution de 1848 en Vendée', *Revue du Bas-Poitou*, 61e–62e année (1948–9), p. 37.

50 Denis, *Royalistes de la Mayenne*, p. 417.

51 Reports of procureurs of the Republic in AD, IV, 1V 163, dated July–August 1880.

52 AD, IV, 3M 333 bis, sub-prefect Redon to prefect, 22 November 1889.

53 Cited in P. Fourcault, 'Aspects de la vie chrétienne de 1830 aux lois de la séparation', in G.-M. Oury (ed.), *Histoire religieuse du Maine* (n.p.: n.d. [1978]), p. 229.

54 *Semaine religieuse du diocèse de Rennes*, 12 August 1893, pp. 697–8.

55 AN, F^{19}, 5622, sub-prefect Dinan to prefect, 7 May 1902.

56 Clipping from *L'Arvor*, 23 March 1902 in AN F^7, 12542. On anti-Semitism see the *professions de foi* in ibid. and the *Journal de Rennes*, 28 April 1898.

57 Cited in M. Lagrée, *Mentalités, Religion et histoire en Haute-Bretagne au XIXe siècle. Le diocèse de Rennes, 1815–1848* (Paris: 1977), p. 281.

58 Cited in Y. Le Gallo, 'Aux sources de l'anticléricalisme populaire en Basse-Bretagne: un recteur sous la Troisième République', *Bulletin de la Société archéologique du Finistère*, xcix (1972), p. 803.

59 Quotations from obituaries in the *Semaine religieuse du diocèse de Laval*, 24 September 1881, p. 790; 20 August 1882, p. 727; 30 December 1882, p. 167; and 14 April 1883, p. 407.

60 P. Pierrard, *Histoire des curés de campagne de 1789 à nos jours* (Paris: 1986), p. 179.

61 Fourcault, 'Aspects de la vie chrétienne de 1830 aux lois de la séparation', pp. 230–1; Anon., 'Les étapes de la reprise, 1802–1850', in G.-M. Oury (ed.), *Histoire religieuse de la Bretagne* (n.p.: 1980), pp. 307, 339; and, especially, C. Langlois, *Le Diocèse de Vannes au XIXe siècle, 1800–1830* (Paris: 1974), pp. 523–9.

62 Cited in Lagrée, *Diocèse de Rennes*, p. 293.

63 Le Gallo, 'Aux sources de l'anticléricalisme populaire en Basse-Bretagne', *passim*.

64 J. Quellieu, *Bleus, Blancs, Rouges. Politique et élections dans le Calvados, 1870–1939* (Caen: 1986), pp. 135–43.

65 On electoral and religious behaviour, see notes 38 and 41; on professional structure: AD, M, 6M 34, Récapitulation suivant les professions . . . du recensement de 1851; on literacy: AD, M, 6M 37, Récapitulation . . . recensement de 1866.

66 Ministère du Travail et du prévoyance sociale, *Album Graphique de la statistique générale de la France. Résultats statistiques du recensement de 1901* (Paris: 1907), *passim*.

2

Large landed property and its influence in nineteenth-century Burgundy

Pierre Lévêque

Even if one considers only the two departments of the Côte d'Or and the Saône-et-Loire, Burgundy exhibited remarkable diversity in the structure of landed property, as it did in its landscape and its rural economy.[1] Large-scale property was present everywhere, but its importance varied greatly from one region to another. In analysing such property, we are obliged by the incomplete state of scholarly research to concentrate on the first half of the nineteenth century, for which we can both establish a fairly precise inventory of large landed properties and analyse in a concrete way the methods employed by their owners to establish and exercise their power. For the later period, we shall have to be content with an evaluation of the solidity – or fragility – of this hold in the face of the major tests constituted by the rise of democracy and the great agricultural depression.

The *structure* of landed property under the censitary monarchy is well documented by the registers of the first cadastral survey, carried out in Burgundy between 1821 and 1847. For the time of the cadastral survey, that is, on average, about 1830–55, we can draw up maps at cantonal or sub-cantonal level: the first shows the proportion of the surface area occupied by *cotes*[2] of more than 50 hectares;[3] the second, in calculating the lower limit of 'large-scale property' (that is, the minimum that allowed its owner to live, if he so desired, without working with his hands, and thus to be a 'notable'), takes into account the fertility of the soil, the rate of return on agriculture and the land tax per hectare;[4] the third, necessarily less precise, deducts – as far as possible – the properties devoted entirely to forestry (and thus not leading to subjection of a peasantry) from large-scale property in general.[5]

Such large-scale property was dominant in the southwest of the former province of Burgundy, where it exceeded 40 per cent of privately owned land in a dozen cantons comprising the south of the *arrondissement* of Autun and

Map 2.1 Agricultural regions

Map 2.2 Cantons and sections of cantons

Table 2.1 *Arrondissements* of Autun and Charolles

No. of *cotes* of more than 500 hectares	62
No. of corresponding properties	44
– owning 500–1,000 hectares	22
– owning 1,000–2,000 hectares	10
– owning 2,000–3,000 hectares	5
– owning 3,000–5,000 hectares	6
– owning more than 5,000 hectares	1

the north of that of Charolles. In this area were to be found some powerful concentrations of landed property, as indicated in Table 2.1. The largest single *cote*, that of the Comte de Charrin at Charmoy (canton of Moncenis), amounted to 1,945 hectares. But usually, and especially in cases of properties of over 100 hectares, the land belonging to one owner was spread over several communes, thus resulting in multiple *cotes*. The greatest landed fortune, that of the Comte Mayneaud de Pancemont, consisted of more than 6,300 hectares spread over 16 communes of the Charollais and centred around his château at Génelard (canton of Toulon-sur-Arroux). The communes themselves, in this region of *bocage* countryside and dispersed habitat, were usually very large and contained a considerable number of large properties: in that of Issy-l'Évêque (7,114 hectares, of which 6,980 were in private hands), we find 19 of more than 100 hectares and 8 of between 50 and 100, occupying in all 87.5 per cent of privately owned land. The lords of the soil were thus not faced by a numerous and coherent group of peasant proprietors; small-scale property, of the level of the family farm which could ensure the economic independence of its owners, covered less than a tenth of the surface area of the Autunois and the northern Charollais. It was indeed a region of *hiérarchie*.[6]

Conversely, the limestone regions of the Côte d'Or (Châtillonnais, Montagne, haut Auxois, plaine calcaire, Arrière-Côte) were an area of 'rural democracy' (not, of course, implying any equality between *laboureurs* [better-off peasants] and *manouvriers* [agricultural labourers]). In only a few cantons did large-scale property exceed 20 per cent of the surface area; if forests are excluded even this anomaly disappears, and we are confronted by a good 15 cantons below the 20 per cent mark. Doubtless large confrontations of landed property were not entirely absent: the Comte de Grancey enjoyed more than 5,000 hectares spread over 7 communes around his château, and the Marquis de Courtivron some 2,000 hectares in 4 communes. But these were essentially forests; forests occupied 74 per cent of the total surface area of *cotes* of more than 200 hectares in the Montagne dijonnaise,[7] and more than 92 per cent in the canton of Laignes. Notables might even be wholly absent: of the 114 communes of the Châtillonnais, 42 had no large property at all, even wooded. And where they were present, they had to coexist with a solid group of *laboureurs*, of *propriétaires-cultivateurs* each owning a few dozen hectares, and another group of *manouvriers* each with a hectare or so. Small and very

Map 2.3 Area occupied by *cotes* of more than 50 hectares

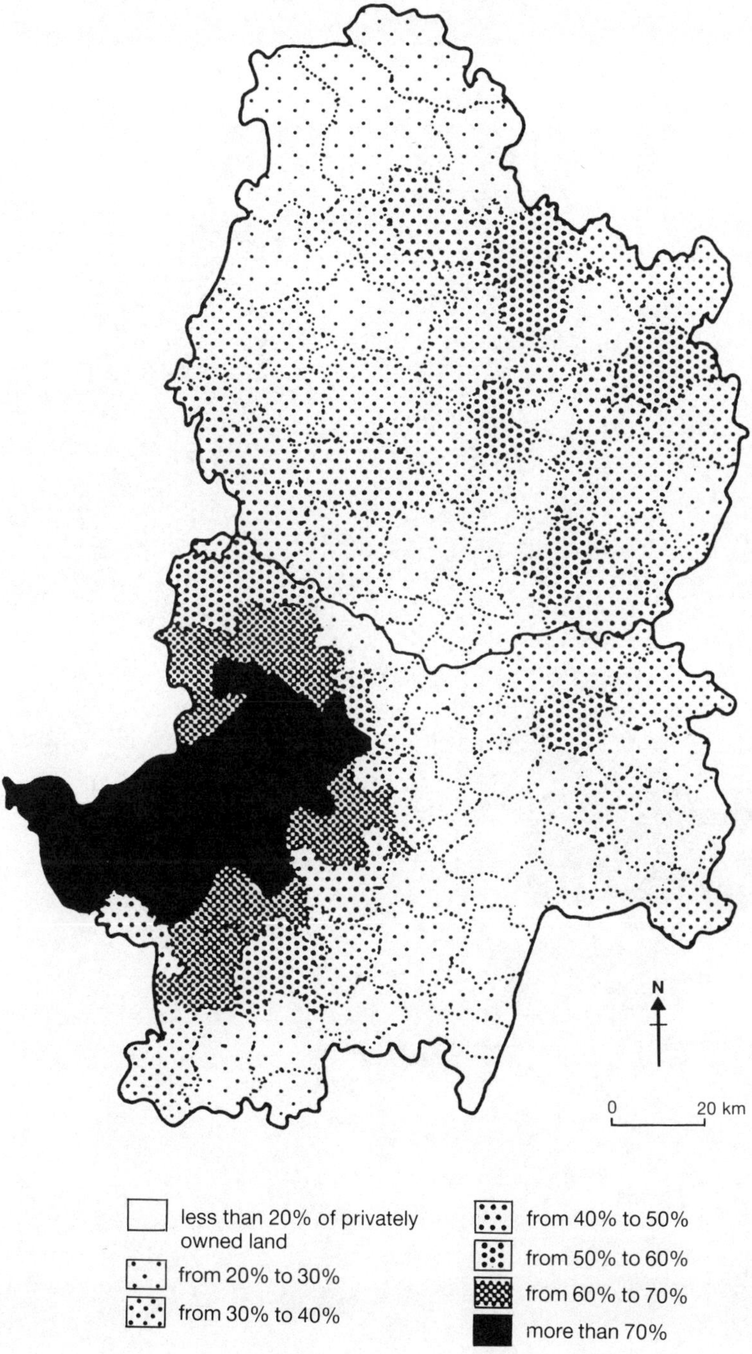

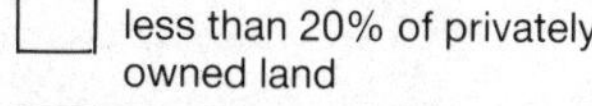

Map 2.4 Large-scale property at the time of the cadastral survey

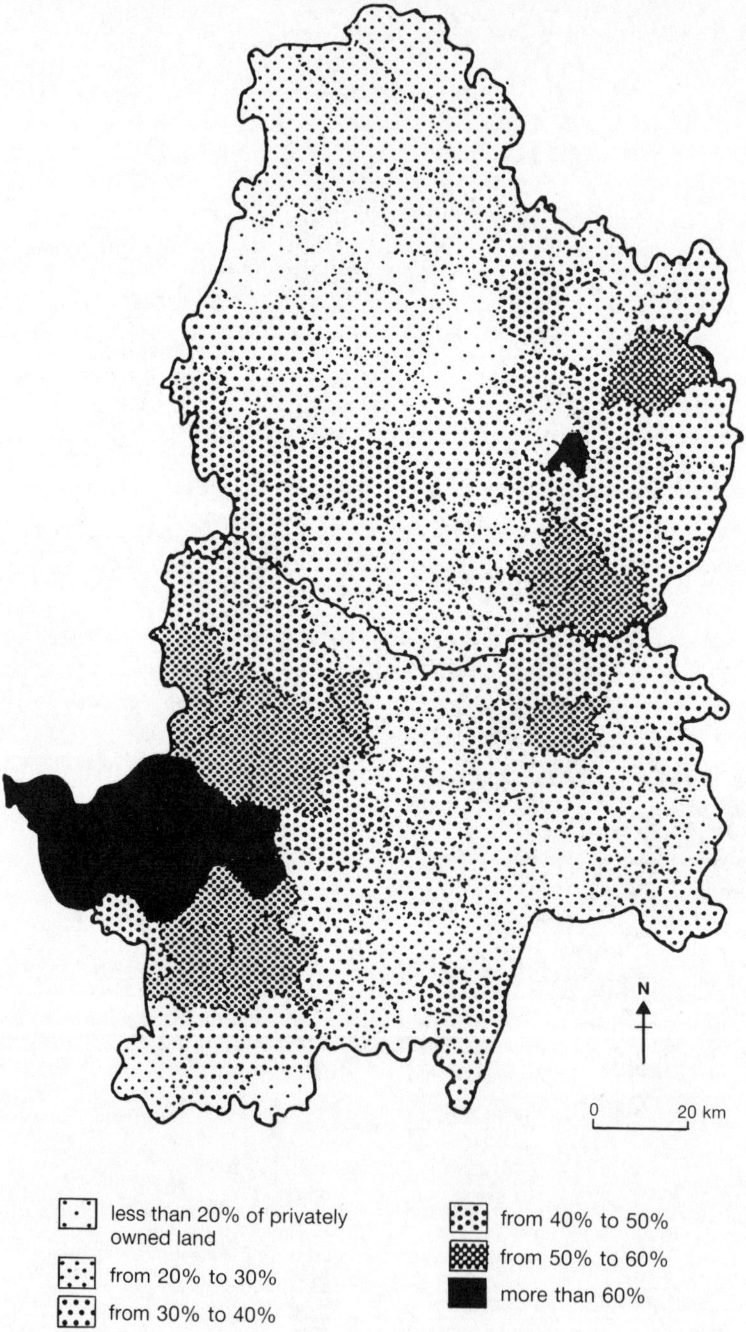

N

0 20 km

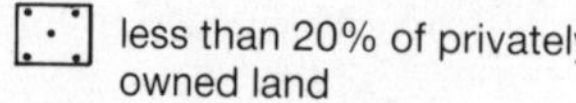

less than 20% of privately owned land

from 20% to 30%

from 30% to 40%

from 40% to 50%

from 50% to 60%

more than 60%

Map 2.5 Large-scale property at the time of the cadastral survey in % of cultivatable land in private ownership, excluding forests

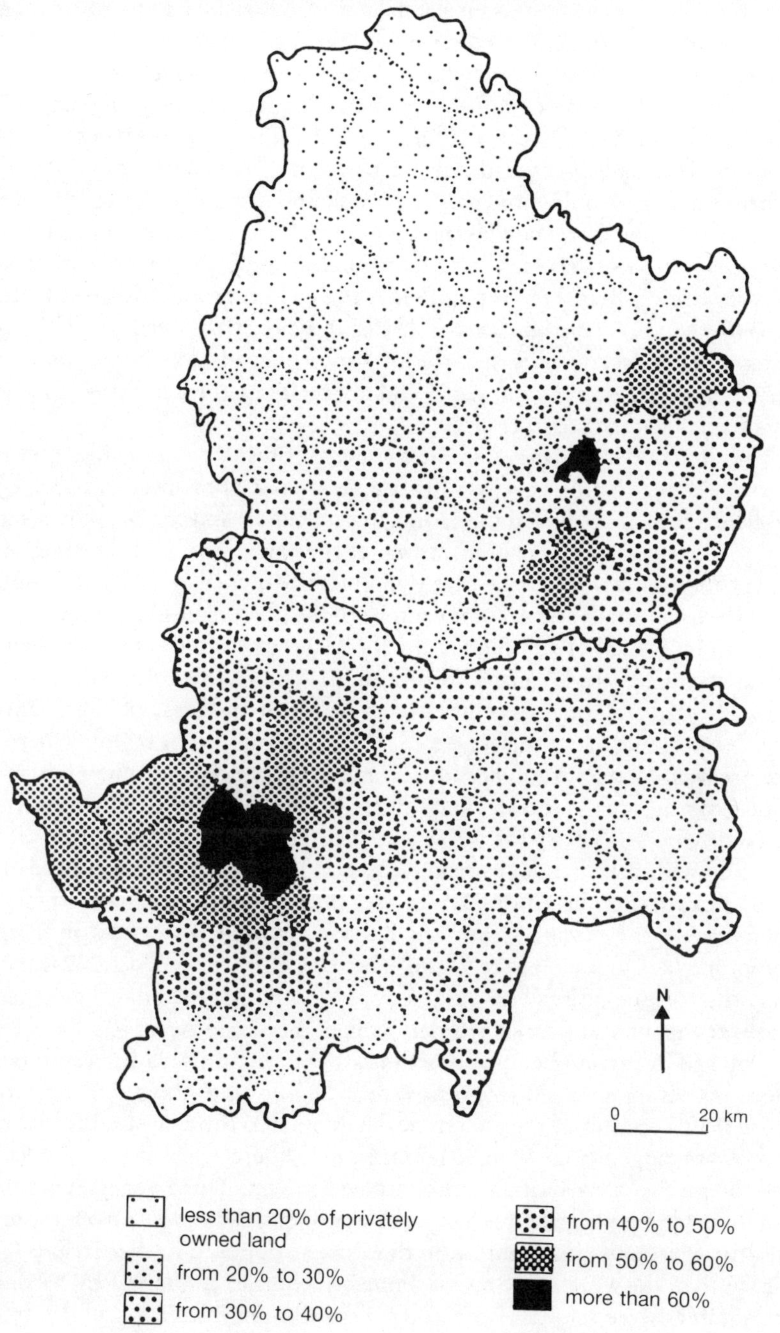

small property thus covered well over half of agricultural land, to say nothing of intermediary properties of between 20 and 80 or 100 hectares, which in this case were very often in peasant hands and which jacked some of its owners into the property franchise (200 francs in direct taxes).

Another zone of rural democracy, though more dispersed, was located in the south and southeast of the Saône-et-Loire, covering a part of the Charollais and Mâconnais hills and several cantons of the Bresse region. Large-scale property covered only 10 per cent of the canton of Chauffailles (where there were only nine *cotes* in excess of 60 hectares), 16 per cent of that of Tramayes (the Comte de Pierreclos with 282 hectares, and Lamartine with 119 at Saint-Point, seemed almost magnates), and 18 per cent of that of Beaurepaire-en-Bresse (15 *cotes* of more than 50 hectares, only one of which, the 346-hectare *cote* of the Comte de Beaurepaire, was over 100). The major difference between this area and the limestone plateaux was that it possessed a very dense rural population, which did not facilitate the emergence of a well-established 'peasant aristocracy'.

The remainder of the two departments presented a whole range of intermediary situations between the two extremes of property structure just described. On the plains of the Saône, in the Auxois and the Brionnais, large-scale property was rarely absent. It was even very important in the regions of Arnay and Épinac (where the MacMahon family owned 3,700 hectares spread over 15 communes), and in some cantons of the plain around Dijon, where the large *cotes* (even after subtracting the forests) represented often over half the privately owned land (cantons of Mirebeau, Dijon-Ouest II, Nuits II). The major landed holdings were inferior to those of the west of the Saône-et-Loire, but could nevertheless exceed 1,000 hectares in a region where the hectare was worth more and produced more revenue. In the richest part of the wine-growing area – Côte de Nuits and Côte de Beaune especially – 8 per cent of landowners (that is, the large and medium proprietors, almost all not working with their hands) were in receipt of 55 per cent of the revenue of the land; a calculation based on surface area only conceals their importance. In some cases, one comes across a collection of large properties in a single commune (at Ouges, close to Dijon, 12 proprietors exceeded 1,000 francs of cadastral revenue). Elsewhere, one vast property perpetuated the old seigneurial *réserve*: one such, at Cléry on the left bank of the Saône, occupied 116 hectares out of 126 in private hands. Sometimes it was surrounded by a number of more modest domains; at Époisses, near Semur-en-Auxois, 530 hectares – more than a quarter of the commune – belonged to the château, but six other properties ranged from 40 to 80 hectares. Elsewhere again, 'rural democracy' and 'hierarchy' shared out a canton between them. Three general comments can be made, however. First, large-scale property was often strongest in the wealthiest regions (for example, in the Côte as opposed to the Arrière-Côte, the south of the wine-growing Mâconnais in contrast to the north). Secondly, the notables were very rarely absentees. Thirdly, they often found themselves confronted by a numerous class of small, sometimes even medium, proprietors working their own land. Needless to add, the power relations between them were almost infinitely variable.

Along with other documents such as the censitary electoral lists, the cadastral survey allows us to sketch out a sociology of the large landowners. If we exclude the hospitals and hospices (those of Dijon and Beaune were particularly well provided for), we can try to estimate the proportion of the land held by nobles – or those claiming to be nobles – and that held by *roturiers* (generally bourgeois, but also including wealthy peasants). In only a few regions did the 'nobility' own more than half the surface area of the large *cotes* (more than 50 hectares): in the west, in the Morvan and the pays d'Arnay (nearly 59 per cent in the latter, thanks particularly to the landed wealth of the MacMahon family); in the east, on the plains of the Saône, except around Chalon (62 per cent in the extreme north of the Côte d'Or, 58 per cent in the Bresse); and finally, in a few marginal areas of the wine-growing areas of the Côte d'Or and the Charollais.[8] By contrast, the nobility's part fell to about a third in the Autunois, in the east Charollais and the Clunysois, in the Châtillonnais and the haut Auxois. It was often, though not always, the possession of large forests that gave nobles the statistical advantage. Overall, however, non-noble large-scale property was more extensive (55 per cent of the surface area of *cotes* above 50 hectares for the two departments).

But non-noble property was also less concentrated. With only 28 per cent of the large *cotes*, the nobility appropriated 45 per cent of their surface area. The average noble *cote* (of those over 50 hectares) was 216 hectares, compared with only 103 hectares for non-nobles. This contrast is confirmed by an analysis of the censitary electorate, of which landed proprietors constituted a massive majority (78 per cent at the beginning of the July Monarchy, 77 per cent at the end), members of the economic professions usually only reaching the censitary threshold by virtue of the land tax they paid.[9] The censitary requirement can in fact be considered as roughly proportional to the value of the landed property of those whose political domicile was in the department. The proportion of nobles rises as one goes up the censitary scale: for 1846/7, they constituted 3.2 per cent of electors paying from 200 to 1,000 francs in direct taxes, 30.5 per cent of electors paying between 1,000 and 3,000 francs and 70.1 per cent of those paying more than 3,000 francs. Beyond the 10,000-franc limit there were only nobles: five of them in 1831/3 (with, in first place, Comte Mayneaud at Génelard: 13,694 francs), two in 1846/7. It is thus possible to think of the body of large landowners as a pyramid, of which the lower levels are largely occupied by the bourgeoisie and even, to a lesser degree, by the peasantry. The noble presence begins to assert itself halfway up. Nobles alone, or almost alone, occupy a very pointed apex.

Were these bourgeois and nobles local men? Specific examples can give the impression of a fairly strong Parisian presence: in the canton of Verdun-sur-le-Doubs, for example, for *cotes* above 100 hectares, Parisians held 62 per cent of privately owned land; in that of Saint-Germain-du-Bois, nearly 50 per cent. But for the Châtillonnais as a whole, the proportion falls to 18.7 per cent of the total surface area of *cotes* of over 200 hectares, as against 60 per cent for Burgundians; for the Autunois and the Charollais, it falls to 20.7 per cent for *cotes* over 500 hectares (57.6 per cent for the Burgundians). A calculation involving all *cotes* above 50 hectares, which brings in the middle bourgeoisie and the peasant aristocracy, further emphasizes the preponderance of local men, as Table 2.2 shows.

Except in the Semurois the proportion owned by Parisians (usually nobles) is modest. The landowning influence of Dijon declines rapidly outside the *arrondissement*. The influence of Lyons is very weak, even in the Clunysois and the vineyards of the Mâconnais.[10] All in all, around 1830 the landed notables (even if it is not immediately clear that they actually lived on their properties, and *a fortiori* that they took an active interest in them) belonged chiefly to Burgundian families as far as their usual place of residence was concerned.

Table 2.2 Percentage of the total surface area of *cotes* over 50 hectares

	Arrondissements		
Residence of owner	*Dijon*	*Semur-en-Auxois*	*Autun*
Dijon	31.0	9.5	4.0
Arrondissement capital	n.a.	7.2	19.8
Within the canton	33.5	41.5	36.2
Rest of department	15.3	15.7	15.1
Total, local men	**79.8**	**73.9**	**75.1**
Paris	13.5	20.5	9.0
Rest of France	6.5	3.5	12.9
Residence unknown	0.2	2.1	3.0

Large-scale property in Burgundy around 1830, whether noble or bourgeois, covered 37 per cent of the privately owned land (representing 1.36 per cent of the *cotes* for landownership). Did the 2,500 or so owners[11] of such property constitute the real ruling class? In a region where more than 80 per cent of the population lived in the countryside, and where in 1851 nearly two thirds of the active male population worked the land, one is tempted to give an immediate affirmative answer: it seems obvious that the authority of landed notables must have gone without saying in such a society.

This apparent truism needs to be qualified, however. We shall try to do this by distinguishing (following Jean Lhomme) three aspects of power: economic, social (better still, sociocultural) and political.[12]

The exercise of *economic* power depended in the first place on the way that properties were farmed: direct cultivation, tenanting, or sharecropping. For various reasons, in particular the frequent geographic dispersal of the largest agglomerations of landed property, direct cultivation was rare. It was evidently practised by the richest of the *propriétaires-cultivateurs*, whose number is very difficult to ascertain: possibly more than a thousand, but most of them were in the category of medium rather than large landowners. Some notables, usually those of modest standing, cultivated their property directly, sometimes with the help of a *maître-valet* who controlled the farm labourers. The agronomist Victor-Prosper Rey thought they owned a tenth of the land in the Autunois, with an average of 50 to 70 hectares each.[13] Finally, cultivation '*à prix d'argent*' was common in the vineyards of the Côte d'Or: for an annual salary payable quarterly, the *vigneron* was responsible for every aspect of cultivation and for the grape harvest. Naturally the major landowners – Ouvrard at Clos-Vougeot, for example – did not deal directly with the labourers, who were under the authority of a manager. But whatever the technical aspects of the system, the relationships to which it gave rise were capitalist in nature, and in a labour market swamped by overpopulation the employer had little difficulty in laying down the law.

Most of the large domains, however, were cultivated indirectly. Tenant farming for cash rents (including sometimes certain services in labour and in kind) was easily the commonest system, except in wine-growing areas and in the west of the Saône-et-Loire.[14] But it was rarely a case of tenant farming on the classic English model, with vast farms managed by veritable agricultural entrepreneurs, well provided with equipment, stock and capital. A few hundred tenant farms at the very most were larger than 100 hectares, and the immense majority ranged from 10 to 50. In the Bresse, for example, 'an ordinary domain contains 15 or 16 hectares of arable, and 4 or 5 of pasture'.[15] This division into small units was true of the very largest properties. That of the Comtesse de Berbis at Lachaux (canton of Pierre-de-Bresse), put up for sale in 1847, comprised 11 farms even though it consisted of 394 hectares of arable and pasture 'in a single unit'.[16] Sometimes owners even had recourse to leasing '*en détail*': peasants whose holdings were inadequate would round off their farm by renting a few hectares. These '*fermiers propriétaires*' were particularly numerous in the most densely populated rural areas. This system, seemingly a disincentive to innovation and contrary to economic logic, in fact allowed the notables, either directly or via their managers, to guarantee themselves simultaneously both a whole clientele of small and medium farmers (kept well under the thumb thanks to the short duration of most leases) and also a higher income, since land was more in demand and attracted higher rents when leased in detail rather than in large units.[17] Whereas capitalist tenant farmers were rare and could impose conditions, the plethora of small peasants was willing to pay a high price for self-sufficiency – even if this was not the economic independence which in peasant eyes could be guaranteed only by ownership of the land.

The subjection of the sharecropper, supposedly the 'associate' of the landowner, was even greater than that of the small tenant. In the wine-growing areas of the Saône-et-Loire (and the south of those of the Côte d'Or),

Map 2.6 Indirect cultivation in 1851

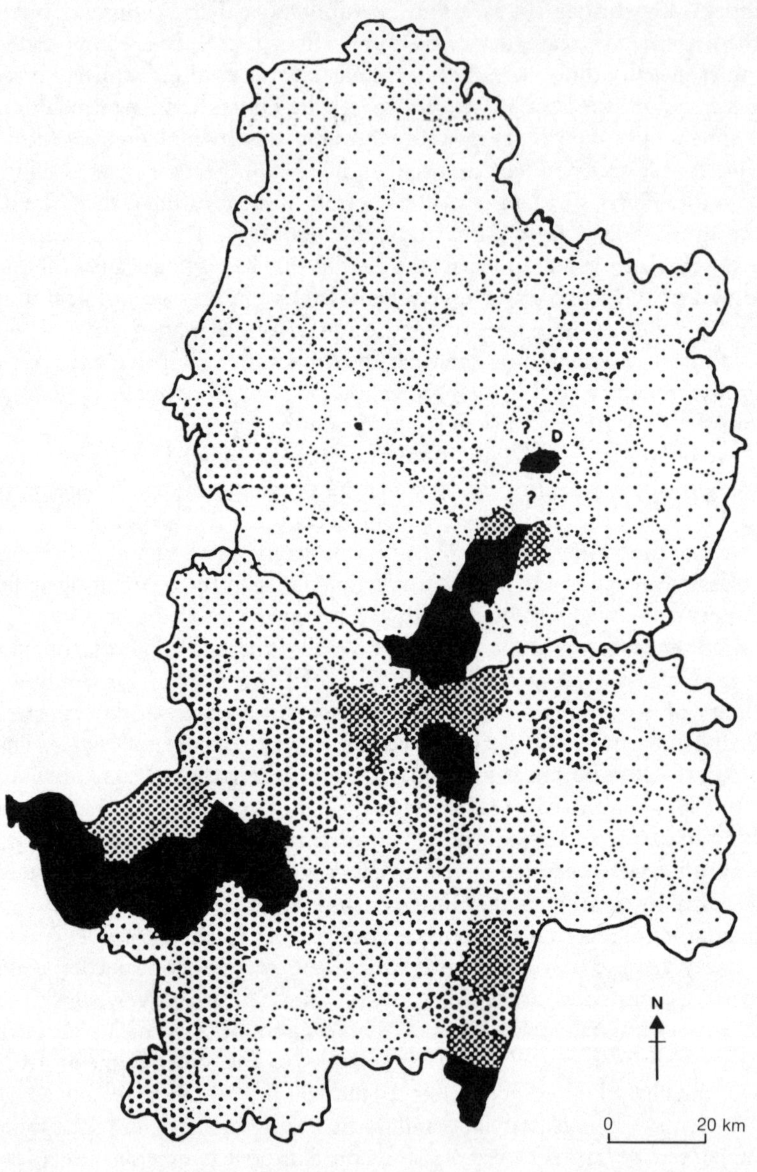

more than 5 *métayers* per *fermier*
from 5 to 2 *métayers* per *fermier*
from 2 to 1 *métayers* per *fermier*
from 1 to 2 *fermiers* per *métayer*
from 2 to 5 *fermiers* per *métayer*
more than 5 *fermiers* per *métayer*

cultivation for half-shares by '*vignerons*' and 'grangers' was the normal means of exploiting the great vineyard properties, which were divided into small units of 2 to 5 hectares consonant with the labour power of a family. In theory, the *vigneron* had only to give up half his harvest and to pay a cash 'condition' of 80 to 300 francs. In practice, he was forced in bad years to seek a loan from his landlord, and to deliver his wine to the latter to settle the loan. It was thus the owner who commercialized the wine, admittedly with storage costs but also with the advantage of selling when the price was high, whereas the actual producer found himself tied to the land by his debt, often for life: a relative security was paid for by complete subjection. This subjection was also found, in an even more intense form, on the vast domains of the Autunois and the Charollais where, in a dozen cantons, sharecropping was more extensive (sometimes much more) than tenant farming, and *a fortiori* than direct cultivation. Most large landowners, not caring to take personal charge of the management of a number of medium-sized farms (20–80 hectares) often scattered over several communes, dealt through local businessmen, known as farmers-general, who paid them a fixed rent and received from the share-croppers half the harvest, a cash payment known locally as '*belles mains*', and various payments in kind and labour services. This system, though considered by most agronomists (despite their attachment to the existing social order) to be oppressive of those who worked the land and detrimental to agricultural progress, nevertheless guaranteed the masters of the soil a regular income with a minimum of bother, if at the cost of a kind of sharing of economic power.

Outside the wine-growing areas, which were suffering from a long-term depression, large landowners under the Restoration and the July Monarchy enjoyed a certain prosperity. There are two major pieces of evidence for this: they managed almost everywhere to maintain their hold on the land and they were able to increase their income. In 10 cantons or sub-cantons, the cadastral registers drawn up in 1822/3 were redone between 1842 and 1847; in the space of 20 years, the proportion of privately owned land occupied by the largest *cotes* remained unchanged (38.6 per cent). Over the same period, the rent from 20 properties belonging to the Dijon hospital in the plain and the Montagne increased by 24 per cent (while the cost of living remained stationary), and information collected for other agricultural areas (except wine-growing ones) tells a similar story.[18]

This economic prosperity enabled notables who wished to do so to exercise *social* power of a traditional kind, in some ways not unlike that of the seigneurs of the *ancien régime* – a power which tended to spread beyond the boundaries of the domain and beyond any purely economic control, to take in the inhabitants of the village as a whole. The seigneurial regime having disappeared, the large landowner no longer held at his disposal any legal authority, such as police or judicial powers. He was therefore obliged to make an even greater effort to build up among the rural population (even those who were theoretically 'independent'), by very diverse means, the voluntary acceptance of his dominant position, in a framework of reciprocal rights and duties.

The example of Édouard Carrelet de Loisy, son of a *conseiller au Parlement* and a very wealthy landowner in the Autunois (with about 3,000 hectares and paying 3,508 francs in direct taxes), is a perfect illustration of this concept of authority. Wealth was for him 'a public duty', bringing with it definite obligations. He strove to establish with his peasants social relations in which deference did not exclude a certain cordiality. Thus he devoted 'whole hours to listening to their complaints, their requests, taking an interest . . . in their family and in the conduct of their affairs'. For her part, the lady of the château, for example, (still in the Autunois) Madame d'Esterno or (in the Mâconnais) Madame de Lamartine, mother of the poet, devoted herself untiringly to charitable works, giving alms to the poor and visiting the ill and the crippled. Concerned for the intellectual, but above all the moral and religious, development of the villagers, the lord took an active interest in education (the 'obscurantist' attitude was very rare among Burgundian notables). Carrelet de Loisy thus established at Saint-Émiland, near his château at Épiry, a girls' primary school run by nuns, and paid its running costs. Jean-Hugues Magnin-Philippon founded a public library at Lux. In the small industrial town of Lacanche, Madame de Caumartin, widow of an ironmaster, established a school at her own expense and spent 60,000 francs on the construction of a new church. At Grosbois-les-Tichey, near Seurre,

> the chief landowner is M. le comte Dugon, whose presence . . . is a great boon to the parishioners, both because of his good example and because of the material benefits which he brings to the inhabitants, and he is at the same time a source of much pleasure to the *curé*, who without this family would find the parish rather a tedious one.

The alliance of presbytery and château, where it existed, evidently reinforced the influence of both, and gave a religious consecration to the authority of the master of the soil. He tried, furthermore, in his own interest but sometimes also in that of the peasants, to promote agricultural progress: Carrelet de Loisy forced his tenants and sharecroppers to adopt 'sound methods' and distributed free to neighbouring farmers the lime produced by the kiln that he had had built. The defence of economic interests even at that time took the form of collective action, through agricultural societies of which the archetype was that of Autun. The moving spirits were a group of nobles and bourgeois, passionately devoted to agronomy; they worked to disseminate knowledge of new developments and to reward 'progressive' farmers (who often turned out, it is true, to be their own members or their tenants) and managed to set in motion, between 1833 and 1848, the modernization of a part of the countryside of the *arrondissement*.[19]

All these activities, usually linked with the idea of paternalist duty, brought some notables a genuine popularity in their villages, whose inhabitants considered them as their natural leaders. This was the ideal-type of social power.

Where local *political* power was concerned, it was the legislation of the censitary monarchy which conferred it on large landowners, under the authority, it is true, of the prefects and sub-prefects. The departmental and *arrondissement* councils, nominated by the government under the Restoration, included in 1827/9 45.5 per cent proprietors out of the 112 councillors whose profession is given, as against 8 per cent merchants and manufacturers (most of whom also owned land and forests); the other councillors were mostly retired army officers, magistrates, or members of the legal profession, all owning considerable amounts of land, and often paying more than 1,000 francs in direct taxes. The election of these local government bodies, established by the law of 1833, was by electoral colleges not very different from those which chose the deputies, and did not involve any radical change: it is true that proprietors as such fell to 23.2 per cent in 1842/5, but businessmen gained only slightly, and members of the liberal professions and civil servants, especially (43.7 per cent) barristers, notaries, or magistrates, all had close connections with the land. Three quarters of councillors had annual incomes (essentially from the land) in excess of 5,000 francs, implying ownership of some fairly large domains (16 per cent were even over the 20,000-franc mark). Given that the post-1831 election of municipal councils by about a third of adult males helped the poorer elements only very briefly, and that the notables won impressive victories as early as 1834 and 1837,[20] one must conclude that the union of Jean Lhomme's 'three kinds of power' meant that between 1815 and 1848 the hegemony of large landowners in the two Burgundian departments rested on apparently solid foundations. As we shall now see, however, this hegemony had its limitations and weaknesses.

The *economic* influence of landed notables varied widely, as we have seen, according to region. In the Châtillonnais and the Montagne, they were surpassed by the ironmasters, who were of course themselves landowners, but most of whom came together in 1845 in the powerful Châtillon-Commentry company, whose interests increasingly diverged from those of the rural population. Even in the Autunois, where they were stronger and better organized, the lords of the soil had to coexist with the Schneider family of ironmasters, which occupied the deputy's seat from 1842 onwards. Income from the land, restricted by the slowness of the agricultural revolution, a slowness partly attributable to the excessive division of farms, did not grow as fast as did the profits of capitalist enterprise, and this retardation would lead in the long term to the relative effacement of traditional notables. For the moment, the latter were deeply divided by the tariff issue: owners of vineyards, looking to regain their foreign markets, joined with large trading interests in calling for free-trade treaties, whereas owners of cereal and pasture land allied with the ironmasters in the protectionist camp. Finally, in areas where small proprietors and *manouvriers* were numerous, the initiatives of large landowners in scientific agriculture could, where they clashed with communal rights such as those of common grazing, lead to sharp conflicts and endanger the peaceful exercise of 'social power'.

The exercise of such power was further compromised by a much more general phenomenon: the *absenteeism* of major landowners. Their physical presence in the village was of course not always beneficial. Some were local tyrants, like Léger Guyotat of the château de Ménessaire in the Morvan, who ruled by authoritarianism, threat and sanction rather than by paternalism.[21] As far as one can tell, however, this was true only of a small minority. But the notables who resided permanently or for long periods on their estates seem to have been a minority as well. Complaints about this were common. Here we shall mention only two complementary analyses of the subject. First, that of the *curé* of the overpopulated Morvan commune of Anost, who not only observed such absenteeism but went on to denounce its consequences:

> Where there are poor people, Providence . . . has been careful to put *large fortunes* close by to succour them with their excess. But what happens? The inheritors and owners of these immense fortunes live in Paris and make no effort at all to come to the help of the poor in those parishes where they are so well provided with the goods of this world.[22]

Non-residence was here seen as damaging a providential social harmony by preventing the notable from fulfilling his charitable duty. A few years later the sub-prefect of Autun, reflecting on the development of 'socialist ideas' in the west of the Saône-et-Loire, blamed the 'absentee landowners who live in the major towns or the best parts of the department'; with 'honourable exceptions', they

> provide little employment for the population and absorb all the revenue. They bring to agriculture neither technical knowledge nor capital. . . . This region presents a certain similarity with the situation in Ireland.[23]

Absenteeism was here seen as responsible for economic stagnation. It did in fact mean that almost all the profit from the land was not reinvested, especially where, as was often the case in these areas, there was systematic use of farmers-general, who were uniquely concerned with immediate profits: 'these rental agents take no interest in agriculture, often living a long way from their sharecroppers and rarely visiting them', and even if they did have the necessary capital they would not use it for long-term improvements, which would only lead to an increase in rents and thus, they imagined, a reduction in their profits.[24] Even outside the latifundia and sharecropping regions, managers and intendants found themselves accused of playing an equally negative role. At Labussière-sur-Ouche (canton of Pouilly-en-Auxois), where a great Parisian notable, Jean-Baptiste Gauthier, had acquired almost all the arable and pasture land of the former Cistercian abbey, he had 'changed manager several times. One after another they have acquired great importance in the region, and all have been cordially detested by the inhabitants', particularly the penultimate one, who rounded out his income by usury and who, according to the prefect, 'is regarded as a local plague'.[25] It would of course be unwise to generalize. But it does seem the case that absenteeism (which must have concerned at least two thirds of the surface area of the great domains of the Dijonnais, more than 56 per cent of that of the Semurois and nearly 61 per cent of the Autunois) tended to nullify the social power of landowners, by all too often transforming a patriarchal-type system into one of pure economic exploitation without any appreciable services in return.

As for *political* power, it was imperilled by the deep fault-line running through the world of the notables in general and that of the landed notables in particular: on one side the victims and enemies of the French Revolution, very numerous in the old nobility and supported by a majority of the clergy; on the other the supporters and beneficiaries of the new social order, a majority among the bourgeoisie, basing themselves on the principles of 1789 and readily affecting a religious indifference lamented by many *curés* on the occasion of pastoral visits or diocesan inquiries. This division was of course manifest in the legislative elections of the Restoration which, except in 1815 and 1824, and in all *arrondissement* electoral colleges save that of Autun, saw the victory of the liberals. But it is also clearly evident in the composition of departmental and *arrondissement* councils. At the end of Charles X's reign, nobles comprised 44.3 per cent of their membership. At the same time, some 10 per cent of the mayors in each department had a noble title or a 'de' before their name. The revolution of 1830, followed by the two laws governing the franchise for elections to local bodies, triggered an anti-legitimist and anti-noble reaction of surprising violence. Among departmental and *arrondissement* councillors, the proportion of nobles fell to about 9 per cent and – despite the 'appeasement' attempted by Molé and Guizot – stayed at that level in the 1840s. As for the legitimists, they comprised only 12 per cent of the 152 councillors elected in 1842/5. Similarly, the proportion of noble (or pseudo-noble) mayors fell, as early as 1832/3, to less than 3 per cent in the Saône-et-Loire and less than 1 per cent in the Côte d'Or. When the place occupied by the nobility in the group of large landowners (45 per cent of the surface area of the great domains) is taken into consideration, it was clearly under-represented. This ostracism had the effect of undermining the political hegemony of the whole group. On the one hand we find the legitimist notables, often nobles, excluded from political power by a majority of the censitary electorate; supported by the clergy, they were objects of ready suspicion to a rural population whose susceptibilities were easily aroused by anything that smacked of the *ancien régime*. On the other hand we find liberal notables, mostly bourgeois, who dominate elective positions and tend to monopolize political power; but they are themselves split between 'Resistance' and 'Movement', that is, conservatives and left opposition. The former, separated from the legitimists by old hatreds and by their former Voltaireanism, could scarcely count on the eager support of the church; the latter, to combat their rivals' majority, were led to ally with republicans who wanted the abolition of the political monopoly of large landed property.

In other words, the ruling class of the Burgundian countryside had been afflicted, since the end of the eighteenth century, by serious social and ideological antagonisms, and one is tempted to wonder whether, if a major crisis had put its supremacy to the test, it would have been able to overcome its internal division in order to maintain its rule.

The second half of the nineteenth century was in fact marked by the decline of the group of large landowners and the end of their hegemony.

There was, for one thing, a decline in their control of the land. This was a relatively late phenomenon, however. We have seen that they had solidly maintained their position under the Restoration and the July Monarchy. After 1850, both short- and long-term economic factors evolved in a way that was apparently favourable to the peasantry, at least in fertile regions well served by local roads and by railways. The commercialization of agricultural produce became easier, prices rose, productivity increased and the departure of the poorest elements for industrial centres and for the great public works in the cities allowed those who remained to round off their farms. But at the same time land rents, expressed in current prices, continued to rise: between 1847 and 1879, the rent from 20 tenant farms owned by the Dijon hospital increased by another 26 per cent. It is true that this rise was somewhat less than that in the cost of living. Nevertheless, together with the continued prestige conferred by the ownership of broad acres, it was enough to dissuade the majority of notables from giving up their rural holdings in favour of other, more profitable, financial investments, and to persuade others to invest a part of their savings in land. Such at any rate seems to be the conclusion from a comparison of the cadastral survey with the land-tax statistics of 1884,[26] shown in Table 2.3.

In the course of half a century, as Table 2.3 shows, large-scale property (somewhat arbitrarily defined as *cotes* over 50 hectares) declined by 2 percentage points in the Côte d'Or and by less than 5 in the Saône-et-Loire (where it had been more extensive) and the average size of large properties remained about the same. The economic supremacy of the notables in the countryside seems to have remained almost intact.

Such was no longer the case on the eve of the First World War. In the absence of any exhaustive analysis of the cadastral registers of 1913, it is not possible to present an overall statistic for that date, but details from several very different cantons, as indicated in Table 2.4, all suggest the same conclusion.[27]

Table 2.3 Privately owned land: comparison of figures for *c.* 1830 and 1884

	Côte d'Or	*Saône-et-Loire*
(a) *Cadastral survey (c. 1830)*		
Privately owned land (hectares)	669,534	758,695
Cotes over 50 hectares:		
– number	1,735	2,450
– surface area in hectares	230,642	332,194
– % of privately owned land	**34.4**	**43.8**
– average size in hectares	133	136
(b) *1884 statistics*		
Privately owned land (hectares)	684,917	764,264
Cotes over 50 hectares:		
– number	1,695	2,231
– surface area in hectares	223,425	299,338
– % of privately owned land	**32.6**	**39.2**
– average size in hectares	132	134

This time, the landed wealth of the notables has declined sharply. Although varying according to region, the general picture is not in doubt: the effects of partible inheritance (the division of landed property among several offspring) and of the selling-off of large properties in small lots ceased to be almost counterbalanced by new investment in land. The obvious causes were the evolution of the economy (with the multiplication of occasions for profitable investment on the stock exchange and in urban property)[29] and the great agricultural depression. The rental from the 20 properties of the Dijon hospital mentioned earlier fell by 25 per cent between 1879 and 1890, and by another 11 per cent between 1890 and 1907, by which time they had fallen to approximately their 1822/3 level, whereas prices were very much higher. Landowners simultaneously saw their control of the land contract and the purchasing power of their rental income fall. At the same time, the rural exodus put day labourers, farm-servants, tenants and sharecroppers in a better position to bargain over conditions of work and wages, or over the contents of leases. The economic power of the lords of the soil was being progressively eroded.

Table 2.4 Privately owned land: comparison of figures for *c.* 1830 and 1913

	Cadastral survey (c. 1830)	*1913 revision*
Privately owned land (hectares)	173,203	173,482
Cotes over 50 hectares:		
– number	555	436
– surface area in hectares	78,421	63,430
– % of privately owned land	**45.3**	**36.6**
– average size in hectares	141	145

But the loss of *political* power, in their case, considerably pre-dated their economic decline. The decisive event in this respect was the advent of universal suffrage; it was only partially and with difficulty that they were able to bend it to their purposes. As early as the Second Republic, in a good part of the former province, they were unable to withstand the offensive of the republican – and then *démocrate-socialiste* – petite bourgeoisie. Admittedly the elections of 23 April 1848 seemed on balance a great victory for progressive notables, led by Lamartine and most of them comfortably-off landowners; nevertheless Ledru-Rollin and his followers scored impressive successes in the west of the Saône-et-Loire, the Chalonnais, the Bresse and the south of the Côte d'Or. In December 1848 the resounding victory of Louis-Napoleon Bonaparte, won in the future 'red' regions as well as in the more conservative ones, was the result much more of a spontaneous movement of the rural masses fired by the Napoleonic legend than of leadership or pressure exerted by large landowners, many of whom had in fact come out for Cavaignac.

But it was the election of 13 May 1849 which revealed most clearly the limitations of the landowners' influence. In the Côte d'Or the candidates of the Party of Order were victorious. But the split between those conservatives who accepted the Revolution, known as the 'blues', and those who did not, known as the 'whites', cost them two seats which went to the 'reds'. Significantly, the Party of Order got its best results in the Châtillonnais and the Montagne dijonnaise, regions of conservative 'rural democracy', where the presence of notables was discreet (most of their property was forested); it had slight or mediocre success in the cantons of the plain, the wine-growing areas and the southwest (astride the Auxois and the Morvan), where large-scale property was very much more visible. The case of the Saône-et-Loire was clearer still. In the Bresse, the Chalonnais and the Mâconnais, but also in latifundia and sharecropping regions in general, the Party of Order, the rallying-point for large landowners, was overwhelmed. It could offer resistance only in a few cantons near Autun, where the nobles and great bourgeois of the *arrondissement* capital were well organized and to a certain extent present in the countryside, and in the Brionnais, an area of very high religious practice, where the clergy could lend effective assistance to the defence of the established order. Everywhere else, *démocrate-socialiste* militants, mostly from the petite bourgeoisie, were able in a period of severe economic crisis to channel to their ends the aspirations for social change of indebted small peasants, sharecroppers, poor tenants and wine-growers on sharecropping leases. The only reassuring elements in this grim picture were the national victory of the Party of Order and the presence at the head of the state of an enemy of the 'reds' in whom diverse elements could see their salvation, and also the fairly acceptable results of the departmental and municipal elections of the previous summer. The 'social power' maintained by some notables, and the habit of entrusting to them the defence of local

Map 2.7 Elections of 13–14 May 1849: *démocrates-socialistes*

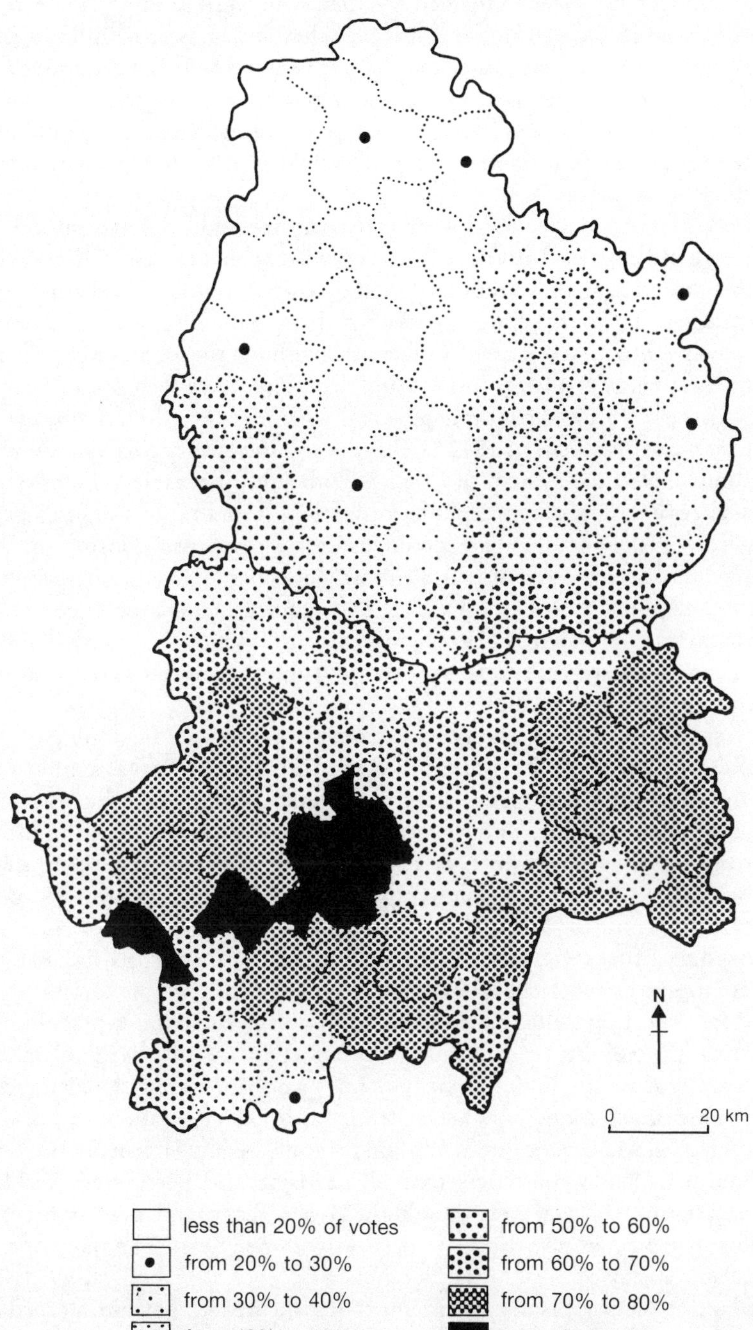

economic interests, made possible the continuation, in the departmental and *arrondissement* councils, of a majority of men who were certainly somewhat less well placed in the hierarchy of incomes than under Louis-Philippe, but most of whom (63 per cent as against 74.7 per cent in 1842/5) were above the 5,000-franc mark; 81 per cent of departmental councillors had even been censitary electors before 1848.[29] This was a relative success, but it could not hide the seriousness of the electoral defeat (14 'reds' out of 20 representatives) suffered in the spring of 1849.

In this situation, the Second Empire seems at first sight to have embodied the revenge of the great landowners. Allied with Schneider and Chagot, the kings of iron and coal, they recovered their quasi-monopoly of parliamentary representation. The only republican elected, Joseph Magnin, was in any case one of their own. Local elected bodies, throughout the regime, contained three times as many nobles as in 1848 and distinctly more than under Louis-Philippe (nearly 15 per cent); 'proprietors' with no other designation were also more numerous than in 1842/5. But the significance of this victory was ambiguous. Given the system of official candidates, it was very largely the consequence of the support of the administration. If traditional notables were able almost everywhere in the countryside to recapture control of the electorate, it was very often only in a subordinate position to the government executive, its prefects and sub-prefects, and thanks to the adherence of the peasant masses to Bonapartism, a 'popular' ideology which was not that of the lords of the soil, who were more attached to legitimism or, more often, to an ultra-conservative liberalism.

The fragility of their hegemony was evident from the very beginning of the Third Republic. Despite the support of the monarchist national assembly and the governments of Moral Order, they were unable to withstand the offensive of the republicans of the '*couche sociale nouvelle*', who were all the more dangerous to them in the countryside in that unlike the 'reds' of 1848–51 they could scarcely be accused of being a threat to property. Between 1871 and 1877, traditional notables lost control of the majority of municipal councils and mayoral offices (now elected), and almost all their parliamentary representation; the few large landowners who were elected, like Lamartine's friend Henri de Lacretelle, got in as republicans. Apart from a few similar exceptions, the nobility in particular was under threat as a symbol of the former ruling class. In 1880, the proportion of nobles among departmental and *arrondissement* councillors had fallen from 15 per cent (at the end of the Second Empire) to 2.3 per cent; in 1913 there would be none left at all. By then even bourgeois landowners (less than 20 per cent) had been overtaken by doctors, pharmacists and vets (totalling 23 per cent), and even more by members of the economic professions (nearly 28 per cent). The days of the political supremacy of the large landowners were over.

By adapting themselves to new circumstances, however, they did succeed in retaining a part of their *social* power. Where the great domain was preserved almost intact, and all the more so where it stayed in the hands of the same family, habitually resident, the traditional methods of paternalism were far from having lost their effectiveness at a local level. Noble mayors (elected by their fellow citizens) were twice as numerous in 1913 as in 1833 (46 as against 23), admittedly for more than 1,300 communes. However, through the complex mechanisms of inheritance and sale, the phenomenon of absentee-ism, of which there is a lot of evidence in the available local studies, seems to have developed considerably.[30] With the systematic use of managers, increasing mobility and the breaking-up of properties, and the growth of the independent middle peasantry, communes susceptible to patriarchal rule by a great notable became increasingly rare. By the same token, the alliance between château and presbytery lost its effectiveness. Not that the clergy gave up; in conflict with the anticlerical republican authorities, it was more than ready to lend a hand to conservative landowners. But outside a few pious regions like the Brionnais its influence, to judge from the taking of Easter communion and attendance at Mass, was in steady decline. In the diocese of Autun, Easter communion rates fell between 1840 and the eve of the First World War from 65.4 per cent to 40.8 per cent; in that of Dijon, between 1839 and 1921/6, from 43.8 per cent to 23.5 per cent. At the same time, all publicly owned schools had been secularized. As for private schools run by the religious orders, the protection and financial support of certain notables and the zeal of their wives had helped them to get established and to survive, but they were almost all closed down at the beginning of the twentieth century.

Although they experienced a serious defeat in this area, a number of large landowners, sometimes supported by their managers, succeeded in maintaining and even extending a powerful instrument of social influence: the agricultural associations. These were in the first instance the former agricultural societies, control of which had been a source of sometimes very sharp conflict between republicans and monarchists. In 1880, the four *arrondissement* committees of the Côte d'Or still had conservatives as presidents: the Comte Sixte de Saint-Seine, the Comte Henri de la Ferrière, the Vicomte de Vergnette-Lamotte and Achille Maître, a Catholic notable of the Châtillonnais. In the Saône-et-Loire at the same time, republicans controlled the societies of Louhans and Mâcon (the latter created by them in 1879); in the Charollais, however, the *comice agricole* presided over by the landowner and republican deputy Bouthier de Rochefort was confronted by the '*comice libre agricole*' under the control of his political enemies, while the agricultural society of Chalon and the much more important one at Autun continued as in the past to bring together the principal notables and their chief tenants. It was often the organizers of these societies who contributed, after the passing of the 1884 law, to the creation of agricultural syndicates. These were intended to bring together a much wider clientele, by offering various services to peasants (purchase of fertilizer and equipment, dissemination of technical developments, insurance, credit) and by defending their economic interests.

Furthermore, the great Catholic and conservative landowners were able to create stronger organizations in this field than were their opponents, drawn mostly from the republican, later radical, petite bourgeoisie, and despite the administration's support for the latter. It is possible that in this period of depression the apoliticism affected by these 'agrarians' (who were in fact hostile to the regime) seemed to many farmers a guarantee of independence in the face of a government to which most of them were prepared to give their votes but which they were easily disposed to suspect of not doing enough for agriculture. However that may be, at the beginning of the twentieth century agricultural syndicalism in the Côte d'Or was dominated by the Union Régionale de Bourgogne Franche-Comté, whose president was the Comte Lejéas, a Bonapartist by tradition, lord of the château of Aiserey in the plain near Dijon. A number of syndicates in the Saône-et-Loire were also affiliated to it, while others (21 as early as 1900) belonged to the powerful Union du Sud-Est, founded at Lyons in 1888. All were thus linked with the central union in the rue d'Athènes, close to the aristocratic Société des Agriculteurs de France. Officially, this syndicalism 'in no way represents an oligarchy of landed proprietors, but a broadly based rural democracy'.[31] In practice, it enabled a section of the traditional notables to retain, and indeed to strengthen, their social influence over a peasantry which, by its progressive accession to landownership, had more and more escaped from their economic power, and which the victory of the Republic had by and large removed from their political control.

The history of the great Burgundian landowners of the nineteenth century is profoundly marked by the French Revolution. The Revolution was a severe blow to those of them who had been seigneurs, by abolishing their *legal* authority over their tenants as a whole and by ending the often very lucrative dues that they extracted from them. It modified the power relationships between nobles, who saw their patrimony on the whole dilapidated, and bourgeois, who extended theirs thanks to the sale of *biens nationaux*. By the bitter and recurrent nature of the political struggles to which it gave rise, it produced a durable split in the class of landed notables: 'whites' on one side and 'blues' on the other. It thus undermined their power. Most peasants felt an instinctive distrust for the 'whites', and to a certain extent for the clergy, suspecting them of dreaming of a return to the *ancien régime*. The memory of the burdens of the seigneurial order and of the extensive domination exercised in the province by the aristocracy through the Estates and the Parlement created an objective solidarity between the majority of country-dwellers and the liberal landowners. The 'historic bloc' typical of the countryside in the West, uniting clergy, nobility and peasantry under the banner of traditional Catholicism, did not exist in Burgundy. It is no surprise that, in spite of the post-1848 coming together of legitimists, Orleanists and Bonapartists, the representatives of the republican petite bourgeoisie, with deep roots in rural society and skilful at invoking the heritage of the Revolution, were fairly easily able, even before the traditional notables suffered the harsh consequences of economic depression, to appropriate their local political power.

But although they were weakened, the great landowners did not disappear. And for those who had remained faithful to the land the turn of the century brought new possibilities of action, symbolized by syndicalism. By agreeing to renounce domination and to content themselves with mere influence, they and their descendants were able to play a far from negligible role in agricultural organizations: the evolution of society brought them closer to the well-off farmers who now had the village almost to themselves and who had gone conservative. The twentieth century in Burgundy was marked not so much by the '*fin des paysans*' as by the end of a centuries-old conflict between peasants and the lords of the great domains.

NOTES

1 See Maps 2.1 (agricultural regions) and 2.2 (cantons and sections of cantons).
2 The cadastral survey was carried out at the level of the commune. Each person holding land in that commune had a single *cote*, which consisted of the total amount of land he held in that commune and the total tax he paid on it. He might very well own land in another commune or communes, in which case he would have a separate *cote* for each commune. (Editors' note.)
3 See Map 2.3. The figures are for the total area of privately owned land held in units of over 50 hectares, as a percentage of the total area of privately owned land (i.e. taxable land less communal land and canals).
4 See Map 2.4. The lower limit thus ranges from 15 hectares in the richest wine-growing districts to 120–130 hectares in the poorest regions of the Châtillonnais or the Autunois.
5 See Map 2.5. Derived from Map 2.4 (but the wooded part of the great domains can often only be estimated; consequently all the absolute figures and the percentages correspond to Map 2.4 unless indicated to the contrary).
6 This terminology is borrowed from Pierre Barral, *Les agrariens français de Méline à Pisani* (Paris: 1968), pp. 41–63.
7 Cantons of Grancey-le-Château, Is-sur-Tille, Selongey and Saint-Seine-l'Abbaye.
8 See the map in Pierre Lévêque, *Une société provinciale: la Bourgogne sous la Monarchie de Juillet* (Paris: 1983), p. 677.
9 In the Côte d'Or, as late as 1846, only 112 of those paying the *patente* (less than 13 per cent of the total number of electors who owned a business) paid a *patente* of over 200 francs.
10 See Lévêque, *Une société provinciale*, pp. 99–101.
11 The 1851 census gives, for the two departments, 218,305 proprietors for 365,209 *cotes foncières*, i.e. 59.8 per cent. Applying this coefficient, one would arrive at about 2,500 proprietors for the 4,148 large *cotes*. Since large proprietors held land in several communes much more often than did small ones, this is a maximum figure.
12 J. Lhomme, *La grande bourgeoisie au pouvoir (1830–1880)* (Paris: 1960), pp. 59–71.
13 *Bulletin de la Société d'Agriculture d'Autun* (1855), pp. 59–63.
14 See Map 2.6.
15 C. Ragut, *Statistique du département du Saône-et-Loire* (Mâcon: 1838), p. 541.
16 *Le Courrier de la Côte d'Or*, 19 January 1847.
17 At Romenay (canton of Tournus), the average rent per hectare for a property over 20 hectares was 45 francs; it was 55 francs for properties under 20 hectares (Archives Départementales du Saône-et-Loire [hereafter ADSL], M, *usages locaux*). In the canton of Dijon-Est, according to the office of direct taxation, a 100-hectare property rented as a whole would fetch an average of 4,083 francs; divided into 10 farms of 10 hectares each, it might

bring in 5,416 francs (Archives Départementales de la Côte d'Or [hereafter ADCO], SM 15675).

18 Lévêque, *Une société provinciale*, pp. 123–4, 281–3. The rental income of the Dijon hospital has been studied by G. Martin and P. Martenot, *Contribution à l'histoire des classes rurales en France au XIXe siècle: la Côte d'Or* (Paris: 1909), pp. 104–17.

19 ibid., pp. 137–44, 261–2, 278, 417–20.

20 ibid., pp. 518–19.

21 The case of Ménessaire has been studied by M. Vigreux, initially in his *Mémoire de diplôme d'études supérieures*, 'Évolution de l'économie et de la société rurale dans une commune du Morvan (Ménessaire) au XIXe siècle' (Paris: 1957): and subsequently in his doctoral thesis, *Paysans et notables du Morvan au XIXe siècle* (Château-Chinon: 1987), p. 190.

22 Archives du Diocèse d'Autun. Pastoral visitation of 1842.

23 Archives Nationales, F 1b I 162[6]. Report of 22 March 1850.

24 ADSL, série M, *état-civil, statistiques et nomenclatures*. Report of the commission of inquiry of the *arrondissement* council of Charolles for the canton of Gueugnon, October 1850.

25 ADCO, 2J[6]I. Report of the prefect of the Côte d'Or, 14 April 1840.

26 Excluding communal land (and other property assimilated to it). For 1884, its surface area (total surface area and that over 50 hectares) has been calculated by approximation from the cadastral registers and the article by J. de Crisenoy, 'Statistique des biens communaux et des sections de communes', *Revue générale d'administration* (1887), pp. 257–77. The 'Tableau par département des cotes comprises dans les rôles de l'année 1884, divisées par catégorie et d'après leur contenance' can be found in the collection of *Documents statistiques réunis par la direction générale des contributions directes sur les cotes foncières* (Paris: 1889), tableau 12.

27 The cantons concerned are those of Arnay-le-Duc, Liernais, Mirebeau, Saint-Jean-de-Losne and Saulieu in the Côte d'Or, La Chapelle-de-Guinchay, Issy-l'Évêque, Saint-Germain-du-Bois and Verdun-sur-le-Doubs in the Saône-et-Loire.

28 In 1890, urban property represented 49.09 per cent of the fortune of residents of Dijon who died in that year, stocks and shares 22.24 per cent, rural property only 5.03 per cent (from P. Gonnet, 'La société dijonnaise au XIXe siècle', thesis, typescript, 1974, pp. 1144–51).

29 For a full presentation of the election results of the Second Republic, see P. Lévêque, *Une société en crise: la Bourgogne au milieu du XIXe siècle (1846–1852)* (Paris: 1983), chs II, IV, V and pp. 481–511. For May 1849, see Map 7.

30 In particular the following *mémoires de maîtrise* by students at the University of Dijon: M. Barlet, 'La vie politique dans le canton d'Arnay-le-Duc de 1870 à 1914' (1974); C. Bonnot, 'Le canton de Verdun-sur-le-Doubs: vie économique, sociale et politique de 1870 à 1914' (1976); A. Colin, 'Le canton de Liernais de 1880 à 1914' (1983); C. Gaudillère, 'Le canton de Saulieu de 1880 à 1914, étude sociale et politique' (1974); and C. Rabut, 'La société rurale dans un canton de la Bresse du Nord (1830–1914), Saint-Germain-du-Bois' (1970).

31 Comte de Rocquigny, *Les syndicats agricoles et leur oeuvre* (Paris: 1900), p. 393.

3

The Périgord: landownership, power and illusion

Ralph Gibson

One of the most durable myths about the Périgord (now the department of the Dordogne) is that it used to be an area of large-scale property, dominated by great landowners and particularly by an aristocracy dedicated to throne and altar. This ruling class is believed to have dictated its will in the nineteenth century – at least until the Third Republic – to a mass of sharecroppers, farm-workers, rural artisans dependent upon it for employment, and even small proprietors whose holdings were not large enough to give them real economic independence. This was in fact widely believed at the time. In 1843 an inspector of primary schools attributed the educational backwardness of the department to the fact that 'property here is highly concentrated: whole communes, even cantonal centres, belong entirely to one or two people. The great landowners look askance on the idea of their sharecroppers' children going to school.'[1] This image of a very uneven distribution of landed wealth has been refurbished by René Pijassou, the only authoritative modern writer on the Périgord,[2] and it is widely believed by *périgourdins* today – strengthened by the portrait of the evil Comte de Nansac in the highly successful television adaptation of Eugène le Roy's novel *Jacquou le Croquant*, and of the wicked marquis in *Histoire d'Adrien*, the first French film to be made with patois-speaking actors. Everyone simply assumes that land was concentrated in the hands of an aristocratic few, and that only the Third Republic brought a modicum of social justice to the Périgord.

This has been an extraordinarily potent myth in the politics of the area, but there is very little evidence that it bears any relationship to reality. Let us remember in the first place that nineteenth-century France, when compared with most other countries of Europe, was the homeland of small peasant proprietorship. It is of course true that this image was grossly exaggerated by republican ideologues who wished to believe that the Revolution had established the social base for a property-owning democracy. When Michelet wrote in 1844 that 'the land of France belongs to 15 or 20 million peasants who work it themselves; the land of England belongs to an aristocracy of 32 thousand people who get others to work it for them',[3] he was simply making it up as he went along (the figures came out of his head). But the contrast with the United Kingdom is indeed striking: in France, in 1882, 40 per cent of the land was owned by the richest 100,000 landowners; the English New Domesday Survey of 1873 showed 80 per cent of the land owned by the richest 7,000.[4] Some regions of Europe, like the south German states or parts of northern Spain, may have had a higher proportion of peasant landownership than the French average, but as a general rule France, although not the peasant democracy of jacobin mythology, had less concentration of agricultural capital and more peasant proprietors than most of the rest of Europe.

France itself knew regional differences in the concentration of landownership – though not as massive, or as crucial for national history, as in Germany, Spain and Italy. The first national figures on the surface area of large holdings appeared in 1884, and they form the basis of Map 3.1 on page 81.[5] The map is to a certain extent misleading, inasmuch as the large holdings in the Alps and the Pyrenees were mostly communal lands, and thus represent the very reverse of a concentration of landownership; in the Landes, the large properties were largely scrub and pine forest. So long as these distortions are borne in mind, however, the map gives a reasonable picture of the distribution of relatively large-scale landownership in France. The classic area of large landed domains was the Centre, as the black blob on the map clearly indicates. Burgundy, which Pierre Lévêque examines in this volume, was an area of fairly large concentrations (Saône-et-Loire: 29.2 per cent; Côte d'Or: 31.5 per cent), whereas the West, discussed here by Donald Sutherland, on the whole was not. The Dordogne was absolutely not such an area: 12.2 per cent of the surface area was owned in tax units of over 100 hectares – less than half the national average, and 71st out of 87 departments. Earlier figures, going back as far as 1826, produce a similar if less dramatic conclusion.[6] Whatever figures one takes, it is clear that this supposed home of great landowners was in fact always below the national average for the concentration of landownership – in a country which was itself at the bottom of the European league.

Given this situation, and the frequent connection between large landownership and sharecropping, it is not surprising that the Dordogne was not really sharecropping country. The illusion that it was, however, does have some sort of basis in fact. It was an area where there was more sharecropping than elsewhere, as the 1851 census clearly demonstrated (see Table 3.1)[7].

Table 3.1 Distribution (%) of agricultural population (1851 census)

	Dordogne	*France*	*Pos./86*
Propriétaires-cultivateurs	48.4	35.2	26
Fermiers	3.7	12.7	72
Métayers	24.5	6.9	6
Journaliers	12.4	30.1	82
Domestiques	10.6	13.5	55
Bûcherons, charbonniers	0.5	1.6	57

Map 3.1 Large-scale property in France, 1884

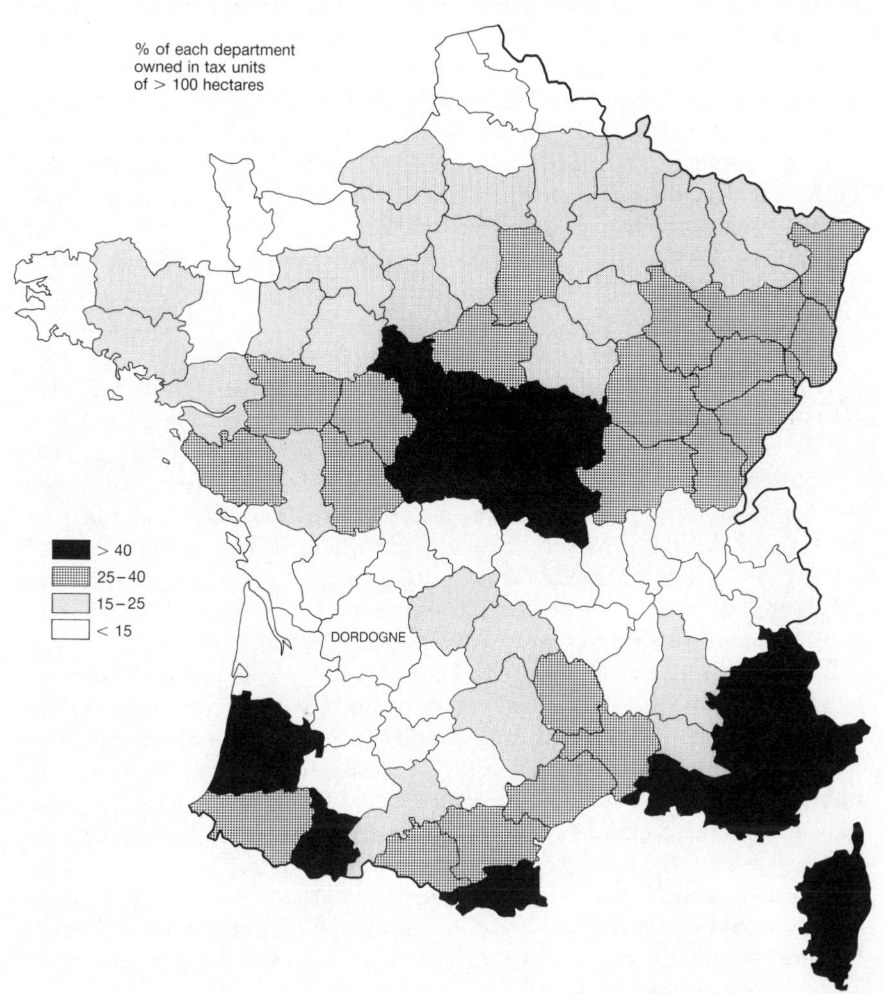

Source: Ministère des Finances, *Documents statistiques réunis par la direction générale des contributions directes sur les cotes foncières*, Paris: 1889, pp. 52–55.

The illusion was compounded by the fact that the average *métairie* covered 20–25 hectares, whereas a *petit propriétaire* would scratch a living out of very much less – such that the quarter of the population who were *métayers* probably farmed a greater area than the half who were *propriétaires-cultivateurs*. But if we are interested in the people rather than the land, the significant point is that there were twice as many of the latter: the Dordogne countryside was characterized not so much by sharecroppers as by poor peasants owning some land, some of them enough to be economically independent, some of them making up the balance in a black economy (odd-jobbing, poaching, charity, and so on) of which very little trace survives in the documents. An analysis at communal level makes this equally clear: in 46.6 per cent of communes, in 1851, *propriétaires-cultivateurs* were a majority of the agricultural population, as against only 13.4 per cent in which a majority were *métayers*. Agricultural inquiries tell us a not dissimilar story: in 1862, 33.0 per cent of the active agricultural population in the Dordogne were farming exclusively their own land, as against 24.5 per cent in France as a whole; twenty years later, the figures would be 46.5 per cent and 30.9 per cent.[8]

The classic source for the study of the notables of the first half of the nineteenth century is the electoral lists of the Restoration and the July Monarchy.[9] As Table 3.2 shows, an analysis of the Dordogne lists for 1829 and for 1840/1 does not reveal very many large *cotes* – and thus not very many large properties, since the great bulk of direct taxation fell on land. (For an explanation of the term *cote*, see Chapter 2, note 2.)

The most heavily taxed man with his political domicile in the department was Robert Paul Coignet, captain in the engineers and director of the asphalt mines at Pyrimon-Seyssel in the Ain, paying 10,947 francs in direct taxes, but he figured on the Dordogne lists only because he had married into the old noble de Beaumont family; most of his property was in the Ain. The next most heavily taxed (at 4,947 francs) was Armand Nicolas le Roy, Comte de Barde. The '*grands notables*' of the Périgord were thus small beer, at least if we compare them with some of those brought to light by André-Jean Tudesq. The electoral lists for the Dordogne – even though they reveal some sizeable fortunes – thus do not suggest that it was a region of truly enormous accumulations of landed wealth.

Table 3.2 Number of *cotes* in Dordogne electoral lists, 1829 and 1840/1, by size of *cote*

	1829	*1840/1*
200–300 francs		1,230
300–500 francs	632	899
500–1,000 francs	373	566
1,000–2,000 francs	161	273
>2,000 francs	29	40
Total	1,195	3,008

Table 3.3a Percentage of privately owned land held by largest landowner

	0–5	*5–10*	*10–20*	*20–30*	*30–50*	*>50*	*Total*
Ist *cadastre*	64	251	168	37	23	1	543
1913 revision	125	248	123	33	12	2	543

Table 3.3b Percentage of land tax paid by most heavily taxed landowner

	0–5	*5–10*	*10–20*	*20–30*	*30–50*	*>50*	*Total*
Ist *cadastre*	61	231	187	47	15	2	543
1913 revision	110	240	141	37	13	2	543

Table 3.3c Percentage of land tax paid by three most heavily taxed landowners

	0–10	*10–20*	*20–30*	*30–40*	*40–50*	*>50*	*Total*
Ist *cadastre*	22	227	178	70	29	17	543
1913 revision	66	264	130	49	24	10	543

Table 3.3d Area in hectares owned by largest landowner

	0–50	*50–100*	*1–200*	*2–300*	*3–400*	*>400*	*Total*
Ist *cadastre*	41	153	223	81	24	21	543
1913 revision	89	167	189	53	28	17	543

At the risk of overkill, one can turn to the massive cadastral registers themselves.[10] This has the advantage of enabling fairly direct comparisons to be made between the period when the first cadastral survey was carried out in the Dordogne (1810–46), and the first systematic revision (1913). The comparisons are not always of like with exact like, particularly because the first *cadastre* lumped buildings and land together, but in a very rural department like the Dordogne the consequent distortion is not all that serious. A series of tables (3.3a–d) sums up the situation. The figures are for the number of communes in each category.

These statistics (though somewhat indigestible) should put paid to the idea that the Dordogne was typically an area of large landed property. In brief, in the first half of the nineteenth century:

- in 94 per cent of communes, the largest landowner owned less than a quarter of the land;
- in 93 per cent of communes, the most heavily taxed landowner paid less than a quarter of the land tax;
- in 97 per cent of communes, the three most heavily taxed landowners between them paid less than half the land tax;
- in 36 per cent of communes, the largest landowner held less than 100 hectares;

- and finally (not shown in the above tables): only 14.4 per cent of privately owned land was held in units of more than 100 hectares. (In the Loir-et-Cher, studied by Georges Dupeux, the comparable figure was 47.9 per cent.)[11]

The tables also make it clear that in the Dordogne, as in the rest of France, agricultural capital was being de-concentrated at a fairly rapid rate in the course of the nineteenth century. This development should not be supposed to have been universal: in 38 per cent of communes, the proportion of the surface area owned by the largest landowner in fact increased between the first *cadastre* and the 1913 revision; in 39 per cent, the proportion of land tax paid by the most heavily taxed landowner increased; in 33 per cent the proportion paid by the three most heavily taxed landowners together increased. The general trend, however, was in the opposite direction, as a glance at Tables 3.3a–d will readily show. This was partly due to the partible inheritance provisions of the Napoleonic code – Tocqueville's famous *machine à hâcher le sol*. The importance of this factor should not, however, be overestimated, since family limitation and the reconstruction of properties by judicious marriages were often effective counters – especially in a region accustomed before the Revolution to primogeniture. More important may have been a process of disinvestment from the land by the rural bourgeoisie, to which we shall return.

Fiscal statistics, censuses, electoral lists and cadastral surveys thus all reinforce the conclusion that the Périgord was a region of relatively small-scale property, in a country not noted for large accumulations of land. That does not mean, of course, that there were not some very major landowners, or that some of them were not able to exercise considerable power over the rural population. The landed notables of the Périgord were, however, at least in the first half of the nineteenth century, a deeply divided lot. The basic division was not of wealth, nor even of relations entered into in the process of production, but of estate. For France as a whole, Tudesq has argued that aristocracy and upper bourgeoisie were fairly rapidly fused into '*le monde des grands notables*'.[12] But in the Périgord, under the July Monarchy at least, distinctions of estate were crucial, and were largely determinant of political ideology and of the influence that notables could exert over the mass of the population.

The dividing line between nobles and bourgeois was of course very unclear at the time, and it remains so to historians. I have decided to consider as noble those whose families voted with the second estate in 1789, or had been the object of an official *maintenu* of their nobility under the *ancien régime*. This kind of definition is much contested, on the grounds that any nobility is constantly changing and renewing itself, and that the French nobility continued to do precisely that in the course of the nineteenth century.[13] While that is undoubtedly true, in practice it is essential to have a fairly rigid definition of who was noble, if one is going to make any quantified statements at all.

What then can we say about the nineteenth-century role of those families which had been officially noble in 1789? To a very considerable extent they had, by hook or by crook, survived the scourge of the Revolution with much of their landed property intact. They figure prominently among the *censitaires* of the Restoration and the July Monarchy, particularly at the higher levels, as Table 3.4 shows.

Nobles were evidently a minority of electors (particularly of those engaged in professional or economic activities) – but the higher one went in the tax bracket the more prominent they became, and at the very highest levels they constituted a majority. In 1829 they made up 20.4 per cent of the electorate but were responsible for 30.9 per cent of the land tax paid by electors; in 1840/1, they constituted 10 per cent (of a much larger electorate), paying 21.0 per cent. Of those paying over 1,000 francs in direct taxes, they represented (even by my fairly rigorous definition) 48 per cent in 1829 and 29 per cent in 1840/1 – though their number remained rock-steady at 92.

These were fairly respectable percentages by comparison with other departments.[14] A full national comparison is not possible, since electoral lists have not always survived. There is however a curious document deposited in the Bibliothèque Nationale: in 1820 the genealogist Hozier borrowed from the Ministry of the Interior the electoral lists for all the departments and transcribed, rather indiscriminately, all the names that he considered relevant

Table 3.4 Nobles in the electoral lists of the Restoration and the July Monarchy

(a) *Profession*

	1829		*1840/1*	
	Noble	*Roturier*	*Noble*	*Roturier*
Proprietors	76	436	213	1,638
Title only given	110	139	26	71
Liberal professions	17	222	10	511
Civil servants	10	37	5	87
Armed forces	28	27	31	79
Industry and commerce	0	93	2	335
Total	241	954	287	2,721

(b) *Tax bracket*

	1829		*1840/1*	
	Noble	*Roturier*	*Noble*	*Roturier*
200–300			38	1,192
300–500	64	568	61	838
500–1,000	85	288	96	470
1,000–2,000	72	89	66	207
>2,000	20	9	26	14
Total	241	954	287	2,721

Table 3.5 Percentage of nobles among largest landowner in each commune

(a)	*% of land owned by largest landowner*						*All*
	0–5	*5–10*	*10–20*	*20–30*	*30–50*	*>50*	*communes*
1st *cadastre*	20.3	31.9	51.8	52.2	77.3	0	39.6
1913 revision	11.2	21.4	30.1	39.4	58.3	100.0	23.2

(b)	*% of land tax paid by most taxed landowner*						*All*
	0–5	*5–10*	*10–20*	*20–30*	*30–50*	*>50*	*communes*
1st *cadastre*	16.4	30.7	46.5	55.3	93.3	50.0	38.5
1913 revision	11.8	22.1	26.2	40.5	53.8	100.0	23.4

(c)	*hectares owned by largest landowner*						*All*
	0–50	*50–100*	*1–200*	*2–300*	*3–400*	*>400*	*communes*
1st *cadastre*	14.6	18.3	47.5	56.8	54.2	76.2	39.6
1913 revision	17.8	14.4	28.6	47.2	35.7	41.2	23.2

for his studies of the French nobility.[15] If the total number of names transcribed is expressed as a proportion of the total population, the Dordogne comes out 11th of the 83 departments for which the statistics are usable, and 10th if the number of *censitaires* in the department is taken as the denominator[16] – suggesting a disproportionate noble presence. The procedure is a rough and ready one, but the result is plausible. The Périgord was not a region of great landed aristocrats, but it was one of *hobereaux*: relatively impoverished nobles of only local importance. There were more of them than in most other parts of France, but relatively few *grand seigneurs*.

The *cadastre* tells a not dissimilar story, summarized in Table 3.5. Clearly, the richer the largest landowner in a commune was, the more likely he was to be a noble. In all, the nobility (rigorously defined) owned at the time of the first *cadastre* almost exactly 10 per cent of the privately owned land in the Dordogne. The largest or richest landowner was a noble in nearly two communes out of five; by 1913 this figure had fallen to just under a quarter. These statistics reinforce conclusions from the electoral lists that there were in the Dordogne quite a lot of nobles, but not particularly rich ones. They were *hobereaux*, but for whom (as has been said of the Spanish *hidalguía*) 'how nourishing was the crust of black bread eaten beneath the genealogical tree'.[17] It is a gross exaggeration to say that they lived on crusts of bread, but many of them did have some difficulty in living in the style they thought proper; it was particularly hard on noble girls, many of whom remained unmarried for want of an adequate dowry, with sad consequences of which I have written elsewhere.[18]

The comparison of the first *cadastre* with the 1913 revision suggests a fairly clear decline in the proportion of the land owned by families who had been noble in 1789. Conspicuous consumption, negligent management, agricultural crisis, mortality, contraception, and the attractions of city life all combined to impoverish, extinguish, or remove from the scene a certain number of noble families. The phylloxera was often the *coup de grâce*, as probably in the case of la Lardimalie, the very old seigneurial property of the Foucauld de Lardimalie, bought around 1880 by M. Honoré Secrestat, who had made a fortune in the Bordeaux liqueur trade.[19] One can in fact accumulate examples of the breaking up and sale of noble properties and châteaux, to make it look as though the nineteenth century was fatal to the Périgord nobility. Its decline should not, however, be exaggerated. On the eve of the First World War, *ancien régime* noble families still provided the largest landowner in nearly a quarter of communes – and if one were to include other families who certainly wished by that stage to be regarded as noble the figure would be considerably inflated. Old aristocratic families in fact often showed a greater determination to hang on to their ancestral lands than did non-noble proprietors whose links with the land were of a more purely economic kind.

We have seen that the Périgord, in the early nineteenth century, was marked by the presence of a considerable number of noble families, whose estates were not very large by national (and especially international) standards, but who were a very visible element of rural society; their presence declined in the course of the century but remained important until at least the First World War. Classic sources such as the electoral lists and the *cadastre* make it equally clear, however, that most of the important landowners were *not* nobles of any kind: they were what was called at the time 'bourgeois', and I shall apply to them the term 'rural bourgeoisie'.

The members of this class had three distinguishing marks: (a) they were not noble; (b) they drew the greater part of their revenue from the soil; and (c) they did not work with their hands. Some of them had a liberal profession, such as barrister or doctor, but this was usually an honourable pastime or a means of acquiring a political clientele rather than the main source of their income. Most of the 'notables' of the countryside belonged to this class. This is very obvious if we consider the electoral lists. Even if we exclude those paying under 300 francs in direct taxes (a category into which a certain number of wealthy peasants and others who worked with their hands probably crept), a large majority of the *censitaires* were not noble but bourgeois (see Table 3.4): 80 per cent in 1829, 86 per cent in 1840/1. Only in the over-2,000 franc bracket did nobles outnumber bourgeois. It is true that were we to use a less rigorous definition of noble and to include those of noble pretensions and fellow-travellers, these percentages would fall somewhat; but there would still be a crushing majority among the landed notables of the Périgord who were in no sense noble, and who indeed – as we shall see – belonged to a very different world. The *cadastre* tells a similar story.

Non-nobles were the most important landowners in three communes out of five in the first half of the century, and in three out of four at the end of it (see Table 3.5). The presence of this rural bourgeoisie was almost universal. In 1855 the *évêché*, in one of its periodic questionnaires to the clergy, included the question 'Are there any bourgeois in the parish?' The survey did not cover the whole of the diocese or department, but its results are striking: 177 *curés* replied that there were one or more 'bourgeois' families, as against only 67 who replied that there was 'peu de bourgeoisie' or none at all.[20] To the clergy of the time, the term clearly meant someone who drew his living from the land – hence replies such as: 'The inhabitants are all engaged in agriculture, which doesn't prevent there being a lot of bourgeoisie.'[21] The *curés* were hypersensitive to the existence of this class (for reasons that will become apparent). They were in fact more sensitive to it than historians have tended to be: this massive social group, which numerically dominated most of the French countryside in the first half of the nineteenth century, has been very largely ignored.[22]

The rural bourgeoisie was very badly hit, however, by the evolution of the French economy in the second half of the century, and particularly by the extended agricultural crisis which began in the late 1870s. The rural exodus was making labour scarcer and more expensive, and the selling price of agricultural produce was steadily falling. More seriously still, the interest rate in other sectors was much higher – above 5 per cent, while knowledgeable estimates put it at between 2 and 3 per cent in agriculture.[23] At the same time there was a considerable peasant demand for land, such that many bourgeois could and did sell up; as a 1912 inquiry reported, 'it is the medium landowners, the old bourgeois of former times, who are today most ready to sell their land, and it is from them that the very small peasants usually purchase the plots destined to round off those they already possess'.[24] A whole social class, once dominant in the countryside, was in the process of liquidation in the late nineteenth century; its representatives sold up and abandoned the countryside for the town, often investing their capital in *rentes* or in Russian bonds – which is why they never forgave the Bolshevik revolution.

I have spent a long time on establishing the social structure of the Périgord notables, if only because there is so much misconception about it. The Périgord was not a region of great landowners: the concentration of landownership there was slight even by French standards. There was a fairly large number of nobles by comparison with other parts of France, but they tended to be relatively small fry, *hobereaux* rather than *grands seigneurs*. Numerous though they were, however, they were outnumbered by the rural bourgeoisie, a large and amorphous class to which most notables in the first half of the century (and not only in the Périgord) can be ascribed. Most notables were bourgeois; most of the land not in peasant hands belonged to them. Some bourgeois attached themselves more or less successfully to the aristocracy; most retained a distinct sense of non- and even anti-noble identity.

To what extent were the disparate elements of the Périgord notables able to exercise power over the mass of the population? We have seen that local tradition ascribes a great deal of power to noble landowners, at least before the Third Republic. The durability of this belief is perhaps attributable in part to the extraordinary pullulation of châteaux in the Dordogne. Legend has it that *le bon Dieu*, when sowing châteaux all over France, had found a gaping hole in his sack while over the Périgord and emptied the lot before returning for a new one.[25] Whatever the reason, the Périgord is certainly château country: the *Annuaire des châteaux* of 1888/9 lists more of them for the Dordogne than for any but three other departments.[26] This architectural heritage may have caused historians to posit a level of noble influence and power which did not exist in the nineteenth century. The ability of nobles to get others to do their will was in fact limited by two factors: first, they owned only a small proportion of the land; and secondly, they were cordially detested by the mass of the population.

It is possible that nobles in the seventeenth century, at the time of the great *jacqueries* in the southwest, had possessed a real 'vertical solidarity' and allied themselves with the Périgord peasantry against the fiscal exactions of a centralizing state.[27] By the time of the Revolution, however, the Périgord was the scene of a passionate anti-seigneurial movement. The resentment was so strong that it dominated the peasant mentality of the Dordogne for the following century, and beyond. It meant easy pickings for republican propagandists. In 1849 – when the Dordogne was one of 16 departments to give an absolute majority to Ledru-Rollin's *démocrates-socialistes* – *montagnard* propaganda owed much of its success to the claim that a victory for the Party of Order would bring back feudal dues and privileges, the tithe and the *corvée*. Peasants on the banks of the Dordogne were convinced that the Marquis de Gourgues, one of the Party of Order candidates, kept in his château a hundred yokes, to which – in the event of victory for his party – the peasants would be attached to plough the fields of the former *grand seigneur*.[28] In 1877, according to the prefect, propaganda against the candidate of the *seize mai* was along the lines that 'if M. Raynaud is elected: war will break out immediately; the *curés* will be masters of the government; the nobles will be re-established with the tithe and seigneurial dues'; the prefect asserted that these rumours were believed and did cause peasants to vote for the Republican candidate.[29] The old legend about tithes and dues died hard: in the Popular Front election campaign in the Dordogne in 1936, the moderate candidates were presented as 'l'homme du château', ready to establish 'le temps des seigneurs'.[30] So did the other chief element in anti-noble propaganda in the nineteenth century: the anti-patriotism of the nobility. In 1870 it was widely believed in the Dordogne that the nobles (and *curés*) were in league with the Prussians. The same rumours were common elsewhere, but here it led to a peasant mob in the commune of Hautefaye lynching a local noble and burning him alive; four peasants were guillotined in the village square, but a *curé* of the environs reported: 'The moral sense of the peasant is so perverted that he regards those executed as martyrs; it would be dangerous to maintain the contrary.'[31] Similar echoes of noble emigration and the army of the princes were still loud in 1914, when it was widely rumoured that Kaiser Wilhelm II and his suite had installed themselves in the château de Lamberterie, whence they sallied forth at night, and that in the morning the sandy driveway bore the traces of his spurs and of the satin slippers of his ladies.[32]

Republicans of the Second and Third Republics were thus able, by exploiting atavistic peasant fears of seigneurial jurisdiction and by playing on a rather newer fear of the nobility as an enemy fifth column, to direct peasant antagonisms onto the nobility in particular, and away from wealthy landowners in general. This kind of propaganda succeeded, not because it corresponded to a real threat, or because it promised to remedy a genuine exploitation, but because it appealed to a distorted and impassioned folk memory. For the nobles of the Périgord were far from being the major exploiters of the peasantry. They did indeed own 10 per cent of the land, but they clearly owned less than did non-noble landowners – many of whom were or would become republicans. When in around 1880 M. Honoré Secrestat bought up the old seigneurial domain of la Lardimalie, he immediately established himself as the permanent and solidly republican mayor of the commune; similarly, one M. Simonnet, *ancien négociant*, who had purchased the château of Vendoire and disposed of 150,000 francs in revenue, was considered by the sub-prefect in 1878 a 'devoted republican'.[33] It would be easy to multiply these examples. Republican landowners under the Third Republic were certainly exploiting the peasantry on a wider scale – and perhaps more intensively – than was the nobility. Furthermore, the real enemy of the peasant – at least in the first half of the nineteenth century – was not the great landowner (whether noble or bourgeois) but the *usurer*. As the prefect reported in 1812: 'It would be difficult to paint in too strong colours the evil that this odious traffic does to the department.'[34] In his Easter letter of 1852, the bishop could still refer to 'the usurer, that notorious daylight robber . . . who in our diocese has caused more tears to be shed than there are stars in the firmament or leaves in our forests'.[35] The problem declined fairly rapidly in the second half of the century, as peasant wealth increased and other sources of credit became available, but until then it was usury, not the rents or sharecropping of the great landowner, that represented the real form of exploitation.

What I am suggesting is that when republican propaganda turned the animosity of peasants against the nobility, it was in fact blinding them to their real enemies. In the first half of the nineteenth century, the most dangerous enemy was the usurer. Later, it is clearly true that landowners who rented land or let it out for sharecropping were indeed extracting surplus value from the peasantry (as they always had). But such landowners were more likely to be bourgeois than noble, and they might well be republican. Republicanism in the Dordogne was thus what might be termed a 'deflecting ideology'. It had the objective function of deflecting peasant animosity from usurers and non-noble landlords onto the specific group of the nobility (and clergy). The nobility were not the major exploiters of the peasantry, but they were the major recipients of peasant suspicion and hostility. They were thus largely without influence on the mass of the population. This was particularly clear where national politics were concerned. A large majority of Périgord nobles were legitimists, but (with the exception of the 1871 elections) they had little success in getting the peasants to support the cause of Henri V – such that the sub-prefect of Bergerac could write in 1876 of the Marquis de Saint-Exupéry that he had 'very extensive relations in legitimist circles, but consequently very little influence on the elections'.[36]

There were of course isolated communities in the Périgord which gave the lie to any generalization about the nobility's lack of influence. Such an *isolat* was the parish of Bourniquel, which was, according to the vicar-general in 1863,

> excellent in all respects. This is attributable to the able ecclesiastics who have always directed the parish, and to the examples which the population, composed almost entirely of sharecroppers and small proprietors, receives from the family that inhabits the château.

It was the château de Cardou, and the family were the Saint-Exupéry. In 1838 they owned 371 hectares in the commune (42 per cent of privately owned land), and more than a hundred hectares in neighbouring communes. The family was furiously active in religious matters; Jacques de Saint-Exupéry was a vicar-general of the diocese from 1858 to 1879. Thus in 1855 96 per cent of adults made their Easter communion, and in 1879 everyone except four men and two women (in 1874 the diocesan average was 57 per cent). The political influence of the Saint-Exupéry at a local level was equally strong: in the 1877 elections, of 63 electors on the roll, 60 voted for the anti-republican candidate; before the First World War the Republic never got more than a third of the vote, and usually a good deal less. *Volens nolens* (and probably the former), the peasantry of Bourniquel accepted the religious and political direction issuing from the château de Cardou.[37] As the local schoolteacher remarked bitterly in 1912,

> the lord of Cardou is for them a sacred personage, and absolutely indispensable to their existence! 'Qué fayant, si nosté ségnour nous quittaros!!' (*verbatim* from one of the rare peasant proprietors in the commune whose fortune is sufficient for him to be independent).[38]

There were other comparable cases of noble influence and power in the Périgord. Such families, however, were a small minority: the vast majority of the nobles of the Périgord exercised very little influence at all; peasants might respect them personally, but treated them generically with extreme suspicion and rejected all that they stood for.

Where the noble remained an isolated figure, without influence on the peasant mentality, the rural bourgeois held the peasant in a kind of ideological thrall. It was under the July Monarchy that the influence of the rural bourgeoisie reached its apogee. The revolution of 1830 may not have been a bourgeois revolution in the Marxist sense, but in the Dordogne at least its chief significance was that it established the ideological hegemony of non-noble landowners in the countryside. The 1830 revolution meant that the anti-legitimist, anticlerical rural bourgeoisie, now visibly backed by the state, could exercise immense influence over the peasantry. The anguish of the clergy in the face of the aggressive Voltaireanism of most rural bourgeois under the July Monarchy makes this particularly clear. According to one *curé*,

> the bourgeois class makes it a point of honour to despise religion and its ceremonies. If there are a few bourgeois in a parish, they affect never to enter the church, and to criticize the priest in the exercise of his functions. All these sarcasms have completed the destruction in the mind of the simple and naive peasant of all respect for the religion of his fathers.[39]

According to another: 'The bourgeoisie does not set the example, the people would be better if they were not dragged along by those they regard as wiser than themselves.'[40] Answers to the 1841 episcopal inquiry are full of this kind of comment. Often terms like 'the rich', 'les messieurs', 'the principal inhabitants' are substituted for 'bourgeois', but the object remains the same – thus: 'The greatest obstacle to the progress of religion comes from the example of the principal inhabitants, who do not go to church.'[41] The anticlericalism of the rural bourgeoisie (although somewhat shaken by the red menace of 1849) was maintained into the Second Empire and often continued to determine the religious behaviour of the peasantry. In 1855 the *curé* of Saint-Priest asked the bishop to preach, during his pastoral visit, on the example of the bourgeoisie, 'for it is certain that the poor man would follow the example of the rich and that if the bourgeois went to church the sharecropper would do the same'.[42] Indeed, the Voltairean ideology of the rural bourgeoisie lasted almost as long as the class itself. It was, clearly, another case of a 'deflecting ideology': this pre-republican anticlericalism served the objective function of diverting potential antagonisms from the owners of large properties onto the clergy, and at the same time established an ideological solidarity between bourgeois and peasant, with the clergy and nobility for a common enemy.

The influence of the rural bourgeoisie was not, furthermore, confined to its anticlericalism. In 1851 the prefect attributed Louis-Napoleon's massive majority in the plebiscite to the bourgeoisie,

> which has directed the election in the Dordogne. It is in immediate contact with the peasants and has over them the influence which education and wealth confer, an influence which is not diminished by the distrust that the aristocracy inspires in the people.

In 1867 his successor could still write that

> the spirit of the population, generally apathetic and indifferent in the Dordogne, is characterized above all by a complete absence of spontaneity. The people of the countryside, extremely ignorant, are under the influence of a few bourgeois, notaries, doctors, or proprietors, who may be considered the real leaders of public opinion.[43]

Under the Third Republic this influence would decline, as the rural bourgeois sold up and left, perhaps also as the *instituteurs*, the black hussars of the Republic, took the influence of the centralized republican state further and further into the countryside. But for much of the century, if anyone exerted an ideological hegemony over the peasant in the Dordogne, it was the rural bourgeoisie.

At one point at least in the century, however, no local ruling class exercised much power or influence over the peasantry at all. The Dordogne was one of the 16 departments in the south of France which in May 1849 – despite heavy administrative pressure to the contrary – gave absolute majorities to the *démocrates-socialistes*. All eight deputies from the department belonged to that political formation. The top *démoc-soc* candidate received 62,184 votes, the best-placed conservative only 45,909 (the Marquis de Gourgues finished bottom of the conservative list . . .).[44] In voting this way, the peasants of the Périgord appear to have been supporting a programme that was very radical indeed. Conservatives and government administrators were so traumatized by the sudden appearance of rural revolution in their midst that they may have exaggerated its radical content, but the voice of their panic often rings true. According to the procuror-general at Bordeaux,

> the most extravagant promises have been spread abroad, and the most chimerical fears stimulated . . . . The fears stimulated are the re-establishment of the tithe and the *corvée* by the former nobles and bourgeois. The promises spread abroad are the restitution of the 45 centimes land tax and of the *milliard* of the émigrés in favour of those who work with their hands, and progressive taxation.[45]

This programme was radical enough, but what really worried conservatives was the *démocrate-socialiste* attack on private property. In a rural society where a significant minority of peasants owned land, and where the ruling passion of all the rest was to acquire it, socialists evidently did not envisage communal ownership of the means of production. They did, however, violently attack *large-scale* property; as the procuror-general continued in the report quoted above: 'It is reported that they went so far as to promise to those who possessed nothing the sharing out of the land.' The most detailed report on this element of distributive socialism in *démocrate-socialiste* propaganda in 1849 came from Lorenzo Theulier, who had himself been a fairly advanced republican candidate in the April 1848 elections:

> Poverty and the love of property were also exploited. Sharecroppers were promised that they would be exempt from all taxation, that they would have the sole enjoyment of properties now farmed on half shares and that they would be maintained for ten years, despite the landlord, in possession of the *métairie*. . . . Face to face or in private meetings, things went much further. They asserted that the law would authorize the spoliation of the rich, whose properties would be divided up among those who worked the land. They knew that the mere thought that someone might touch his property would put the peasant off completely. The leaders, while still promising that his ardent desire for property would be satisfied, got round this difficulty very cleverly. They established that all properties up to 30,000 francs in value would be inviolable. Only the rich would be dispossessed. It was a *jacquerie* that they were preaching, more or less openly.[46]

There seems little doubt that democratic-socialism meant to the peasants not only protection against the evil designs of the nobles, and not merely relief from hard times (for example, the end of the 45 centimes tax), but also a radical redistribution of landed wealth in the countryside. The owners of concentrations of landed wealth, whether noble or bourgeois, were quite unable to do anything about it. This may have been because those concentrations were relatively slight; Alain Corbin has suggested for the neighbouring Limousin that the absence of great landed notables was one reason for its role as a heartland of the left (the *limousin* departments of the Haute-Vienne and the Creuse were equally *démoc-soc* in 1849).[47] At any rate, all they could do for the moment was to look to the centralized state to save them. At first this meant simply the physical force at the disposal of the conservative Second Republic, which duly closed down newspapers, dissolved political clubs and generally did its best to neutralize the mechanisms of *montagnard* propaganda. But as Lorenzo Theulier wrote in July 1851,

> one cannot hide from the fact that the apparent calm of the socialist party is only the immobility of the tiger watching the approach of its prey. 1852 is still the lottery of pillage for which the tickets are being given away free.[49]

Elections were scheduled for May, and it seemed to conservatives that the red wave that had submerged the south in 1849 would spread to the rest of the country. Some other way of stopping it would have to be found.

In the Dordogne, the means of canalizing if not stopping peasant unrest were in fact to hand. For only five months before they voted for the redistribution of landed wealth, the peasants of the Périgord had voted massively for Louis-Napoleon Bonaparte as president of the Republic: 88.1 per cent as against 74.2 per cent in France as a whole.[49] They would give him similar support in 1851 and 1852. In the immediate aftermath of the coup, the procuror-general, so shortly before trembling at the prospect of social revolution, could write of his region that 'the most complete order and calm have not ceased one instant to reign throughout its entire extent'.[50] Manifestly, peasants saw in the nephew of the great emperor the same thing that they saw in the *démocrates-socialistes*: the enemy of the rich and powerful of all kinds. This was a popular Bonapartism – 'the guarantee of equality . . . the peasantry's revenge against the age-old domination of the notables'.[51] Peasants voted for Louis-Napoleon, not because they were constrained to do so (certainly not the case in 1848), nor really because of memories of Napoleonic *gloire* (since many of them scarcely knew what 'France' was), but because they contrived to perceive him as the enemy of nobles in particular, and of the rich in general.

The notables themselves, however, were willing to go along with the Second Empire, because its objective function was to ensure that there was no social revolution in the countryside. They had no particular affection for Napoleon III, and the legitimist nobility frankly detested him – to the point, in one case, of covering the floor with five-franc pieces in order to trample daily on the face of the *usurpateur*.[52] The vast majority of Périgord notables nevertheless rallied to the Empire, not because they liked it, but because it defended them from what they believed, rightly or wrongly, to be the very real menace of social revolution. Bonapartism turned out to be, in fact, the ultimate 'deflecting ideology'. Without it, the Dordogne would certainly have seen a violent class war in the countryside in 1852, perhaps even more severe than that which did in fact take place in the southeast.[53]

The ability of the major landowners of the Périgord to get the mass of the population to do their will was thus incomplete and variable. They did not own enough of the land to be in a position to exercise direct economic power over everyone: sharecroppers and day labourers may have been economically dependent, but the important and growing minority of independent land-owning peasants (perhaps a majority by the time of the First World War) was less manipulable and its members were themselves increasingly able to manipulate opinion as the century progressed. The old nobility, faithful to its legitimist ideology, was absolutely unable to influence the hearts and minds of the peasants. The rural bourgeoisie, in normal times, did indeed exert considerable ideological hegemony in the countryside. When, however, the Second Republic opened a Pandora's box of discontents that must have been smouldering there long before, even they were unable to stop the explosion of democratic-socialism; had popular Bonapartism not arrived to deflect peasant discontents, the Dordogne would certainly have seen a civil war. Under the Third Republic, this rural bourgeoisie began to disappear, its place taken by commercial wealth (like that of Honoré Secrestat) which bought up some old estates, but perhaps above all by a class of landed peasants which saw its interests as being served by the Republic. The former legitimized their landed wealth in peasant eyes by a more or less explicit adoption of republicanism. Nobles clung on grimly, to much of their land and rather more of their legitimist ideology, but without any more influence or power than they had had a century before.

In general, the exercise of power in the Périgord countryside seems to have been determined to a considerable degree by major ideologies, in particular republicanism (subsuming anticlericalism and anti-noble sentiment) and popular Bonapartism. I have not really examined in this chapter *why* these ideologies were locally so successful; perhaps that is the next task. What is clear, however, is that those who were able to manipulate them were able to exercise power, while those who flew in the face of them could not.

NOTES

1 Archives Départementales de la Dordogne [hereafter ADD], 1T 20.

2 R. Pijassou, *Regards sur la révolution agricole en Dordogne* (Périgueux: 1967), esp. p. 10.

3 J. Michelet, *Le peuple* (Paris: 1946), p. 32. There is no source for Michelet's figures; the most comprehensive study on which he could have drawn, Patrick Colquhoun's *A Treatise on the Wealth, Power and Resources of the British Empire* (London: 1815), p. 126, estimated the nobility and gentry at 47,425 families.

4 Ministère de l'Agriculture, Statistique agricole de la France publiée par le Ministère de l'Agriculture, *Résultats généraux de l'enquête décennale de 1882* (Nancy: 1887), p. 278 (I have made some risky assumptions about the relation of the number of *cotes* to that of individual owners); F. M. L. Thompson, *English Landed Society in the Nineteenth Century* (London: 1963), p. 27.

5 Ministère des Finances, *Documents statistiques réunis par la direction générale des contributions directes sur les cotes foncières* (Paris: 1889), pp. 52–5.

6 ibid., *passim*; see the map for 1826 in G. Dupeux, *La société française, 1789–1960* (Paris: 1964), p. 118, and that for 1842 in A.-J. Tudesq, *Les grands notables en France (1840–1849): étude historique d'une psychologie sociale*, 2 vols (Paris: 1964), Vol. I, p. 99.

7 Statistique de la France, 2e série, Vol. II, *Territoire et Population* (Paris: 1855), pp. 150–1.

8 Statistique de la France publiée par le ministre de l'Agriculture, du Commerce et des Travaux Publics, *Agriculture. Résultats généraux de l'enquête décennale de 1862* (Strasbourg: 1868), pp. 194–7; Ministère de l'Agriculture, Statistique agricole de la France publiée par le ministère de l'Agriculture, *Résultats généraux de l'enquête décennale de*

1882 (Nancy: 1887), pp. 186–9. The second line includes a few cultivating with the help of a *maître-valet*. The bottom line includes a considerable but unspecified number of females.

9 For 1829: ADD, E supplément (Hautefort); for 1840/1: ADD, 2Z 61 – except for the electoral *arrondissement* of Périgueux II, of which the only known copy is in private archives no longer accessible; I have a photocopy which I am happy to make available. Remember that the franchise was fixed at 300 francs in direct taxes until 1830, and at 200 francs thereafter.

10 ADD, sous-série 63P. I have excluded a small number of communes for which the *matrice* is missing either for the original *cadastre* or for the revision, and a small number where boundary changes make comparison impossible.

11 G. Dupeux, *Aspects de l'histoire sociale et politique du Loir-et-Cher 1848–1914* (Paris and The Hague: 1962), p. 99.

12 Tudesq, *Les grands notables*, Vol. I, pp. 8–9.

13 Most recently by D. Higgs, *Nobles in Nineteenth-Century France: the Practice of Inegalitarianism* (Baltimore, Md and London: 1987), p. 5.

14 R. Gibson, 'The French nobility in the 19th century – particularly in the Dordogne', in J. Howarth and P. Cerny (eds), *Elites in France: Origins, Reproduction and Power* (London: 1981), pp. 5–45 (and esp. p. 16).

15 Bibliothèque Nationale, Nouvelles Acquisitions Françaises 22284.

16 Archives Nationales [hereafter AN], F Ic II 52 (for the number of electors in each department).

17 Raymond Carr, 'Spain', in A. Goodwin (ed.), *The European Nobility in the Eighteenth Century* (London: 1953), pp. 43–60; the quotation can be found on p. 55.

18 Gibson, 'The French nobility in the 19th century – particularly in the Dordogne', pp. 18–19.

19 Pijassou, *Regards sur la révolution agricole en Dordogne*, p. 16.

20 Archives du Diocèse de Périgueux [hereafter ADP], C 44, 49, 55, 55 bis, 355.

21 ADP, C 394 (Cazoulès). (This is actually from a parallel inquiry of 1863, of which only fragments survive.)

22 Some brief recent treatments: E. Weber, *Peasants into Frenchmen. The Modernization of Rural France, 1870–1914* (London: 1977), pp. 236–40; M. Agulhon, *La vie sociale en Provence intérieure au lendemain de la Révolution* (Paris: 1970), pt 4, ch. 3; M. Agulhon *et al.*, *Apogée et crise de la civilisation paysanne, 1789–1914* [Vol. III of *Histoire de la France Rurale*, ed. G. Duby and A. Wallon] (Paris: 1976), pp. 95–6.

23 Weber, *Peasants into Frenchmen*, p. 239.

24 Ministère de l'Agriculture, Direction de l'enseignement et des services agricoles. Office des renseignements agricoles, *Enquête sur les salaires agricoles* (Paris: 1912), p. 138. See also (published by the same body) *La petite propriété rurale en France: enquêtes monographiques (1908/9)* (Paris: 1909), p. 68.

25 G. Rocal and J. Secret, *Châteaux et manoirs du Périgord* (Paris: 1938), p. 3.

26 *Annuaire des Châteaux et des Départements*, 1888–9, 2e année (Paris). The Gironde, the Calvados and the Maine-et-Loire had more.

27 Y.-M. Bercé, *Histoire des Croquants. Étude des soulèvements populaires au XVIIe siècle dans le Sud-Ouest de la France*, 2 vols (Paris and Geneva: 1974), Vol. I, pp. 127–34.

28 AN, BB 30 359.

29 ADD, 3M 60.

30 J.-Y. Lachaudru, *Le Front Populaire en Dordogne* (Bordeaux: 1971), p. 72.

31 ADP, C 55 bis (Saint-Pardoux, Mareuil). See also J.-L. Galet, *Meutre à Hautefaye* (Périgueux: 1970) and G. Marbeck, *Cent documents autour du drame d'Hautefaye* (Périgueux: 1983). On the *rumeur infâme* in general, see F. Boulard, *Matériaux pour l'histoire religieuse du peuple français, XIXe–XXe siècles. Région de Paris, Haute-Normandie, Pays de Loire, Centre* (Paris: 1982), pp. 76, 147, 319, 320, 342, 344, 369, and J. M. Villefranche, *Curés et Prussiens*, 2nd edn (Bourg: 1877).

32 Rocal and Secret, *Châteaux et manoirs du Périgord*, p. 63. See also J.-J. Becker, *1914: Comment les français sont entrées dans la guerre* (Paris: 1977), pp. 418–20.

33 ADD, 3M 173, 175, 189, 203, 227. The system did not perhaps work indefinitely: in 1944, the lads of the communist *maquis* were all for burning la Lardimalie to the ground; it was only their officers that prevented them.

34 AN F Ic III Dordogne 7 (rapport du premier trimestre, 1812 – *et passim*).

35 *Mandement . . . pour le saint temps de Carême* (13 February 1852), p. 9.
36 ADD, 3M 165.
37 ADP, D6, C42, 47, 108, 310, 351; ADD 63 P48, 115, 311; 3M 58, 62, 64–6, 70, 73, 75–8, AN, F19 2806.
38 *Beaumont: monographies historiques et géographiques des communes du canton de Beaumont établies par les instituteurs respectifs des différents communes en 1912* (Bayac, Dordogne: 1985), Vol. I, pp. 64–5.
39 ADD, V 276* (Saint-Sulpice-d'Excideuil) – 1838.
40 ADP, C 43 (Quinsac, Champagne-de-Belair) – 1841.
41 ADP, C 43 (Cadouin). For the 1841 inquiry in general, see C 42, 43, 49, 218, 253 (questions 41 and 43).
42 ADP, C55.
43 AN, F Ic III Dordogne 7 (for both quotations).
44 *Echo de Vésone*, 20 May 1849 (the results in AN, C 1331 are defective).
45 AN, BB 30 359.
46 AN, BB 30 374. Similar proposals were made elsewhere, e.g. in the Allier; see T. R. Forstenzer, *French Provincial Police and the Fall of the Second Republic* (Princeton, NJ: 1981), p. 134.
47 A. Corbin, *Archaïsme et Modernité en Limousin au XIXe siècle, 1845–1880*, 2 vols (Paris: 1975), esp. pp. 226–77 and p. 991.
48 AN, BB 30 374.
49 AN, B II 980.
50 AN, BB 30 374 (report of 3 February 1852).
51 R. Rémond, *The Right Wing in France from 1815 to de Gaulle*, tr. J. M. Laux (Philadelphia, Pa: 1966), p. 142; see also the contribution of Roger Magraw to T. Zeldin (ed.), *Conflicts in French Society* (London: 1970), esp. pp. 171–2.
52 *L'Express*, 27 May 1983, p. 99.
53 See T. W. Margadant, *French Peasants in Revolt: the Insurrection of 1851* (Princeton, NJ: 1979); M. Agulhon, *La République au village: les populations du Var de la Révolution à la Seconde République* (Paris: 1970); P. Vigier, *La Seconde République dans la région alpine*, 2 vols (Paris: 1963); and much else.

GERMANY

4

The social and political power of the Prussian Junkers

Hanna Schissler

No other social class in the history of Germany has possessed so problematic an image as that of the Prussian Junkers – the large landowners of northeastern Germany. Representing the authoritarian and anti-liberal traditions within German history, the Junkers have been reproached for having acquired their economic and social status at the expense of other social classes and for playing a substantial part in the downfall of the Weimar Republic. These views, based essentially on the history of the later nineteenth century and of Weimar, serve to attribute to the Junkers the character of a pre-fascist social class. Historians agree that the Junkers represented a great burden – economic, social and political – for Prusso-German history. The bill for preserving the Junkers as a social class was also presented during 12 years of National Socialist dictatorship and two world wars, and finally paid off through defeat and destruction. It has frequently been noted that the Junkers were able not only to survive under changing circumstances but also to maintain their influence and power even when prevailing currents flowed against them, as, for example, in the first years of the Prussian reforms or at the end of the nineteenth century.[1]

The Prussian Junkers of East Elbia were a regionally based lesser nobility whose wealth and power were founded upon landownership. In many respects, and especially as regards landownership, agricultural activity, relative position of power and historical importance, they are comparable with the English landed gentry. Their economic, political and social importance remained intact even in the nineteenth and early twentieth centuries, but Germany's defeat in the Second World War marked the end of the Junkers as a social class.[2]

What justifies the effort expended today, almost half a century after the

Junkers' downfall, in continuing to discuss them? Why have they not been allowed to come to rest in the moth-ridden closets of the past, since they obviously have no part to play in the present, at a time when the issues preoccupying the German people are clearly of a totally different nature from the outdated rulership of a pre-industrial ruling class?

It is of some interest to observe how, after 1945, a historical-political consciousness that was struggling for a democratic and liberal self-awareness allowed the undesirable features of German history to coalesce in the portrayal of the Prussian Junkers.[3] This in no way implies that such features were *not* present, for they certainly were; even into the twentieth century the power of the Junkers relied on an extremely repressive social system and on unbending exploitation. The three-class system of franchise secured for the Junkers an antiquated political dominance within the German Empire. State subsidies maintained a social class and an economic system which, without such help, would have foundered long before in a free market and which were able to enjoy an artificially sustained financial security at the expense of industry and the working class.[4] The Junkers' practice of calling on the state was extremely successful. In serving as a model to others it has also had a lasting influence on German political culture, one of whose characteristic features has been the expectation of economic, social, or political solutions via state intervention.[5] Such patterns of behaviour have become ingrained over centuries.

In recent years – to be precise, in discussions involving British historians – the so-called '*Sonderweg*' debate, that is, the debate over a supposed special path of development in German history, has been revived.[6] The historical role of the Junkers is automatically introduced into any discussion of the question as to why liberalism had so little chance of success in Germany, a question raised almost thirty years ago by Ralf Dahrendorf.[7] As H. A. Winkler put it a few years ago: 'It would be far easier to write about the history of Great Britain without Scotland or the United States without the Southern States than to write on the history of the German Reich without referring to East Elbia.'[8]

The historical employment of the Junkers within the '*Sonderweg*' thesis leads one easily to forget, however, that the Junkers were not always reactionary, illiberal and economically backward; that for a time they were a decisive factor in the country's economic development and that in the first half of the nineteenth century they displayed the features of an open social class, otherwise presumed to exist only in the admired ideal of English landowners. The '*Sonderweg*' thesis, in contrast to recent attempts once more to fuse German desires with Prussian history, is in my opinion an important start to this interpretation, which nevertheless is not wholly unproblematical.

The Prussian Junkers may be investigated via numerous paths. Many questions arise. How did the Junkers successfully maintain their ruling position into the twentieth century? How great was their ability to adapt to altered economic circumstances and conditions which threatened their political or economic position? How, and by what means, were they able to maintain their standing as an estate (*Stand*) and their social exclusiveness? Given that in the eighteenth and nineteenth centuries industrialization and revolution shook the economic basis of all European pre-industrial elites and threatened their claims to power and dominance, how and with what consequences, counter-strategies and attempts at consolidation did the process unfold for the Junkers? How did they, as a social class, experience and digest the rise and fall of their economic power? What role did they *really* play in German history, in its divergence from a supposed model of 'western' democracy? Were they an inherently conservative force? Is it possible to specify the ways in which the Junkers can be held responsible for the failed attempts to democratize German society? If we set aside the fixation on the Prussian Junkers' historical merits or transgressions and attempt to widen the perspective, another question then arises: was the re-feudalization of society a distinctively Prusso-German phenomenon, or was it not perhaps, as the American historian Arno Mayer, like Josef Schumpeter before him, has suggested, a feature present throughout Europe?[9]

It is necessary first of all to pull back from any associations, whether apologetic or critical, which are intended to legitimize the significance of the Junkers, and instead to assess their effect upon German history in a more precise manner.

From the sixteenth century onwards, as part of the economic differentiation between east and west, agricultural activity in East Elbia became heavily commercialized and export-oriented.[10] Within East Elbia the ruling system was characterized by the principles of *Gutsherrschaft* and *Gutswirtschaft*; descriptions abound of the social figures of the wilful and despotic Junkers on the one side and the subservient peasant population on the other.[11] But how did this system of rule, dominance and obedience develop and what functions did it possess? At the apogee of the system in the eighteenth century, the *Gutsherrschaft* implied a profusion of seigneurial rights – low-level jurisdiction, control over the forces of law and order, rights of patronage, and rights of control over the peasant population with regard to change of ownership, permission to marry and geographical mobility. Apart from manorial rights (dues), there also existed compulsory labour service, the reality of which varied widely according to the peasant's property rights. During the secular process of commercialization, the *Gutswirtschaft* (the lord's economic control of the estate) and the *Gutsherrschaft* (his political power) had expanded considerably. In the course of this process, the whole peasant population became *erbuntertanen*: that is, peasants were restricted in their personal mobility, bound to the land and subject to forced labour. Forced labour resulted from property rights. Hereditary servitude followed directly as a result of the personal power relationship between nobles and peasants. This personal dependency and forced labour were to be ended via a complicated process, which set in on the sovereign domains in the eighteenth century, began on the Junkers' estates after 1800 during the Prussian reforms and was concluded in the middle of the nineteenth century.[12]

The principal characteristic of the Junkers' *Gutsherrschaft* was the instrumentalization of sovereign rights for economic purposes.[13] This also accounted for the particular harshness of noble–peasant power relations and the ambiguity of these relations in the age of Enlightenment, economic liberalism and citizen emancipation. Personal servitude and forced labour appear to our contemporary consciousness as objectionable social configurations, surpassable only by real serfdom, as in the case of the Russian peasantry, or actual slavery. The development of servitude and forced labour in Prussia was a gradual process, neither having been characteristic of earlier times. The *Gutswirtschaften* were formerly run by free labourers. It was not until the agrarian upswing in the sixteenth century that it appeared worthwhile to tie the peasants to the land, exploit their labour, decrease their ownership rights and occasionally buy them out or drive them off their property. The full development of the lords' political power was an accompaniment to the boom, experienced by the *Gutswirtschaften* in the sixteenth century and stimulated by the increase in demand, rather than in any way a prerequisite for it.[14]

In the sphere of mentality, it was the Reformation that lent countenance to the development of the Junkers' power.[15] The Lutheran doctrines of obedience and submissiveness to authority were invaluable ideological gains for the nobles, since they made suppression and obedience appear legitimate and in accordance with the 'natural' religious order. Lutheranism, as Otto Hintze stated, with its tendency to suffering obedience, its passiveness and self-restraint, facilitated the oppression of the peasant population. The custom of rule was able to emerge in the same way as did some of the features of the peasant's mentality, which implanted subjection in their religious consciousness. The orthodox character of Lutheranism complied with the specific needs of forming a hierarchical society.

The question thus arises: how did the state react to the expansion of the Junkers' power? The economic and social structures which developed in the royal domains were essentially the same as those on the estates of the nobility. The sovereign had no genuine interest, in this respect, in preventing the process of subjugation and oppression of the peasant population in the initial phase of expansion of the *Gutsherrschaft*. He profited from the agricultural boom in the same way as the Junkers and accordingly acted in much the same way as far as the sovereign domains were concerned. It was not until the eighteenth century, with the introduction of state laws protecting the peasantry, that this process was counteracted.

This leads on to the question of the relationship between the Junkers and the central political authorities. The question of *Gutsherrschaft* played an important role in the relationship between the Junkers and state authority.

For centuries, there were enormous tensions between the absolute rulers and the nobility, the main issues at stake being taxes and military service.[16] These disputes were decided on the back of the peasant population and at the expense of the cities. Since the sovereign and the nobility shared broadly the same economic interests in the expansion of the *Gutswirtschaften* and the recruiting of peasants as a reliable and available labour force, from 1653 onwards the questions of tax guarantees were regularly solved via a compromise in which the Junkers guaranteed the taxes and the state authority renounced the process of nation-building. State authority ended at the gates of the estates.

In the course of the eighteenth century the aggressive, rebellious nobility became the mainstay of the Prussian state.[17] The nobility's concessions on the issue of estate-based taxation made the development of the Prussian army financially possible, and after decades of opposition it allowed itself to be integrated into the officer corps of the king's army. The list of concessions and privileges which the absolute monarchy offered the nobility as its part of this compromise is a long one. It granted the nobility preferential treatment in the state bureaucracy and military and allowed it to expand further the *Gutsherrschaft* (with the exception of the state's own laws protecting the peasantry). Finally, it gave the nobles secure control of their property, which guaranteed their monopoly over estate ownership, offered them a chance to transform their land into entailed estates and provided them with exclusive credit institutions backed by state subsidies: the *Landschaften*.

Adapting slightly the contemporary term 'military industrial complex', one might best describe the conditions of Junker power in the eighteenth century as a 'military agrarian complex', as brilliantly described by Otto Büsch. Monarchical absolutism gave the nobles a free rein on their estates, or at least, with the one exception of *Bauernschutz*, did not stand in their way. In return, the Junkers agreed to let themselves be integrated into the absolutist state through military and bureaucratic service.

There can be no question that the close relationship between the agrarian and military spheres was responsible for the inflexibility of the Prussian social structure in the eighteenth century. It is no coincidence that it was only after the overwhelming defeat of the Prussian army by Napoleon that it was possible to carry out reforms in the agrarian structure, specifically with regard to private estates. Prussian absolutism pursued a political policy of maintaining the class system, which was above all beneficial to the nobility. It not only established for the nobility a monopoly over estate ownership but also guaranteed them, as part of common law, 'preferential entitlement to the most honoured offices of the state'. In other words, from the middle of the eighteenth century onwards this policy reserved for the nobility all appointments to the officer corps and gave them priority over administrative posts.[18]

At a local level, the Junker developed a double role as both military commander and holder of local power on his estate. This resulted in the development of a unique collective mentality among the Junkers, characterized by a special familiarity with power at all levels of social, military and political life. It also meant a militarization of civil rule. The Junkers had undoubtedly been strengthened by their struggle with absolutism. In the last decades of the eighteenth century and throughout the nineteenth, their magic bastions of power and influence were the landed estate, the officer corps and the state bureaucracy.[19]

By 1800, according to contemporary estimates, the number of families belonging to the nobility was around 54,000.[20] Of these, around 20,000 were to be found in the old Prussian provinces. The nobility constituted approximately 1 per cent of the total population, but in some provinces the proportion was considerably lower. At the end of the eighteenth century the nobility contained many distinct subdivisions. The 'magnates', especially those from Silesia but also to a certain extent those from East Prussia, stood out from the rest of the nobility in terms of both the level of their wealth and their political and social independence. Numerically, however, they were of little consequence. Approximately one quarter of the nobility could be considered prosperous, while about one half were moderately so and a further quarter were less well off.[21] What cannot be quantified are the numbers of lesser and lower nobility who had fallen on hard times and who were distinguished from the common rural population only by their class-consciousness.

Until the October Edict of 1807 the nobility, according to common law, was set apart from other classes within Prussian society. The nobles were nevertheless an 'open class' in so far as they were willing and able to assimilate émigrés, the newly ennobled and eventually, in the wake of the agrarian reforms of 1807, also middle-class estate owners.[22] In this respect the Prussian nobility can be distinguished from the much more exclusive nobility of, for example, Westphalia,[23] and was not very different from the English gentry. However, both the existence of a personal *Standschaft*, which characterized them corporatively and which outlasted the reforms, and the more rigid segregation from other social classes marked a fundamental difference between the nobility of Prussia and that of England.

Although relatively few in number, the eighteenth-century Prussian nobility exercised enormous control over the land. Of all the land put to agricultural use, 4.5 per cent was part of the royal domains and approximately another 4.5 per cent was owned by cities and foundations. A further 11 per cent was directly owned and managed by the nobility. The remaining 80 per cent was worked by peasant farmers on the basis of a wide variety of property and legal rights. The nobility and landlords possessed various rights over this 80 per cent, most often including ultimate ownership rights which resulted in service and tax obligations on the part of the peasant farmers. These obligations were removed in the course of the agrarian reforms (this occurring on the domains in the last third of the eighteenth century and on the private estates in the first half of the nineteenth). Besides the royal domains, which were heavily concentrated in East Prussia, there existed, especially in Silesia, extensive manorial estates and rural freeholdings.[24]

At the end of the eighteenth century the system of *Gutsherrschaft* and *Gutswirtschaft* was in serious difficulties, due chiefly to the growing indebtedness of Junker estates stemming from enormous speculations in previous years.[25] It was also at this time that the failure of the absolutist policies to conserve the estates became obvious. Another factor contributing to the Junkers' precarious position was the numerical expansion of the nobility, caused by the immigration of Polish and French nobles, by generous policies of ennoblement, especially during the reign of Frederick II, and finally by the natural expansion of well-established families.

The agricultural upturn which occurred during the last third of the eighteenth century was substantially achieved on the basis of the established social structure. This fact made it difficult at the beginning of the nineteenth century for agrarian capitalism to make a breakthrough. Massive, economically based protests were mobilized against the agrarian reforms. The agricultural expansion had ambiguous consequences for the constitutional rights of workers. On the one hand, 'rational landlords' endeavoured to free their peasants from subservience and to run their estates more profitably with emancipated wage-earning labourers. More sweeping, however, was the attempt on the part of estate owners to make more use of compulsory services and exploit them more effectively. Even though compulsory socage carried out reluctantly by the peasants was less effective and less profitable than free wage labour, it was still cheaper for the estate owner who was entitled to make such demands than the expensive conversion to a wage economy.

Around 1800, approximately one tenth of all nobles' estates were in middle-class hands. After 1807, the abolition of the nobility's monopoly over estate ownership, coupled with the collapse of the market for landed estates (which had been inflated by speculation), resulted in a surge of new middle-class ownership of estates once reserved for the nobility. An indication of the extent of the incursion of middle-class capital into estate ownership even before 1807 is that private mortgages accounted for a 307-million-thaler share, while the value of bonds from the nobles' credit institutions, the *Landschaften*, which were publicly circulating in 1805 amounted to only a 53-million-thaler share.[26] After 1807 approximately one third to one half of all aristocratic estate owners were bought out by the middle class.

Noble rule and inequality between the estates were generally under pressure in the age of the French Revolution. The Prussian reforms, conceived of as a modernizing force to prevent something worse, had considerable effect on the Junkers and on agrarian society in general. Far from eradicating the Junkers, however, as some of them feared would happen, the reforms made possible efficient measures for the improvement of Junker estates. But what the reformers *did* do was allow bourgeois landowners access to the formerly closed estate of the Junkers.

The timing of the agrarian reforms was in many ways inconvenient for the estate owners, for they occurred at a time when a radical secular change in the agrarian economy was beginning to take shape and when profits and the value of contracts slumped. This coincided with the collapse of the market for landed estates, which had become inflated by speculation. The resistance of estate owners to the reforms was intense and extremely successful.[27]

In any case the transformation of the nobility from an estate into a property-owning ruling class no longer defined exclusively by noble birth, the legal emancipation of labourers and the transformation of peasant land into private property were all undertaken in such a way as to make the hardships of transition easier for the landowners. The Junkers were able to boycott reforms of the state's political constitution almost entirely.[28]

The agrarian reforms after 1807, owing to the extent and type of the compensations paid by the peasants, promoted the accumulation of capital and private landownership in the hands of capitalist agrarian entrepreneurs. The delays to and the implementation of liberal economic reforms, along with a conservative political power structure, meant that the reforms led to a multitude of opportunities for feudal and capitalistic exploitation by the estate owners. The legal means for the proletarianization of a large proportion of the rural population was also made possible. The agrarian reforms provided a *de facto* and *de jure* framework for the comprehensive breakthrough of capitalism into the agrarian economy.[29]

From an economically privileged and legally secure class, the Junkers evolved in the nineteenth century into a distinct economic class which continued to enjoy preferential economic status. Resistance to those reforms which, after 1807, dismantled the legal basis of the class structure were of no avail. However, resistance *did* achieve notable success, first in securing concessions for the landowners as regards the preservation of their estates and the partial maintenance of compulsory peasant labour, and secondly in preserving the status of the estate owners as a distinct economic class. The assimilation of middle-class estate owners, who had been entering the estate-owning class in large numbers, succeeded to all extents and purposes in the course of the 1820s and 1830s. In this way, the Junker nobility was able completely to impose its value system onto the emerging estate-owning class. During the 1820s, when the Junkers faced a deep economic crisis which only the most viable estates survived, the whole process of forging a new, transformed agrarian class took place.

During the reform period the compromise between landed elite and monarchy was revitalized – at the expense of the peasants and agrarian workers. These were, indeed, the conditions of bureaucratic rule: the bureaucracy needed an ally in order to make a breakthrough and secure its own power, but the bourgeoisie was not available to serve as such an ally at the beginning of the nineteenth century. The bureaucracy's claims to power meant essentially the continuation, modernization and rationalization of monarchical absolutism.[30] Potential bourgeois demands, for the parliamentarization of political rule, for example, or for the state to give up its regulation of political and social processes, could hardly have supported the bureaucracy in an effective way. This situation, along with the prevailing power relations and the fact that Prussia's high officials came mainly from the landed nobility, necessarily put the bureaucracy into contact with the Junkers, placing both groups in the same camp. The Bonapartist alternative of a coalition with the urban and rural lower classes against the Junkers and the monarchy was not a realistic option at this historical moment.

The bureaucratic climbdown in the area of local power reform (the *Gendarmerie-Edikt*) was the price to be paid for carrying out the reforms to the economic and social structure (the *Oktober-Edikt* and the *Regulierungsedikte*). Local power rights survived not only the reform period but also, to a certain extent, the revolutionary period.

It was in the 1850s and 1860s that the Junkers reached the peak of their economic power. On the supply side, factors contributing to this economic power were extremely low wage levels and an abundance of agricultural labourers, both resulting from population expansion and pauperism. On the demand side, the repeal of the Corn Laws in Britain in 1846 and the development of an internal market played a determining role. The economic significance of the East Elbian Junkers would never be greater.[31] Through its exports, the agrarian sector contributed substantially to general economic growth and also indirectly to industrialization. Junker ties to international trading networks transmitted British demand onto the German market.[32]

There could hardly have been a worse time to try to take away the Junkers' power than the revolution of 1848. Given the great economic importance of East Elbian agriculture, which lasted into the 1870s, a coalition against the Junker elite was of necessity unstable and fragile. It is easier for a class to maintain its social and political dominance when it has legitimized itself through economic success. For the Junkers this was the case in the 1850s, in contrast to their position of defensive reaction during the reform era; or, as Eckart Kehr remarked, 'Conservatism remained active because it was part of a large, modern, agrarian class, not because it was feudal.'[33]

When in the 1870s the terms of trade turned against the East Elbian Junkers, and even more so during the severe crisis of the 1890s, they relied upon that compromise with the central political authority which had always served to consolidate their power and economic success. From the middle of the 1870s onwards, the Junkers demanded and obtained protective tariffs. Protectionism was costly both for the state and for society and was carried to such an extreme that by 1931 German grain prices were 300 per cent over the world market level. For consumers and taxpayers, and in particular for the mass of workers but also for small agrarian producers dependent on cheap imported fodders, the economic and social consequences of these protectionist policies were only too obvious.[34]

In all industrializing countries, agriculture has always been the long-term loser during economic development, with agricultural growth rates, profitability, productivity, profit margins and volume lagging behind their industrial equivalents and the percentage of agricultural workers in the labour force declining. The East Elbian Junkers were confronted with precisely these structural problems in the years of acute agricultural crisis.[35]

The Prussian Junkers had not to any great extent developed the ability either to compromise with other groups in society or to identify personal interests with those of the nation as a whole. Over the centuries they had become accustomed to reducing their resistance on the condition that they be given privileges at the expense of other social classes. Because their interests were always particular rather than national, they were never able to reach a consensus with society as a whole. In accepting compromises over their rights to rule, the Junkers were offered, by way of appeasement, privileges in exchange for compliance. As a result, even in the nineteenth and twentieth centuries, they were accustomed to seeking aid from the state whenever a crisis arose. As a rule they always got what they wanted. Political compromise with other classes in society was not part of the repertory of Junker rule. In the decades in which attempts at liberalization in Germany might have had some chance of success, the Junkers were economically too powerful and, as their economic fortunes began to wane, Prussian conservatism had already given shape to the German Empire.

NOTES

1 Parts of this chapter are taken from H. Schissler, 'The Junkers: notes on the social and historical significance of the agrarian elite in Prussia', in R. G. Moeller (ed.), *Peasants and Lords in Modern Germany: Recent Studies in Agricultural History* (Boston, Mass.: 1986), pp. 24–51.

2 ibid., pp. 36 ff. See also F. L. Carsten, *Geschichte der preussischen Junker* (Frankfurt am Main: 1988).

3 Most clearly in the case of Hans Rosenberg, 'Die Pseudodemokratisierung der Rittergutsbesitzerklasse', in H. Rosenberg (ed.), *Machteliten und Wirtschaftskonjunkturen: Studien zur neueren deutschen Sozial- und Wirtschaftsgeschichte* (Göttingen: 1979), pp. 83–101.

4 H.-J. Puhle, *Agrarische Interessenpolitik und preussischer Konservatismus im wilhelminischen Reich, 1893–1914*, 2nd edn (Bonn: 1975).

5 K. Rohe, 'Zur Typologie politischer Kulturen in westlichen Demokratien. Überlegungen am Beispiel Grossbritanniens und Deutschlands', in H. Dollinger *et al.* (eds), *Weltpolitik, Europagedanke, Regionalismus: Festschrift für H. Gollwitzer* (Münster: 1982), pp. 581–96; K. H. S. Dyson, 'Die Ideen des Staates und der Demokratie. Ein Vergleich "staatlich verfasster" und "nichtstaatlich verfasster" Gesellschaften', *Der Staat*, 19 (1980), pp. 485–515.

6 D. Blackbourn and G. Eley, *Mythen deutscher Geschichtsschreibung. Die gescheiterte bürgerliche Revolution von 1848* (Frankfurt: 1980), translated and expanded as *The Peculiarities of German History* (Oxford: 1984). The publication of this book set off a rather tumultuous debate in West Germany over the German '*Sonderweg*': see, for example, H.-U. Wehler, ' "Deutscher Sonderweg" oder allgemeine Probleme des westlichen Kapitalismus?'

and H. A. Winkler, 'Der deutsche Sonderweg: eine Nachlese', both in *Merkur*, 35 (1981); D. Langewiesche, 'Entmythologisierung des "deutschen Sonderweges" oder auf dem Wege zu neuen Mythen?', *Archiv für Sozialgeschichte*, 21 (1981), pp. 527–32; *Kolloquien des Instituts für Zeitgeschichte: Deutscher Sonderweg – Mythos oder Realität?* (Munich: 1982); J. Kocka, 'Der "deutsche Sonderweg" in der Diskussion', *German Studies Review*, 5 (1982), pp. 363–79; B. Faulenbach, ' "Deutscher Sonderweg". Zur Geschichte und Problematik einer zentralen Kategorie des deutschen geschichtlichen Bewusstseins', *Aus Politik und Zeitgeschichte*, 15 August 1981, pp. 3–21.

7 R. Dahrendorf, *Gesellschaft und Freiheit* (Munich: 1961).

8 Winkler, 'Der deutsche Sonderweg', p. 796.

9 A. J. Mayer, *The Persistence of the Old Regime: Europe to the Great War* (London: 1981); J. A. Schumpeter, *Capitalism, Socialism and Democracy*, 5th edn (London: 1976).

10 H. Rosenberg, 'Die Ausprägung der Junkerherrschaft in Brandenburg-Preussen, 1410–1618', in Rosenberg, *Machteliten und Wirtschaftskonjunkturen*, pp. 24–82; H. Schissler, *Preussische Agrargesellschaft im Wandel. Wirtschaftliche, gesellschaftliche und politische Transformationsprozesse von 1763–1847* (Göttingen: 1978), pp. 59 ff.; W. Abel, *Agrarkrise und Agrarkonjunktur. Eine Geschichte der Land- und Ernährungswirtschaft Mitteleuropas seit dem hohen Mittelalter*, 2nd edn (Hamburg: 1966), pp. 103 ff.

11 Rosenberg, 'Die Pseudodemokratisierung der Rittergutsbesitzerklasse'; R. M. Berdahl, 'Preussischer Adel: Paternalismus als Herrschaftssystem', in H.-J. Puhle and H.-U. Wehler (eds), *Preussen im Rückblick* (Göttingen: 1980), pp. 123–45; Schissler, *Preussische Agrargesellschaft*, pp. 66 ff.

12 R. Koselleck, *Preussen zwischen Reform und Revolution. Allgemeines Landrecht, Verwaltung und soziale Bewegung von 1791 bis 1848*, 2nd edn (Stuttgart: 1975), pp. 487 ff.; Schissler, *Preussische Agrargesellschaft*, pp. 105–44; H. Harnisch, *Kapitalistische Agrarreform und industrielle Revolution* (Weimar: 1984); C. Dipper, *Die Bauernbefreiung in Deutschland 1790–1850* (Stuttgart: 1980).

13 Most convincingly described by Rosenberg, 'Die Ausprägung der Junkerherrschaft'.

14 F. L. Carsten, *The Origins of Prussia* (Oxford: 1954); Rosenberg, 'Die Ausprägung der Junkerherrschaft'.

15 See three essays by O. Hintze in his *Regierung und Verwaltung. Gesammelte Abhandlungen*, Vol. III (Göttingen: 1967): 'Geist und Epochen der Preussischen Geschichte' (p. 3); 'Die Epochen des evangelischen Kirchenregiments' (pp. 56 ff.); and 'Kalvinismus und Staatsräson in Brandenburg zu Beginn des 17. Jahrhunderts' (pp. 259, 264).

16 Carsten, *Origins of Prussia*; Rosenberg, 'Die Ausprägung der Junkerherrschaft'.

17 O. Büsch, *Militärsystem und Sozialleben im alten Preussen, 1713–1807* (Berlin: 1962); Hintze, 'Geist und Epochen'; and O. Hintze, 'Die Hohenzollern und der Adel', also in Hintze, *Regierung und Verwaltung*, pp. 30–55.

18 H. Rosenberg, *Bureaucracy, Aristocracy and Autocracy. The Prussian Experience, 1660–1815* (Cambridge, Mass.: 1958).

19 ibid., Busch, *Militärsystem.*

20 According to L. Krug, *Abriss der neuesten Statistik des preussischen Staates*, 2nd edn (Halle: 1805); also G. Hassel, *Statistischer Umriss der sämtlichen europäischen Staaten im Hinsicht ihrer Grösse, Bevölkerung, Kulturverhältnisse, Handlungen, Finanz- und Militärverfassung, und ihrer aussereuropäischen Besitzungen* (Braunschweig: 1805). This calculation includes, however, the exceptionally numerous Polish nobility of the newly acquired provinces of Neuostpreussen and Südpreussen, with about 29,000 and 5,000 noble families respectively. On the situation of the East Elbian nobility around 1800, see F. Martiny, *Die Adelsfrage in Preussen vor 1806 als politisches und soziales Problem* (Stuttgart: 1938).

21 G. Cybulka, *Die Lage der ländlichen Klassen Ostdeutschlands im 18. Jahrhundert* (Braunschweig: 1949); Schissler, *Preussische Agrargesellschaft*, pp. 78 ff.; Koselleck, *Preussen zwischen Reform und Revolution*, pp. 78 ff.

22 Koselleck, *Preussen zwischen Reform und Revolution*, pp. 507 ff.; Schissler, *Preussische Agrargesellschaft*, pp. 164 ff.

23 H. Reif, *Westfälischer Adel 1770–1860. Vom Herrschaftsstand zur regionalen Elite* (Göttingen: 1979).

24 Schissler, *Preussische Agrargesellschaft*, pp. 72 ff.

25 M. Weyermann, *Zur Geschichte des Immobiliarkreditwesens in Preussen* (Karlsruhe: 1910).

26 Schissler, *Preussische Agrargesellschaft*, p. 84.
27 U. Wiese, 'Zur Opposition des ostelbischen Grundadels gegen die agraren Reformmassnahmen, 1807–1811', dissertation, University of Heidelberg, 1935.
28 Koselleck, *Preussen zwischen Reform und Revolution*, pp. 448 ff.
29 Schissler, *Preussische Agrargesellschaft*, pp. 145 ff., 164 ff.
30 Rosenberg, *Bureaucracy, Aristocracy and Autocracy*.
31 G. Hermes, 'Statistische Studien zur wirtschaftlichen und gesellschaftlichen Struktur des zollvereinten Deutschlands', *Archiv für Sozialwissenschaft und Sozialpolitik*, 63 (1930), pp. 131 ff.
32 R. H. Dumke, 'Anglodeutscher Handel und Frühindustrialisierung in Deutschland, 1822–1865', *Geschichte und Gesellschaft*, 5 (1979), pp. 182 ff.
33 'Neuere deutsche Geschichtsschreibung', in E. Kehr, *Der Primat der Innenpolitik*, 3rd edn (Berlin: 1976), p. 258; see also Rosenberg, 'Die Pseudodemokratisierung der Rittergutbesitzerklasse', p. 84.
34 H.-J. Puhle, *Politische Agrarbewegungen in kapitalistischen Industriegesellschaften* (Göttingen: 1975), p. 50; H. Rosenberg, 'Zur sozialen Funktion der Agrarpolitik im Zweiten Reich', in Rosenberg, *Machteliten und Wirtschaftskonjunkturen*, pp. 102–17.
35 Max Weber, 'Entwicklungstendenzen in der Lage der ostelbischen Landarbeiter', in Max Weber, *Gesammelte Aufsätze zur Sozial- und Wirtschaftsgeschichte* (Tübingen: 1924), pp. 470–507; Puhle, *Politische Agrarbewegungen*, pp. 36 ff.; Hermes, 'Statistische Studien', p. 135.

5

The landed elite of Hesse-Cassel in the nineteenth century

Gregory W. Pedlow

LANDOWNERSHIP IN HESSE-CASSEL

At the end of the eighteenth century the small landed elite of Hesse-Cassel consisted almost entirely of nobles. Peasants owned approximately 90 per cent of the non-forest land, but most of these holdings were small, scattered and often burdened with manorial dues and services to the state or local landlords. This pattern of landownership was typical of the system of *Grundherrschaft* (landlordship) prevalent in western and southern Germany, in contrast to eastern Germany with its system of *Gutsherrschaft* (estate lordship), which was characterized by large noble estates and a peasantry heavily burdened with services to landlords and owning little land of its own.

The eighteenth-century pattern of landownership in Hesse-Cassel – large numbers of small and medium-sized peasant holdings and a small number of large estates – remained intact throughout the nineteenth century despite major agrarian reforms and attempts to rationalize landholdings, as can be seen in Table 5.1, which shows the distribution of landholdings in the Cassel Administrative District (previously the electorate of Hesse-Cassel) at the beginning of the twentieth century.[1]

Table 5.1 Landownership in 1907

Type of holding (in hectares)	*Number*	*Area (hectares) used for agriculture*	*% Share*
Parcelled holdings (under 2)	76,220	47,524	9.6%
Small peasant holdings (2–5)	25,597	83,565	16.9%
Medium peasant holdings (5–20)	22,177	216,412	43.7%
Large peasant holdings (20–100)	3,463	109,904	22.2%
Large estates (100+)	223	37,991	7.7%
Total	127,680	495,396	100.1%

Almost all large estates were in the hands of the nobility or the royal family at the end of the eighteenth century. Very few bourgeois owned landed estates even though there were no longer any restrictions upon the purchase of estates by non-nobles. Thus the rolls for the knights' tax (*Rittersteuer*) at the beginning of the nineteenth century list only five non-noble individuals owning land that was comparable in value to the estates of the nobility and there were few, if any, large landholdings that were not subject to the knights' tax at that time. Unlike Prussia and other parts of northern Germany, Hesse-Cassel had not experienced waves of speculation in landed estates during the late eighteenth century. Hessian nobles tended to cling to their estates as long as possible and if forced to sell, generally did so to other nobles, particularly to other branches of the same family.[2]

Comprehensive landholding statistics are available only for the mid-nineteenth century. By this time bourgeois ownership of large landholdings had probably increased since the late eighteenth century, but nobles still predominated among private individuals owning large estates, as can be seen in Table 5.2, which shows the owners of large landholdings in surveys taken in 1865 and 1895 (the latter survey was more comprehensive and included more landholdings).[3]

Relatively few bourgeois owned large tracts of land in the nineteenth century. In 1865 bourgeois owned only 5 estates with more than 200 hectares of land, and none of these was larger than 300 hectares. In contrast, nobles owned 59 estates larger than 200 hectares, 39 of which were larger than 300 hectares. Thirty years later the number of estates in bourgeois hands had increased considerably, but most of these holdings were relatively small, less than 200 hectares in size. The largest estates still remained in the hands of the nobility. Thus in 1895 bourgeois owned only 2 estates that were 300 hectares or more in size, while nobles owned 55. Another symbol of the nobility's continued domination of large landholdings in the late nineteenth century

Table 5.2 Ownership of large estates

Size in	*1865*		*1895*	
hectares	*Nobles*	*Non-nobles*	*Nobles*	*Non-nobles*
100–199	63	32	56	69
200–299	20	5	34	12
300–399	14	0	10	1
400–499	10	0	10	0
500–599	2	0	8	1
600–699	2	0	7	0
700–799	3	0	3	0
800–899	1	0	4	0
900–999	0	0	1	0
1,000+	7	0	12	0
Total	122	37	145	83

was the ownership of landed estates that bore the prestigious historic title *Rittergut* (knight's estate), which had previously brought with it many fiscal privileges. In 1895 nobles still owned 106 out of the 133 *Rittergüter*.[4]

Within the nobility the most important landholding group was the *Althessische Ritterschaft*, the traditional knighthood of the old Hessian provinces of Upper and Lower Hesse. Originally consisting of all nobles eligible to sit in the Hessian Estates in the sixteenth century, the *Ritterschaft* had gradually become a privileged group of families within the nobility; prospective new members had to show proof of four generations of noble ancestry, own a landed estate and be accepted by a majority vote of the existing membership. Numbering 181 adult males in the roll of nobles compiled in 1835, the Hessian *Ritterschaft* owned 40,600 hectares of land in the mid-1860s.[5]

Numerically small but individually quite wealthy, the five families of *Standesherren* (former ruling families who had lost their sovereignty during the Napoleonic era but had retained important fiscal and social privileges) owned another 12,300 hectares. Former imperial knights (18 adult males in 1835), who had also lost their rights of sovereignty during the early nineteenth century, owned another 4,400 hectares. The small knighthood (26 adult males in 1835) of the Hessian territory of Schaumburg, a small enclave in Hanover, owned 1,900 hectares, and the remaining nobles not affiliated with any corporate body of nobles (245 adult males in 1835) owned 5,900 hectares. Altogether the various groups of nobles owned approximately 7 per cent of the total land in Hesse-Cassel in the mid-nineteenth century but comprised only 0.3 per cent of the population.[6]

The nobility placed great value on its ties to the land, especially the members of the older families in the Hessian *Ritterschaft*. These families demonstrated a high degree of continuity in their landownership. Of the 101 estates owned by members of the knighthood in the 1860s, 84 were still in the hands of the knighthood in 1895 (and of the 17 that were lost, only 7 came into the hands of non-nobles). During this period knights added another 7 estates, giving them a total of 91, only 10 less than in 1863. Furthermore, the 84 estates that had remained in the possession of the same family throughout this period had increased substantially in size (an average of 22 per cent) through land purchases and the division of common lands. The continuity of the knighthood's landownership was much greater than that of non-nobles during this period. In an 1851 survey of large landholdings excluding those of the knighthood, non-nobles owned 186 estates over 50 hectares in size. The owners of 123 of these estates were listed in an 1895 survey, and only 49 of these estates were still owned by the same family as in 1851.[7]

The strength of the knighthood's bonds to its estates was not just a nineteenth-century phenomenon. Most of the estates owned by knights had been in the possession of the same family for hundreds of years. Thus only 21 of the 101 estates held by knights in 1863 had been owned by different families a century earlier.[8]

Despite the turmoil of the early twentieth century in Germany, the knighthood's landholdings remained quite steady. In 1929 knights owned 87 estates, only 4 fewer than in 1895. However, there had been more turnover in estates because of the extinction of several noble lines. Thus between 1895 and 1929 knights lost 12 estates but gained 8.[9]

Why had the Hessian knighthood been so successful in preserving its landholdings in the eighteenth and nineteenth centuries? One very important reason was the influence of the state. In the late eighteenth century, when landowners in much of northern and central Germany were experiencing severe financial problems from indebtedness and falling grain prices, the Hessian government – flush with funds from British subsidy payments for the use of Hessian troops during the American Revolution – made large amounts of capital available at low interest, enabling landowners to consolidate their debts and reduce the burden of interest payments. Whereas in Prussia nobles were able to use new sources of credit to speculate in estates because fiefs had become allodial, the Hessian government clung to the feudal system as long as possible, which hindered speculation in estates because most were fiefs and could not be sold or even mortgaged without royal consent. Nobles' fiefs did not become allodial until 1848.[10]

Even if there had been no feudal ties, however, it is unlikely that many nobles would have voluntarily alienated their landholdings. Most families had owned their estates for centuries and many nobles bore the same names as their estates. The long-lasting ties between noble families and their estates were made possible by the unrestricted marriage system of the Hessian nobility, which did not practise primogeniture and therefore made no distinctions between eldest and younger sons. All were free to marry, and approximately seven out of every ten noblemen did so. Without primogeniture and its attendant limitations on marriage by younger sons, families did not become extinct as quickly as in other parts of Europe. Even though individual branches died out, the family as a whole lived on and maintained strong bonds with its estates. In Prussia, by way of comparison, estates changed families through inheritance more frequently. Many new owners did not feel close ties to their recently inherited estates and were therefore willing to sell them. So by the late nineteenth century, very few Prussian estates had been in the same family for at least a century, whereas continuous ownership of an estate for three or four centuries was quite common among Hessian noble families.[11]

One additional reason for the strong degree of continuity in the landownership of the Hessian nobility was the use of *Fideikommisse* (entails). Once the feudal system ended in 1848, making fiefs allodial, nobles began to entail their estates to keep them in the family. This practice was not generally followed by bourgeois landowners. At the end of the nineteenth century there were 71 *Fideikommisse* in the territory formerly belonging to the electorate of

Hesse-Cassel: 42 were owned by members of the *Ritterschaft*, 11 by *Standesherren* or members of the former ruling family, 13 by other nobles, and only 5 by bourgeois. In many cases a *Fideikommiss* included more than one estate, so most noble estates were entailed by the end of the nineteenth century.[12]

Unlike entails in other parts of Europe, Hessian *Fideikommisse* did not include primogeniture. Under the Hessian system of equal inheritance, families had originally divided landholdings equally among the sons, but once there were more sons than estates, they practised a system of joint ownership of estates. The estates were generally farmed by a leaseholder, and the joint owners shared in the annual profits. Shares of an estate were passed on to the next generation and thus sometimes became smaller each generation as they were divided among several sons, but at other times the shares increased as individuals died without male heirs and their shares were inherited by other members of the family.[13]

SOURCES OF POWER FOR THE LANDED ELITE

At the end of the eighteenth century, the landed nobility was in a very strong position in Hesse-Cassel. One of its most important sources of power was the traditional manorial or 'feudal' system of peasant dues and services. In the eighteenth century most peasants did not own their land completely. Although they worked the land without interference and could sell it or pass it on to their heirs, they still owed certain obligations to the original owners of the land in return for the hereditary right of use. Therefore landlords had the right to collect a wide range of dues and services from peasants. Such payments had originally been established centuries earlier and were recorded in land records, so landlords could not arbitrarily increase the burden on peasants. On the other hand, because dues and services were officially recorded as obligations resting on particular pieces of land, they had a strong legal basis and could be enforced in courts of law, when necessary.[14]

Very few of these obligations resulted from serfdom. Some individuals were still nominally serfs in Hesse-Cassel, but their 'servitude' consisted solely of a small annual fee and an additional payment by the heirs after a serf's death. Much more important to landlords were the annual quitrents paid by peasants for the hereditary use of their land. Quitrents were paid in both cash and produce. The size of these payments had been fixed generations or even centuries earlier and could not be changed by landlords, so inflation had substantially eroded the value of the cash portion. In contrast, the produce portion of quitrents remained a valuable part of the landlord's annual income. Other forms of annual hereditary rents existed in bewildering variety, but most were quite small and therefore neither particularly burdensome to peasants nor particularly important for landlords. In many villages, however, landlords were also entitled to collect a portion of the harvest (up to one tenth) and these tithes represented both a burden to peasants and an important source of income for landlords.

One of the most important aspects of the manorial system as a source of power for landlords was labour services. In terms of economic benefits, labour services were not tremendously significant for landlords, because peasants performing services generally worked only halfheartedly at best. In addition, landlords often had to provide substantial amounts of food and drink to the peasants performing services, and in some cases this was worth as much as, if not more than, the value of the labour being supplied. Psychologically, however, services were extremely important as a source of power for noble landlords. When a peasant had to work in the landlord's field on specified days sowing seed or bringing in the landlord's harvest even though he had not yet been able to do the same work on his own land, his subservient position was clearly demonstrated.[15]

In addition to the right to collect the various forms of dues and services from peasants in the surrounding villages, estate owners from the *Ritterschaft* also possessed the right of seigneurial justice in the eighteenth century, giving them direct judicial authority over local peasants in civil and sometimes also criminal cases (although generally not including the right to impose the death penalty). These landlords could therefore use their own courts to obtain judgments against peasants who fell behind in their payments.

Manorial dues also contributed to the economic strength of the nobility. At the end of the eighteenth century, income from dues and services comprised between one third and one half of estate owners' annual landed income. Peasant payments were frequently in kind rather than in cash, and although the quantities of produce delivered by each individual peasant were small, the overall totals were large enough to enable a landlord to participate actively in the grain market, even if his own estate was being farmed by a leaseholder, as was generally the case. Not all of the grain collected from peasants found its way onto the market; some of the produce was consumed by the noble family or paid out as salaries to servants and officials.[16]

In addition to the dues and services collected from the peasantry, nobles derived considerable income from their own holdings, particularly rents from the demesne portion of estates and income from forests (such as hunting fees and wood sales). Hessian estate owners were generally absentee landlords. Most nobles pursued a career in some form of government service for at least part of their lives and therefore had to be away from their estates. Relatively few nobles ran their estates themselves. Those landowners who were unable or unwilling to run an estate personally faced the choice of hiring an administrator, renting the estate as a whole to a bourgeois leaseholder, or renting it in small parcels to local peasants. The most common course of action was to lease the estate as a whole; this was the simplest option because it did not require close supervision of the estate, which was ideal for an owner who was away pursuing a career in government service. Although leasing an estate in parcels to local peasants might bring in more income, this course of action was also more dangerous because of the difficulty in collecting rents from so many individuals.[17]

During the nineteenth century, revenues from landlords' own holdings increased substantially, making them less dependent upon income from manorial dues and services. The main reasons for this increase were rising rents for estates and increased profits from forests, as wood harvests multipled owing to the application of more scientific methods of forestry. Thus even before peasant dues and services were abolished by the nineteenth-century reforms, their importance had been declining.[18]

In addition to their economic power as owners of large estates and their psychological power as the recipients of dues and services from the peasantry, members of the landed elite possessed considerable political power through their representation in the Hessian diet and their strength within the bureaucracy. In the late eighteenth century the Hessian *Landtag* had only two estates: the prelates' and knights' chamber and the towns' chamber. The prelates' and knights' chamber consisted almost entirely of members of the knighthood, either as representatives of the nobility itself or of various institutions run by nobles. The only non-noble was a representative of the University of Marburg. The diet's presiding official, the *Erbmarschall* (hereditary marshal) was also a nobleman, and nobles dominated the *Landtag*.[19] Within the bureaucracy, most of the top offices were filled by nobles, and nobles held approximately one half of the offices in the upper bureaucracy at the end of the century. One key local office, the *Landrat* (county councillor), was reserved for members of the landed nobility during this period.[20]

A further source of power for landed nobles, but one that is hard to measure because it was not contained in any legal code, was the long tradition of deference to nobles by peasants after centuries of economic, legal and political subservience. Although eroded by the influence of the French Revolution and nineteenth-century reforms, peasant deference to the landed noble elite remained an important factor throughout the nineteenth century.

There were some paternalistic aspects to the nobility's power over peasants in the late eighteenth and early nineteenth centuries. During years of bad harvests, for example, noble landlords often reduced the amounts of grain owed to them by local peasants or at least made no serious attempt to collect the grain owed them, waiting instead until the following year when the harvest was likely to be better. Landlords also frequently made special concessions to their 'subjects'. Thus the von Buttlar-Elberberg family always sold wood at special low prices to the villages that had been under its jurisdiction, even after the right of seigneurial justice was abolished by the government. Many noble families also assisted local charities or provided direct financial assistance to needy peasants. Some of the more prosperous nobles were also important sources of credit for local peasants, lending money at reasonable rates at a time when there were few other non-usurious sources of credit available.[21]

CHALLENGES TO THE NOBILITY'S POWER DURING THE NINETEENTH CENTURY

The nineteenth century witnessed the continual erosion of the traditional sources of power of the landed nobility in Hesse-Cassel. The first losses had actually come at the end of the eighteenth century. In 1797 the government abolished the office of *Landrat*, reducing the nobility's influence at the local level of government. The following year saw the abolition of a minor tithe, the *Kleezehnt*, which had been imposed upon clover planted on fallow fields to enrich the soil and tended to discourage peasants from taking this very beneficial step. During debates in the diet on the issue of the clover tithe, the knighthood's leader, hereditary marshal Ludwig Freiherr von Riedesel, had argued in favour of the immediate abolition of this tithe, stating: 'It is well known that foolish ideas are becoming commonplace among our subjects and are making them rebel against their masters. We nobles must therefore take steps to prevent this unrest and draw our subjects closer to us.'[22] Disregarding this plea, Riedesel's fellow nobles continued to demand compensation, which they did not receive when the government abolished the clover tithe in 1798. The economic loss to landlords was not very great, but as a symbol of things to come the abolition of the clover tithe was very important.

The first significant reforms came after France occupied Hesse-Cassel in 1806 and then incorporated it into the new kingdom of Westphalia, ruled by Jerome Bonaparte. The Westphalian constitution of 1808 abolished serfdom, which had existed in name only, but peasants took this reform to mean that they no longer had to perform labour services for landlords, which was a significant economic blow. Even though landlords were still legally entitled to peasant labour services, enforcement had become very difficult because landlords had lost the right of seigneurial justice, one of their most important sources of power and prestige and the only way they could achieve swift judgments against peasants who were in arrears or who refused to pay manorial dues any longer. The new constitution also provided for the abolition of the entire system of manorial dues and services but did so in a cautious manner, calling for the compensation of landlords. With no lending institution established to facilitate the process of abolition, manorial dues generally remained intact. Despite its theoretical links to the French Revolution, the Westphalian government had not undertaken radical reforms because it respected and needed the power and authority of the traditional landed elite. King Jerome attempted to give his court legitimacy by filling it with members of the old nobility, and the new regime also needed the services of nobles in the bureaucracy and officer corps. Furthermore, much of the value of the estates that had been confiscated from the Hessian royal family by the French government resulted from peasant dues and services, and the French government did not want to reduce the value of these estates, which it had given to members of the new French imperial nobility (high-ranking officers and civil servants).[23]

Following the collapse of King Jerome's government and the return of Elector William I from exile in 1814, most of the Westphalian reforms were nullified. However, the elector did retain some reforms that strengthened the central government. Thus he refused to restore the right of seigneurial justice to noble landlords and retained both a new tax on individuals and a new land tax that had replaced the older and lower knights' tax. Nobles complained about their lost rights and some nobles refused to pay their taxes in protest, but the opposition soon collapsed.[24]

In 1815 the elector convened the estates to discuss a new constitution for Hesse-Cassel in fulfilment of promises he and other German rulers had made at the Congress of Vienna. The *Landtag* of 1815–16 consisted of the traditional two estates of nobles and towns plus a new third estate, the peasantry. Nobles objected strongly to the addition of the peasants, correctly seeing this change as a diminution of their power, particularly since the estates sometimes held joint sessions where voting was by head rather than by estate. The government's constitution committee presented a draft constitution in 1816, which eliminated separate representation for the estates but still guaranteed seats for the nobility (one third of the total). Noble deputies objected strongly to these reforms and one warned, 'What caused the revolution to occur so quickly in France? Without a doubt the fact that all the notables were placed together in a single chamber!'[25] The nobles demanded that voting take place by estate rather than by head when matters concerning privileges were discussed. Noble opposition slowed the deliberations on the new constitution, and eventually the elector dismissed the estates – which had also been pressing for separation of his personal wealth from that of the state – before they had completed their discussions on a constitution.[26]

During the 1820s the political influence of the nobility declined as it became embroiled in quarrels with the new elector, William II (who ruled from 1821 to 1830 and then turned over the government to his son Frederick William, remaining 'co-ruler' in name only until his death in 1847). William II had arbitrarily curtailed several important traditional rights of the nobility and was also very unpopular because of the influence of his mistress, Emilie Ortlöpp, whom he had named the Countess Reichenbach. He also ennobled several of his mistress's favourites and declared them to be knights, despite strong objections by the existing members of the knighthood.[27]

Because of William II's many affronts to the nobility, traditional ties between the monarchy and nobility had been weakened by 1830. One angry noble wrote:

> Monarchs should recognize what a vital source of support they have in the nobility of their countries, they should bear in mind that only the nobility would be willing to support them against an uprising of the populace, and they should take to heart the tragic examples of Charles I of England and Louis XVI of France. But no, monarchs are rushing to their destruction. They trample upon the only individuals who remain loyal and support the monarchy against demagogic intrigues. The nobility is truly foolish for remaining loyal to a prince who rewards loyalty with such ingratitude.[28]

Widespread unrest broke out in the summer of 1830, after news of the revolution in Paris reached Hesse-Cassel. Much of the agitation in Hessian towns concerned the elector's highly unpopular mistress and the desire for a constitution, but there was also considerable unrest among the peasants in the mediatized territories acquired by Hesse-Cassel in 1815. These peasants greatly resented the heavy burden of their labour services to the *Standesherren*. Elsewhere in Hesse the peasants were calmer but did draw up petitions protesting the heavy burden of taxes and other obligations to the government and, to a lesser degree, manorial dues and services.

To restore order the elector quickly agreed to summon the estates for the first time since 1816, and in October 1830 the *Landtag* began to draft a constitution. The delegates elected by the nobility were not prepared to support the monarchy blindly; in fact most were moderate liberals prepared to work together with the bourgeoisie against the unpopular elector to achieve reforms. Even conservative nobles realized that the so-called 'spirit of the times' required reforms rather than unyielding defence of traditional privileges. As one noble wrote before the opening of the *Landtag*: 'It is much better for us to act honourably for the benefit of all by giving up obsolete things rather than waiting until they are taken from us by force.'[29]

By January 1831 the *Landtag* had drafted a constitution that was quite liberal for its day. The new legislature would have only one chamber rather than the upper and lower chambers common in many nineteenth-century German constitutions. There would no longer be any separate voting by estates; all delegates would sit and vote together. Under the new constitution the number of noble delegates was larger than in the past, but this gain was outweighed by large increases in the number of delegates from the towns and peasantry, making the nobility a minority in the legislature (with approximately one third of the delegates). Despite this reduction of the nobility's political power, nobles remained very influential in the 1830s because they often elected moderate delegates, generally civil servants, who cooperated well with the middle class and frequently held positions of leadership in the *Landtag*.

The constitution of 1831 took another step that undermined one of the traditional sources of the landed nobility's power when it declared that manorial dues and service could be abolished, and a few months later the newly elected legislature began to consider measures to carry out this provision of the constitution. None of the delegates from the nobility opposed reforming the manorial system. Their main concern was to protect the economic interests of landlords by obtaining the most favourable redemption terms possible. The noble delegates were unsuccessful in their efforts to give both landlords and peasants the right to request the redemption of dues and services (the new law gave this right solely to the peasants), but were able to defeat attempts to reduce the level of compensation for landlords from 20 times the annual value of the dues or services (as proposed by the original draft of the bill) to only 18 times.[30]

During the crucial debates of 1830 and 1831 the delegates from the nobility had demonstrated considerable moderation and willingness to cooperate with the bourgeoisie. This spirit of cooperation was rooted in the nobility's alienation from the monarchy during the 1820s, in the many ties of occupation or even marriage that bound nobles and bourgeois, and in their common fear of the lower classes.[31]

Although peasants were now able to eliminate their dues and services to noble landlords, most landlords remained bound to the state by the ties of the feudal system. These ties often caused financial difficulties for noble landowners, because they still needed the government's permission before they could borrow money against their estate or alienate it, and such permission was becoming increasingly difficult to obtain. Furthermore, many of the peasant redemption payments to noble landlords were being held by the state credit institution set up to facilitate the redemption process, the *Landeskreditkasse*, because the payments redeemed dues or services that were part of a fief that had originally been granted by the ruler to a particular noble family. As long as the state was still part-owner (as feudal lord) of these peasant payments, it refused to allow the *Landeskreditkasse* to distribute such funds to noble families. To clear up these problems, the nobility pleaded for an end to the entire feudal system on several occasions during the 1840s, but the government took no action. Thus on the eve of the revolution of 1848, nobles were once again alienated from the government, this time for economic reasons rather than questions of privilege and status.[32]

The widespread unrest that broke out in March 1848 in both the cities and the countryside quickly brought change to the government and the legislature. The elector found himself forced to appoint a new liberal cabinet. And in the *Landtag* a prominent liberal nobleman became the legislature's new president.

One of the first issues addressed by the new government was the complete abolition of the system of manorial dues and services, for peasants had been upset by the slow pace of reform after the first redemption law of 1832. As in the debates of 1831–2, there was no resistance to this reform from the noble deputies. In fact, many nobles welcomed the end of the feudal system because they would thereby gain complete control over their own estates, which were often held as fiefs from the state subject to numerous restrictions.

Nobles had been right not to resist reform of the manorial system, for the end of peasant dues and services actually contributed to the improvement of the landed nobility's economic condition during the nineteenth century. Because landlords received compensation in cash for the loss of dues and services, they were able to use this large influx of funds to eliminate accumulated debts burdening their estates, to purchase additional land (occasionally entire estates but generally small parcels from local peasants in order to round out and enlarge the nobles' own holdings), or to invest in government securities. Very little of the redemption funds was invested in industries such as railroads, the only exceptions being investments in nobles' own estate-related manufactories producing, for example, bricks or beet sugar.[33]

Despite the nobility's willingness to support reforms in 1848, its continued existence as a privileged political group soon came under attack from both the liberals and a new, more radical group of delegates known as the democrats, who advocated a truly representative government with deputies elected solely on the basis of population. In August 1848 debate in the *Landtag* began on a new election law, which called for an end to the nobility's separate representation. The most prominent noble in the legislature, its president Ludwig von Baumbach-Kirchheim, supported the elimination of seats for the nobility, arguing: 'There can no longer be any special representation. It is the task of the nobility and of the knighthood to become part of the people and to have the same representatives as the rest of the population.'[34] Baumbach's willingness to sacrifice the nobility's representation in the *Landtag* was not unconditional, however; he argued that because Hesse-Cassel did not have a two-chamber system of government, there must be separate representation for large landowners once representation for the nobility ended. This desire was shared by many of the liberal delegates from the bourgeoisie, who feared the radicals' call for complete democracy. Thus the election law proposed by the liberals called for separate representation for the wealthiest taxpayers in each district, who would represent both landed and commercial interests. The radicals were outraged by the thought of replacing separate representation for nobles with separate representation for the rich, and one delegate, Carl Winkelblech, declared:

> If we must have a privileged class in the legislature, then I strongly believe that the nobility should keep its seats. The nobility has already lost its privileges in society, and it is neutral in the coming struggle between the working class and the upper bourgeoisie.[35]

During the autumn of 1848 most noble delegates had opposed the liberals' proposed law, hoping to obtain greater representation for large landowners.

However, by early 1849 the possibility of achieving this aim seemed remote because of the prevailing sentiment inside Hesse-Cassel and the decisions of the Frankfurt Parliament. Fearful of the radicals' demands for complete democracy, the noble deputies supported the liberals' proposed law as the lesser of two evils, and on 2 February 1849 the measure passed, ending separate representation for the nobility. The devastating impact of the election law of 1849 upon the nobility's power was clearly demonstrated when the first legislature elected under the terms of the new law assembled in July 1849. Only one nobleman was present: the liberal civil servant Moritz von Schenck zu Schweinsberg, who had been elected by the wealthy taxpayers of his district.

The elimination of the nobility's representation in the *Landtag* should not be seen as a triumph for a new, dynamic bourgeoisie of merchants and manufacturers, which Germans term the *Besitzbürgertum* (economic bourgeoisie). Instead it was the traditional *Bildungsbürgertum* (educated bourgeoisie) of civil servants, lawyers, professors and teachers that dominated the Hessian legislature in the mid-nineteenth century. After the first election held under the terms of the electoral law of 1849, the delegates to the *Landtag* consisted of 12 mayors, 10 lawyers, 8 educators (3 professors, 2 school principals and 3 teachers), 4 civil servants, 4 farmers, 3 estate owners, 2 pastors, 2 brewers, 1 mill owner, 1 journalist, 1 cloth manufacturer, 1 merchant and 1 doctor.[36]

The nobility's political eclipse was not permanent, for the era of reaction began in 1850 when Elector Frederick William appointed the strongly conservative Hans Daniel Ludwig Hassenpflug to head a new government to replace the liberal 'March Ministry' that had come to power in March 1848. Strong opposition to Hassenpflug's decrees from the legislature, the bureaucracy and even the officer corps led to a major constitutional crisis in Hesse-Cassel, which was settled by the intervention of troops from the German Confederation to restore order at the request of the Hessian government. Many liberal officials, including some nobles, were forced from office. In 1852 Hassenpflug proclaimed a new constitition without consulting the *Landtag*. The new constitution established a bicameral legislature, which restored the nobility's political power. In fact, now that nobles controlled one of the two chambers of the legislature, they had even more political power than in the past.[37]

The outlook of most noble delegates was now quite different from that in the 1830s and 1840s. The constitutional struggles of 1850 had marked a turning-point in the political activities of the nobility. Up to that year the leading noble politicians had been liberals, but the defeat of liberalism in 1850 encouraged conservative nobles to become more actively politically, while disheartening the liberals. One of the most prominent liberal nobles, Ludwig von Baumbach-Kirchheim, had already given up the struggle and emigrated to the United States. Furthermore, the government forbade civil servants –

generally the most liberal members of the nobility – from sitting in the legislature without the government's permission; this measure aided conservatives in dominating the elections for representatives from the nobility. The rising tide of conservatism among nobles was also marked by the establishment of a conservative pressure group known as the Loyalty League (Treubund, which was short for the Bund der Treue mit Gott für Fürst und Vaterland) in November 1850, with nobles in the key leadership positions.[38]

Contrary to Hassenpflug's expectations, the conservative noble deputies in the upper house did not prove to be unquestioning supporters of the government. When he presented the constitution to the new legislature for ratification, the upper house was far more critical than the lower house and made numerous suggestions for changes that would give more power to the legislature. Even though the noble delegates in the upper house were far from liberals, they valued their newly regained political power and did not want the legislature to be nothing more than a rubber stamp for the government.[39]

Beginning in 1852 the upper and lower houses worked to revise the government's constitution, trying to make it acceptable to both chambers and to the government. By the summer of 1857 the two houses had reached agreement, but the government resisted some of the changes and debate on the constitution continued. Meanwhile the delegates in the lower house were growing restless, in great part because of the efforts of exiled liberal leader Friedrich Oetker to convince the delegates that the only acceptable constitution for Hesse-Cassel was that of 1831 together with the reforms of 1849. By 1859 Oetker had succeeded; the lower house voted to rescind its earlier approval of the revised version of the constitution of 1852 and soon afterward the lower house appealed to the diet of the German Confederation to force the restoration of the constitution of 1831.

Stunned by the lower house's sudden change of course, the delegates of the upper house soon found themselves becoming mere spectators as a new constitutional crisis developed in Hesse-Cassel and quickly became caught up in national politics. The revised version of the constitution of 1852 took effect on 30 May 1860, but after new elections the legislature found itself hamstrung by the lower house's announcement that it was not a 'legitimate assembly' and therefore could not work on the legislature's business. Following the dissolution of the legislature and new elections in 1861, the protests continued. Now Prussia began championing the cause of the Hessian liberals, and by the spring of 1862 the Federal Diet forced the elector to restore the constitution of 1831 along with the electoral reforms of 1849. Once again the nobility was without representation.[40]

When the new legislature opened in October 1862, only two nobles were present. Both were liberals who had been elected to represent the wealthy taxpayers of their districts. The new legislature immediately began to work on an amendment to the election law, because when the government restored the constitution of 1831 and the election law of 1849, it insisted that the decisions of the Federal Diet concerning the political rights of the *Standesherren* and imperial knights be respected. The government's actual proposal went even further and called for the restoration of representation for all nobles who had been guaranteed seats by the constitution of 1831. After much heated discussion on this issue, the legislature finally approved a new law restoring limited representation to the various groups of nobles, although far less than set forth in the constitution of 1831. Beginning in 1863 the nobility would be guaranteed 8 delegates out of the total of 56.[41]

In the final three years of Hesse-Cassel's independent existence, the nobility – now a tiny minority with little influence – played a very small role in Hessian politics. The spirit of cooperation between noble and bourgeois delegates in the 1830s had long since vanished, as both groups had become polarized during the constitutional crises, with the bourgeoisie moving to the left and forming two parties, the liberals and the democrats, while the nobility moved to the right (with the exception of a few nobles who sided with the liberals; these nobles had been elected by wealthy taxpayers, not by their fellow nobles). These three main groups of delegates did not see eye to eye on the most important issue of the 1860s – national unification. The bourgeois liberals called for German unification under Prussian leadership, the democrats distrusted Prussia and continued to call for greater social and political reforms, and the nobles remained Hessian patriots. In 1862 a number of nobles banded together to form the Hessenverein, a conservative pressure group that opposed German unification.[42]

When Hesse-Cassel was finally forced to choose sides in the conflict between Austria and Prussia in the summer of 1866, the liberal majority in the legislature called for the elector to stop mobilizing in support of Austria and return to a position of neutrality. Both the nobles and the democrats opposed this motion. In replying to the liberals on 15 June 1866, the leading noble spokesman, Otto von Trott zu Solz, noted that:

> It has been jokingly suggested that the far right and the far left are united here; I have always found this far left to be honourable, one always knows where one stands with them, and in this case I see Herr Trabert [leader of the democrats] as a true Hessian and a true German and believe that under no circumstances does he want to be made into a Prussian, a feeling that I naturally share with him.

Trott criticized Prussia's alliance with Italy against a fellow German power and closed with a strong attack on Bismarck's policies and a prophetic warning to the liberals:

> Frederick the Great has often been called the gravedigger of German unity, but I find that Bismarck is its real gravedigger. You think that the Prussian government may change, that a different one may come to power, but the

whole policy of Prussia is that of Emperor Napoleon, it is that which leads to caesarism. If Prussia succeeds in accomplishing what it has set out to do, do not be so naive as to think this is being done for the benefit of liberalism. You will soon see what kind of politics you will have under Bismarck's regime.[43]

The combination of radicals and conservatives was not strong enough to block the liberals' motion, which passed 35–14. All of the delegates representing the nobility voted against the motion; only the two liberal nobles elected by other groups supported it. The motion had no impact on the elector's actions, however, and he continued to support Austria. One day later Prussian troops began to occupy Hesse-Cassel and the elector was soon a prisoner on his way to Prussia.

Austria's defeat at Königgrätz on 3 July sealed Hesse-Cassel's fate, and on 8 October 1866 Prussia annexed Electoral Hesse. Although the Prussian takeover was initially a major shock to Hessian nobles, they gradually adjusted, particularly after the outbreak of war against France in 1870 inspired a tremendous outburst of German nationalism. The adjustment to Prussian rule was made easier by the pro-noble policies followed by the Prussian government. Noble landowners benefited from Prussian legislation that was often more favourable to large landowners than Hessian laws had been. Thus after 1866 landowners were able to eliminate traditional peasant rights in nobles' forests, which had previously hindered the application of more modern methods of forestry. The rationalization of agriculture was greatly aided by laws that divided common lands and made both peasant and noble landholdings more efficient through the exchange of parcels of land to end the previous quilt-like patterns.[44]

The advent of Prussian rule also gave nobles a greater voice in local government, with guaranteed seats in the provincial assembly. In addition, nobles gained much greater influence on the local administrative organs. The Prussian preference for landed nobles in the office of *Landrat* resulted in a large increase in the number of Hessian nobles holding this influential office. In 1865 only 6 of the 21 Hessian *Landräte* were nobles, but by 1900 16 of the 22 *Landräte* in the Cassel Administrative District came from the nobility.

The gain in positions as *Landräte* was not matched in other portions of the bureaucracy. The nobility's importance in the Hessian bureaucracy had already declined during the first half of the nineteenth century as bourgeois came to fill an ever greater percentage of the positions, including many of the top offices that had previously been held by nobles, and the Prussian takeover of 1866 reduced the nobility's representation in the bureaucracy even further, at least initially. The greatest blow to noble civil servants in 1866 was the elimination of the Hessian diplomatic corps, which had been a very popular career choice for nobles. Furthermore, the highest ranking positions in the bureaucracy, where the nobility's representation had been strongest, had either been eliminated (in the case of ministers) or filled by officials brought in from Prussia to ensure the bureaucracy's loyalty to its new master. As time passed, however, Hessian nobles again began to advance to leading positions in the provincial bureaucracy and one noble, August von Trott zu Solz, even became a Prussian minister in 1909.[45]

In politics the nobility never regained the position it had held at the beginning of the nineteenth century, but the advent of Prussian rule brought greater involvement of large landowners at the local and provincial assemblies. Large landowners also began to play an important role in the agrarian movements that swept Germany in the late nineteenth century, which put them at the head of large numbers of peasant members.[46]

By the late nineteenth century the Hessian landed elite – still composed primarily of nobles – had been surprisingly successful in remaining a powerful local elite. Although nobles were no longer in the dominant position they had held at the end of the previous century, they had weathered a series of reform movements and considerable economic change. Much of their success was due to their flexibility; during times of unrest they did not attempt to cling futilely to their inherited privileges but accepted reforms while working to achieve the most favourable terms possible. When their political power gradually declined, they sought to form new alliances with other classes, including, at times, the lower classes. Although cooperation between nobles and the lower classes remained limited in the legislature, noble landowners eventually recognized their common interests with the peasantry and soon played a leading role in the growing agrarian movements of the late nineteenth century. Just as important as the nobility's political flexibility was its economic conservatism. Hessian nobles remained strongly attached to their estates and did not enter into the speculation in land that swept portions of northern and eastern Germany at times. This combination of flexibility and conservatism enabled the Hessian nobility to retain considerable influence as a local landed elite.

NOTES

1 'Verbreitung der landwirtschaftlichen Gross-, Mittel- und Kleinbetriebe Preussens über das Staatsgebiet: Nach dem Ergebnis der landwirtschaftlichen Betriebsstatistick von 1807', *Zeitschrift des königlich preussischen Landesamts*, 52 (1912), pp. 95, 104–9.

2 Staatsarchiv Marburg (hereafter cited as StAM), Rechnungen II, Kassel 199 and Treysa 15, 1808 Rittersteuer accounts. For speculation in landed estates during the late eighteenth century in northern and eastern Germany see Wilhelm Abel, *Agrarkrisen und Agrarkonjunktur. Eine Geschichte der Land- und Ernährungswirtschaft Deutschlands seit dem hohen Mittelalter*, 2nd edn (Hamburg: 1966), pp. 202–8; Hanna Schissler, *Preussische Agrargesellschaft im Wandel. Wirtschaftliche, gesellschaftliche und politische Transformationsprozesse von 1763–1847* (Göttingen: 1978), pp. 82–3; Johannes Ziekursch, *Hundert Jahre Schlesischer Agrargeschichte: Vom Hubertusberger Frieden bis zum Abschluss der Bauernbefreiung*, 2nd edn (Breslau: 1927), p. 58; U. J. Seetzen, 'Über dem Handel mit Langüter', *Annalen der niedersächsischen Landwirtschaft*, 3 (1801), pp. 90–1.

3 StAM 30 (Statistische Kommission), Rep. II, K1. 6, Nr 5, Übersicht der grösseren Ökonomien in Kurhessen, 1865; *Handbuch des Grundbesitzes im deutschen Reiche*, Vol. 11, pt 1, *Regierungsbezirk Kassel* (Berlin: 1895), pp. 1–109.

4 ibid.

5 The roll of nobles (*Adelsmatrikel*) from 1835 is located in StAM 300 (Hessen-Rumpenheim, Geheimes Kabinett), Abt. 11, C 32, Nr 6; landownership statistics from the nineteenth century are found in StAM 30, Rep. II, K1. 6, Nr 7, 9.

6 ibid. The population figure of 0.3 per cent is an estimate because the role of nobles includes only male nobles aged 18 and above, whereas the available overall population statistics for Hesse-Cassel group together all males over 14 (202,244 in the census of 1827). Bruno Hildebrand, *Statistische Mittheilungen über die volkswirtschaftlichen Zustände Kurhessens* (Berlin: 1853), p. 40.

7 StAM 30, Rep. II, K1. 6, Nr 12, Verzeichnis der 100 und Mehr Acker haltenden Güter und Grundbesitzungen von Privaten mit Ausschluss der Ritterschaft, 1851; *Handbuch des Grundbesitzes*, Vol. 11, pp. 1–109.

8 Eighteenth-century estate ownership has been compiled from the cadastres in StAM, Kataster I and from Heinrich Reimer, *Historisches Ortslexikon für Kurhessen* (Marburg: 1926).

9 *Niekammers landwirtschaftliche Güter-Adressbücher*, Vol. 6, no. 2, *Regierungsbezirk Kassel* (Leipzig: 1929).

10 For the loans made by the Hessian state to large landowners see Joseph Sauer, *Die Finanzgeschäfte der Landgrafen von Hessen-Kassel* (Fulda: 1930), p. 36; StAM Rechnungen II, Kassel 51, 52; StAM 12, Kriegszahlamt Rechnungen, Nr 8300–8342; StAM 300, Abt. 11, C 8, Nr 5; StAM 17c (Lehensrepositur), Generalia, Nr 229.

11 For the marriage and inheritance practices of the Hessian nobility see Gregory W. Pedlow, 'Marriage, family size, and inheritance among Hessian nobles, 1650–1900', *Journal of Family History*, 7, 4 (1982), pp. 333–52; for the low continuity of ownership of Prussian estates see Hansjoachim Henning, *Sozialgeschichtliche Entwicklungen in Deutschland von 1815 bis 1860* (Paderborn: 1977), pp. 87–91. By 1885 only 13 per cent of the estates in East Prussia had been in the hands of the same family for at least 50 years. J. Conrad, 'Agrarstatistische Untersuchungen', *Jahrbücher für Nationalökonomie und Statistik*, 3rd series, Vol. 2 (1891), p. 831.

12 Otto Stahl, *Denkschrift über Fideikommissrecht und Fideikommisswesen im Gebiet des ehemaligen Kurhessen* (Cassel: 1902), pp. 57–8.

13 Pedlow, 'Marriage, family size, and inheritance', pp. 344–9.

14 For the manorial system in Hesse-Cassel see Eihachiro Sakai, *Der kurhessische Bauer im 19. Jahrhundert und die Grundlastenablösung* (Melsungen: 1967), pp. 10–12; Hans L. Rudloff, 'Die gutsherrlich-bäuerlichen Verhältnisse in Kurhessen', *Schmollers Jahrbuch*, 41 (1917), pp. 116–24; Hans Lerch, *Hessische Agrargeschichte des 17. und 18. Jahrhunderts* (Hersfeld: 1926), pp. 12–23.

15 For examples of the kinds of services that were required of peasants and the food and drink landlords often had to supply in return see StAM Kataster I, cadastres of Aue, Betzigerode, Bischhausen, Eschwege, Harmuthsachsen, Kirchheim, Nentershausen, Schachten, Solz and Stammen.

16 For the importance of peasant dues and services to landlords see Gregory W. Pedlow, *The Survival of the Hessian Nobility, 1770–1870* (Princeton, NJ: 1988), pp. 126–7.

17 An 1865 survey of large estates shows that 27 were run by the owner, 9 run by an administrator, 134 leased as a whole, and only 8 leased in small parcels. StAM 30, Rep. II, K1. 6, Nr 5.

18 Pedlow, *Survival of the Hessian Nobility*, pp. 137–8.

19 For the influence of the nobility in the diet during the late eighteenth century see Charles W. Ingrao, *The Hessian Mercenary State: Ideas, Institutions, and Reform under Frederick II (1760–1785)* (Cambridge: 1987); Adolf Lichtner, *Landesherr und Stände in Hessen-Cassel, 1797–1821* (Göttingen: 1913).

20 *Hessen-Casselischer Staats- und Adresskalender* (Cassel: 1764–1806).

21 For examples of reductions in peasant dues see the account books of the von der Malsburg-Elmarshausen and von Buttlar-Elberberg families, Archiv der Familie von der Malsburg-Elmarshausen, Schloss Elmarshausen, and StAM, 340 v. Buttlar-Elberberg, Rechnungen.

When Geheimer Rat Wilhelm von Baumbach-Ropperhausen died in 1805, his estate included almost 10,000 thalers in debts owed him by local peasants and townsmen. The rate of interest on these loans averaged only 3.85 per cent, well below the normal rate of 5 per cent. Elmarshausen archive, list of income for Baumbach's heirs.

22 Cited in Lichtner, *Landesherr und Stände*, p. 63.

23 For the limited nature of Westphalian reforms see Helmut Berding, *Napoleonische Herrschafts- und Gesellschaftspolitik im Königreich Westfalen, 1807–1813* (Göttingen: 1973), pp. 108–11.

24 StAM 5 (Geheimer Rat), Nr 6886.

25 Hellmut Seier and Winfried Speitkamp (eds), *Akten zur Entstehung des kurhessischen Verfassungsentwurfs von 1815/16* (Marburg: 1985), p. 194.

26 Winfried Speitkamp, *Restauration als Transformation: Untersuchungen zur kurhessischen Verfassungsgeschichte 1813–1830* (Darmstadt and Mainz: 1986), pp. 287–333.

27 StAM 16 (Innenministerium), Rep. X, K1. 16, Nr 33; Archiv des ritterschaftlichen Stiftes Kaufungen, 3504 Oberkaufungen, Rep. VI, Gef. 12–14, Nr 31, 34.

28 StAM 340 v. Baumbach-Kirchheim, Nr 12.

29 StAM 340 v. Eschwege, Nr 22.

30 *Verhandlungen des kurhessischen Landtags*, 15 December 1831, pp. 1118–29, 5 April 1832, p. 1760.

31 Many nobles and bourgeois worked together in the bureaucracy and officer corps, and intermarriage increased throughout the nineteenth century. Thus 36 per cent of the noblemen born between 1800 and 1849 married bourgeois women; the percentage increased to 49 per cent of noblemen born between 1850 and 1899. Women were less likely to marry outside the nobility; for the cohorts born between 1800 and 1849 and between 1850 and 1899 the percentages of noblewomen marrying bourgeois were 30 and 36 per cent respectively. Pedlow, 'Marriage, family size, and inheritance', p. 338.

32 See the complaints made at the annual meeting of the delegates from the knighthood on 29 March 1847 and the motions made by noble deputies in the legislature on 22 October 1847. Kaufungen Archiv, Rep. VI, Gef. 2–3, Nr 7; *Landtagsverhandlungen*, 22 October 1847, p. 32.

33 Hessian nobles' three main uses of the redemption payments – reducing debts, buying land and purchasing bonds – correspond to those of the *Standesherren* of southern Germany; see Harald Winkel, *Die Ablösungskapitalien aus der Bauernbefreiung in West- und Süddeutschland: Höhe und Verwendung bei Standes- und Grundherren* (Stuttgart: 1968), pp. 150–61.

34 *Landtagsverhandlungen*, 15 August 1848, pp. 11–12.

35 ibid., 21 December 1848, p. 26.

36 Philipp Losch, *Die Abgeordneten der kurhessischen Ständeversammlungen von 1830 bis 1866* (Marburg: 1909), pp. 1–61.

37 Philipp Losch, *Geschichte des Kurfürstentums Hessen, 1803 bis 1866* (Marburg: 1922; reprint edn, Cassel: 1972), pp. 254–9; Eberhard Radbruch, 'Offiziere im Konflikt um Gehorsamkeit und Gewissen: Die Haltung des kurhessischen Offizierkorps im Verfassungskonflikt von 1850', *Geschichte in Wissenschaft und Unterricht*, 19 (1968), pp. 137–45. The new upper house contained 10 representatives from the knighthoods, approximately 8 upper nobles, representatives from each of the three major churches in Hesse-Cassel and a delegate from the university.

38 For the Treubund's membership see StAM 300, Abt. 11, C 7, Nr 13. Never a very effective pressure group, the Treubund dissolved in 1853.

39 See, for example, Otto von Trott zu Solz's speech of 13 August 1853 against any lessening of the *Landtag*'s power over the budget. *Landtagsverhandlungen*, 13 August 1853, p. 6.

40 Losch, *Geschichte des Kurfürstentums*, pp. 312–16.

41 Salomon Hahndorf, *Der kurhessische Landtag von 1862–63* (Cassel: 1863), pp. 17–20.

42 Nicholas M. Hope, *The Alternative to German Unification: The Anti-Prussian Party – Frankfurt, Nassau, and the Two Hessen, 1859–1867* (Wiesbaden: 1973), pp. 174, 182, 193, 323–5.

43 *Landtagsverhandlungen*, 15 June 1866, pp. 32–3.

44 Otto Bähr, *Der hessische Wald: Eine Darstellung der im vormaligen Kurfürstenthum Hessen am Walde bestehenden Rechtsverhältnisse* (Cassel: 1879), pp. 17–18; Kurt Scharlau, 'Landeskulturgesetzgebung und Landeskulturentwicklung im ehemaligen Kurhessen seit

dem 16. Jahrhundert', *Zeitschrift für Agrargeschichte und Agrarsoziologie*, 1 (1953), pp. 144–5.

45 *Königlich preussischer Staatsdienst-Kalender für den Regierungsbezirk Kassel* (Cassel: 1867–1914).

46 Bodo von Trott zu Solz led the spread of the Raiffeisen movement in Hesse, which established credit unions to provide low-interest loans to small farmers. He was supported by a number of other noble landowners. Other nobles were active in the Agrarian League. Karl von Baumbach, 'Bodo von Trott zu Solz', in Ingeborg Schnack (ed.), *Lebensbilder aus Kurhessen und Waldeck, 1830–1900*, 6 vols (Marburg: 1939–58), Vol. 2, pp. 375–80; Hans-Jürgen Puhle, *Agrarische Interessenpolitik und preussischer Konservatismus im wilhelminischen Reich, 1893–1914*, 2nd edn (Bonn-Bad Godesberg: 1975), p. 313.

6

Peasants and rural notables in the Bavarian Palatinate 1816–1933

Jonathan Osmond

Wine has always played a major role in the history of the Palatinate. When the French annexed the territory in 1797 and amongst other things abolished the tithe so hateful to the wine-growers, the following autumn saw great celebration:

> On 2 October [1798] the wine harvest began. There was much wine and good wine. As a good republican, the landlord of the Anchor wrote on the door of the wine press room, 'for the first time freedom from the tithe'. Never was there such a joyous vintage; everywhere one could see tricolour flags and ribbons – on the barrels, on the horses, on the whips, etc. In the evening, celebrations with fireworks.[1]

No less was the conviviality half a century later. Thus wrote Friedrich Engels on the rebellion of 1849:

> Anyone who has seen the Palatinate even once will understand that in this wine-producing and wine-loving province any movement inevitably assumes a most cheerful character. The ponderous, pedantic Old-Bavarian beer-souls had at long last been shaken off and merry Palatinate wine-bibbers appointed in their place. . . . The first revolutionary act of the people of the Palatinate was to restore the freedom of the taverns; the entire Palatinate was transformed into one enormous pot-house and the quantities of strong drink which were consumed 'in the name of the people of the Palatinate' during those six weeks were beyond all calculation.[2]

Unfortunately, wine was not always a democratic beverage. In 1935, amid great festivity, *Gauleiter* Josef Bürckel named the stretch of vineyard down the eastern side of the Haardt hills 'the German Wine Road'. The designation prevails to this day, and in 1985 celebration of the fiftieth anniversary caused great local controversy, because of the National Socialist origins of the term.[3] So wine still has strong political resonance, even if some of the crasser manifestations have departed. In 1933, for instance, the Palatine vintage received the official sobriquet of '*Gleichschalter*' to commemorate Nazism's consolidation of power.[4]

Wine is central to an understanding of the character, politics and social relations of the Palatinate. But though viticulture is its most distinctive economic contribution, this is not – nor was it in the past – solely a wine-growing region. To understand local patterns of landownership and power, one must also raise one's head from the glass.

In the century under discussion the Palatinate was a region with a large number of owner-occupier smallholders and a much smaller number of rural non-noble notables, whose property was modest compared with that of estate-owners in many other parts of Germany. These notables were able in large measure to fulfil their economic and social ambitions, although that might mean conflict either with their peers, or with their social superiors and inferiors, or with all of them. In particular, it might mean conflict with the Bavarian state. They also had authority in that their power was recognized as legitimate. Their economic interests were seen – not always correctly – as generally consonant with those of the smaller landholders. This was by no means an unchanging position, however. Indeed during this period there took place one mass demonstration, one major uprising, two political coups and several periods of military rule, not to speak of the effect of two major wars. One of the main arguments of this chapter is that in the course of these upheavals, and of the less violent but no less important changes wrought by demographic growth and industrialization, the notable class – while maintaining much of its economic power – was gradually displaced from its authoritative position. Because of the relative power of the smallholder class and changing political circumstances, it was possible for humbler landholders to exert a considerable degree of influence.

The Bavarian Rhine Palatinate had its origins in the treaty of 1816 between Munich and Vienna, which finalized the territorial negotiations after the overthrow of Napoleon. It covered the territory from Homburg in the west, along the border with Alsace to the Rhine, northwards almost as far as the Hunsrück. Despite the loss of some territory and French military occupation from the end of the First World War to 1930, the Palatinate remained Bavarian until the Third Reich, when it was effectively removed by *Gauleiter* Bürckel from Munich's control. After the Second World War it came to form part of the new West German *Land* of the Rhineland-Palatinate.[5]

The Napoleonic occupation and the Bavarian takeover were crucial to local landownership. The French had already done the job of abolishing feudal obligations and tidying up the multitude of petty lordships which had occupied the territory, and the Wittelsbach monarchy did not reconstitute them. Hence this was a consolidated territory free of a nobility yet subject to a crown.[6] Under the Bavarian monarchy it was possible to achieve noble status, and indeed many civil servants and rural notables were so elevated, but this should not disguise the major change which had taken place.[7] As important was the Bavarian recognition of the Palatinate's distinctive institutions, very different from those of the adoptive parent state. Already, prior to the French occupation, customary partible inheritance had prevailed throughout most of the Palatinate and it had been further entrenched by the introduction of French law. Furthermore, the entire legal system after 1816 remained based on the Napoleonic Code until the introduction of the German Civil Code in 1900. These provisions, collectively known as the 'Rhenish institutions', were guaranteed in the Bavarian constitution of 1818 and jealously guarded by the landowners of the Palatinate.[8]

The Palatine population was divided almost equally between Protestants and Catholics. Neither church could rely on much in the way of landed estate or authority vested in the state. Popular devoutness, however, and allegiance to one denomination or the other were quite strong, especially around the beginning of this period. The main Catholic areas were in the east and south and in some parts of the central Palatinate. Elsewhere Protestants predominated, but there were also many mixed communities.[9] It is a common feature of Palatine villages to have both sizeable Protestant and Catholic churches. Antagonism between Protestants and Catholics rarely appeared in violent form, but in most towns and villages the local elite tended to come mainly from one church. Whether this was Catholic or Protestant varied, however, so that social predominance was not uniformly tied to confession.[10]

The population of the territory in 1816 was approximately 420,000. It grew, despite high levels of emigration at times of economic or political crisis, to 580,000 in 1840, 615,000 in 1871, nearly 940,000 in 1910 and 980,000 in 1935. Indeed, throughout the period under consideration the Palatinate was the most densely populated of the Bavarian governmental districts. In the early nineteenth century the population was predominantly rural and agricultural. In 1840 just over two thirds of the population was engaged in agricultural production, and half of these people could be classed as 'farmers' of one degree or another and their dependants. By the 1880s the agricultural proportion was down to just over one half and by 1907 to less than two fifths. Industrial production, particularly chemicals and engineering, had now assumed predominance.[11]

This broad outline does not, however, reflect the complex economic and social reality. In the late eighteenth century Palatine peasants were very much dependent on subsidiary occupations, and this remained typical of the area.[12] On the eve of the First World War the Palatinate was a densely populated region of many sizeable towns and villages with mixed Protestant and Catholic populations, possessing a good network of transport and financial facilities. It had some mineral resources and specialist manufactures, but in general its own industries were mixed and small-scale. Only at the chemical works of BASF in Ludwigshafen and perhaps in some of the metalworking concerns could one talk of a substantial factory labour force. Most labour was employed in small concerns, in artisanal production, in the service sector, as outworkers (particularly in the Pirmasens shoe industry), or in many cases in a combination of some or all of these. And over one third of the labour force worked partly or wholly on the multitude of farms which characterized the Palatine landscape.

It was an area of mixed farming, and the small farmers generally aimed for a balanced income from different types of culture. Apart from the localized specialities of wine and tobacco – both produced mainly in the east – all crops were found throughout the region. There existed a broad distinction, however, between the eastern and western districts, the Vorderpfalz and the Westrich. The former enjoyed a warmer climate and more fertile soil, and was more suited to intensive cultivation. It benefited too from nearer urban markets and the Rhine waterway. The Westrich was not so blessed. The poorer soil lent itself to extensive rather than intensive cultivation and the harvest came several weeks later than on the Rhine plain.

About half the Palatinate's arable land was devoted to cereals, with rye the most widely grown. Otherwise the nineteenth century saw a huge increase in potato-growing, to the point where by the end of the century the proportion of the area devoted to potatoes was the highest in Germany. Potato-growing was particularly important in the western district of Homburg. Most of the harvest was used or sold as fodder, but distilleries took up part of the crop, and there was a surplus of quality produce for human consumption.

Cash crops, including rape, hemp, hops and tobacco, declined in importance during the course of the nineteenth century, and fruit-growing was also very undeveloped. Livestock and dairy farming, on the other hand, expanded steadily. It is clear that even in the early nineteenth century the small farmers of the region were producing for markets, albeit on a very small scale, and displaying adaptability as far as climate and terrain allowed.

Two distinctive aspects of the landscape converged on the edge of the Rhine plain: the forest and the vineyard, both captured in the name of the celebrated wine village, Forst. The Palatinate was one of the most wooded regions of Germany, with the mixed forest of the Palatinate Forest stretching from the Westrich to the Haardt. However, forest and woodland made up only 12 per cent of the land of the agricultural holdings. In 1908 fully 88 per cent of the forest was in the possession of the state, the Crown personally, local authorities, or public and private institutions. The remainder was in private hands, generally on the larger holdings. The vineyard region, by contrast, was divided into tiny plots, of which there were about 30,000 by the end of the nineteenth century.[13]

Turning now to more detailed questions of landownership, the French occupation and the Bavarian settlement promoted the creation of a rural notable class and a large population of smallholders. Thus Haasis in his studies of Rhenish liberal democracy argues that the selling-off of noble and ecclesiastical land from 1800 created a propertied bourgeoisie which was at this stage at least wedded to democratic principles.[14] Similarly Faber notes the Bavarians' concern for 'the political and also personal expectations of the Rhenish notable stratum and that there would be no "denapoleonization", as was feared under the pressure of agitation by German national patriots'.[15] Similarly, looking at the administration rather than at landholding as such, Mack Walker suggests the creation of a notable class: 'in the separately administered Palatinate, where French administrative law prevailed, the provincial administrators . . . assumed stronger control over community affairs.'[16] One example of this role was in the establishment in 1816 of the Palatine *Landrat*, a council of 20 members chosen by the king from 40 candidates elected indirectly from high tax payers.[17]

Certainly several notable families established themselves by purchasing land in the wake of French reform. The auctioning of the Deidesheim lands of the prince bishop of Speyer was the beginning of the famous vineyards of the Bassermann-Jordan, Buhl and Deinhard families.[18] Their and others' villas still display the wealth and presumptions of these so-called 'bottle barons'.[19] The families, especially the Buhls, as a consequence came to play an important economic and social role in the region and also to possess a political voice at national level. They began as 'democrats', but in the course of the century, particularly after 1849, moved towards a conservative National Liberalism.[20]

The other effect of the French occupation was to perpetuate partible inheritance. Under this system a holding was divided amongst the heirs (usually the children) on the death of its owner, or very often before. The house and surrounding land went to one of the heirs, not necessarily the eldest but one who had continued to live with the parents and work the holding. This system explains the great fragmentation of property in the region and the prevalence of very small farms. By 1907 nearly 90 per cent of the agricultural land was cultivated in units of less than 20 hectares, compared with a Reich average of nearly 50 per cent, and over 40 per cent in units of under 5 hectares, compared with a Reich average of 16 per cent. Both the number of dwarf holdings of under 2 hectares and the area that they represented had been increasing.[21]

In practice, the system did not mean that property was split several ways with each generation. Heirs frequently sold their shares, either to siblings or outside the family, and marriage too acted as a consolidating factor. Inheritance also worked in a form of continuous cycle, with a farmer adding to his property in the middle years, later to shed it gradually to his offspring.[22] A specific example may serve to show how inheritance practice could operate. An arable property of 41 hectares, a fair size for the region, came to belong to

Rudolf Hamm, a young peasant leader of the 1920s, in the following fashion. Hamm's grandfather moved from Pfeddersheim, near Worms, in 1874 to buy the Deileisterhof, near Zweibrücken in the southwestern Palatinate, as French families sold up after the Franco-Prussian War. Shortly afterwards he bought another nearby farm. One farm was now let, and the other worked. The grandfather had four children: Hamm's father received the Deileisterhof, Hamm's aunt the other farm, and the other two children were portioned off with the proceeds of the sale of the Pfeddersheim property. Hamm then took over the farm before his father's death. So even though the inheritance was divided between the heirs, there was no fragmentation, and the effects of the procedure were not dissimilar from those of the *Anerbenrecht* (one heir and portioning off) common in Bavaria.[23]

There were some instances of customary impartible inheritance – a kind of entail – but they were confined to a few larger farms in certain localities and to one village: Gerhardsbrunn on the Sickinger Höhe between Zweibrücken and Landstuhl. Interestingly, though, it was this village which was the home of another prominent peasant leader, Karl Munzinger, so there is a lot to suggest that inheritance procedures which, customarily or deliberately in individual cases, avoided fragmentation and alienation helped form a class of medium farmer notables, below the wine barons but later in contention with them.[24]

The selling of land during the French occupation did not, of course, create a rural bourgeoisie from nothing. In the light of the market in land which followed the later peasant emancipation elsewhere in Germany, one might assume that the flow of land onto the market helped to consolidate rather than create a class of rural notables. Moreover the division of land on inheritance had existed before the French came, and presumably peasants in those days had found ways to avoid the worst effects of fragmentation. What the French period did, however, was to establish the Palatinate, apart from the forest, as an area of predominantly owner-occupied small to medium holdings, fragmented strip holdings, and a lively market in land. The smallest of the holdings were unable to support a family by themselves, hence the complicated interlocking of different economic activities in the region. The smallest vineyards in the right locations could, however, still be quite remunerative, and the larger ones could develop a wealth and prestige disproportionate to their actual size. The larger arable and livestock farms too, though tiny compared with estates elsewhere in Germany, brought to their owners influence and authority, if not necessarily great wealth.

Within the Palatinate there were various levels of political and social authority. To begin with, the region was governed by the monarchy of a state geographically distant and distinct in many vital respects. In the regional capital of Speyer on the Rhine, this state installed an administration which reflected Bavarian rather than Palatine priorities. Of the governors of the Palatinate during the nineteenth century only one – Franz Alwens from 1846 to 1849 – was a born Pfälzer. Most of the rest were Catholic Bavarian nobles.

The bureaucracy which served these governors was again appointed by and largely drawn from Bavaria.[25]

There was a degree of local self-determination in the *Landrat* and this was dominated by the notables of the region. At town and village level, mayors and councils were elected by citizens, and also constituted a local oligarchy, in charge of law and order, appointments to certain posts, agricultural controls, and education. Of the village of Maudach, Catt comments that 'Council members were drawn from a restricted number of families, basically the larger farming families; this continued throughout the nineteenth century. The position of mayor was almost hereditary.'[26] And this was the position in a village where even the larger farming families were smallholders by most European standards.

Local power and authority were expressed in terms of economic clout, the provision of employment, political and social patronage, and actual participation in political decision-making at local, regional, or national level. Too sharp a distinction should not be drawn between rural and urban power. Even before industrialization the Palatinate was densely populated with generally large settlements. As industry developed in the region, the interlocking of town and country changed and became in some ways more complex, but it did not disappear. The wine trade required urban participation, and other agricultural pursuits developed industrial links too. A prominent local dignitary and Reichstag deputy of the 1920s, Albert Zapf, for instance, was the owner of a sugar refinery at Frankenthal and the political associate of many of the agrarian notables.[27] Of course, larger factories, notably BASF, altered structures of power, but even here a large part of the factory labour force commuted from villages where they retained plots or vineyards.

Political developments came into play both as reflectors of underlying changes and as themselves instigators of change. A number of important political episodes or developments of the nineteenth and twentieth centuries can usefully be considered for their relationship to questions of landownership and power. These were the Hambach Festival of 1832; the Palatine uprising of 1849; the reconstitution of politics from the 1890s to the First World War; the separatist *putsch* of 1923; and the growth of Nazism from the late 1920s. Others might well be included, but cannot be so here for reasons of space.[28]

The Hambach Festival of 27 May 1832 was a planned demonstration at the ruins of the Max-Burg at Hambach outside Neustadt, billed as the 'National Festival of the Germans'. Between 20,000 and 30,000 people, not all from the Palatinate, gathered to hear speeches about democracy, freedom and German unity. The event derived inspiration from the July revolution in France two years earlier, but also concerned specific grudges with the Bavarian government and was timed to counter celebrations of the Bavarian constitution. These grievances were about censorship – which was in fact lighter in the

Palatinate than elsewhere in Bavaria – and the tariff boundary imposed around the Palatinate in 1829.[29] This had occasioned numerous petitions from all over the Palatinate during the autumn and winter of 1830. The petition from Neustadt, to take a single example, bore 54 signatures, mainly from the commercial urban middle class. Some larger wine-growers were among the signatories, many more of whom had other links with the wine trade.[30]

The most vocal participants at the Hambach Festival were lawyers, journalists, Protestant clergymen and students, but it also drew a much wider social participation, which had more to do with economic distress. The tariff had hit the small wine-growers and tobacco-planters particularly hard, and thousands of wine-growers converged on Hambach with black banners proclaiming 'The wine-growers must mourn'.[31] An unsigned letter from a wine-grower reached the Bavarian king:

> Your Majesty!
> You will have heard about the May Festival in Neustadt: on account of the tariff. There were abusive things said about you. Get rid of the tariff from Rhine Bavaria! That will stop all the unrest! Get rid of the tariff! . . . Away with the tariff, away with it! A warning from your most humble and obedient servant and most loyal subject: do away with the tariff, or there will be dire consequences.[32]

Unrest was fuelled by severe rural impoverishment, especially in the Westrich. In numerous localities so-called trees of freedom were erected, as in the 1790s, and several mayors and other officials were ousted from office. Although the wealthier landowners of the Vorderpfalz were generally not prominent in their participation, they were still at this stage broadly aligned with the liberal journalists. The vineyard owner Johannes Fitz led the small growers of Dürkheim with their black banner.[33]

In the aftermath of the demonstration the Bavarians sent in the army, effectively imposed martial law and rounded up liberal agitators. The repression had an interesting effect. Those liberal deputies who had been prominent at Hambach, particularly the lawyers, found themselves harassed and excluded from important offices. This, according to Faber, meant that from the late 1830s 'wealthy landowners, not least from the "wine aristocracy" of the Vorderpfalz, won a numerically greater influence among the deputies'.[34] Thus Hambach and its repression strengthened the landowners, although they had themselves had objections to the tariff and were in many cases sympathetic to liberal demands.

It was in 1849, rather than in 1848, that the Palatinate witnessed most disturbance. Beginning as a rebellion against the Bavarian refusal to recognize the new Reich constitution, the uprising rapidly developed into a wider conflict which Droz interprets as a struggle for separation from Bavaria in which the bourgeoisie was not interested.[35] The battles in the Palatinate drew in many participants from outside the region, among them Engels. His analysis of the situation was that the provisional government, which he admired personally but found incompetent, failed to draw upon the potential support of the peasantry:

> In the Palatinate it was not so much particular classes of the population as particular districts which, governed by local interests, declared themselves against the movement, some from the first and others little by little. Certainly the townspeople of Speyer were reactionary from the start; in Kaiserslautern, Neustadt, Zweibrücken, etc., they became so with the passage of time; but the main strength of the reactionary party was to be found in agricultural districts spread over the whole of the Palatinate. This confused configuration of the parties could only have been eliminated by one measure: a direct attack on the private property invested in mortgages and mortgage-usury, in favour of the debt-ridden peasants who had been sucked dry by the usurers. But this single measure, which would immediately have given the whole of the rural population a stake in the uprising, presupposes a much larger territory and more developed social conditions in towns than is the case in the Palatinate. It was only feasible at the beginning of the insurrection.[36]

This was a perceptive analysis. Engels recognized the strength of local authority in the towns and districts and the refusal of even the smaller farmers to participate. He might also have mentioned that the large wine-growers were now certainly not in the progressive camp. He was right too that a peasant uprising at the beginning would have had an impact, but the fact that it did not occur was surely significant.

According to Haasis, after 1849 the Palatine notables went 'in droves into the reactionary camp'.[37] Even if one stops short of expressing it as strongly as this, it is nevertheless clear that up to and beyond the foundation of the German Empire, the agrarian and wine-growing grandees of the Palatinate became more and more part of the right wing of National Liberalism. In political terms, after 1871 National Liberalism had a virtual monopoly of electoral success and local control. And far from operating through strict party discipline, National Liberalism at local level consisted largely of a club of notables, whose economic and political activities went hand in hand.

This cosy world came under threat once more in the 1890s, as smaller landowners moved to a broader participation in local political power. In the 1890s agricultural crisis and Caprivi's trade policy provoked an upsurge of organized agrarian protest. In the Palatinate it mobilized more of the small farmers, but was still essentially dominated by the larger owners. There was a change, however; the National Liberal notables were gradually displaced from their political pre-eminence by younger arable farmers organized in the Agrarian League (Bund der Landwirte).[38]

This process was taken even further after the strains of the First World War, and patterns of deference and allegiance were shaken up irrevocably. In the years 1918–20 a new organization was formed – the Free Peasantry (Freie Bauernschaft) – which claimed to represent the small farmers in a peasant trade union.[39] Out of control of the agrarian notables, it generated a now large popular membership and organized delivery strikes and other direct action against the controlled agricultural economy of the early Weimar Republic. The Free Peasantry relied very much on demagogic local leadership, which came from middling farmers – both Protestant and Catholic – not previously associated with the notables. Labour relations now also came to the fore, both in the form of antagonism between peasants and urban workers, and within the rural sector itself. An agricultural employers' association was formed for the first time, encompassing the large vineyard owners and some of the larger arable farmers.[40]

The major political consequence of the growth of the Free Peasantry was the collaboration of its leader, Franz Josef Heinz, with the French occupying force. Heinz led a separatist *putsch* in late 1923, which established a government for several months before his assassination in January 1924 and the final defeat of the separatists in the following month. His regime had generated popular hostility rather than approval, but it had relied for its initial success on the support – particularly Heinz's own local support – of the small peasantry. It would not have been conceivable without the strains of the controlled economy and the inflation.[41]

The failure of the separatists exposed agrarian politics to increasing fragmentation into sectional interests, a process exacerbated by growing agricultural depression. One example of this was the dispute which raged from the late 1920s between the smaller and the larger wine-growers. The former, mainly in the southeastern Palatinate, had planted American vines because they were cheaper and more prolific. This, and the fact that the American vines were of lower quality, enraged the larger vineyard owners of the Haardt, who had enough sway with the government to effect the ripping-out of the American vines. This understandably led to still further rural unrest.[42]

The confusion and fragmentation of the late 1920s left the way wide open to political exploitation by the Nazis. They managed to ride the tide of agrarian discontent and scored some of their greatest electoral successes among – mainly – the Protestant small farmers of the Palatinate. Forlorn attempts by persevering representatives of both the Free Peasantry and the older Agrarian League to stem the tide came to nothing.[43]

To conclude: from the beginning of the nineteenth century to the National Socialist seizure of power a smallish group of middling bourgeois owners consolidated its economic and social power through the purchase and development of small but for the area relatively large concerns. The arable and dairy farmers, most of whom were personally involved in the running of their farms, managed to achieve a reasonably sound economic performance, with its consequent social advantages. They were not immune, however, from problems of prices at times of economic crisis – particularly in the late nineteenth century and from the late 1920s. In a rather different position were the vineyard owners. Their concerns were smaller than those of the farmers, but – situated as they were on prime land – they could derive considerable profit and an exalted social position from the wine trade. Even they, however, were adversely affected by conditions in the early 1830s and indeed the 1930s.

Both these groups, but particularly the vineyard owners, initially attached themselves to political liberalism, which had been the basis of their social advance. This began to change by 1832 and the process was more or less completed by 1849, as they came to espouse a more defensive attitude toward their economic position. They later became identified with the agrarian right of the National Liberal Party, which in elections maintained a comfortable monopoly of political power. This position of power was eroded in the 1890s by the growth of political Catholicism, social democracy and particularly agrarian protest. Although at first there was no clear dividing line between the National Liberals and the Agrarian League, by the eve of the First World War the agrarian notables had politically eclipsed the 'wine barons'.

After the First World War the challenge came from even further down the social scale. Populist agrarian protest, led by smaller peasants, damaged but did not destroy the authority of the estate owners and the 'wine barons'. When the increased involvement of small farmers came up against the agricultural crisis from the mid-1920s, however, the organizations built up after the war could not cope. Also a failure were the attempts to found peasant parties. Some of the agrarian notables and some small farmers threw in their lot with the National Socialists, but more importantly that party began to gather electoral support among the aggrieved peasant population at large. This then fuelled a movement which completely changed the political framework within which agriculture operated. The economic position of the farmers then gradually improved, but not without an exodus of many people from agriculture into urban employment.

From the perspective finally of small farmers, it is possible to adopt in part a Bonapartist framework of interpretation. It was patently not the case that the peasants were without 'manifold relations with one another',[44] but their economic vulnerability meant that throughout this period they were unable to represent themselves politically. Until the 1890s, even with an extended franchise, the peasants generally deferred to the authority of the rural notables, and such sporadic unrest as there was in the countryside was uncoordinated and produced no concrete results. The Agrarian League opened up the scene, but even it – like the National Liberals – was inadequate, since it involved minimal involvement by the people themselves and was in any case almost exclusively Protestant and inattentive to the small wine-growers. After the First World War the Free Peasantry, and other associations heavily influenced by its structure and tactics, provided an opportunity for democratic participation and direct action, based on an ideology of class struggle. What it could not do, however, was win the struggle. As soon as it tried through the separatist Heinz to establish a political authority, it failed miserably. The result was a growing confusion and fragmentation, to which the only solution was a dictatorship pledged to represent the peasantry in a society free from class struggle altogether.

NOTES

1 H. G. Haasis, *Morgenröte der Republik: Die linksrheinischen deutschen Demokraten 1789–1849* (Frankfurt am Main: 1984), p. 139. Translated by the author.

2 Friedrich Engels, 'The campaign for the German Imperial Constitution', in K. Marx and F. Engels, *Collected Works* (London: 1978), Vol. 10, p. 187.

3 G. List (ed.), *'Deutsche, lasst des Weines Strom sich ins ganze Reich ergiessen!': Die Pfälzer und ihre Weinstrasse – ein Beitrag zur alternativen Landeskunde* (Heidelberg: 1985).

4 J. Mathäss, ' "Trinkt mehr Pfälzer Wein": 80 Jahre Weinwerbung im Dienst steigenden Pro-Kopf-Verbrauchs', in List, *Deutsche, lasst des Weines Strom*, p. 190.

5 Bayerisches Hauptstaatsarchiv, Munich [hereafter BH], MInn 34 562/II, King Max Josef to the Ministry of the Interior, 20 February 1817; K.-G. Faber, 'Die südlichen Reinlande 1816–1956', in F. Petri and G. Droege (eds), *Rheinische Geschichte*, Vol. 2 (Düsseldorf: 1976), pp. 367–474.

6 C. Dipper, *Die Bauernbefreiung in Deutschland 1790–1850* (Stuttgart: 1980), pp. 50–3.

7 'Edict über den Adel im Königreiche Bayern', in P. J. Siebenpfeiffer (ed.), *Handbuch der Verfassung, Gerichtsordnung und gesammten Verwaltung Rheinbayerns*, Vol. 1 (Zweibrücken: 1831–2), pp. 51–2. For instance, Walter Ritter von Lichtenberger, National Socialist chairman of the Pfälzer Bauernschaft from 1930, was Ritter of the Max-Josef Order.

8 Bavarian constitution of 26 May 1818 and supplementary laws, in Siebenpfeiffer, *Handbuch der Verfassung*, Vol. 1, pp. 18–120; French laws applying to Rhine departments, in ibid., pp. 170–204.

9 BH, MH 784, 'Statistische Notizen des Rheinkreises 1816–22'; *Statistisches Jahrbuch für das Königreich Bayern*, Vol. 11 (Munich: 1911), pp. 24, 35; E. O. Bräunche, *Parteien und Reichstagswahlen in der Rheinpfalz von der Reichsgründung 1871 bis zum Ausbruch des Ersten Weltkrieges 1914: Eine regionale partei- und wahlhistorische Untersuchung im Vorfeld der Demokratie* (Speyer: 1982), pp. 15–23.

10 See C. S. Catt, 'Farmers and factory workers: rural society in Imperial Germany: the example of Maudach', in R. J. Evans and W. R. Lee (eds), *The German Peasantry: Conflict and Community in Rural Society from the Eighteenth to the Twentieth Centuries* (London: 1986), pp. 150–2.

11 W. Herzberg, *Das Hambacher Fest: Geschichte der revolutionären Bestrebungen in Rheinbayern um das Jahr 1832* (Cologne: 1982 [reprint of 1908 edn]), p. 13; *Statistisches Jahrbuch für das Königreich Bayern*, Vol. 6 (Munich: 1901), p. 15; *Statistisches Jahrbuch für das Königreich Bayern*, Vol. 11, p. 30; and see J. Wysocki, 'Die pfälzische Wirtschaft von 1871 bis 1939', *Beiträge zur pfälzischen Wirtschaftsgeschichte* (Speyer: 1968), pp. 237–9.

12 Dipper, *Bauernbefreiung*, p. 50.

13 For more detail and sources see J. Osmond, 'The free peasantry: agrarian protest in the Bavarian Palatinate, 1893–1933', DPhil thesis, University of Oxford, 1986; and J. Osmond, *Rural Protest in the Weimar Republic: The Free Peasantry in the Rhineland and Bavaria* (forthcoming).

14 H. G. Haasis, 'Winzer in der Frühzeit der Pfälzer Demokratie (1789–1849)', in List, *Deutsche, lasst des Weines Strom*, pp. 20–41; Haasis, *Morgenröte der Republik*.

15 Faber, 'Die südlichen Rheinlande', p. 375. Translated by the author.

16 M. Walker, *German Home Towns: Community, State, and General Estate 1648–1871* (Ithaca, NY and London: 1971), p. 272.
17 Faber, 'Die südlichen Rheinlande', p. 377.
18 Haasis, 'Winzer in der Frühzeit der Pfälzer Demokratie', pp. 35–6.
19 For instance, the villa in Wachenheim designed by Eisenlohr for the Wolf family. See *Frankfurter Allgemeine Zeitung*, 18 September 1986, no. 216, p. R1.
20 Haasis, 'Winzer in der Frühzeit der Pfälzer Demokratie', pp. 25–6; Faber, 'Die südlichen Rheinlande', pp. 413–15.
21 A. Müller, *Die Grundlagen der pfälzischen Landwirtschaft und die Entwicklung ihrer Produktion im 19. Jahrhundert bis zur Gegenwart* (Naumburg a. S.: 1912), pp. 31–49.
22 Catt, 'Farmers and factory workers', pp. 138–9.
23 Interview with Herr Rudolf Hamm at the Deileisterhof, near Zweibrücken, 29 August 1978.
24 L. Mang and T. Zink, *Das Wirtschaftsleben der Pfalz in Vergangenheit und Gegenwart* (Munich: 1913), pp. 122–4.
25 W. Schineller, *Die Regierungspräsidenten der Pfalz* (Speyer: 1980).
26 Catt, 'Farmers and factory workers', p. 147.
27 Bundesarchiv Koblenz, NL 227 Nachlass Albert Zapf.
28 For detail on the period 1893–1933 see Osmond, *Rural Protest*.
29 BH, MInn 34562/3: 'Organisation der Regierung des Rheinkreises', vol. 3, 1825–32; MInn 45516–7: 'Verhältnisse im Rheinkreis', vol. 1 (1830–2), vol. 2 (1833–6); *Hambach 1832: Anstösse und Folgen* (Wiesbaden: 1984); *Hambacher Fest 1832–1982: Freiheit und Einheit Deutschland und Europa* (Mainz: 1983); Herzberg, *Das Hambacher Fest*; Haasis, *Morgenröte der Republik*, pp. 182–90.
30 BH, MInn 34 562/II: petitions against the '*Maut*', September–December 1830.
31 Faber, 'Die südlichen Rheinlande', p. 388; *Hambacher Fest 1832–1982*, p. 148; Haasis, 'Winzer in der Frühzeit der Pfälzer Demokratie', p. 33.
32 Haasis, 'Winzer in der Frühzeit der Pfälzer Demokratie', p. 33. Translated by the author.
33 ibid.
34 Faber, 'Die südlichen Rheinlande', p. 391. Translated by the author.
35 J. Droz, *Les Révolutions Allemandes de 1848* (Paris: 1957), pp. 606–8; and see BH, MInn 45368: *Amts- und Intelligenzblatt der provisorischen Regierung der Rheinpfalz*, no. 1, 22 May 1849; MInn 45531–5: 'Pfalz, Unruhen wegen der deutschen Verfassungsfrage', 5 vols, 1849–51.
36 Engels, 'The campaign for the German Imperial Constitution', pp. 190–1.
37 Haasis, 'Winzer in der Frühzeit der Pfälzer Demokratie', p. 26.
38 Bräunche, *Parteien und Reichstagswahlen in der Rheinpfalz*; J. Osmond, 'A second agrarian mobilization? Peasant associations in South and West Germany, 1918–24', in R. G. Moeller (ed.), *Peasants and Lords in Modern Germany: Recent Studies in Agricultural History* (London: 1986), pp. 173–4.
39 ibid., pp. 177–82; Osmond, *Rural Protest*.
40 Archive of the Verband der Pfälzischen Industrie e. V., Neustadt an der Weinstrasse, Ka: Kreisarbeitgeberverband für Land- und Fortstwirtschaft, Wein- und Gartenbau in der Pfalz, 1921–33.
41 BH, MA 107 668 'Heinz-Orbis, "Präsident der autonomen Republik Pfalz": seine Erschiessung und andres, 1924–32'; Osmond, *Rural Protest*; J. Osmond, 'Peasant farming in South and West Germany during war and inflation 1914 to 1924: stability or stagnation?', in G. D. Feldman, C.-L. Holtfrerich, G. A. Ritter and P.-C. Witt (eds), *Die Deutsche Inflation: Eine Zwischenbilanz* (Berlin and New York: 1982), pp. 289–307; G. E. R. Gedye, *The Revolver Republic: France's Bid for the Rhine* (London: 1930), pp. 214–34; Rudolf Hamm, *Freie Bauernschaft, Heinz-Orbis und Separatismus* (Deileisterhof: 1930). At the time of writing this chapter, the author had not yet been able to consult Gerhard Gräber and Matthias Spindler, *Revolverrepublik am Rhein: Die pfälzischen Separatisten von 1923/24 und ihre Feinde: Eine deutsche Geschichte* (forthcoming).
42 BH, MInn 71713: 'Unruhen, Demonstrationen in der Pfalz, 1921–32', part 3.

43 Landesarchiv Speyer, T63: 'Landwirtschaftliches Vereins-, Verbands- und Gerwerkschaftswesen', nos 87–95, 142–84, 188–90: 'Pfälzer Bundschuh, 1933'.

44 Karl Marx, 'The Eighteenth Brumaire of Louis Bonaparte', in Karl Marx and Friedrich Engels, *Selected Works in Three Volumes*, Vol. I (Moscow: 1969), p. 478.

GREAT BRITAIN AND IRELAND

7

Landownership and the exercise of power in an industrializing society: Lancashire and Cheshire in the nineteenth century

Eric J. Evans

I

In any discussion over the relationship between landownership and power, it is tempting to see nineteenth-century Britain as a special case. It was the first nation to experience an industrial revolution and, while recent writing has stressed this revolution's 'evolutionary' nature, it cannot be disputed that the process of industrialism greatly expanded opportunities for wealth creation in the non-landed sector of the economy.[1] It has been tempting to follow Marx's massive, over-simple schema and characterize nineteenth-century Britain as witnessing a struggle for power between 'landed' and 'bourgeois' property. Economically determined 'historical forces' ensured that the former was bound to lose and, on this analysis, nineteenth-century British society is studied in order to understand the process whereby the landed classes lost their grip on power.

Britain was also special in a second sense. Its landed class was unique in exercising virtually independent political power at the centre from the late seventeenth century. The so-called 'Glorious Revolution' of 1688 confirmed Parliament's central role. Despite recent, and not very successful, attempts at a 'conservative' reaction in eighteenth-century political studies, the story thereafter is one of declining royal power and the increasing control of Parliament by members and clients of the immensely wealthy leading families of England and Scotland.[2] By the beginning of the nineteenth century, royal power was in irreversible decline and the emergence of cabinet government had strengthened the control of the dominant political groups over the structure of central power. Lord Liverpool in the 1820s was able to dictate to King George IV who should, and who should not, be in his government.[3]

The study of power in nineteenth-century Britain should, therefore, also show how the landed classes lost their control over Parliament to the bourgeoisie. This chapter attempts to demonstrate that the links between landownership and power proved much more tenacious even in the world's first industrial nation than might be assumed. It does so by paying particular attention to two of the counties of England at the heart of the industrialization process: Lancashire and Cheshire, in the northwest of the country.

The conventional wisdom once was that the 1832 Reform Act, which substantially increased both the middle-class vote and the number of parliamentary seats in urban areas where industrial and commercial interests predominated, began a process of transfer of power from the aristocracy to the middle classes. This view has long since been exploded.[4] Landowners continued to be substantially the most numerous social grouping among MPs. Of the 14 ministries in office between the Reform Acts of 1832 and 1867, only the two led by Robert Peel did not have aristocratic prime ministers. Peers of the realm were in a substantial majority in all the cabinets of the period. Though the first Reform Act was, in considerable measure, a concession to the 'new' forces of industrial Britain, it was a witting and measured one which aimed to leave the landed interest in control, and succeeded in doing so.[5]

The repeal of the Corn Laws in 1846, which ended protection for arable farmers from most foreign competition and which has similarly been seen as the economic counterpart by the middle classes of their assault on the constitution in 1832, also needs to be put into appropriate context. Despite the vigorous and well-publicized work of agricultural protection societies and a parliamentary campaign of considerable skill, orchestrated by Benjamin Disraeli, the removal of agricultural protection was not uniformly opposed by the landed interest.[6] It is also clear that during the period of so-called 'High Farming' in the 1850s and 1860s many landowners benefited handsomely from their investments. It seems that both the total acreage and the proportion of land given over to arable increased in the twenty years after the repeal of the Corn Laws.[7] Probably for the first time in English history, the acreage under crops exceeded that under grass during the 1850s, realizing the dreams of the agricultural improvers of the late eighteenth century who had wrestled with problems of food supply and how to feed a rapidly growing population. Little of the agricultural supply evidence in the mid-nineteenth century suggests a landed interest under pressure.

The larger landowners also remained in control of those important local social institutions upon which the exercise of power ultimately rested. For the 350 or so landowners in the middle of the nineteenth century who owned

10,000 acres or more, power radiated outwards from the great country houses such as Alnwick in Northumberland (home of the Duke of Northumberland), Chatsworth in Derbyshire (Duke of Devonshire), or Knowsley in Lancashire (Earl of Derby). Such houses provided the local community with both a political and a social focus. The regular and opulent dances and balls, given for the local gentry, high-status employees like land agents and solicitors, and also perhaps leading professional men like lawyers and doctors, were not just vehicles for ostentation and conspicuous consumption. They symbolized the cohesion of the local community[8] and they could also be the occasion for practical social or political decisions, such as the negotiation of a marriage contract or decisions about which candidates might be suitable to put forward at a forthcoming election.

Similarly, the lavish staffing levels of the larger country houses were maintained to show visitors that their hosts were folk of influence and power. The names of titled figures donating substantial sums at the head of subscription lists for private charities fulfilled the same purpose. Those in receipt of charity, of course, would be expected to show due deference to the giver. Gentry families for their tenants and the clergy for the community more generally aped this kind of conspicuous hospitality and benefaction, though on a necessarily more modest scale. By no means all of the owners of 10,000 acres or more were aristocrats, but, significantly, the life-style expected of a man of wealth in the countryside was related not so much to title as to ownership of landed property.

Sir Gilbert Scott, who had considerable experience in designing or improving the houses of the great, explained their social significance:

> a landed proprietor is especially in a responsible position. He is the natural head of his parish or district – in which he should be looked up to as the bond of union between classes. To him the poor man should look up for protection; those in doubt or difficulty for advice; the ill-disposed for reproof or punishment; the deserving, of all classes, for consideration and hospitality; and *all* for a dignified, honourable and Christian example.[9]

The development of sport with a social function also played an important role in the exercise of power by the landed classes. Between the mid-eighteenth century and the mid-nineteenth, as D. C. Itzkovitz has shown, hunting was transformed from a pastime attractive only to a minority of country squires into a major social event in which the greater landowners participated fully and in which the appointment of a Master of Foxhounds became a decision of considerable social significance.[10] Hunting developed particularly in the East Midlands and 125 packs of hounds were known to be in existence by 1866. The hunt united landowners and tenant farmers, and humbler members of the rural community were encouraged to be supporters and followers. Itzkovitz maintains that hunting developed a stabilizing mystique which 'raised it to the level of a unique social institution' and F. M. L. Thompson argues that 'the fox did more for the unity and strength of the landed interest than rent rolls'.[11]

It is significant that among the most notable foxhunters were Anglican clergymen. The social cohesion upon which the exercise of landowner power rested was widely believed by contemporaries to depend upon harmonious relations between church and state. Many of the most fervent upholders of the old order during the reform crisis of 1827–32 believed that the repeal of the Test and Corporation Acts (1828) and the passage of Roman Catholic Emancipation (1829) were bigger blows to the landed interest than was the Great Reform Act.[12] The revival of the Church of England, after threats to its status as the established church were deflected by a reform of its institutions in the 1830s and 1840s,[13] strengthened the position of landowners in rural society.

The right to present clergymen to vacant livings in the Church of England was, in the mid-nineteenth century, a jealously guarded piece of patronage vested, for the most part, in the landed aristocracy and the more substantial gentry. Over 7,000 of the 11,300 Anglican livings were in lay hands, and, unsurprisingly, some of the best-endowed rectories and vicarages went to the younger sons and close relatives of great landowners.[14] In addition to clerical duties, many rectors and vicars were leading figures in local educational initiatives and also in the administration of many of the multifarious charities and benefactions which grew up in Victorian England. The clergy's mediating role between rich and poor in the village community had come under severe attack during the period of parliamentary enclosure in the late eighteenth and early nineteenth centuries,[15] but the church rode out the storm and the more tranquil relations between church and state from the 1840s and 1850s undoubtedly help to explain the more harmonious relations which obtained within rural society by the third quarter of the nineteenth century. Ecclesiastical patronage was a factor in the exercise of landed power at the local level.

The overall picture of the exercise of landed controls, however, should not be painted as one of cloying harmony, unremitting duty on the part of the landowners and grateful deference on that of the lower orders. As Thompson has sardonically pointed out, while foxhunting might be a socially unifying force, neither shooting rights nor the preservation of game were.[16] Both were jealously guarded preserves of the landowners and acts against poaching were seen as 'blatantly discriminatory class legislation'. By 1911, Thompson calculates, there were twice as many gamekeepers in post as rural policemen. The majority of landowners, in his view, were unconcerned about threats to their power, had no need of systematic 'social control' and could easily accommodate both such respectful and orderly agricultural trade unionism as developed in the 1870s[17] and the rash of tenants' rights movements in the 1880s. 'In the eyes of the generality of landowners', Thompson writes,

> the function of their estates was to provide the income to support their life style; the function of the countryside was to provide good sport . . . either . . . the majority of landowners neglected their social responsibilities towards the majority of the people living on their estates, because they were indifferent, lazy, or self-centred, or . . . the majority declined to abuse the power of property by interfering in other people's lives.

Either way, the picture built up of nineteenth-century English rural society is one of complacent authority, only weakly and ineffectually challenged.

The most concerted challenge to the powers of the landed classes, ironically, came from urban middle-class professionals and intellectuals. This was the unrepresentative social group which dominated the land reform movement. Radical urban intellectuals had read enough political economy to believe that their landed opponents belonged to a world on the way out, but they never conquered their bemusement at the self-assured way the landowners retained powers they neither earned nor discharged with social responsibility.

G. C. Broderick wrote a scholarly study in 1881 of English land and English landlords which nevertheless made its polemical purpose plain:

> The love of power will always be gratified by the possession of land. The man with a real taste for county business, local government and estate management will cling to his paternal acres. . . . Happily, the last and present generations have witnessed a wonderful change for the better in the fulfilment of territorial obligations. Few country gentlemen now regard themselves as mere receivers of rent.[18]

Broderick's solution was what he called a 'new land system'. This would be based on free trade in land, the abolition of the Game Laws and the ending of restrictive practices, such as strict settlement and entail, which were widely used to keep great estates intact for the benefit of the male heir. It would also involve greater security for tenants, who farmed between 75 and 80 per cent of England's usable land. Broderick and his land-reforming allies perceived an increasing incompatibility between the economic and the political worlds, and sought to resolve it by subjecting the latter to the dominant nostrums of the former: free trade and the resolution of the market.

This was the route mapped out more than thirty years earlier by the much more famous radical free trader Richard Cobden, who noted in 1849 that 'the citadel of privilege . . . is so terribly strong owing to the concentrated masses of property in the hands of the comparatively few'.[19] The National Freehold Land Society, established in that year, Cobden saw as an appropriate vehicle to aid his grand design 'to place . . . political power in this country in the hands of the middle and industrious classes . . . by constitutional and legal means'. Land reformers unhesitatingly linked land with privilege and, what to them was much worse, with *unearned* and *hereditary* privilege. John Bright, likewise, beat the anti-aristocratic drum and looked beyond the repeal of the corn laws to a more thoroughgoing assault on the aristocracy:

> I conceive there is no delusion so great as that of believing that the great and the mighty of the earth will ever be the true, sincere, and disinterested friends of the middle classes, either in this or in any other kingdom.[20]

Landowners were a special target for attack not just because of the power which they exercised but because their right to it was not justified by the labour and effort which, to a strident strain of both nineteenth- and later twentieth-century thinking, should properly precede success. Joseph Chamberlain, the Birmingham screw manufacturer, who made so good that he contrived to split both landowners' political parties in the course of one spectacularly counterproductive career, recalled the Sermon on the Mount, but without the charitable message of its originator. The great landowners of Britain, he asserted, 'toil not, neither do they spin'.

Though their remedies proved unpalatable in the nineteenth century, the diagnosis of the land reformers was sound enough. Land meant power, and large holdings of land were concentrated in a small number of families. According to John Beckett's recent calculations from the famous statistics published in John Bateman's *The Great Landowners of Great Britain and Ireland* (1883), which unfortunately omits London, 1,688 families owned between them 43 per cent of the United Kingdom's 33 million or so acres. Of these, 331 owned more than 10,000 acres each. The ten estates which totalled more than 60,000 acres each were all owned by peers.[21] The seven wealthiest, the Dukes of Westminster, Buccleuch, Bedford, Devonshire and Northumberland, the Earl of Derby and the Marquis of Bute, were all worth more than £150,000 a year in land alone by the early 1880s.[22] The Westminster estates were worth more than a quarter of a million, including as they did most of Belgravia, Mayfair and other prime London sites. Each of these men had very substantial additional income from mines, commercial enterprises and stocks, and it is easy to conclude that they were among the wealthiest individuals of the time not just in Britain but in Europe as a whole.

The yeomanry and substantial squirearchy of later nineteenth-century Britain, defined as those owning between 300 and 3,000 acres (or receiving up to £3,000 a year in rent), comprised just over 12,000 members. Few worked their own land; it has been estimated that about 90 per cent of it was tenant-farmed. The bulk of small-scale family-based farming was done by the 240,000 or so who owned between 1 and 300 acres. As had been the case since medieval times, these small proprietors linked their landownership with a wide variety of ancillary sources of income. Many were craft manufacturers, whose activities by the 1880s were facilitated by an extensive railway network.

Of those categorized as 'landowners', 72 per cent were not so in the generally accepted sense. They were either domestic house owners or cottagers, owning between them less than half of 1 per cent of all the land itemized in Bateman's survey. A further 4.4 per cent was owned by institutions such as the church, or Oxford and Cambridge colleges. For practical purposes, therefore, land in private ownership was owned by only 255,263 of the United Kingdom's 34.8 million people, while 95 per cent of that quarter of a million owned less than 300 acres each, representing just under 26 per cent of the land.

What might be defined as 'great landownership' (total holdings in excess of 10,000 acres) was spread reasonably evenly across England, although, thanks to the Duke of Northumberland's immense holdings, the county which bore his name stood out with 51 per cent of its acreage held in 'great landownership'. At the other end of the spectrum, and understandably, given rental values and the pressure for building land, great landownership was less prominent in the southeast. Only 4 per cent of Middlesex, 9 per cent of Essex and 11 per cent of both Kent and Surrey was held in estates of more than 10,000 acres. Of England's 40 counties, 31 had between 15 and 30 per cent of their land held in estates of more than 10,000 acres.

II

The adjacent counties of Lancashire and Cheshire, and in particular the heavily urbanized areas of southeastern Lancashire and northeastern Cheshire, stand out of course as the birthplace of the world's first industrial revolution. They do not, however, stand out as regards great-landowner concentration. From my own analysis of Bateman, it appears that Cheshire had six landowners who owned more than 10,000 acres in the county;[23] their holdings totalled 77,131 acres (12.6 per cent of the total acreage). Lancashire had eight, totalling 151,818 acres (15 per cent of the total acreage) but dominated by the Earl of Derby's 57,000 acres, more than twice as much as was owned by his nearest rival, the Earl of Sefton.[24] Residential great landownership was substantial in Cheshire, where all of the county's leading six lived in the county, and in Lancashire, where all but the Duke of Devonshire of the leading eight were resident.

In the revised version of his survey Bateman included all owners of land in excess of 200 acres. In Lancashire and Cheshire 230 owners were thus identified, of whom 28 owned land in both counties. Unfortunately, only owners in excess of 300 acres had holdings in different counties separately identified. As might be expected, Lancashire's overall landownership figures are distorted by the presence of some 76,000 'cottager' owners of less than an acre. The great majority of these were town-dwellers from the industrialized southeast of the county. Their mean holding was less than a fifth of an acre.

The extent of social leadership, of course, is more effectively estimated by counting landowners resident in their respective counties. Many substantial proprietors owned land in various parts of the country. Making no allowance for the ambivalence of the returns in the 2,000–3,000-acre category, 65 landowners with 2,000 acres or more are known to have been resident in Lancashire and 38 in Cheshire. Of these, 10 residents in each county owned more than 10,000 acres in all, while 35 Lancashire and 22 Cheshire residents owned between 3,000 and 10,000 acres. Some of the largest proprietors of all were so because of holdings in Scotland. The Banks family of Winstanley Hall owned fewer than 3,000 acres near Wigan but almost 70,000 in remote Ross-shire. The Earl of Crawford and Balcarres lived at Haigh Hall with a home estate of 1,900 acres. The remainder of his property was ancestral land in Scotland.

The aristocracy and gentry of Lancashire and Cheshire, though modest in number, possessed enormous social influence. On these leading landed families devolved the major administrative and paternal responsibilities of the counties: the magistracies, responsibility for a substantial tenantry and rural workforce, either parliamentary duties or responsibility in the selection of MPs and parliamentary candidates. To these would be added myriad tasks and perquisites traditionally associated with being a great figure in the local community. In Lancashire, especially, such duties were likely to be onerous since substantial gentry figures were rather thin on the ground. The county had twice the national average of those owning between 1 and 100 acres (who would not share in these privileges and responsibilities) and a commensurately smaller proportion of those in the 300- to 3,000-acre bracket who might, for want of a better term, be described as 'middling gentry'.[25]

Lancashire's landed class engaged in a wide range of economic activities, and mobility both into and within it was pronounced. Land, industry and commerce were, to a substantial degree, interdependent and this helps to explain why the exercise of power in nineteenth-century Britain was attended with such limited hostility between the middle and upper classes.

Few of the larger Lancashire landowners by the last quarter of the nineteenth century had fortunes based exclusively on agricultural land. Land remained the basis of status, but a combination of poorer-quality soils than were commonly found in the midlands and the southeast and great opportunities for alternative investments made other prospects seem attractive. The Earl of Derby's gross income in 1900 was about £300,000 a year, getting on for half of which derived from urban rentals in Liverpool, Manchester, Salford, Bolton and Bury.[26] The Duke of Devonshire's immensely, if temporarily, profitable investments in the shipyards of Barrow and in the Furness railway company in the 1850s and 1860s have recently been brought to wider attention.[27] On a more modest scale, the Lilford family made a substantial fortune out of mining around Atherton, Westhoughton and Leigh between 1836 and 1892. This they used to buy Lilford Hall and move away from the spoil heaps to aristocratic Northamptonshire.[28]

In some ways the most dedicated entrepreneurial landowner in Lancashire in the nineteenth century was Alexander Lindsay, sixth Earl of Balcarres. In 1780, Balcarres married the heiress of the extensive coal-mining estate near Wigan held by the long-established Lancashire gentry family, the Bradshaighs. For the next 45 years, Balcarres committed himself to a huge range of industrial and entrepreneurial enterprises, from coal and cannel in Wigan and Wales to sugar in Jamaica, taking in a few opportunities opened up by young Mr Pitt to trade with France on the way.

Balcarres was an inveterate, and somewhat incautious, risk taker and, though his business acumen kept him afloat, he did not reap all the rewards of his enterprise. Nevertheless, he firmly believed that his business activities were much more than an individualist whim. He had a strong patriarchal sense and took the view that the future prosperity of the aristocracy was intimately bound up with industrial enterprise. As he wrote to his son in January 1822:

> The basis of our fortune is our coal and cannel mines, colliers we are and colliers we must ever remain. The value of our lands and buildings are deeply dependent on our colliery and we must never lose sight of the principle that coal must ever be the foundation of our prosperity.[29]

Coastal resort development provided tempting opportunities for established Lancashire landowners in the middle of the nineteenth century. The fortune of the Scarisbricks, an old Catholic gentry family from west Lancashire, was transformed from the 1840s when partnership with the Hesketh enabled the families to acquire 97 per cent of the land at North Meols. From this base, Southport developed dramatically as a fashionable resort.[30] The involvement of another, but more substantial, old Catholic family, the Cliftons, in the development of Lytham on the Fylde coast was also the route to greatly increased social and political influence in the second half of the nineteenth century.

Ample scope was afforded established landed families to diversify their economic activities, but the opportunities for movement *into* the landed classes in nineteenth-century Lancashire were even greater. Landownership was not a closed caste, and recent attempts to minimize the extent of social mobility in early modern Britain rest upon unacceptably narrow definitions of social exclusivity.[31] As R. O. Knapp's detailed researches into 118 Lancashire families who rose in status between 1540 and 1870 show, mobility was extensive.[32]

No fewer than 55 of Knapp's 'rising families' came to prominence towards the end of his period of study, that is, after 1760. Whereas successful farming or small landowning families could achieve elite status by land purchase in earlier centuries, this was no longer so easy from the late eighteenth, when both the purchase price and subsequent investment requirements to maintain profitability increased costs dramatically. Those who had made their fortunes in industry or commerce found things easier. For them, 35-years purchase, which is what Lancashire land regularly cost during the Napoleonic wars, was manageable for businessmen anxious to establish themselves in polite society. During the boom of the 1860s, land became even more expensive. Henry Ward, a cotton magnate in Blackburn whose family had been obscure local yeomen, laid out more than 45-years purchase on 2,200 acres in Clayton-le-Dale in 1866.

Twenty-five of Knapp's post-1760 rising landed families owed their success to cotton textiles in south or east Lancashire. County society had to accommodate itself to rough and not-so-rough entrepreneurs with the arrival of magnates like the Bazleys, Gregs and Woods. For some, the urbanizing northwest was not good enough. Lancashire land was only a staging post on a journey of geographical, as well as social, mobility southwards to warmer climes and gentler manners. The Gregs of Styal first bought land at Reddish and then moved to Coles Park, Herefordshire. Sir Thomas Bazley, who had been chairman of the Manchester Chamber of Commerce and had replaced a fellow Anti-Corn Law Leaguer, Sir John Potter, as the town's MP from 1858 to 1862, retained 5,000 acres in Lancashire when he moved to Moreton-in-Marsh (Gloucestershire) later in the 1860s. Clearly, the industrial revolution, in creating new sources of wealth, diminished neither the attraction of land to those in search of status and respectability nor its availability, if at high prices. It was the established yeoman who was priced out of further consolidatory purchases in the middle of the nineteenth century.

One of the most direct ways in which power was exercised in the nineteenth century was through the office of Justice of the Peace. JPs in the eighteenth century had fulfilled a huge variety of both judicial and administrative tasks. They dispensed justice at local Quarter Sessions; they adjudicated on poor law relief entitlement; they might intervene in wage disputes between master and servant; they licensed alehouses; they supervised highway repairs. The beginnings of the administrative reform movement in the nineteenth century did not at first reduce their influence. Some survived even the advent of elected county councils in 1888. Justices of the Peace were the only agencies of authority which many ordinary folk ever saw. Admission to the judicial bench was a sure indication of status and worth.

Only landowners could become JPs. The statutory requirement for service was ownership of land worth at least £100 a year or, as a useful device for training up the sons of the great to a life of influence and service to the community, the reversion to an estate of £300. Admission to the ranks was carefully controlled. As land values increased sharply at the end of the eighteenth century, Lords Lieutenant became choosy about appointing those who only just qualified. More owner-occupiers would not normally do. Humphrey Senhouse, a leading Cumberland landowner, smartly advised his Lord Lieutenant, Lord Lonsdale, in 1831 of local freeholders: 'There is not a single permanent resident either in Keswick or its vicinity whom I think properly qualified for the office of acting magistrate.'[33]

The going rate for magistracy in the 1820s and 1830s depended much on regional variation but seems to have been of the order of £1,000 to £2,000 a year in land. The only numerically significant exceptions to the landed monopoly until the 1840s were beneficed clergy of the Church of England, and even they were life-tenants of their benefices. Anglican clergy were widely regarded as reliable, more than averagely conscientious, by no means too soft on 'sensitive' rural crimes such as poaching and other infringements of the Game Laws, securely anti-reformist when necessary and anyway, in the better-endowed rectories from which they were drawn, likely to be close relatives of the aristocracy and leading gentry.[34]

In predominantly rural counties, which were still the great majority until the end of the nineteenth century, landed domination of the bench survived intact throughout the century. In Cheshire, not only did landowners continue to rule rural society, but their influence in new towns such as Crewe, the railway centre, and Birkenhead, the new shipping town, was most extensive down to 1888.[35] In Parliament, landed influence blocked until 1888 all attempts to establish locally elected county councils with wide and integrated responsibility. Suggestions that the property qualification for magistracy be removed were not received kindly either. The fact that such a qualification comfortably outlasted that for MPs, which was abandoned in 1858 – the first of the Chartists' Six Points to be accepted – shows the importance which a landowners' parliament attached to local leadership.

In Lancashire, however, different guidelines necessarily applied. As late as 1831, the county magistracy contained only one industrialist, a brewer. Problems of public order and a rapid development of industrial wealth came together in the 1830s to effect a dramatic change in the overpopulated and under-policed Salford hundred. In this decade, 61 cotton manufacturers were put on the bench and a further 47 were appointed from mercantile or commercial backgrounds. By 1851, entrepreneurs provided 85 of the 156 magistrates in the division. By contrast, 85 per cent of magistrates in the Leyland hundred at the same date were landowners.[36]

While John Walton has noted that the 'vast majority' of Lancashire's magistrates on the eve of local government reform were 'industrialists, merchants, bankers and professionals',[37] this certainly did not mean that their influence was evenly spread across the county. It largely reflected the need of thickly populated areas for many magistrates. The paucity of contests for seats on the new Lancashire county council in the 1890s and the presence on that council of some of the longest-established landed gentry families is further evidence of propertied accommodations and the relative rarity of conflict between land and capital.

The influx of industrial and trading wealth did not pass without adverse comment, however. During one of the many parliamentary debates which touched on the respective spheres of influence of land and industry, the Tory MP for North Lancashire, J. Wilson Patten, noted gloomily in 1863 that his county could now boast only 200 landowners on the bench, whereas the manufacturers had 400. Separation of influence could assuage injured pride, however, and in rural Lancashire the landed interest maintained more or less unchallenged control over the daily lives of its citizens. Probably a greater worry was the growing inequity of political representation among county magistrates. Appointment to the bench was a jealously guarded element of political patronage which increasingly favoured the Tory Party as its hold on county seats in Parliament tightened. In Lancashire, where appointments were the responsibility of the Chancellor of the Duchy of Lancaster and thus even more directly political, the prosperous shipping magnate William Brown, who represented South Lancashire as a Liberal, complained that the chancellor 'did not seem disposed, as he ought to be, to appoint magistrates recommended by the Liberal party'.[38]

The themes of separation and accommodation are also well accented in the parliamentary history of these two counties up to the second Reform Act of 1867 and even, though the emergence of a sizeable working-class electorate altered perspectives substantially, beyond it. Before 1832 in Britain, as is generally known, the distribution of parliamentary seats bore little relation to either population or property. The norm was for seats either to be directly owned or, in the case of many counties, indirectly controlled by great magnates. Lancashire and Cheshire conformed to this pattern closely enough, though the existence of Lancaster, Liverpool and Preston as three of only two dozen or so parliamentary boroughs with electorates in excess of 2,000 made for more disputed elections and a greater general liveliness than was entirely good for the bank balances of the political protagonists.

Even in rapidly industrializing Preston, which saw 9 contested elections out of a possible 13 between 1780 and 1831, however, great magnate influence was strong. One of the two seats was held on Derby patronage, in the persons first of the earl's son and later of his brother-in-law. The other seat was held for much of the period by a self-made cotton manufacturer from Bolton, John Horrocks, whose firm was from the 1790s the largest employer in the town. Horrocks bought himself onto the Preston Corporation and thence, with corporation backing, obtained nomination for the parliamentary seat. The Earl of Derby tried to destroy this upstart, first by founding his own cotton mill, which failed, and then by supporting Horrocks's main rival. Only when Horrocks obstinately refused to fold under magnate pressure did the earl agree with Preston Corporation to share the borough seats between them. It was Lancashire's first political accommodation between cotton and land.[39]

Elsewhere, matters were less contentious. Newton-le-Willows, a borough which would be disenfranchised with parliamentary reform in 1832, had only about fifty electors. Since Newton was controlled by the Legh family of Lyme who filled it with family or relatives, those electors were never called upon actually to elect. The 100 electors of Clitheroe remained similarly undisturbed and Wigan had elections only when the Balcarres coal interest superseded the Leighs of nearby Hindley in 1820.

Most prestige attached to the two Lancashire county seats. Lancashire's two members had been drawn, by long-standing agreement, one from the Derby family and one from the local gentry. For most of the period before 1832, the gentry representative was John Blackburne of Hale Hall near Widnes, owner of 3,000 acres. Only twice between 1780 and 1832 did Lancashire's 8,000 county electors have the opportunity to vote.

Cheshire, which had only four seats before 1832, was divided between the county's leading landowners, more or less by agreement. The county seat was shared between the Egertons (one of the wealthiest commoner families in England), Crewes, Cholmondleys and Davenports. All owned more than 10,000 acres; all resided in Cheshire; all were firm Tories. The most influential Cheshire family of all, the Grosvenors of Eaton Hall whose leading member was Marquis of Westminster, lavished their attentions on the borough of Chester, one of whose seats they held rock-solidly in the Whig interest without a break from 1715 to 1874.

Before 1832, land was effectively all that mattered in the distribution of parliamentary seats. After the first Reform Act, matters were more complicated, partly because new industrial and commercial interests were enfranchised, partly because such interests often needed clear delineation from nearby landed influence and partly because of the increasing polarization of politics into Whig-Liberal and Conservative camps. Lancashire made a net gain of nine borough and two county seats; Cheshire, in addition to two more county seats, welcomed the silk town of Macclesfield and the cotton town of Stockport to its parliamentary complement.[40]

The extent to which electoral power remained vested in old, landed hands may in part be gauged by the number of parliamentary elections which, following the pre-1832 norm, remained uncontested. Only just over a half of all constituencies, on average, had a contested election on the nine opportunities which general elections afforded between the first two Reform Acts of 1832 and 1867.[41] The new, urban seats of Lancashire and Cheshire polled on an average of 7.3 occasions out of this possible 9. Blackburn and Stockport had an election on every occasion and Bolton, Macclesfield, Manchester and Rochdale missed only 1.

Rural Lancashire and Cheshire told a different story. Though county electorates were generally larger on average – North Lancashire's was six times as large as Bolton's in 1832 and virtually the same size as Manchester's – polling took place only on an average of 2.5 occasions. No contest at all was held in the overwhelmingly rural seat of North Lancashire. Local election committees comprising leading landed proprietors organized the nominations and, by 1852, they had agreed to run an established Tory squire, J. Wilson Patten (later created Lord Winmarleigh by Disraeli), in harness with a

Whig magnate. Guided, no doubt, by the enormous recent Devonshire investment in the boom town of Barrow, the unopposed Liberal MP from 1857 to 1868 was Lord Spencer Cavendish, later better known as the Marquis of Hartington and eighth Duke of Devonshire.[42]

On closer study, however, this use of polling frequency may be misleading. If the relative absence of elections in rural seats indicates the need for compromise within the landed elite in the interests of economy, their relative frequency in industrial Lancashire and Cheshire may reflect initial jockeying for position within an alternative elite. Electoral contests in the middle of the nineteenth century often indicated power struggles *within* the middle classes and not always across orthodox party lines. The famous Manchester election of 1857, for example, saw the ejection of the sitting 'Manchester school' radicals Thomas Gibson and John Bright, in the intellectual heartland of *laissez-faire* liberalism, by chauvinistically inclined Palmerstonian liberals.[43] It should have indicated to Bright, though in fact it did not, the futility of mounting a frontal attack on the aristocracy via land reform campaigns when he could not carry the middle classes with him. The survival of the aristocracy at the centre of political life throughout Victorian Britain owes more than a little to the self-confident and recurrently assured certainty with which the intellectual middle classes kicked the football of class hostility into their own net.

On the other hand, it might be objected that the football net was anyway placed at the bottom of a fairly steep gradient. Just as much new wealth in the seventeenth and eighteenth centuries found its way into land as the necessary qualification for power and prestige, so nineteenth-century mill owners, whether Liberal or Conservative, who did not choose to buy large tracts of land might nevertheless demand political recognition in their urban localities by seeking nomination for a borough seat. If successful, they stood a good chance of assimilation within the existing power structure as 'mill-owning squires'.

Some of these, like the Tory William Feilden, who represented Blackburn in the 1830s and 1840s, came from an established local landed background. Others, like the Liberal Charles Hindley, who represented Ashton-under-Lyne from 1835 until his death in 1857, and the Macclesfield silk manufacturer John Brocklehurst, who was the town's MP at the same time, did not.[44] Some, like the Feildens and Hornbys in Blackburn or Henry Ashworth at Turton near Bolton, were paternalist employers seeking to recreate in an urban environment both the caring and the controls which they believed to be the bedrock of deference and acquiescence in rural England.[45] Others, like Ashton's puritanical cotton-spinning magnate Hugh Mason, relied on the iron laws of political economy.[46] Either way, captains of industry demanded recognition from, and assimilation into, an existing political elite, entry into which had widened both practically and psychologically in 1832.

Thus, although Patrick Joyce's calculations show parliamentary candidates from industrial and commercial backgrounds in the northwest between 1860 and 1890 outnumbering those from the landed elite by two to one, it should not necessarily be inferred that the new men were challenging the existing power structure.[47] However distasteful it might have been to Cobden, Bright, John Stuart Mill and their lesser-known land-reforming colleagues like John Howard and George Argo, industrial wealth in Lancashire did not necessarily entail anti-aristocratic hostility.

Land purchase remained attractive to businessmen and industrialists until the great depression in arable prices began in the mid-1870s. Only then, and almost for the first time in modern British history, did landed property seem an undesirable speculation, although rates of return had been lower on land than on many other forms of investment for many years. If land were not purchased, furthermore, surrogate forms of social pre-eminence, like the creation of a model industrial estate or the holding of aldermanic or other civil office, were now more prized. This theme could be embellished in many different ways but it should be reiterated that industrialists had no need to take the aristocracy on. The transition from feudalism to capitalism, if such a crude and misleading model is applicable at all, is certainly not operable with inevitable class conflict built into it. In Britain at least, too many 'feudalists' were themselves capitalists with extensive mining, banking, or urban development interests which they carefully nurtured.

For their part, 'capitalists' could choose either assimilation within, or separation from, landed society with ever fewer risks to their status and self-regard. Some, no doubt, considered themselves superior to idle landlords. In their turn, representatives of established county families, like the Cliftons of Lytham, might evince county hauteur and find the driving of 'bargains' by mere 'cotton spinners' disagreeable. As Lady Clifton remarked in 1868: 'We have the misfortune to belong to a county where merchants and wealth are far above, in their own opinion, the aristocracy and the old landed gentry', but Lancashire merchants could live with such flea-bites.[48]

For land reformers towards the end of the nineteenth century, beached after the never particularly strong tide of class conflict between land and industry had ebbed, it was all too perplexing. Like frustrated intellectuals in all generations, they fell back on the last refuge of the scholar: the plea for re-education in the ways of rationality. James Howard MP chided tenant farmers with a lack of understanding of their own interest. Did they not know that their 'stock in trade is liable to confiscation'? Were they not aware that 'the little band of law reformers in their efforts to bring about needful changes have received but little aid from popular support'?[49] The Scottish farmer George Argo admitted the 'great indifference' which accompanied discussions of the land question but asserted that the indifference was

> exactly proportional to the ignorance and prejudice that exist respecting it. Were the people alive to their interest in the matter, did they not see the

degraded and degrading position our country holds on the question, as it appears to dispassionate observers who have given attention to the subject, they would demand land reform with a voice that would cause the most sacred recesses of obstructive stolidity to quake.[50]

Such aristocratic quaking as there was came in response to inexorable economic pressure, not to anti-landlord lectures. As over political questions in 1832 and 1867, the landed classes proved themselves far less 'obstructively stolid' than they were depicted in the hostile caricature of liberal radicals. The depression of agricultural prices and the consequential decline in land values, much more severe in the arable areas of the south and east than in the northwest, but far from negligible even there, induced Parliament to pass legislation which sanctified custom between landlord and tenants. The Agricultural Holdings Act of 1883 put teeth into an earlier piece of legislation from 1875 by ensuring that landowners compensated tenants for improvements made to their land during a tenancy. The Ground Game Act of 1881 removed one of the few persistent national irritants in relations between landlords and tenants by allowing tenants to destroy rabbits and hares on their farms without first asking the landowner's permission. Potentially more favourable to the land reformers, yet going much less far than they wanted, was the Settled Land Act of 1882 which put the management of estates into the hands of the tenant for life, as if it were indeed a freehold. It even allowed the outright sale of land given certain safeguards.

The problem for landlords, however, was not how to defend their remaining privileges of settlement, primogeniture and entail against radical attack but how to find purchasers for estates which, because of the slump in prices (English wheat declined from about 56 shillings per quarter in the early 1870s to less than 25 shillings in the mid-1890s), were disastrously unprofitable. The usual palliatives of 'nursing' ailing tenants by rent abatements and the cancellation of arrears were no longer sufficient. Landlords across swathes of England were forced to take land into hand for which they had no use, and to await more favourable opportunities later to sell it off – usually to sitting tenants. This happened, spurred both by the first genuinely anti-landlord legislation – Lloyd George's in 1909 – and by the modest recovery of prices before the First World War.

Sales of estates proceeded apace after 1918 and it was not until after the end of the First World War, in which, symbolically, so many sons of the gentry and aristocracy were killed, that the great age of landlord power finally ended. Between 1914 and 1980, the proportion of land in owner occupation leapt up from 14 per cent to 65 per cent.[51] Farms of between 100 and 500 acres became much more common as the twentieth century developed. The old aristocratic estates, upon which so much political and social influence had ridden during the nineteenth century, were retrenched and rationalized in the twentieth, though rarely entirely sold off.

Economic success for titled families necessitated ever greater reliance on business. This development was satirized by W. S. Gilbert in *The Gondoliers* as early as 1889, in the figure of the Duke of Plaza Toro, supposedly Spanish but in caricature an English nobleman fallen upon hard times who hawks his title around the boardrooms of the City of London, exploiting the supposed softness of the English for a title. Paradoxically, as its economic fortunes waned, the numbers of the peerage increased with many more creations from the worlds of business, industry and, latterly, even the performing arts. There were more than 1,200 titles in existence in 1980, compared with just over 500 in 1900 and only about 170 in 1780. Certain established estates, like Bryanston and Stowe, were converted into schools while others, such as Alton Towers and the Peel family residence at Drayton Manor, near Tamworth (Staffordshire), became pleasure parks. In some sense, therefore, though with precisely the opposite effect to those intended by the land reformers of the 1880s, the land was given back to the people.

The primacy of land, and the power which went with it, therefore, was ended by the collapse of prices and not by direct bourgeois challenge. In Lancashire and Cheshire, at least, power continued to be exercised through wealth and by many well-established and acknowledged social institutions and reciprocities at least until the end of the nineteenth century. The industrial revolution, even in its heartland, brought far fewer conflicts between landed and bourgeois forms of wealth than was once thought. Though some regional segregation was seen, with a predominantly bourgeois magistracy, for example, in southeast Lancashire, the social influence of land proved remarkably resilient in early industrial England.

NOTES

1 N. F. R. Crafts, *British Economic Growth during the Industrial Revolution* (Oxford: 1985) and 'British economic growth, 1700–1831, a review of the evidence', *Economic History Review*, 2nd series, xxxvi (1983), pp. 177–99; E. A. Wrigley, *Continuity, Chance and Change: The Character of the Industrial Revolution in England* (Cambridge: 1988).

2 The protagonist of a briefly fashionable view was J. C. D. Clark, *English Society, 1688–1832* (Cambridge: 1985) and *Revolution and Rebellion: State and Society in the Seventeenth and Eighteenth Centuries* (Cambridge: 1986). The 'orthodox' view is perhaps best represented by J. Cannon, *Aristocratic Century* (Cambridge: 1984) and H. T. Dickinson, *Liberty and Property: Political Ideology in Eighteenth-Century Britain* (London: 1977).

3 A. S. Foord, 'The waning of the "influence of the Crown" ', *English Historical Review*, lxii (1947), pp. 484–507. N. Gash, *Lord Liverpool* (London: 1984).

4 See, among an extensive literature, J. Cannon, *Parliamentary Reform, 1640–1832* (Cambridge: 1973) and M. Brock, *The Great Reform Act* (London: 1973). For a contemporary statement suggesting that things remained much as they had been, see C. Greville, *Memoirs*, 8 vols (London: 1888), Vol. III, p. 30.

5 Brock, *Great Reform Act*, pp. 314–36; E. J. Evans, *The Forging of the Modern State: Early Industrial Britain, 1783–1870* (London: 1983), pp. 212–18.

6 N. McCord, *The Anti-Corn Law League, 1838–46* (London: 1958); D. A. Hamer, *The Politics of Electoral Pressure* (Hassocks, Sussex: 1977), pp. 58–90.

7 G. E. Mingay (ed.), *The Agrarian History of England and Wales*, Vol. 6, *1750–1850* (Cambridge: 1989) [hereafter *Ag. Hist. 6*], p. 31.

8 D. C. Moore, 'The landed aristocracy', in G. E. Mingay, *The Victorian Countryside* (London: 1981), pp. 367–82; *Ag. Hist. 6*, p. 915.

9 M. Girouard, *The Victorian Country House* (Oxford: 1971), p. 2.

10 D. C. Itzkovitz, *Peculiar Privilege: a Social History of Foxhunting, 1783–1885* (Hassocks, Sussex: 1977).

11 ibid., p. 176; F. M. L. Thompson, *English Landed Society in the Nineteenth Century* (London: 1983), pp. 144–6.

12 J. Cannon (ed.), *The Whig Ascendancy* (London: 1981), p. 102; G. I. T. Machin, *The Catholic Question in English Politics, 1820–30* (Oxford: 1984); *John Bull* (London), 21 April 1828, p. 124.

13 W. O. Chadwick, *The Victorian Church*, Vol. I (London: 1966); Olive J. Brose, *Church and Parliament: the Reshaping of the Church of England 1828–60* (Stanford, Calif.: 1959), esp. pp. 120–77.

14 E. J. Evans, *The Contentious Tithe: the Tithe Problem and English Agriculture, 1750–1850* (London: 1976), pp. 1–15; P. Virgin, *The Church in an Age of Negligence, 1700–1840* (Cambridge: 1989), pp. 134–70, 276–84. See also A. Haig, *The Victorian Clergy* (London: 1974).

15 E. J. Evans, 'Some reasons for the growth of anti-clericalism in England, *c.* 1750–1850', *Past and Present*, 66 (1975), pp. 84–109; W. R. Ward, 'The tithe question in England in the early nineteenth century', *Journal of Ecclesiastical History*, xvi (1965), pp. 67–81; Virgin, *The Church in an Age of Negligence*, pp. 109–30.

16 F. M. L. Thompson, 'Landowners and the rural community', in Mingay, *The Victorian Countryside*, pp. 457–74.

17 J. P. D. Dunbabin, *Rural Discontent in Nineteenth-Century Britain* (London: 1974), pp. 62–129 and 'The revolt of the field', *Past and Present*, 26 (1963), pp. 68–97; P. L. R. Horn, *Joseph Arch* (Kineton, Oxfordshire: 1971) and 'Agricultural trade unionism and emigration, 1872–81', *Historical Journal*, xv (1972), pp. 87–102.

18 G. C. Broderick, *English Land and English Landlords* (London: 1881), pp. 457–8.

19 Cobden to John Bright, 1 October 1849 in J. Morley (ed.), *The Life of Richard Cobden*, 2 vols (London: 1896), Vol. ii, p. 53. See also 'America' in *The Political Writings of Richard Cobden*, 2 vols (London: 1903; rpt 1969), pp. 117–18, in which he castigated 'displays of wanton extravagance' and 'exhibitions of prodigality and insolence' by an 'idle, debauched and worthless' aristocracy.

20 J. Thorold Rogers (ed.), *Speeches of John Bright*, 2 vols (London: 1868), Vol. ii, p. 53. On Bright's specific proposals for free trade in land see *Public Letters of John Bright* (London: 1895; rpt 1969), p. 187: Bright to G. W. Sanders, 2 November 1873.

21 J. Bateman, *Great Landowners of Great Britain* (London: 1883), p. 501–28.

22 *Ag. Hist. 6*, p. 619.

23 Bateman, *Great Landowners, passim.*

24 ibid., pp. 127, 401.

25 ibid., *passim.*

26 R. S. Churchill, *Lord Derby, King of Lancashire* (London: 1959), p. 95.

27 D. Cannadine, 'The landowner as millionaire: the finances of the Duke of Devonshire, *c.* 1800–1926', *Agricultural History Review*, xxv (1977), pp. 77–91 and *Lords and Landlords: the Aristocracy and the Towns* (Leicester: 1980), esp. pp. 285–92.

28 G. Rogers, 'Social and economic change on Lancashire landed estates during the nineteenth century', PhD thesis, University of Lancaster, 1981, p. 351.

29 John Rylands Library, Manchester, Crawford MSS 23/14/10, cited in S. Walker, 'The eighteenth-century landowner as entrepreneur: the business career of Alexander Lindsay, sixth Earl of Balcarres, 1785–1825', PhD thesis, University of Lancaster, 1988, p. 108.

30 J. Liddle, 'Estate management and land reform politics: the Hesketh and Scarisbrick families and the making of Southport, 1842–1914', in D. Cannadine (ed.), *Patricians, Power and Politics* (Leicester: 1982), pp. 134–66.

31 Notably by L. Stone and J. C. Stone, *An Open Elite? England, 1540–1880* (Oxford: 1984). For critiques of this view, see E. Spring and D. Spring, 'The English landed estate, 1540–1879 – a review', *Albion*, xvii (1985), pp. 149–66 and L. Bonfield, 'Affective families, open elites

and strict family settlement in early modern England', *Economic History Review*, 2nd series, xxxix (1986), pp. 341–54.

32 R. O. Knapp, 'The making of a landed elite: social mobility in Lancashire society', PhD thesis, University of Lancaster, 1970, esp. pp. 436–43.

33 Thompson, *English Landed Society*, p. 110.

34 Evans, 'Some reasons for the growth of anti-clericalism in England'; D. Foster, 'Class and county government in early nineteenth-century Lancashire', *Northern History*, ix (1974), p. 51.

35 W. H. Chaloner, *The Social and Economic Development of Crewe, 1780-1923* (Manchester: 1950), pp. 104–221; J. M. Lee, *Social Leaders and Public Persons* (Oxford: 1963), p. 5.

36 D. Foster, 'The changing social and political complexion of the Lancashire Magistracy', PhD thesis, University of Lancaster, 1971, pp. 274–7.

37 J. K. Walton, *Lancashire: A Social History, 1588–1939* (Manchester: 1987), p. 223.

38 Foster, 'Lancashire magistracy', p. 234.

39 R. G. Thorne (ed.), *History of Parliament: The House of Commons, 1790–1820*, 5 vols (London: 1986), Vol. ii, pp. 236–7.

40 Brock, *Great Reform Act*, pp. 160–230; H. J. Hanham, *The Nineteenth-Century Constitution* (Cambridge: 1969), pp. 262–8.

41 Evans, *Forging of the Modern State*, p. 384.

42 J. Vincent and M. Stenton (eds), *McCalmon's Parliamentary Poll Book: British Election Results, 1832–1918* (Hassocks, Sussex: 1971), p. 162 and Cannadine, *Lords and Landlords*, pp. 84–7. Marquis of Hartington was the title bestowed upon the eldest son of, and heir to, the Duke of Devonshire; Cavendish was, of course, the family name.

43 K. G. Robbins, *John Bright* (London: 1978), pp. 125–6; F. W. S. Craig, *British Parliamentary Election Results, 1832–85* (London: 1977), p. 206.

44 ibid., pp. 31, 49, 198.

45 P. Joyce, *Work, Society and Politics: The Culture of the Factory in Later Victorian England* (Hassocks, Sussex: 1980), pp. 9–16.

46 Walton, *Lancashire*, pp. 234, 245.

47 Joyce, *Work, Society and Politics*, pp. 201–39.

48 G. Rogers, 'Lancashire landowners and the Great Agricultural Depression', *Northern History*, xxii (1986), p. 286.

49 J. Howard, *A Paper on Impediments to the Development of British Husbandry* (Bedford: 1873), p. 7.

50 G. Argo, *Our Land Laws: Or a Plea for Land Reform* (Aberdeen and Edinburgh: 1877), p. 28. See also the case for 'informing' English farmers of the malign influence of the land laws, in C. Whitehead, *The Evil Influence of Entail and Strict Settlement upon Agriculture* (London: 1883), p. 42.

51 J. V. Beckett, *The Aristocracy in England, 1660–1914* (Oxford: 1986), pp. 474–81 and Thompson, *English Landed Society*, pp. 333–4.

8

Landownership and power in nineteenth-century Ireland: the decline of an elite

K. Theodore Hoppen

Because the power of landlords in Ireland experienced substantial diminution in the last quarter of the nineteenth century it is tempting to dissect the resulting corpse with the sole intention of laying bare such dormant pathological weaknesses as might have rendered the eventual collapse probable, even inevitable. But while this is a reasonable procedure in the sense that all developments grow out of certain potentialities, yet the most striking aspects of landlordism during the two decades which followed the Great Famine of 1845–9 were strength, prosperity and optimism. Until the 1870s it would, indeed, be quite misleading to exaggerate the problems of landownership or to see proprietors as already moving remorselessly down the escalators of power, influence and wealth. Rather was the earlier period one of advance as well as retreat, of consolidation as well as withdrawal, of success as well as failure. This does not mean that combustible materials were ever in short supply. But a good deal of complicated manipulation was required before elements separately safe and controllable could begin to combine into a compound capable of biting deep into the central core of landed confidence and power.

That they would ever so combine was for long neither obvious nor probable. Just as wealth and sociopolitical influence constituted the twin and connected pillars of proprietorial strength, so any effective attack required the marriage of economic and other considerations. Not only was this easier said than done but even its very perception took time. The most notable characteristic of popular politics in the first half of the century was the almost unbridgeable gulf which lay between those seeking agrarian and those seeking constitutional change. Until the Famine the widespread, though sporadic, unrest which was a recognized feature of Irish rural life and which since 1760, had manifested itself especially in the activities of secret societies was predominantly localist, fissiparous and uncoordinated.[1] The complaints varied according to region and to time, but were usually specific rather than

Map 8.1 Irish landownership in the 1870s. The numbers under the names of the counties indicate the number of owners of land in that county over one acre. The numbers after the owners' names are the number of acres they held in the county.

Source: Finlay Dun, *Landlords and Tenants in Ireland*, London: Longmans, Green, 1881, frontispiece.

general: excessive rents, evictions, the shortage of potato ground for labourers, tithes, employment and so forth. They involved no single-minded assault on landlords or landlordism as such, but instead reflected tensions between all sections of rural society, between labourers and farmers as much as between proprietors and anyone else.

Although the social arrangements of the countryside were extremely complicated they were ultimately based upon the existence of three identifiable, if often overlapping, groups: landlords, tenant farmers and landless labourers.[2] All ranged along a wide spectrum. Landlords could own anything from a few hundred to many thousands of acres. Farmers could be substantial men employing hired help or (more typically) occupiers of 10 or 15 acres worked entirely by themselves and their families. Some labourers regularly rented tiny patches of potato ground *from farmers* by annual agreement (an obvious source of tension); many others depended exclusively on regular or irregular wages from those needing hired help. Thus labourers often had an 'interest' in occupying land, farmers often let out some of the land they themselves rented, while so many proprietors were farmers in their own right that demesnes and home farms probably accounted for not less than 15 per cent of all agricultural land.[3] Such blurring at the edges makes precise estimates of the size of each group difficult, especially in the early years when statistics of any kind were few and unreliable. What cannot, however, be doubted is that a significant shift in relative numbers took place in the decade after the Famine and that this shift was of enormous significance for the fate of the landowning community. Within an overall context of general population decline (from over 8 million in 1841 to less than 4 million in 1901) several important developments stand out. While the proportion of all occupied males engaged in farming activities fell from more than seven tenths in 1841 to three fifths in 1881, the proportion of all such so engaged living outside towns of 2,000 and more inhabitants remained steady. Within this sector, however, farmers came to form a steadily increasing proportion, while labourers declined, not only absolutely but relatively also. Though the data have their complications it would seem that, while in 1841 farmers and their 'assisting relatives' constituted only about two fifths of the occupied male farming population, already by 1881 this had risen to more than three fifths, that is, to a majority. What this meant was that the post-Famine period was, above all, a time of growing demographic triumph on the part of farmers – as opposed to labourers. Economic power was added to numerical growth in that the size of farms increased (by 1891 some 32 per cent were over 30 acres as opposed to 17 per cent in 1841) and farmers, though not until *after* the Land War of 1879–82, were able to secure for themselves a larger slice of the agricultural cake. Thus, while during the two decades beginning in the mid-1850s total rent in real terms rose slightly and gross farming profits fell by about an eighth, thereafter economic relativities turned somersault as, between the mid-1870s and 1905–10, rent declined but farming profits in real terms notched up an enormous increase of 70 per cent or thereabouts.[4]

This did not of course mean that all farmers suddenly found themselves in a situation of comfort. Not only were conditions still often harsh but the improvement was far from evenly distributed. And, in any case, the temporal lag between the farmers' growing demographic importance and their later economic triumphs gave an edge to those discontents which many of them felt during the immediate post-Famine years when landlords were proving themselves relatively more successful in benefiting from the rising agricultural prices of the time. While, therefore, during the first half of the century proprietors had been only one among many targets of attack and had faced a divided agrarian population in which farmers and labourers pursued different ends and were often locked in mutual combat, thereafter a more simple and potentially dangerous antagonism between farmers and landlords became the norm as labourers were rendered ever more socially marginal and politically ineffective. It was this development which, above all, made it possible to mount that marriage between economic and political agitations which had been so lacking in earlier years. But before this could happen both agitations had to be defined in new ways and rendered effective by new methods of participation and propaganda.

It has in recent years become almost an orthodoxy to see the Famine as providing little more than a continuation of social and economic changes which had been in train at least since the agricultural collapse brought about by the ending of the Napoleonic wars.[5] And it is true that the subdivision of holdings was less severe before the late 1840s than was once thought and that, in consequence, consolidation thereafter was neither immediate nor extreme. The rise in population too had come to a virtual halt by the year 1840 and perhaps even a little earlier. But the initial insistence by revisionists that a significant movement away from tillage and towards the kind of pasture farming which became so important in the late nineteenth century had already begun between 1815 and 1845 has failed to gain anything like universal acceptance.[6] Whatever else may have happened there can, however, be no doubt as to the enormity of population loss by emigration and death, the subsequent shift away from labour-intensive tillage to capital-intensive cattle and sheep farming, the gradual consolidation of holdings, and the ever greater standing of the farmer within rural society. But the Famine also had an effect upon the landowning sector. Although the size of this elite group in the early years of the century cannot be precisely established, reasonable estimates suggest that it may have stood at between 8,000 and 10,000 proprietors in all.[7] If this was the case it seems likely that some significant consolidation took place thereafter among those who owned the soil to match that which is known to have occurred among those who rented and farmed it. Tentative calculations suggest that by the 1870s a greater proportion of the land belonged to the largest proprietors than had been the case thirty years before.[8]

In addition, an official inquiry in 1870 for the first time put numerical flesh upon the landed community. In that year only 3,754 persons held estates of more than 1,000 acres (a reasonable if rough and ready bottom line for the maintenance of full landed status) while another 2,683 with between 500 and 1,000 acres stood just outside the gates of complete acceptance and recognition. What the data also reveal is the pyramidal structure of the landowning class: the 303 with at least 10,000 acres possessed more than a third of all agricultural land, while the 741 with over 5,000 acres owned almost a half.[9] And this state of things held good also on the tenant side where in 1871 the tiny minority of farmers (less than 6 per cent) with holdings above 100 acres actually occupied two fifths of the land.[10] Within both groups, therefore, wide differences existed which inevitably resulted in tensions, jealousies and oscillating patterns of influence. What is, however, clear is that the proprietorial community, though often riven by disputes over electoral politics, estate practices, rental behaviour and the like, was (in part simply because of its much smaller size) for many years far more coherent as a social and political entity than the tenant community where the larger men – often operators of extensive grazing ranches – were regarded with great suspicion by their less substantial fellows. And it was only when something like unity could be achieved among farmers as a whole that really effective and general tenant action proved sustainable for even short periods.

What the Famine did for the overall position of Irish landowners was to act as a Darwinian agent weeding out the weak and reinforcing the strong. Despite much contemporary and later folklore many landlords had become financially emaciated by the 1840s. In some cases this was undoubtedly the result of simple extravagance, in others of inefficiency and neglect, in yet others of an inability to realize maximum realistic rents because of the delayed falling-in of middleman leases by which in the late eighteenth century large tracts had been let out for fixed amounts to so-called middlemen who then sublet to a hierarchy of small farmers at variable (and often rising) rents.[11] Already in 1844 the Courts of Chancery and Exchequer had 1,322 estates in their charge with a total rental of £904,000.[12] Yet already too, Irish landlords as a group had come to be seen as rapacious, extravagant and masters of limitless wealth. This was a belief held not only by tenants and by nationalist politicians but also by many of the leading British statesmen of the day, so that, when the Famine occurred, the prime minister, Lord John Russell, was far from alone in his initial determination to ensure that the landed community should be made to pay for relief and that the government should give as little as possible for something he believed to be the result of proprietorial greed and mismanagement. Certainly many English and Scottish politicians themselves owned land in Ireland. Certainly too there continued to be a good deal of feeling that attacks on property rights across the Irish Sea might prove an exportable commodity. But after the 1840s Irish proprietors as a body never enjoyed total support at either Westminster or Whitehall (indeed one English Liberal chief secretary in 1855 expressed the view that those who behaved 'outrageously' virtually 'deserved to be murdered') – something too easily forgotten in an age when a belief in the sacredness of property constituted perhaps the dominant creed of those in control of the state.[13]

This does not, of course, mean that landlords were without power or wealth. By the 1850s, when the weakest had gone to the wall and their estates had begun to be bought up by their more successful colleagues under the provisions of the Encumbered Estates Act of 1849, they together enjoyed a gross annual rental of something in the region of £10 million, and this at a time when total United Kingdom central expenditure on civil government amounted to £6.6 million and even the Royal Navy cost only £5.8 million a year.[14] By then it is probably reasonable to identify that mythical beast, the 'typical' landlord, as a man holding some 2,000 acres, and the 'typical' farmer as the tenant of something like 15 acres or perhaps a little more, a difference which alone gave the proprietors very considerable power and influence over many aspects of rural and national life. And the fact that most were members of the (Anglican) Church of Ireland set further barriers between them and those from whom they received their incomes.[15] Given that their tenants were essentially independent small producers, Irish landlords were able to achieve dominance and exercise power by means of a wide (but not limitless) variety of strategies. Thus, although, on the one hand, they could not resort to the very direct methods open to those involved in wage-labour relations with their tenants, they did, on the other, possess greater potential control than elites faced with producers enjoying ownership and paying no rents. In the Irish case landlords sought dominance through the legal rights they enjoyed over their properties, through informal economic and social influence, through their control of local administration, justice and electoral politics, and by being able to act as brokers between their tenants and the apparatus of the contemporary state.

None of these methods was without its problems. In law proprietors enjoyed almost limitless rights. They could raise rents as they pleased. Because fewer and fewer tenants held by lease they could evict after only the shortest of delays. They could insist on good farming practices. They could demand deference and subservience. In fact, however, the exigencies of practical reality rendered such powers less complete than theory alone might suggest. Rents could not float unendingly away from the level of agricultural prices. Large-scale evictions could severely reduce revenue. The achievement of good practices demanded vigilance and efficient management. As a result, the limited evidence available for the half-century before the Famine does not suggest that rents (especially on the larger estates) were raised with rapacious abandon. Indeed, actual rents paid seem *in general* by the 1840s to have been very much in line with the official government land valuations of the day, though after the Famine they undoubtedly began for a time to grow more rapidly than gross farming profits.[16] Not only, however, did farmers in the 1850s and 1860s have substantial grounds for complaint with respect to overall rent movements, but the erratic and sudden manner in which individual increases were often implemented caused further resentment still. Incomprehensible differences existed between neighbouring estates and 'the greatest dissimilarity' could be found 'between the rents paid by different tenants' with identical holdings.[17] When, therefore, the agricultural depression of the late 1870s produced a dramatic collapse in prices and threatened to bring about an actual fall in profits, farmers of all kinds had little hesitation in concluding that it was the landlords who should be made to pay.

In the case of post-Famine evictions there was, however, an even more notable gulf between legal potential and actual practice. Though most tenants held only 'from year to year' and though vast numbers of 'ejectments' and notices to quit were issued at all times, the number actually put out of their holdings and not readmitted was, once the effects of the Famine had worn off, remarkably small, running in the quarter-century beginning in 1854 at an average annual rate of 1.36 per 10,000 holdings above one acre in size.[18] Indeed, well-known horror stories of mass evictions by such as Lord Leitrim, William Scully and J. G. Adair stand out precisely because of their rarity.[19] The real reason for the large-scale issue of notices to quit lay in their usefulness as a means of control, as a threat to those in arrears, those running down the soil, those refusing electoral support, and so on. And as such they proved a valuable if rebarbative tool of estate and political management. Thus, even if most tenants did not enjoy 'fair' rents (and many small tillage farmers found it virtually impossible in bad times to pay any rent at all), 'fixity of tenure' – the second of the so-called 'three Fs' which constituted the main platform of the Tenant League of the 1850s – was an undoubted fact. The third 'F' was 'free sale' or the ability of tenants to 'sell' an 'interest' in their holdings upon peaceably giving these up to their successors. This curious practice usually went under the names of 'tenant right' or the Ulster Custom, though it was present to a lesser degree in many other parts of the country. Its curiosity lay both in the many different ways it could be interpreted and in its implicit recognition that tenants somehow possessed property rights in land they did not own. It was thus very different from the contemporary English practice of mere compensation for unexpired improvements (though this was also often involved) – something English politicians were very slow to grasp. And though it was the incoming tenant who made the payment it is clear that his ability to do so depended to a large degree upon landlords charging a rent lower than it would otherwise have been.[20]

Now, although at least two of the 'three Fs' were, in varying degrees, actually available to many tenants by the 1850s and 1860s, tension arose out of a clash between the farmers' demand that they be granted to them by law and the landlords' insistence that they remain no more than concessions. What, therefore, to one side was a set of firm customary 'rights' (which the law unfortunately failed to recognize) was for the other a voluntary benevolence useful in the exercise of influence and control. In truth the customs themselves were neither very old nor very precise and their history reveals above all the Irish tenants' success in inventing traditions and then rapidly encasing these in a thoroughly bogus yet revered antiquity. At the same time, however, the agitation to enshrine them in law represented at first no outright attack upon the principle of landlordism as such. What it did represent and reflect was a set of cross-cutting contradictions. On the one side, landlords were fiercely determined to do away with anything that smacked of customary duties and to confine their obligations to matters of strict legal contract (while still making voluntary concessions); on the other, tenants demanded the extension of custom as a matter of right while at the same time also insisting that the law be changed to subsume a whole army of customary practices. The chronology of the ensuing conflict is revealed in the passing of Deasy's Act in 1860 which denigrated custom, and later of the Land Acts of 1870 and 1881 which effectively transformed the 'three Fs' into legal obligations. Though less alliterative there were of course many other non-contractual privileges which proprietors were often prepared to grant: the cancellation of arrears, the free use of demesne grazing, permission to cut turf, the giving of dowries to tenants' daughters, and so on. But while all these things represented useful methods of ensuring control they also all suffered from a common and gradually emasculating defect, namely, that what was granted too widely and too regularly came to be seen, not as a concession, but as a customary right.

It is of course hardly surprising that few of these benevolences lacked an ulterior motive. The six months or more by which Irish tenants were generally permitted to delay rent payments (the so-called 'hanging gale'), though it provided free credit for farmers, gave landlords a useful reserve weapon against the recalcitrant. Indeed, it was precisely those landlords who behaved most 'generously' who thereby put themselves in a position to take the most severe action against those who disobeyed their demands. And even certain things which might readily be regarded as generosities by one side were seen very differently by the other. Thus, although Irish landlords invested less in improvements than their English counterparts (a rational enough decision on economic grounds – though it earned them a reputation for meanness), it was often those who tried hardest to secure better agricultural practices, by means of grants for fences, the squaring of fields, drainage and fertilizers, who incurred the most opprobrium. It was often by contrast (as astonished observers uncomprehendingly reported) the most neglectful proprietors who were the most popular – for at least they eschewed minute interference and patronizing zeal.[21]

Because proprietors for long dominated local administration and justice they could and did secure favours for 'respectable' tenants in the shape of jobs, grants and lenient sentences. County grand juries were entirely in landlord hands until 1898 and even the increasingly important and partly elected poor law boards set up in 1838 did not really move out of their control until the 1880s.[22] But though most Justices of the Peace were either landlords or their dependants (agents, Protestant clergymen and the like), on a national level the development of a sophisticated and professional state apparatus proved more of a weakness than a strength. The establishment of the Irish (later Royal Irish) Constabulary in 1836 removed the maintenance of law and order into bureaucratic and centralized hands. A growing civil service and the introduction of stipendiary magistrates made it more difficult for landlords to monopolize local power with all their old crudity and disregard for legal forms. Of course many stipendiaries and senior civil servants themselves came from gentry backgrounds (and the whole business undoubtedly served as a huge system of relief for younger sons), but they were subject to public rules and procedures which did not always allow for the undiluted transformation of proprietorial imperatives into immediate reality. The state, in other words, was more and more establishing itself as an alternative centre of influence and power and as such was not automatically prepared to dance to the landlord tune.[23]

Just as the growth of the state's power to some extent undermined the unique and all-embracing nature of landlord patronage and influence, so also did the development of alternative and rival sources of authority within society as a whole. Outside the northeast the overwhelming majority of the people were Roman Catholics, adherents of a church that was, slowly but more or less steadily throughout the early and mid-nineteenth century, becoming more administratively and socially influential and efficient. Its bureaucratic structures were reformed and improved. Its relentless assault upon, and eventual defeat of, those at best quasi-Christian beliefs and practices which had once constituted an almost alternative religiosity in the Irish countryside concentrated spiritual authority upon itself alone. Its clergy increasingly came from the prosperous farmer class and therefore began more and more to act as the educated shock-troops of tenant (*not* labourer) demands and aspirations. Though the political power of the priesthood fluctuated with events and was always far from absolute (another fact that contemporary Englishmen never found it easy to accept), the clergy undoubtedly exercised much social influence and equally undoubtedly constituted an important counterweight to landlord dominance and control.[24] To some extent allied with the priests was the rising class of rural shopkeepers who in many parts of the countryside were the chief suppliers of credit to all but the largest farmers. Although some were certainly rapacious in the interest rates they charged, on the whole they provided a useful service and, like all creditors, exercised a degree of influence over those to whom they had granted loans.[25]

Amid all its objective power and wealth what the landed community most lacked was something intangible but increasingly important: an attractive (or even a neutral) image. Not only at home but in Britain too, Irish landlords stood condemned as constant evictors, as demanders of excessive rents, as extravagant and inefficient, though the truth in most cases – especially after 1850 – was often otherwise. Above all they were constantly denounced for being absentees and spending their time and profits in the fleshpots of London and the watering places of the continent. But this too was somewhat wide of the mark. The larger landlords often owned several properties (sometimes on both sides of the Irish Sea) and could clearly 'reside' on only one of them. And, as an official inquiry revealed in 1870, almost half lived on their estates constantly while only about an eighth could be described either as 'resident usually out of Ireland but occasionally on their property' or 'rarely or never resident in Ireland'.[26] Yet, though absenteeism was far from rare in England, English landlords enjoyed quite a different reputation in this respect.[27] In both countries it was frequently the wealthiest landowners – by definition often absent from many of their properties – who charged the lowest rents and provided the greatest concessions and benefits to their tenants.[28] But despite all this, image was frequently more important than reality. Indeed, the greatest 'success' of the Irish tenants in the quarter-century after 1850 consisted not simply of having emerged into a post-Famine world in which the previously numerous labourers had been rendered in every way more marginal, but of having begun to win the propaganda battle against the landlords for their own time, for years to come, and in some senses until the present day.

Landlords did not of course stand entirely alone but increasingly relied upon a new breed of professional agents to translate their intentions into effect. Such men were generally of higher social status than their counterparts in England and in substantial properties with non-resident owners acquired virtually proconsular powers.[29] They did far more than collect rents, enforce estate rules and keep financial records. Rather, they were above all the outward and visible signs of proprietorial power, and as such were deeply engaged (together with, on large estates, teams of stewards, agriculturalists, and so forth) in the business of influence. Perhaps the most public forum for their activities in this regard lay in the area of electoral politics. As in England and Scotland the Irish franchise (though *sui generis*) was limited yet large enough to encourage the growth of popular forms of political participation. This the landed community rightly feared and for a long time managed to resist and control with considerable success.[30] But though such resistance depended of course upon the landlords' power over tenant farmers (the bulk of the rural electorate), it was always at its most effective when confined to hints and to coded messages, for overt threats tended to reveal weakness and anxiety rather than strength. Thus at the general election of 1852 the agent for the Clothworkers' Company estate in County Derry 'hoped' that the tenants would give his views 'such weight as they thought right', while Lord Anglesey felt bound 'to let them know what candidates I would recommend'.[31] Frequently, however, things *were* driven further, even though agents often liked to maintain an air of public innocence, as when Thomas Courteney of Longford admitted to an election committee that rent arrears were more generously tolerated from those who otherwise did what they were told.

> Do you call that persecution? – I do not.
>
> Has there ever been any persecution of tenants for voting against the inclination of their landlords? – I do not know what is meant by persecution . . .
>
> Did you ever know a tenant menaced or threatened, if he did not vote as the landlord chose? – I have said to them myself, that if they did not vote as the landlord chose, perhaps they would be sorry . . .
>
> That you would make them sorry? – That is right.[32]

Nor were threats of the most unvarnished kind – that rents would be raised, arrears briskly collected, favours withdrawn, evictions considered – uncommon throughout the century.[33] Lord Erne in 1852 raised the business to a fine art by granting rent abatements (a not infrequent concession in bad times) according to a sliding scale: 15 per cent for those who voted for both Tory candidates, 7.5 per cent for those who voted for only one, and nothing at all for the rest. That non-contractual concessions provided landlords with an important electoral resource can be seen in Lord Londonderry's instructions to his agent to record the names of all those attending tenant-right meetings on the grounds that he 'certainly would not allow those who were present and are in arrears to escape with impunity'.[34] All this seemed quite natural to proprietors whose whole cast of mind led them to see their tenants as so many recalcitrant children in need of guidance from above. Thus Lord Palmerston (who owned widespread acres in County Sligo) refused to allow textbooks in estate schools unless formally approved by himself, while his Whig colleague, Lord Lansdowne, forbade his Kerry tenants from marrying or taking in lodgers without permission.[35]

As long as farmers were relatively weak in the 1830s and 1840s or finding it difficult to share in the growing prosperity of the 1850s and 1860s such things undoubtedly had a real effect, though opposition and resentment were never far below the surface. But just as the Famine had in a sense strengthened the position of those landlords who had survived it intact, so the increasing consolidation of holdings and the creeping effects of the Irish Franchise Act of 1850 (which placed the county electorate almost entirely in the hands of prosperous farmers and thus created a body of voters far more capable of homogeneous mobilization than before) strengthened the potential force for opposition to proprietorial politics. Although, therefore, as late as the early 1870s it would still have been impossible to foresee the Land War explosion that was soon to come, there were straws blowing in the wind for those with eyes to see them. The Liberal victory at the 1868 election was one such: others were the disestablishment of the Church of Ireland in 1869, Gladstone's first

Land Act in 1870 (practically modest but symbolically of great significance), popular enthusiasm for the Amnesty Movement which demanded the release of Fenians imprisoned after their failed rising in 1867, and growing demands for a form of Home Rule. At the election of 1874 the number of landed men returned was substantially lower than it had ever been before – only half compared with seven tenths as recently as 1868.[36]

What was new about the Land War of 1879–82 was the combination of severe agricultural distress and the successful marriage by popular politicians of agrarianism and nationalism. New too was the manner in which the small marginal farmers of the west of Ireland, hitherto a quiescent force, led the way so that the affair could be seen (not altogether accurately) as a great united effort by all sections of the farming community, for their more prosperous fellows elsewhere soon joined in, as did shopkeepers, many priests and even many labourers. Though detailed investigation has made it clear that the land movement was riven by internal tensions,[37] yet, when all is said and done, the mobilization achieved was impressive not only in fact but also – and perhaps more importantly – in public perception. And whereas in the early 1850s political organization had ensued only *after* the rise of tenant-right feelings, in 1879–82 Parnell, Davitt and Devoy (whose coming together had produced an amalgam of political, agrarian and Fenian tendencies) were already in position to take advantage of the rural unrest when it occurred. This, above all, marked the crucial distinction between the economic depression of the late 1870s and that of 1859–64, which, while itself severe, had taken place in a context of political vacuum rather than energy.[38]

Although the landlords hit back with evictions and although the events of the late 1880s showed that they were far from being a totally spent force, yet their own vulnerability to agricultural depression seriously weakened their capacity to ride out the storm. They failed almost entirely to sustain any kind of presence outside Ulster at the general elections of 1885 and 1886. Many were now heavily in debt as they found themselves caught between a widespread tenant agitation for lower rents and the inelastic demands of mortgage repayments and those jointures for widows and younger children with which their estates were almost universally encumbered.[39] On the other side the very experience of the Land War itself reshaped the attitudes and expectations of those who constituted its various *forces de frappe*. In the short run the Land League and its successor the National League were far from being entirely successful and were obliged to accept several bloody noses from the proprietorial side.[40] But the Land Act of 1881 in effect set up a (legal) system of dual ownership with rents now controlled by official bodies rather than by landlords alone. This and the economic depression eventually persuaded landowners to sell out to tenants who were in turn beginning to receive more and more state help with which to purchase their holdings as the century came to a close. And, by providing loans on favourable terms, the government in effect bridged the financial gap which would otherwise have stood in the path of so neat a 'solution' to the problems of the Irish countryside. Over 60,000 tenants applied for money in the 1880s and 1890s and the Wyndham Act of 1903 resulted in more than 200,000 sales. That by the outbreak of the First World War a majority of Irish farmers owned their own holdings[41] was, however, a curious conclusion in the sense that it had virtually nothing to do with the Land League's slogan of 'the Land for the People'. Instead, the land was being handed to the sons of farmers while the 'people' as a whole – and notably the labourers – remained mere spear-holders in the evolving drama. The modest 'proprietors' who emerged from the process, though still envious of the wealthy capitalist graziers who also had much to be thankful for,[42] proved themselves, nonetheless, a force for social and political conservatism in a manner both unsurprising and predictable.

The landowners of Ireland were in the end more the victims of circumstances than the creators of their own downfall. Their actual behaviour during the second half of the nineteenth century with regard to rents, evictions and residence was probably not much worse – and in many cases a good deal better – than that of many of their counterparts on the continent of Europe. Absenteeism was less widespread in Ireland than in Spain, Russia, or France, while the Prussian equivalent of evictions, namely forced sales of peasant properties, actually ran at a rather higher level that did Irish evictions in the late 1850s and 1860s.[43] Situated, however, in an environment where they could – however lengthy their lineage – so easily be depicted as interlopers and strangers, Irish landowners not only failed to protect their power, but also (unlike the Prussian Junkers, for example) failed to insinuate their values into those large sections of society whose interests diverged from their own. Their experience offers especially noteworthy contrasts and parallels with the situation in contemporary England (which itself differed of course from that in Scotland and Wales). The basic structure – landlords, renting farmers, landless labourers – had initially been the same in both countries. And in England too were to be found inter-group tensions, absentees, electoral pressure from above, agrarian violence, sectarian differences, and so on. The chief distinction lay in the fact that there came a moment – probably at some time in the 1880s – when Irish landlords were no longer able to keep the tenantry within the bounds of accepting the fact of landlordism as such. Perhaps it is surprising that this took so long to come about – a reflection of residual landlord strength. But when the end did arrive, it arrived with remarkable suddenness. English landlords, however, remained able to contain English farmers within a species of broad cultural hegemony according to which the latter continued to accept landlordism as a 'normal reality' and in consequence lacked the necessity of creating a new experience and consciousness. Of course there was a price to be paid for this and English proprietors also suffered serious economic decline during the last years of the nineteenth century. Indeed, in the long run English farmers proved themselves perhaps almost as 'triumphant' as their Irish counterparts, but, by doing so within rather than outside the existing normality, most (but not all, for there was some selling-out in England too) remained tenants rather than becoming owners of the soil. In political and social terms the distinction was crucial, in economic terms much less important, for landlords on both sides of the Irish Sea had for years been drifting away from their former position at the economic centre of their localities. But whereas in England they at least continued to be rich men who lived in the countryside (and perhaps in some cases a good deal more than that), in Ireland they simply disappeared. In the Protestant north the process was slower and political power less immediately abandoned. But in the long run the landlords were driven from the soil, from power, and often from wealth, but not – in Ireland – ever from memory.

NOTES

1 See J. S. Donnelly, Jr, 'The Rightboy Movement 1785–8', *Studia Hibernica*, no. 17/18 (1977–8), pp. 120–202; J. S. Donnelly, Jr, 'The Whiteboy Movement 1761–5', *Irish Historical Studies*, 21, 81 (1978), pp. 20–54; J. S. Donnelly, Jr, 'Hearts of Oak, Hearts of Steel', *Studia Hibernica*, no. 21 (1981), pp. 7–73; J. S. Donnelly, Jr, 'Irish agrarian rebellion: the Whiteboys of 1769–76', *Proceedings of the Royal Irish Academy*, section C, 83, 12 (1983), pp. 293–331; J. S. Donnelly, Jr, 'Pastorini and Captain Rock: millenarianism and sectarianism in the Rockite Movement of 1821–4', in S. Clark and J. S. Donnelly, Jr (eds), *Irish Peasants: Violence and Political Unrest 1780–1914* (Manchester: 1983), pp. 102–39; P. E. W. Roberts, 'Caravats and Shanavests: Whiteboyism and faction fighting in East Munster, 1802–11', in ibid., pp. 64–101; M. Beames, *Peasants and Power: The Whiteboy Movements and their Control in Pre-Famine Ireland* (Brighton, Sussex, 1983).

2 See S. Clark, 'The importance of agrarian classes: agrarian class structure and collective action in nineteenth-century Ireland', *British Journal of Sociology*, 29, 1 (1978), pp. 22–40.

3 W. E. Vaughan, *Landlords and Tenants in Ireland 1848–1904* (Dublin: 1984), p. 4.

4 D. Fitzpatrick, 'The disappearance of the Irish agricultural labourer, 1841–1912', *Irish Economic and Social History*, 7 (1980), pp. 66–92; K. T. Hoppen, *Elections, Politics, and Society in Ireland 1832–1885* (Oxford: 1984), pp. 91, 103–5. The picture of rent and profits given here differs substantially from that offered by W. E. Vaughan in 'An assessment of the economic performance of Irish landlords, 1851–81' in F. S. L. Lyons and R. A. J. Hawkins (eds), *Ireland under the Union: Varieties of Tension. Essays in Honour of T. W. Moody* (Oxford: 1980), pp. 173–99 which suggests that between 1852–4 and 1872–4 rents rose by 20 per cent but gross farming profits did so by no less than 77 per cent – both in *current* terms. My figures are based upon new calculations of agricultural output by Dr Michael Turner of the University of Hull ('Towards an agricultural prices index for Ireland 1850–1914', *Economic and Social Review*, 18 (1987), pp. 123–36) which agree broadly with other recent estimates made by Dr Cormac Ó Gráda of University College, Dublin (partly presented in his 'Irish agricultural output before and after the Great Famine', *Journal of European Economic History*, 13, 1 (1984), pp. 149–65) and by Mr Peter Solar of the Catholic University of Louvain. (I am grateful to all three scholars – whose estimates, it should be noted, include potatoes [which Vaughan omitted] – for also supplying me with additional as yet unpublished information.) Although I have used the well-known Sauerback-*Statist* price index (which, with all its faults, remains useful) to produce *real* figures, even in current terms the new estimates would yield, for the period from 1852–4 to 1872–4, an increase in rents of 20 per cent (the same as Vaughan's) but almost no movement at all in gross farming profits. The matter is discussed more fully in my *Ireland since 1800: Conflict and Conformity* (London: 1989), pp. 90–100.

5 R. D. Crotty, *Irish Agricultural Production: its Volume and Structure* (Cork: 1966); P. M. A. Bourke, 'The agricultural statistics of the 1841 census of Ireland: a critical review', *Economic History Review*, 2nd series, 18, 2 (1965), pp. 376–91; F. J. Carney, 'Pre-Famine Irish population: the evidence from the Trinity College estates', *Irish Economic and Social History*, 2 (1975), pp. 35–45; L. M. Cullen, *An Economic History of Ireland since 1660* (London: 1972), pp. 134–5.

6 J. M. Goldstrom, 'Irish agriculture and the Great Famine', in J. M. Goldstrom and L. A. Clarkson (eds), *Irish Population, Economy and Society: Essays in Honour of the late K. H. Connell* (Oxford: 1981), pp. 163–4.

7 J. S. Donnelly, Jr, *Landlord and Tenant in Nineteenth-Century Ireland* (Dublin: 1973), p. 5.

8 Hoppen, *Elections, Politics, and Society*, pp. 106–7. This is true whether one takes a poor law valuation of £2,000 or one of £5,000 as the lowest definition of 'largest' proprietors.

9 Printed confidential 'Return showing the Names of Proprietors, and the Area and Valuation of all Properties in the several counties in Ireland', dated 5 February 1870 in British Library Gladstone papers Add. MS 44613. See also the so-called Irish 'Domesday Book' in House of Commons Paper [hereafter HC] 1876 (412, 422), lxxx. Many large landlords also owned valuable urban properties. For a differently constructed attempt to measure the size of the late nineteenth-century 'Anglo-Irish gentry', see L. P. Curtis, Jr, 'The Anglo-Irish predicament', *Twentieth Century*, no. 4 (1970), pp. 37–63.

10 *The Agricultural Statistics of Ireland for the year 1871*, HC 1873 [C 762], lxix, 383–4, 387.

11 See D. Dickson, 'Middlemen', in T. Bartlett and D. W. Hayton (eds), *Penal Era and Golden Age: Essays in Irish History, 1690–1800* (Belfast: 1979), pp. 162–85; J. S. Donnelly, Jr, *The Land and the People of Nineteenth-Century Cork: the Rural Economy and the Land Question* (London: 1975), pp. 9–14, 50–3, 114–16.

12 Donnelly, *Landlord and Tenant*, pp. 18–19.

13 J. Prest, *Lord John Russell* (London: 1972), pp. 236–53; Hoppen, *Elections, Politics, and Society*, pp. 167–8. The chief secretary was in effect the most important government minister in charge of Irish affairs.

14 Vaughan, 'An assessment of the economic performance of Irish landlords', p. 187; B. R. Mitchell and P. Deane, *Abstract of British Historical Statistics* (Cambridge: 1971), p. 397 (figures for 1853).

15 This had finally become the case in the early eighteenth century, though already by the 1830s between a tenth and a fifth of the land was again in Catholic hands. There is no evidence that Catholic proprietors treated their tenants in any distinct or special way.

16 See note 4 above.

17 The O'Conor Don to W. E. Forster [Jan. 1881], Gladstone Papers Add. MS 44158. The point was widely made, see *Third General Report relative to the Valuations*, HC 1841 [329], xxiii, 594; *Minutes of evidence taken before Her Majesty's Commissioners on Agriculture*, HC 1881 [C 2778-I], xv, 600–1; F. Dun, *Landlords and Tenants in Ireland* (London: 1881), p. 11; A. Shand, *Letters from the West of Ireland 1884* (Edinburgh: 1885), p. 96.

18 T. W. Moody, *Davitt and Irish Revolution 1846–82* (Oxford: 1981), pp. 562–3 (in 1866 there were 549,392 such holdings). It is possible that the official figures given in Moody may slightly underestimate the real level of evictions: see Hoppen, *Elections, Politics, and Society*, pp. 127–8.

19 Even Scully and Adair in the famous Ballycohey (1868) and Derryveagh (1861) evictions actually put out a grand total of 65 families without readmission between them. See H. E. Socolofsky, *Landlord William Scully* (Lawrence, Kans.: 1979), pp. 51–2, and L. Dolan, *Land War and Eviction in Derryveagh 1840–65* (Dundalk: 1980), p. 197; also W. E. Vaughan, *Sin, Sheep and Scotsmen: John George Adair and the Derryveagh Evictions, 1861* (Belfast: 1983). On Leitrim, see S. Clark, *Social Origins of the Irish Land War* (Princeton, NJ: 1979), p. 163.

20 See L. Kennedy, 'The rural economy, 1820–1914', in L. Kennedy and P. Ollerenshaw (eds), *An Economic History of Ulster, 1820–1940* (Manchester: 1985), pp. 38–41.

21 See, for example, D. Thomson and M. McGusty (eds), *The Irish Journals of Elizabeth Smith 1840–1850* (Oxford: 1980), p. 142; F. R. Bertolacci to Sir C. Trevelyan, 21 November 1848, Hampshire Record Office, Broadlands Archive 27M60 box cxix; C. W. O'Hara to I. Butt, 20 January 1865, National Library of Ireland Butt Papers MS 20353; also C. Ó Gráda, 'The investment behaviour of Irish landlords, 1850–75: some preliminary findings', *Agricultural History Review*, 32, 2 (1975), pp. 139–55.

22 D. M. Nolan, 'The County Cork Grand Jury, 1836–1899', MA thesis, University College Cork, 1974; W. L. Feingold, *The Revolt of the Tenantry: The Transformation of Local Government in Ireland, 1872–1886* (Boston, Mass.: 1984).

23 C. Townshend, 'Modernization and nationalism: perspectives in recent Irish history', *History*, 66, 217 (1981), p. 235.

24 Hoppen, *Elections, Politics, and Society*, pp. 171–256; S. J. Connolly, *Priests and People in Pre-Famine Ireland 1780–1845* (Dublin: 1982), *passim*; D. A. Kerr, *Peel, Priests and Politics: Sir Robert Peel's Administration and the Roman Catholic Church in Ireland, 1841–1846* (Oxford: 1982), pp. 1–67.

25 The role of shopkeepers (the most grasping of whom went under the pejorative title of 'gombeenmen') is an area of controversy. See L. Kennedy, 'Traders in the Irish rural economy, 1880–1914', *Economic History Review*, 2nd series, 32, 2 (1979), pp. 201–10; L. Kennedy, 'Farmers, traders, and agricultural politics in pre-Independence Ireland', in Clark and Donnelly, *Irish Peasants*, pp. 339–73; P. Gibbon and M. D. Higgins, 'Patronage, tradition and modernisation: the case of the Irish "gombeenman" ', *Economic and Social Review*, 6, 1 (1974), pp. 27–44; P. Gibbon and M. D. Higgins, 'The Irish "gombeenman": re-incarnation or rehabilitation?', *Economic and Social Review*, 8, 4 (1977), pp. 313–19; L. Kennedy, 'A sceptical view of the re-incarnation of the Irish "gombeenman" ', *Economic and Social Review*, 8, 3 (1977), pp. 213–32; also M. D. Higgins and J. P. Gibbons, 'Shopkeeper-graziers and land agitation in Ireland, 1895–1900', in P. J. Drudy (ed.), *Ireland: Land, Politics and People: Irish Studies II* (Cambridge: 1982), pp. 93–118.

26 *Return, for the year 1870, of the number of landed proprietors in each county, classed according to residence*, HC 1872 (167), xlvii, 775–84 (with sub-100-acre owners excluded).

27 F. M. L. Thompson, *English Landed Society in the Nineteenth Century* (London: 1963), pp. 181–2; R. J. Olney, *Rural Society and County Government in Nineteenth-Century Lincolnshire* (Lincoln: 1979), pp. 24–5, 31.

28 Hoppen, *Elections, Politics, and Society*, pp. 110, 130; Donnelly, *The Land and the People of Nineteenth-Century Cork*, pp. 187–200; D. Jordan, 'Land and politics in the West of Ireland: County Mayo, 1846–82', PhD thesis, University of California, Davis, 1982, pp. 149–50.

29 Donnelly, *The Land and the People of Nineteenth-Century Cork*, pp. 173–87; J. S. Donnelly, Jr (ed.), 'The journals of Sir John Benn-Walsh relating to the management of his Irish estates', *Journal of the Cork Historical and Archaeological Society*, 80, 230 (1974), pp. 86–123, and 81, 231 (1975), pp. 15–42; W. A. Maguire, *The Downshire Estates in Ireland 1801–1845: the Management of Irish Landed Estates in the Early Nineteenth Century* (Oxford: 1972), pp. 183–216.

30 J. H. Whyte, 'Landlord influence at elections in Ireland, 1760–1855', *English Historical Review*, 80, 317 (1965), pp. 740–60; K. T. Hoppen, 'Politics, the law, and the nature of the Irish electorate 1832–1850', *English Historical Review*, 92, 365 (1977), pp. 746–76; K. T. Hoppen, 'Landlords, society, and electoral politics in mid-nineteenth-century Ireland', *Past and Present*, no. 75 (1977), pp. 62–93; K. T. Hoppen, 'National politics and local realities in mid-nineteenth-century Ireland', in A. Cosgrove and D. McCartney (eds), *Studies in Irish History Presented to R. Dudley Edwards* (Dublin: 1979), pp. 190–227; K. T. Hoppen, 'The franchise and electoral politics in England and Ireland 1832–1885', *History*, 70 (1985), pp. 202–17.

31 C. Knox to R. B. Towse, 10 July 1852, Clothworkers' Hall (London) Irish Estate Archives MS Copy Letter-Book 1840–73; Anglesey to A. W. Rutherford, 22 April 1852, Public Record Office of Northern Ireland Anglesey papers D619/23/B/364.

32 *Select Committee on Fictitious Votes, Ireland*, 2nd series, 3rd report, HC 1837–8 (643), xiii, part ii, 39.

33 Hoppen, *Elections, Politics, and Society*, pp. 146–9; K. T. Hoppen, 'Le Elites e L'Influenza Elettorale in Irlanda 1800–1918', *Quaderni Storici*, 23, 69 (1988), pp. 787–807.

34 *Freeman's Journal*, 6 November 1852; R. Kelly to Londonderry, 21 October 1852, Durham County Record Office Londonderry Papers D/Lo/C164.

35 K. Bourne (ed.), *The Letters of the Third Viscount Palmerston to Laurence and Elizabeth Sulivan 1804–1863* (London: 1979), p. 203; J. Godkin, *The Land War in Ireland* (London: 1870), p. 412. H. A. Herbert of Kerry rose early so that he could climb a hill and observe – through opera glasses – which tenants got up and set to work first (Dun, *Landlords and Tenants in Ireland*, p. 80).

36 Hoppen, *Elections, Politics, and Society*, pp. 1–33, 332–9, 436–79.

37 P. Bew, *Land and the National Question in Ireland 1858–82* (Dublin: 1978), pp. 99–232; D. Jordan, 'Merchants, "strong farmers" and Fenians: the post-Famine political élite and the land war', in C. H. E. Philpin (ed.), *Nationalism and Popular Protest in Ireland* (Cambridge: 1987), pp. 320–48.

38 Moody, *Davitt and Irish Revolution*, pp. 117–327; J. S. Donnelly, Jr, 'The Irish agricultural depression of 1859–64', *Irish Economic and Social History*, 3 (1976), pp. 33–54.

39 L. P. Curtis, Jr, 'Incumbered wealth: landed indebtedness in post-Famine Ireland', *American Historical Review*, 85, 2 (1980), pp. 332–67.

40 Donnelly, *The Land and the People of Nineteenth-Century Cork*, pp. 308–76; L. M. Geary, *The Plan of Campaign, 1886–1891* (Cork: 1986), *passim* – though Geary also highlights a good deal of proprietorial timidity. It was prodding from Arthur Balfour as chief secretary (1887–91) which really galvanized the landlords into what was to prove their Last Hurrah.

41 B. L. Solow, *The Land Question and the Irish Economy 1870–1903* (Cambridge, Mass.: 1971), p. 193. In 1920 it was estimated that £83 million had been advanced under the 1903 Act and its 1909 successor and that sums totalling £24 million were pending. Between 1903 and 1920 nearly 9 million acres changed hands and a further 2 million were in process of being sold. In 1923 the Irish Free State introduced completely compulsory purchase and this was also done in Northern Ireland two years later (F. S. L. Lyons, *Ireland Since the Famine* [London: 1971], pp. 214, 595, 696).

42 P. Bew, *Conflict and Conciliation in Ireland 1890–1910: Parnellites and Radical Agrarians* (Oxford: 1987).

43 D. Spring (ed.), *European Landed Elites in the Nineteenth Century* (Baltimore, Md: 1977), pp. 11, 103–4; Vaughan, *Landlords and Tenants in Ireland*, p. 24.

ITALY

9

Commercial agriculture and the crisis of landed power: Bologna, 1880–1930

Anthony L. Cardoza

The province of Bologna provides an ideal setting for exploring the changing relationship between landownership and power in modern Italy. Nestling at the foot of the Apennine mountains in the southeastern sector of the fertile Po Valley, the city of Bologna was the acknowledged, if unofficial, capital of agricultural Italy; the province and the surrounding region of Emilia constituted one of the country's most advanced agricultural areas.[1] As a result, developments in Bologna reflected the larger stresses and strains of rapid but uneven industrialization and political democratization on the peninsula during the first three decades of the twentieth century. Bologna's farm labour unions were the largest and most powerful in the entire country and made the province an early stronghold of the socialist movement. The provincial elite of large landowners and commercial farmers took the lead in founding strong employer organizations and provided both the personnel and the ideas for agrarian interest-group associations that arose at the regional and national levels after 1901. The ensuing confrontation between the propertied classes and organized labour made the province a focal point of social and political conflict in Italy prior to 1914. But above all, Bologna was the cradle of the rural-based fascism that elevated Mussolini's marginal extremist movement into a dominant force on the Italian political scene after the First World War.

Not surprisingly, agriculture left its imprint on all areas of provincial life. Indeed, most of the local populace earned their livelihood directly or indirectly from the land. At the beginning of the twentieth century, over two thirds of the population lived in rural communes of the province with the remainder concentrated in the urban centres of Bologna and Imola. In 1901, 64 per cent of the active population worked in agriculture, less than a quarter in manufacturing; two decades later farming still provided jobs for over half the workforce. Manufacturing played only a marginal role in the provincial economy. In the last decades of the nineteenth century, Bologna registered a modest rate of industrial growth, but even this development was limited to refiners and processors of agricultural products and, to a lesser extent, those mechanical and chemical industries that provided farm machinery and fertilizers. As a result, much of the urban workforce depended indirectly on the countryside. Agriculture also stimulated and sustained most of the commercial activity that revolved around the importation of seed, fertilizers and other farm supplies, and the exportation of local crops.[2]

The primacy of agriculture had always assured the great landowners a powerful role in the province. As one might expect, old aristocratic families had traditionally dominated the structure of landholding in Bologna. On the eve of the French Revolution, the local nobility as a group accounted for nearly three quarters of the private property in the province, while all the largest patrimonies over 500 hectares were in the hands of a more exclusive circle of aristocrats headed by the Hercolani, Malvezzi, Tanari and Isolani families.[3] Descendants of city dwellers who had built up their property more by commercial acquisitions than by feudal concessions, these great families and their fellow nobles provided the overwhelming majority of local notables and administrators who shared power with the high church officials of the Papal States. Bourgeois proprietors, on the other hand, held slightly under a quarter of the private property and the average value of their possessions was only a tenth that of the typical noble holding in 1789.

Much as elsewhere in Europe, Napoleon and the invading French armies seriously disrupted established patterns of aristocratic dominance in Bologna after 1796 by carrying out a number of reforms that swept away noble privileges, rendered alienable all forms of property and guaranteed mortgage credits. The active land market created by these reforms, together with rising agricultural prices, led to a rapid redistribution of land in the province, largely to the benefit of new men. Already by 1804, 42 per cent of the private property in the plains was held by non-nobles, of whom six had amassed holdings that each exceeded 500 hectares.[4]

The Bolognese nobility, however, weathered the storms of the Napoleonic era relatively well. Although their share of the private property declined, leading aristocratic families still controlled over half the land in the decades after 1815 as well as the bulk of large landholdings. Indeed, as late as 1910, titled gentlemen owned 10 of the 12 largest estates in the Bolognese plains.[5] More importantly, the nobility still seemed to set the tone for the hybrid landed elite that dominated public life in the province throughout the nineteenth century. Despite the disappearance of a number of old families, the nobility as a social group continued to enjoy a unique prestige that made it the natural arbiter of elite conduct, education and styles of consumption. Significantly, many of the big new landowners like the Talon, Pizzardi, Salina and Torlonia families sought ennoblement and appear to have embraced aristocratic life-styles, values and institutions in the decades prior to Italian unification.[6]

The history of the Cavazza family suggests that large-scale landownership remained linked to an older process of aristocratic assimilation even at the end of the nineteenth century. Felice Cavazza was a successful local banker who was ennobled in the 1880s for his public services and contributions to charity. Felice's son, Count Francesco Cavazza, moved gradually away from the economic responsibilities and social milieu of his predecessors. Although the bank remained in family hands until after the First World War, Francesco invested heavily in rural properties and by 1914 he had become the second largest landowner in the province. Marriage to Countess Lina Bianconcini provided additional prestige and status by linking the young count to an older family of the Bolognese nobility. As a fitting expression of his wealth and newly acquired noble status, Cavazza purchased and renovated a fifteenth-century walled castle outside the city. Francesco's public career also conformed closely to the ideal of an aristocratic gentleman: he was a major charitable benefactor in the city, a parliamentary deputy from 1913 to 1919 and a leading patron of the arts in Bologna.[7]

Aristocratic influence found further expression in the dominant ideology of Bologna's landed elite, which combined enthusiasm for modernizing agricultural production with the glorifying of traditional patterns of social relations in the countryside. Throughout the nineteenth century, the speeches and discussions in the Agrarian Society of Bologna testified to landlord interest in more efficient methods of cultivation, greater mechanization and larger investments in land reclamation. Moreover, local landowners took part actively in the initiatives sponsored by the government to encourage technical innovation on the farms.[8] Enthusiasm for agricultural modernization, however, coexisted with an ardent defence of a traditional, hierarchical social order in the countryside, a world where the peasant's deference and obedience harmonized with the paternalistic concern of the landlord. Thus, a man like Count Nerio Malvezzi, the scion of one of Bologna's oldest aristocratic families, insisted proudly that he had 'always been a friend of the peasants with whom [he] lived . . . in close contact'.[9]

A similar blend of conservative stability and 'liberal progress' marked the elite's conception of politics. As practised by Bolognese landlords, politics was not an occupation, but rather an 'honorific' pursuit of gentlemen whose financial independence and cultural refinement made them uniquely suited to the task of ensuring the general welfare of society. Count Giovanni Codronchi, parliamentary deputy and local political leader, perhaps captured this sentiment best in a letter to the young Count Nerio Malvezzi in 1884:

> It seems to me that the upper classes have the duty of involving themselves in public life in order to prevent society from falling into the hands of the worst elements. . . . You have an illustrious name and I must invoke

noblesse oblige to induce you to accept an office that will acquire authority and decorum from your name.[10]

Although men like Codronchi and Malvezzi believed firmly in constitutional parliamentary government, they saw little need for the participation of the ignorant masses in the process and felt more comfortable in the system of limited suffrage that prevailed in Italy throughout most of the late nineteenth century.

Such a political system provided the framework for the supremacy of big propertied interests in virtually all areas of public life in the decades after 1861. Large landowners invariably headed the roster of the richest men in the province, presided over the boards of the major local financial institutions as well as the chambers of commerce and served as the chief patrons of Bolognese cultural and social life. With wealth and economic power also came the prizes and rewards of political life. Typically, the public-spirited landowner would serve at various times in his life as a municipal and provincial councillor, mayor of a rural commune and director of one of the province's charitable institutions. Reflecting the close identity between economic elite and political class, most of Bologna's leading parliamentary representatives were also landed gentlemen like Count Malvezzi, Marco Minghetti, Marchese August Mazzacorati and Enrico Pini.[11]

The strong link between landownership and power rested in turn upon a system of social control that found its most important expression in the *mezzadria*. In Bologna and most of the Po Valley, the *mezzadria* was a sharecropping arrangement in which the landlord provided the land with a house, barn, well, and so on, as well as half the seed, while the peasant contributed all the labour power and work animals. As compensation, the landowner received half the gross product along with various supplementary contributions from the peasant, both in kind and in the form of certain free services.[12]

The *mezzadria*, which structured the lives of from half to two thirds of the province's agricultural population in the mid-nineteenth century, gave the landlords tremendous leverage in their dealings with the labour force. By establishing a pattern of highly dispersed settlement, the arrangement discouraged any cohesive peasant community and favoured the growth of scattered and isolated families of cultivators largely at the mercy of their landlords. Since the contracts themselves were renewable on an annual basis and were freely revocable, the landlord was in a position to exercise a great deal of control over all aspects of his tenants' lives. Thus, the landlord or his agent could evict tenants and expel them from the process of production not only for their economic failings, but also on the grounds of immorality or unreliability.[13] Under these circumstances, it was relatively easy for gentlemen politicians to mobilize a rural constituency at election time.

The power and influence enjoyed by the landed elite in the countryside rested on more than the potential economic coercion inherent in the *mezzadria* system. Landlords reinforced peasant dependence by providing various forms of protection to their tenants. Above all, they were patrons who played a crucial role in mediating between their peasants and the various agencies of the Italian state. It was common for the landlord to represent and defend his tenants when they encountered any legal difficulties. Likewise, the tenants relied on the landlord in virtually all matters involving written contracts. Not surprisingly, spokesmen for the landed elite often pointed to these services as proof that the *mezzadria* was not just a business contract but also a source of 'harmony among the social classes' and 'a guarantee of a certain social stability'.[14]

Already in the middle decades of the nineteenth century, however, this idealized world of landlord paternalism and peasant deference and submissiveness had begun to show signs of erosion. Beginning during the Napoleonic era and continuing into the Restoration, a growing number of landlords dismissed their tenants, consolidated their farms and employed large groups of landless day labourers for the cultivation of rice and forage crops. Although the dimensions of this social transformation cannot be measured exactly, they must have been considerable; the changes caught the attention of prominent agrarian leaders like Carlo Berti-Pichat and Marco Minghetti who expressed serious concern both for the plight of many sharecroppers and at the threat to law and order in the countryside posed by a mass of landless labourers, subject to seasonal unemployment and pauperism.[15]

The creation of a unified Italian state and the emergence of a world market for agricultural products after 1860 accentuated these trends by accelerating the commercialization of agriculture in Bologna. Indeed, these changes produced powerful new incentives and pressure to raise productivity and engage in crop specialization. Rising farm prices in the 1860s and 1870s encouraged landowners in Bologna and the Po Delta to embrace a large-scale commercialized pattern of agriculture and to adapt their production to the demands of new national and international markets.[16] The onset of the world agricultural depression, which brought falling prices and sharpened competition in the 1880s, placed even greater pressures on landowners to intensify their methods of cultivation and to develop specialized fodder and industrial crops.

At the same time, new government policies and programmes to combat the crisis provided landowners with additional incentives to modernize their farms. In 1882 the Baccarini Law offered substantial state subsidies and favourable credit arrangements for projects of land reclamation. New agricultural tariffs imposed in 1887 quadrupled duties on imported wheat and rice, and virtually excluded foreign competition in key industrial crops such as sugar beet. Property taxes fell steadily from the mid-1880s until 1910, freeing capital for investments and improvements on the farms of the northern plains. During the same period, the budget of the Ministry of Agriculture nearly tripled, allowing the government to ease farm credit terms and establish experimental stations, technical schools and *cattedre ambulanti* or travelling chairs of agriculture.[17]

Agricultural modernization, however, came increasingly at the expense of social stability in the Bolognese countryside. The trend away from the *mezzadria* meant, first of all, that a growing number of peasant families were pushed off their farms and driven into the ranks of the landless day labourers, already swollen by immigrants in search of work on the vast land reclamation projects of the Po Delta. By 1901, a number of communes in the plains had twice as many day labourers as sharecroppers.[18] While this fate probably befell only a minority of the peasants, most sharecropping families saw the character of their work as well as their relations with the landlords deteriorate in the late nineteenth century. Specialization, for instance, threatened the old balance between crops on which the peasant economy rested. Moreover, some of the most profitable cash crops for landowners, like hemp, meant greater subservience and intensive work for the tenant families. Generally, the commercialization of agriculture entailed more risks, more work and more costs for the sharecroppers.[19] At the same time, these circumstances did little to benefit the new army of day labourers that accompanied the growth of big commercial farms in the plains. On the contrary, the agricultural depression provoked a sharp decline in employment, wages and living standards for rural workers. To make matters worse from the landowners' point of view, these day labourers displayed little of the sharecroppers' affection for the land or their submissiveness to established authority. Faced with living and working conditions that nearly all contemporary observers characterized as intolerable, they responded to their employers with mounting hostility and resistance.[20]

The plight of the landless day labourer, which agrarian leaders had previously viewed as a problem of petty crime and moral degeneracy, took on increasingly ominous economic and social overtones in the 1880s. As that decade unfolded, a small but persistent group of propagandists and organizers began to find a receptive audience for their socialist ideas among the rural labourers of the plains, who had few attachments to traditional values and whose daily existence seemed to be living proof of capitalist exploitation. The first unions or 'leagues of resistance' that they set up provided not only representation in the workplace, but also the institutional framework for a completely new subculture with its own distinctive values, customs and social relations. In an atmosphere of rising hopes and expectations, league leaders became folk heroes who exercised enormous influence over the labourers and were treated with a veneration that in earlier centuries would have been reserved for saints and religious leaders.[21]

Beginning in June 1886 when rice workers went out on strike for higher wages, rural labour agitation became an annual phenomenon in the Bolognese plains. By 1893, some 14 leagues existed in the province; in February of that year they united for the first time in support of a platform of demands for an eight-hour day, differential pay scales and the right to elect their field foremen.[22] This initial unity proved to be fragile and was followed by a three-year period of setbacks and disarray. But in the summer of 1897, the leagues re-emerged with strikes and walkouts that involved both rice workers and labourers employed in the wheat harvest. Even these strikes paled in comparison with the agitation of August 1900 in which over 6,000 labourers participated, the largest single agricultural strike in Italy that year.[23] By the beginning of the new century, Bolognese landowners saw their authority in the fields being increasingly challenged by what had become the strongest socialist labour movement in all of Europe.

The socialist leagues also provided the basis for the first significant political challenge to the landed elite of Bologna. Already in the first years of the new century, the Socialist Party enjoyed a firm hold on the municipal administrations of some half-dozen communes in the plains. Significantly, party efforts met with particular success in those areas where the league leaders were also Socialist candidates. The commune of Molinella, where Giuseppe Massarenti was the mayor, head of the leagues and president of the cooperative, best exemplified this situation. Here, police officials complained, the vast majority of labourers 'follow blindly the counsels, indeed the orders of the Socialist leaders and drag along the hesitant'.[24] While suffrage restrictions still limited the mass base for the party, it was clear that the Socialist Party was emerging as the most dynamic and active political force in the province.

These growing challenges from below coincided with new tensions and divisions within the landed elite itself. The agricultural depression of the 1880s combined with the tariffs and land reclamation legislation to favour the advance of a new group of ambitious rural entrepreneurs. As early as 1881, Marchese Luigi Tanari noted, alongside of traditional landowners like himself who maintained the 'old patriarchal spirit', the presence of a different breed of farmers 'characterized by a greedy industrial spirit which they are injecting into the management of the farms', men whose 'principal infatuations are experimental adventures, rents, and profits'.[25] Sons of wealthy urban merchants or manufacturers, officials from the land reclamation projects, or in other cases enterprising stewards on the large estates, they tended to be big leaseholders rather than property owners. As a rule they shared few of the gentlemanly pretensions or paternal sentiments of the agrarian old guard; they were essentially 'agricultural industrialists' in the business of maximizing profits by increasing production, lowering costs and selling their crops in the most lucrative markets. Running business enterprises rather than peasant households, they began to apply systematic economic calculation to farming and to introduce new crop rotations, machines and chemical fertilizers on an unprecedented scale. These big leaseholders, who numbered fewer than 40 in

1881, grew steadily in number and importance, and by the first years of the twentieth century were managing many of the largest estates in the plains.[26]

The old landholding notables tended to blame the leaseholders for the erosion of the traditional rural order with its stable relationships and fixed patterns of deference. For Marchese Tanari, the leaseholders' 'greedy industrial spirit' was responsible for the 'deteriorating social relations' and the disappearance of the 'old harmony' in the countryside. Echoing these sentiments Count Giuseppe Grabinski denounced in 1892 'the abuses of capital, abuses that too often lead to physical and moral sufferings for the people'.[27] But on the whole, the established landowners were not prepared to halt any of the changes they associated with the big leaseholders. The lure of higher rents or in other cases the competition of industrialized agriculture led more and more landowners to follow the example of the leaseholders. Despite periodic warnings voiced in the Agrarian Society of Bologna, farming the plains increasingly became an industry like any other, in which sound business principles took precedence over the uneconomical considerations of status, prestige and social responsibility.

Partisan government intervention against the socialist labour movement in the 1890s served initially to obscure the tensions between old guard and commercial farmers. Assured of the energetic support of local and national authorities, landowners had few incentives to organize themselves or to develop any coherent, long-term responses to the new economic and political realities in the province. This protective shield disappeared in 1901, however, with the advent of the first of a series of reform governments inspired by the dominant statesman of early twentieth-century Italy, Giovanni Giolitti. Giolitti's resolute commitment to governmental neutrality in labour–management disputes, and the ensuing explosion of strikes and union activity, made it imperative that the landed elite adapt and respond in some fashion, or else face the gradual loss of the prizes and distinctions of public life that had been its exclusive preserve.[28]

Significantly, political liberalization in Rome and the advance of the left locally seemed only to highlight contrasting perceptions within the elite in regard to its proper role and responsibilities in the province. Landed patricians like Count Francesco Cavazza and Count Nerio Malvezzi favoured a conciliatory approach to labour unrest that reflected their particular position in Bolognese society. As the perennial arbiters of local political and cultural life, they preferred to see themselves as members of a disinterested ruling group that stood above the vulgar struggles between capital and labour and concerned itself with the needs of all the people in the province. As a result, they tended to view the strikes and leagues as symptoms of a more general crisis in the countryside that could be overcome only by restoring harmonious relations between proprietors and peasants. Not surprisingly, in their public utterances they looked back to a happier, more tranquil time when the landlord assumed responsibility for the welfare of his dependants and was repaid with their deference and respect. In line with their wider political and social concerns, the older landlords advocated policies to revitalize the *mezzadria* and encourage cooperation and 'harmonious moderation between capital and labour'.[29]

Most of the new commercial farmers recognized none of the old guard's broader social and political concerns. As active entrepreneurs rather than landed notables, they were concerned more with problems of production and markets than with status or political influence. While the absentee landowners might see agriculture as a way of life or the cornerstone of a rural community over which they exercised influence, commercial farmers saw it exclusively as a business in which labourers represented a factor of production and not dependants whose well-being was their responsibility. Accordingly, they looked to a militant and disciplined organization of employers that would defend their immediate economic interests against 'strikes, impositions and disorders'. They wanted an association that would break strikes, eliminate the leagues and reassert agrarian supremacy over the agricultural labour market by 'fighting with equal weapons . . . opposing organization to organization, resistance to resistance'.[30]

The greater prestige and influence of the paternalistic old guard initially ensured that its views prevailed in the earliest organized response of the Bolognese landowners to the socialist labour movement. The first agrarian associations in 1904 were designed to link landowners, leaseholders, sharecroppers and labourers in a single hierarchical agricultural 'sector' in which the different categories could 'share in a peaceful, ordered enterprise united by a common purpose'. Auxiliary organizations of sharecroppers constituted the most innovative feature of the new associations. Conceived as a concrete alternative to the socialist peasant unions, the auxiliaries were to provide institutional channels for 'continual contact and increased familiarity' between landlords and sharecroppers, encouraging 'that mutual trust which is the moral foundation of the *mezzadria*'.[31] Despite their claims about the 'political neutrality' of the auxiliaries, landowners could hardly ignore the possibilities they offered at election time. In a province where the elite had long relied on small political clubs tied to a few notables, the sharecropper organizations potentially fulfilled many of the functions of a mass party in an era of expanding suffrage, since they provided an organized framework for communications, propaganda and electoral mobilization.[32]

While in the short run these agrarian associations enjoyed some success among peasants and at the ballot box, they did not address the underlying structural problems in the countryside associated with commercial agriculture. As a result, they soon fell prey to the mounting hostility of both sharecroppers and big leaseholders. Indeed, the Bolognese leaseholders constituted the vanguard of a new movement of agrarian insurgency in the Po Valley that was directed not only against the socialist labour movement but also against the interest representation of the landed patricians and the political mediation of the old 'parties of order'. This movement had its roots in the major expansion of industrial capitalism into the northern Italian countryside during the first decade of the century. After 1896 exceptional advances took place in Po Valley agriculture that both reflected and stimulated the increasing involvement of commercial farmers with banking interests and industrial supplying and processing sectors. Locally, rising levels of production and the growing interpenetration of agrarian and industrial groups chiefly benefited the large market-oriented leaseholders who were able to increase their wealth and power at the expense of the small producers and less enterprising absentee owners. At the same time, these developments also gave rise to new needs, pressures and problems, spurring commercial farmers to seek an alternative to the inadequate, traditional channels of interest representation and influence at the provincial level and in Rome. Greater vulnerability to market fluctuations combined with the pressing need for an effective organizational counterweight to industrial wealth and organized labour to forge a new interest-group and class consciousness among commercial farmers that transcended old provincial confines. The movement of agrarian insurgency thus was an expression of the changing balance of power within the provincial elites as well as a response to the mounting rigours of economic competition and political lobbying.[33]

With its rhetoric of bourgeois renewal and its advocacy of intransigent resistance, commodity cartels and agrarian political autonomy, the programme advanced by the militant spokesmen for the commercial farmers represented an open repudiation of the Giolitti government's policies of social compromise and a direct challenge to the leadership, methods and ideals of the provincial notables. Predictably, the militants encountered strong opposition from prominent aristocratic landlords like Count Francesco Cavazza and Marchese Giuseppe Tanari. Indeed, the years between 1907 and 1911 witnessed an intense power struggle within the regional and provincial organizations as proponents of bourgeois renewal moved to wrest control from the defenders of class cooperation and deference politics. By 1911 agrarian militants had won a series of victories that marked a crucial turning-point in the evolution of agricultural interest-group politics in the prewar era. During the course of that year, spokesmen for commercial farming interests largely supplanted the old guard of landed notables at the helm of both the regional and the provincial organizations. Under the direction of new men like Lino Carrara and Raffaele Stagni, the agrarian associations dropped all pretence of collaboration and compromise, adopting instead a strategy of direct confrontation with organized labour and governmental authorities.[34]

The organizational triumph of commercial farming interests, however, proved to be a pyrrhic victory for the landed elite as a whole. For the strategy of confrontation was no more effective than class collaboration in stemming the challenge from below. From the outset, the dominant position of the leaseholders within the agrarian association not only alienated the moderate landlords, but also limited its capacity to mobilize the support of that pivotal intermediate class of sharecroppers. As the local prefect observed in 1914, the leaseholders' 'special interest in exploiting the land' led them to treat the sharecroppers with a 'greater severity . . . that then characterizes the entire association . . . so that during electoral campaigns they cannot turn to them for support'.[35]

The estrangement of the sharecroppers was in turn part of a larger political dilemma that confronted the agrarian militants. While rejecting the tutelage of the old parties of order, they were unable to find a viable replacement for them. As an economic lobby representing well-defined interests, the agrarian association could scarcely assume the role of a new political elite capable of winning a broad base of support among the other social groups in the province. In fact, the militants encountered major difficulties in formulating a political programme that went beyond the partisan defence of special interests and entrepreneurial prerogatives. Their narrow corporative vision of social relations left little room for the mass appeals essential to the creation of a conservative majority within an increasingly democratic parliamentary system.

These problems and their disastrous political consequences were strikingly evident in the last two elections prior to the war. The parties of order entered the parliamentary elections of 1913 – the first under a new law that greatly expanded suffrage – fragmented and in disarray. The outcome was predictable; in both the countryside and the city, the left emerged as the chief beneficiary of electoral reform. Apart from the victory of a supporter of Giolitti in an isolated mountain district, just one conservative candidate prevailed. The Socialists swept the remaining six colleges of the province, attracting the lion's share of those voters who cast their ballots for the first time in 1913.[36]

The results from the municipal elections the following year were no less devastating. Of the 61 communes in the province, only 25 now remained in the hands of the parties of order, and of these a mere 3 were in the plains. The Socialists controlled 27 communes, while the remaining 9 were administered by Christian Democratic groups who, according to the prefect, 'generally express socialist tendencies because their supporters belong to the labour organizations'. Capturing 31 of the 50 seats, the left also dominated the Provincial Council and consequently all elective positions on the many local agencies.[37]

The parliamentary and municipal elections clearly demonstrated the inability of either traditional deference politics or agrarian militancy to preserve the power and influence of the landowning classes. In the new era of mass politics ushered in by Giolitti's electoral reform, improvised coalition-building by local notables was no match for the disciplined and well-organized electoral machines of the Socialist Party. While militant spokesmen for commercial farming interests rightly criticized the outdated methods of the moderate old guard, their own strategy of confrontation hardly constituted a viable political alternative. On the eve of the First World War, Bologna's divided and isolated elite appeared powerless to halt the growth of what one contemporary observer described as a socialist 'state within a state with its own special laws and . . . executive organs'.[38]

With Italy's entry into the war in May 1915, new economic conditions, military conscription and state intervention all combined to accelerate important peacetime trends within the propertied classes. Above all, the war accelerated the advance of the big commercial leaseholders, who greatly strengthened their economic position at the expense of the old absentee landlords. With rents frozen at prewar levels as a result of a series of governmental decrees, the leaseholders were in a position to earn huge profits from the sale of their crops as farm prices soared. According to the agricultural expert Arrigo Serpieri, the real income of the commercial leaseholders in the Po Valley more than quintupled during the war.[39]

The leaseholders' enrichment came largely at the expense of the absentee landowners. Governmental decrees, tax policies and price trends all worked decisively to the disadvantage of those landowners who had leased out their lands prior to 1915. Because of the rent freeze, they received none of the financial benefits of soaring farm prices, while they had to shoulder the burdens of increased property taxes and rising living costs. As a result, absentee landlords in the Po Valley saw their real income fall by as much as a third, leading to what Serpieri characterized as a massive 'shift of wealth from the landowner to the leaseholder'.[40]

At the same time, the war created exceptional opportunities for ambitious sharecroppers who had large families or who managed to avoid the draft. Paid a share of the harvest, those fortunate tenants who produced for the market directly benefited from the enormous rise in farm prices after 1914. With a single harvest, they earned sums that previously would have required years of hard work and sacrifices. By 1917 many of them had doubled and sometimes even tripled their prewar incomes. One study of a group of 20 sharecropping families in Bologna, for instance, reported that their net income rose nearly 500 per cent between 1914 and 1918. Similarly, the annual reports of the traditional peasant savings institutions testified to the new-found prosperity of these sharecroppers.[41] As the war wound to a conclusion, the more successful of them began to use their earnings to purchase land, prefiguring what would be the most important social phenomenon in the countryside after the armistice: the emergence of a new rural middle class.

Both developments were temporarily overshadowed in Bologna by the explosion of mass militancy that affected most of the Italian peninsula in 1918 and 1919. For the propertied classes of Bologna, what had been previously a gradual erosion of their power became a full-blown crisis of landlord hegemony in the wake of the war. Fuelled by the experiences of the war and the inspiration of the Russian Revolution, the socialist labour movement advanced a two-pronged attack on the landlords that simultaneously threatened to eliminate the last vestiges of their political power and their control over the land. The parties of order in Bologna confronted an especially formidable adversary in the Provincial Socialist Federation. By the fall of 1919, it had grown enormously in membership largely as a result of support from a union movement representing some 70,000 in the countryside and another 16,000 in the provincial capital.[42] Apart from their numerical strength, the Socialists were distinguished by an increasingly radical posture. In the first half of 1919, the reformist leaders, who had worked closely with the government during the war, lost control of the party organization to more intransigent maximalist elements. With these new men at the helm, the Socialists advanced a programme that violently denounced the war, repudiated any cooperation with 'bourgeois' parties and glorified the dictatorship of the proletariat.[43]

The Socialists provided overwhelming evidence of their political might in the parliamentary elections of November 1919, the first ever with universal manhood suffrage and proportional representation. Nowhere was the defeat of the parties of order or the triumph of the left more impressive than in the province of Bologna. In the capital city, a traditional stronghold of the elite, the Socialists amassed 63 per cent of the vote. The political defeat of the landed classes was even more complete in the countryside, where nearly three quarters of the electorate cast ballots for the Socialist slate. Overall, the old parties of order won only 7.8 per cent of the popular vote and came in a distant third behind the Socialists and the Catholic Popular Party.[44] The Bolognese propertied classes found themselves totally excluded from the Chamber of Deputies for the first time.

As in other provinces of the Po Valley, political developments in Bologna after the war were inseparably linked to the ongoing struggle in the countryside. The stunning success of the Socialists at the ballot box greatly increased the numerical strength of the leagues. One month after the elections, they informed the prefect that they now represented some 40,000 agricultural workers and 9,000 sharecropping families – or, in their words, 'the totality of day labourers and the overwhelming majority of the peasants in the province'.[45] More importantly, the election results of November encouraged local labour leaders to formulate a considerably more radical programme of their own that directly challenged the economic position and managerial authority of the landlords and commercial farmers. Both wage scales and crop shares were made intentionally excessive in order to induce structural changes in the prevailing systems of land tenure and ownership. By sharply reducing the income leaseholders and landowners derived from agriculture, labour leaders sought to compel them to cede their farms to the leagues in the form of collective leases – the first step towards the eventual 'socialization of the land'.[46]

The predictable refusal of the landowners to accept these demands provoked a strike of unparalleled bitterness and violence that made the province the focal point of what was widely perceived as a life and death struggle in the Italian countryside. As the strike dragged on towards summer, the leagues effectively supplanted the police and governmental officials as the real authorities in much of the province. The weak coalition governments in Rome were not prepared to take any strong action against the leagues. Passivity at the top of the state apparatus tended to translate into appeasement of the Socialists by authorities at the provincial level. But in the absence of forceful intervention by the government, the prolongation of the strike favoured the leagues.[47]

By the fall of 1920, Bologna's men of wealth and property felt threatened on a variety of fronts. In the countryside their once unchallenged authority over the land had now been severely challenged by socialist labour leaders who were seemingly determined to exclude them altogether from the productive process. From elective office to honorary positions in the municipal institutions, most of the prizes and distinctions of public life had been lost to the Socialists. With the possible exception of nearby Ferrara, nowhere else on the peninsula did the propertied classes appear to confront a more drastic decline in wealth, power and prestige than in Bologna.[48]

The seeming invincibility of the local socialist movement and the absenteeism of the government destroyed the confidence of Bolognese agrarians in conventional methods of social bargaining and drew them toward more coercive alternatives. Indeed, the key to the rapid emergence of fascism as a major political force in Bologna during the winter of 1920–1 lay in its merger with the propertied classes. Beginning in early 1921, the Bolognese fascists, in collaboration with large landowners and leaseholders, unleashed their own three-pronged attack on the socialist municipal governments, cooperatives and union organizations. Punitive expeditions were directed at strategic targets in the countryside, with the objective of destroying the vital organizational and leadership links of the socialist movement. Selective terror and violence became skilfully coordinated with a campaign by the fascists and their agrarian allies to regiment the day labourers and sharecroppers into 'independent' unions. Before the March on Rome in late October 1922, the offensive had largely achieved its objectives: the destruction of a strong and effective labour movement, the re-establishment of landlord supremacy in the countryside and the installation of the fascists as the new *de facto* rulers in the province.[49]

For landed interests, however, the creation of a stable power structure in the province proved a more prolonged process that involved three separate but interrelated tasks: the establishment of organizational control over the agricultural sector, the domestication of the fascist unions and the development of secure channels of political influence. By the end of 1926, this gradual consolidation of landed power had been largely completed. Through a network of institutions that included commodity associations, the Bolognese

Agrarian Consortium and the Provincial Economic Council, a relatively small group of commercial farming interests, together with the leading manufacturers and banks of the city, was able to extend their control over marketing outlets, agricultural credit and supplies of seed, fertilizers and farm machinery.[50] Likewise, the political structure in Bologna after 1926 was essentially a partnership between the local fascist boss, Leandro Arpinati, and the propertied classes. The latter, in particular, benefited enormously from the elimination of popular suffrage and free party competition which assured them a degree of political influence unparalleled since the late nineteenth century. Approximately half the appointed municipal chiefs or *podestà* in the late 1920s were either agrarian notables or their agents. A similar pattern prevailed on the Provincial Council, where the seats once occupied by popularly elected Socialist representatives were now filled by the 'natural' leaders of the community. Finally, agrarian interests were well represented at the upper levels of the Provincial Fascist Federation by young commercial farmers who were among Arpinati's closest advisers and friends.[51]

Such arrangements did not, however, constitute a simple restoration or return to the past. Under the new regime, agrarian notables no longer had the type of direct control over political decisions that they had once enjoyed through their local liberal-monarchist clubs. They might exercise sizeable influence through the *podestà*, prefecture and provincial federation, but the actual decisions were now made by professional party bureaucrats and state officials rather than through informal understandings between landed gentlemen as in the late nineteenth century. Moreover, in exchange for the strong government they had long sought, agrarian interests had to curb their traditional individualism and accept a level of organizational regimentation, even in their dealings with agricultural labourers. Despite the obvious weaknesses of the fascist unions, landowners and commercial farmers still had to recognize them and at least go through the ritual of negotiating collective agreements with them.[52]

At the same time, the consolidation of the Fascist regime helped to institutionalize a shift in the balance of power within the Bolognese elite that had begun in the first decade of the century. While the propertied classes as a whole benefited from the triumph of fascism, it was the relatively new group of commercial farmers, and not the old guard of absentee landlords, who dominated the main centres of economic power and political influence in the province after 1926. The names of once prominent patrician families had mostly disappeared from the roster of municipal councillors, *podestà* and directors of agrarian organizations. In their place appeared the names of big prewar leaseholders, the sons of an earlier generation of commercial farmers, and young agricultural technicians. The dominant position of commercial farming interests also found expression in the structure of property holdings in the Bolognese plains in the late 1920s. The provincial land registry of 1925 and subsequent additions to it show that many of the most important noble families had given up their estates. Thus, for example, four of the largest aristocratic landowners in Bologna prior to the rise of fascism had all sold their properties by 1927. Significantly, the major buyers of land were either former leaseholders or new joint-stock farm companies.[53]

As these trends in organizational leadership and property holding suggest, the achievement of stability meant considerably more than the restoration of prewar society. It involved not only new institutional arrangements and a new agrarian leadership, but also a fundamental restructuring of power relations within the propertied classes. Such changes were largely the result of political coercion and the authoritarian regimentation of labour. In the countryside, peasant labourers paid for the advance of commercial agriculture in the form of increased exploitation and a diminished standard of living. Policies that crudely rewarded the rich and penalized the weak precluded any genuine social peace and required the presence of a permanent repressive apparatus.[54] When that apparatus finally collapsed under the burdens of military defeat, German occupation and civil war, some of the foremost luminaries of commercial agriculture in Bologna would pay the ultimate price for the advantages they had enjoyed under the Fascist regime.

NOTES

1 The importance of the province and its capital city are amply attested in a variety of sources. See, in particular, Camera di Commercio e Industria della Provincia di Bologna, *Cenno storico sulla Camera di Commercio e Industria di Bologna e caratteristiche del distretto camerale* (Bologna: 1924), pp. 9, 41; Marion I. Newbigin, *Southern Europe: A Regional and Economic Geography of the Mediterranean Lands* (New York: 1932), pp. 171–2; Consiglio Provinciale dell'Economia Corporativa, *La Provincia di Bologna nell'anno decimo. Monografia statistica-economica* (Bologna: 1932); and *La città e provincia di Bologna descritta ne'suoi rapporti storici, statistici, topografici e commerciali* (Bologna: 1889), pp. 3–5.

2 See Giuseppe Puppini, *Le bonifiche in Emilia e Romagna nell'ultimo secolo* (Bologna: 1951), p. 66; Ministero d'Agricoltura, Industria e Commercio, *Censimento della popolazione del Regno d'Italia, 1901*, Vol. III (Rome: 1902), pp. 216–17; G. Medici and G. Orlando, *Agricoltura e disoccupazione*, Vol. I (Bologna: 1952), p. 107; Camera di Commercio, *Cenno storico*, pp. 36–8; Camera di Commercio, *Statistica industriale, Provincia di Bologna* (Bologna: 1898).

3 Renato Zangheri, *La proprietà terriera e le origini del Risorgimento nel Bolognese*, Vol. I (Bologna: 1960), pp. 93–7.

4 Renato Zangheri, *Prime ricerche sulla distribuzione della proprietà fondiaria nella pianura bolognese, 1789–1835* (Bologna: n.d.), pp. 55–63.

5 ibid., p. 66; Luigi Zerbini, *Illustrazione delle principali aziende agrarie del Bolognese* (Bologna: 1913), pp. 6–69.

6 On the enduring importance of the aristocracy, see Dominique Schnapper, 'Storia e sociologia: uno studio su Bologna', *Studi Storici*, viii, 3 (1967), pp. 552–69.

7 See *Il Resto de Carlino*, 14 March 1908; Coriolano Belloni, *Dizionario storico dei banchieri italiani* (Florence: 1951), pp. 63–4 for information on the Cavazza family. For a description and photograph of the Castle Cavazza, see Tryphosa Bates Batcheller, *Italian Castles and Country Seats* (New York: 1911), pp. 108–13. Data on the property holdings of the Cavazza family derive from the Ufficio Erariale di Bologna, 'Catasto dei Terreni', 1924.

8 The speeches given in the Agrarian Society are collected in *Annali della Società Agraria Provinciale di Bologna*. For a discussion of the role of agrarian leaders in the modernizing

activity of the Agrarian Committee see *Annali della Cattedra Provinciale di Agricoltura di Bologna* (1893), p. 5. A more general account of agrarian interest in technical innovation can be found in Giuseppe Carlo Marino, *La formazione dello spirito borghese in Italia* (Florence: 1974), p. 215.

9 Archivio di Stato di Bologna [hereafter ASB], Archivio Privato Malvezzi de'Medici, titolo 28, interview given by Nerio Malvezzi in 1906.

10 ASB, Archivio Malvezzi, letter from Count G. Codronchi, 16 September 1884.

11 Anthony L. Cardoza, *Agrarian Elites and Italian Fascism: the Province of Bologna, 1901–1926* (Princeton, NJ: 1982), pp. 35–7.

12 See Museo civiltà contadina, *Bozze stampa museo civiltà contadina San Marino in Bentivoglio* (Bologna: n.d.), p. 7; Osvaldo Passerini, *Inchiesta sulla piccola proprietà coltivatrice formatasi nel dopoguerra*, Vol. VII (Milan: 1932), pp. 7–20; Aldo Pagani, *Rapporti fra proprietà, impresa e mano d'opera nell'agricoltura italiana*, Vol. XIII (Milan and Rome: 1932), pp. 52–3. For an example of a late nineteenth-century sharecropping contract in Bologna, see Carlo Poni, *Gli aratri e l'economia agraria nel Bolognese dal XVII al XIX secolo* (Bologna: 1963), pp. 231–7.

13 C. Poni, 'Family and "Podere" in Emilia Romagna', *Journal of Italian History*, i, 2 (Autumn 1978), pp. 227–8.

14 *Atti della Giunta per la inchiesta agraria e sulle condizioni della classe agricola*, Vol. II, *Relazione del commissario Marchese Luigi Tanari* (Rome: 1881), p. 224. On relations between landlords and sharecroppers, see Poni, 'Family and "Podere" ', pp. 228–9 and Adrian Lyttelton, 'Landlords, peasants, and the limits of liberalism', in John A. Davis (ed.), *Gramsci and Italy's Passive Revolution* (London: 1979), p. 117.

15 Carlo Berti-Pichat, 'Della tutela dei prodotti campestri', in *Memorie lette nelle adunanze ordinarie della Società Agraria della provincia di Bologna negli anni accademici 1845–1846*, Vol. III (Bologna: 1847), p. 182; Marco Minghetti, "Della proprietà rurale e dei patti fra il padrone e il lavoratore', in *Memorie*, Vol. II (Bologna: 1845), p. 166.

16 Medici and Orlando, *Agricoltura e disoccupazione*, Vol. I, p. 79; Consiglio Provinciale, *La provincia di Bologna*, pp. 589–632.

17 See G. Orlando, 'Progressi e difficoltà dell'agricoltura', in Giorgio Fuà (ed.), *Lo sviluppo economico in Italia*, Vol. III (Milan: 1978), pp. 28–9.

18 Tanari, *Inchiesta agraria*, pp. 428–9; on the growing population of day labourers, see Giovanni Procacci, *La lotta di classe in Italia agli inizi del secolo XX* (Rome: 1970), p. 112.

19 Poni, *Gli aratri*, pp. 104–5.

20 Cardoza, *Agrarian Elites*, pp. 54–5.

21 R. Zangheri (ed.), *Lotte agrarie in Italia. La Federazione Nazionale dei Lavoratori della Terra, 1901–1926* (Milan: 1960), pp. xxiv-xxv, xxxv-xxxviii; Idomeneo Barbadoro, *Storia del sindacalismo italiano dalla nascita al fascismo*, Vol. I, *La Federterra* (Florence: 1973), pp. 66–70, 145–6.

22 Sergio Zaninelli, *Le lotte nelle campagne dalla grande crisi agricola al primo dopoguerra 1880–1921* (Milan: 1971), pp. 143–64; Angelo Bertolini, 'Lo sciopero di Molinella', *Giornale degli Economisti*, xxi (1900), pp. 387–9.

23 On the strikes of these years, see Bertolini, 'Lo sciopero di Molinella', pp. 388–93; Luigi Arbizzani, *Sguardi sull'ultimo secolo. Bologna e la sua provincia 1859–1961* (Bologna: 1961), p. 88.

24 ASB, C6, F2, Police report to prefect, 18 February 1902.

25 Tanari, *Inchiesta agraria*, pp. 229–30, 443.

26 Cardoza, *Agrarian Elites*, pp. 49–53.

27 Tanari, *Inchiesta agraria*, pp. 229–30, 443; Giuseppe Grabinski, *Lo sciopero e la questione sociale nelle campagne* (Bologna: 1888), pp. 7, 29–30, 36.

28 Cardoza, *Agrarian Elites*, pp. 64–75.

29 Enrico Pini, 'Quale deve essere il programma della proprietà agraria in Italia', *Annali della Società Agraria*, xlii (11 May 1902), pp. 223–4.

30 'Di una società mutua fra i proprietari', *Bollettino Mensile del Consorzio Agrario Bolognese*, 31 December 1901.

31 Giovanni Enrico Sturani, *Le consociazioni agrarie della provincia di Bologna. Organizzazione e programma* (Bologna: 1905), pp. 10–13.

32 Cardoza, *Agrarian Elites*, pp. 108–11.

33 ibid., pp. 123–50.
34 ibid., pp. 150–92.
35 ASB, C7, F1, prefect to Ministry of the Interior (no date of day or month) 1914.
36 *Il Resto del Carlino*, 27 October and 3 November 1913.
37 ASB, C7, F1, 'Relazione sulle condizioni politiche della provincia', prefect to Ministry of the Interior (no date of day or month) 1914.
38 *Il Resto del Carlino*, 18 July 1913.
39 Arrigo Serpieri, *La guerra e le classi rurali italiane* (Bari: 1930), pp. 64, 100–2, 116; Utenti Motori Agricoli, *Quarant'anni di motorizzazione agricola in Italia 1928–1967* (Rome: 1968), pp. xvii-xviii.
40 Serpieri, *La guerra e le classi rurali*, pp. 116–18.
41 Passerini, *Inchiesta sulla piccola proprietà*, Vol. VII, p. 33 n.; Serpieri, *La guerra e le classi rurali*, p. 118; Cassa di Risparmio, *La Cassa di Risparmio in Bologna nei suoi primi cento anni* (Bologna: 1937), p. 397.
42 Angela De Benedictis, 'Note su classe operaia e socialismo a Bologna nel primo dopoguerra (1919–1920)', in Deputazione Emilia-Romagna per la storia della Resistenza, *Movimento operaio e fascismo nell'Emilia-Romagna 1919–1923* (Rome: 1973), p. 80; L. Arbizzani, 'Lotte agrarie in provincia di Bologna nel primo dopoguerra', in R. Zangheri (ed.), *Le campagne emiliane nell'epoca moderna* (Milan: 1957), pp. 298–9.
43 Benedictis, 'Note su classe operaia', pp. 84–98.
44 ASB, C5, F1, 'Risultato votazione in Bologna città', 17 November 1919; *Il Resto del Carlino*, 22 and 23 November 1919.
45 ASB, C16, F1, Federterra to prefect, 16 December 1919.
46 Arbizzani, 'Lotte agrarie', pp. 307–8; Barbadoro, *Storia del sindacalismo*, Vol. I, p. 363.
47 Cardoza, *Agrarian Elites*, pp. 278–86.
48 On the situation in Ferrara, see Paul Corner, *Fascism in Ferrara, 1915–1925* (Oxford: 1975), pp. 104–12. Perhaps the most eloquent description of the agrarians' plight remains that of Angelo Tasca in his *The Rise of Italian Fascism* (New York: 1966), p. 95.
49 Cardoza, *Agrarian Elites*, pp. 294–339.
50 ibid., pp. 391–404; Pier Paolo D'Attore, 'Agrari e fascismo. La formazione del regime reazionario di massa (Bologna, negli anni venti)', tesi di Laurea, University of Bologna, 1976, pp. 50–1.
51 ibid., pp. 432–3.
52 See Charles Maier, *Recasting Bourgeois Europe* (Princeton, NJ: 1975), pp. 572, 584.
53 Cardoza, *Agrarian Elites*, pp. 433–5.
54 Maier, *Recasting Bourgeois Europe*, pp. 577–8.

10

The City of the Sun: Red Cerignola, 1900–15

Frank M. Snowden

The South of Italy under the Liberal regime was an area of poverty and economic backwardness, but it did not provide perfect ground for the establishment of revolutionary peasant movements. The essential reason for the failure of stable peasant-based union and political movements was the extreme social 'disaggregation'[1] that characterized the region. In most of the Mezzogiorno there was no sociological foundation for a frontal confrontation between landlords and peasants. Property was fragmented across an entire spectrum that ranged from great *latifondisti* to landless labourers, with a broad range of intermediate strata. As a result, it was difficult for a clear sense of collective identity to emerge. The difficulty was then compounded by the plurality of economic roles that many peasants filled in the course of the agricultural year. It was common for men to combine bewilderingly the roles of dwarf proprietor, sharecropper and day labourer, with the result that the possibility of their recognizing a community of interests with other cultivators was small.

The effects of such 'role fragmentation'[2] in inhibiting mass political organization were reinforced by other aspects of southern Italian life. Poverty and its related disadvantages of malnutrition and insecurity stimulated discontent, but they also removed the economic, physical and psychic resources necessary for sustained political action. Chronic overpopulation and fierce competition for employment and access to the land divided peasants against one another instead of uniting them in opposition to the proprietors. Family ties, patronage networks, paternalism and patriarchy linked people in vertical bonds across class boundaries instead of promoting class solidarity. Illiteracy, isolation and immemorial custom generated acceptance. The influence of the church fostered resignation. Complex differences in contractual terms, in wealth and in life chances promoted division. Social discontent produced deeds of violence and spontaneous, short-lived rebellions but not organized political movements.[3]

A partial exception to the general pattern was provided by the scattered zones dominated by the great estates, or latifundia, which occupied parts of Latium, Sicily, Calabria, Apulia and Basilicata. Latifundia greatly simplified the social structure, producing a pronounced bipolarity between the few great lords and the mass of peasants. Latifundia, moreover, were labour-repressive institutions that relied on physical force and violence, multiplying the occasions for conflict. It was no coincidence that the regions of the South where mass-based socialist movements most successfully challenged the power of property were the latifundist zones of western Sicily and northern Apulia.

Great estates, however, were not standardized economic structures. Although the social history of latifundism is only beginning to be written, it is clear that latifundia varied widely in their social and productive relations. In terms of the stability of lordly power, the most important differences were, first, those distinguishing estates that hired migrant workers from estates that employed a settled workforce; and, secondly, those between estates that recruited peasant cultivators and estates that employed gangs of wage labourers. Migrant workers, employed extensively in Latium and in Grosseto province in Tuscany, were notoriously difficult to organize, while peasant tenants and sharecroppers, who were the dominant labour figures on the Sicilian estates, had a stake in the harvest and in the social order. Such factors greatly limited the scope for peasant militancy. The peasants on the latifundia in Sicily, furthermore, were not a homogeneous class. On the contrary, they were worker-peasants who might own, crop and lease tiny plots and still work as day labourers during the peak seasons of the year.

It is comprehensible, therefore, that the area of the Mezzogiorno that produced the longest and most powerful history of revolutionary farm workers' organizations was Apulia. There the latifundia were distinctive in hiring a settled and wholly proletarianized force of full-time day labourers. In the generation between 1900 and 1922 the Apulian labourers radically challenged the power of property through the most successful anarcho-syndicalist movement in Italian history. The farm workers of Bari and Foggia provinces established a network of stable mass institutions to direct their struggle. Consciously revolutionary in intent with the socialization of the land and the emancipation of labour as their goals, the workers of the Apulian estates presented a formidable challenge.[4]

Most organized of all was the commune of Cerignola in Foggia province, which earned a reputation as the 'fatherland of the farm workers'[5] that served as a model and an inspiration for agricultural labourers throughout the region. At the height of the movement virtually every adult male worker in the township was unionized under the auspices of the Cerignola Chamber of Labour, and on the eve of the First World War the workers elected their own representatives to power in the town hall with a mandate to expropriate the landlords. In pursuing their goals, the *cerignolani* also deployed an imposing arsenal of weapons in the confrontation with the *latifondisti* – sabotage, land occupations and the general strike. The prefect reported of the city in 1920: 'The organization of the working class is perfect.'[6]

The purpose of this chapter is to examine the reasons for the acute instability of the power of the Cerignola landlords. Why were they so signally unable to establish a secure political hegemony? What was the background to the degeneration of social relations to the stark alternatives of rebellion and violent repression? What factors created a situation in which farm workers united in the confident expectation that they could transform their commune into what a local labourer and poet, in the vision of Cerignola without landlords, termed the 'City of the Sun'?[7]

In order to understand the fragility of landlords' power in Cerignola, we shall need to examine the settlement of the township, the position of the estate owners, the relations between workers and employers, and the social structure of the city.

THE FRONTIER

The first essential feature of political life in Liberal Cerignola was its status as a frontier society. Largely settled after Italian unification in the third quarter of the nineteenth century, Foggia province possessed few of the economic, familial and cultural residues of a traditional society. The power of property was not legitimated by what Max Weber terms 'patriarchal authority' – the force of immemorial custom.[8] Modern Cerignola was the product of a peculiarly rapacious form of agrarian capitalism under which the exploitation of labour assumed a naked and brutal aspect.

When peasants in traditional societies are resigned to their condition, it is partly because the inequalities are the inherited and seemingly inevitable parts of a world in which they were born. The existing social order draws strength from the silent ideological force of custom. In Cerignola, by contrast, the landlords were not patriarchs but parvenu entrepreneurs. Landlords and farm-workers confronted each other not in roles handed down from their fathers but as settlers in a new world. Until Unification, Cerignola formed the southern boundary of the enormous sheep walk known as the Tavoliere that covered most of Foggia province – some 3,000 km^2. Planting was limited to designated islands of cultivation. Beyond these, farming was forbidden from the fifteenth century by the Crown, which collected levies on the nomadic herds of sheep brought to pasture from the neighbouring Abruzzi. The word Tavoliere meant 'customs zone'.

The Risorgimento, Italy's 'bourgeois revolution', abolished the dead hand of economic immobilism on the Tavoliere. The customs zone was privatized as the land was sold at public auction and made available for cultivation. A frontier was opened, and the Tavoliere came to be known as the 'Texas of Apulia' and the 'California of Italy'.[9]

The conduct of the land sales concentrated ownership in the hands of a small number of wealthy entrepreneurs. Instead of disposing of the land in small plots and facilitating the creation of peasant proprietorship, the Italian parliament legislated a rapid sale in large blocs to buyers with ready cash or access to credit. The Tavoliere thus provides a dramatic illustration of Gramsci's description of the Risorgimento as a 'revolution without a revolution' or 'passive revolution' by which the old regime was overturned by a narrow ruling class that failed to give the masses a stake in the new order. The result, in Gramsci's words, was 'the endemic rebelliousness of the popular classes'.[10]

Cerignola illustrates Gramsci's comments. In one of the largest communes in the kingdom, the decades following the abolition of the sheep regime in 1865 witnessed the creation of what many observers described as a 'pathological' social structure.[11] The designated latifundists of the Bourbon Tavoliere were joined by a small but wealthy class of capitalist investors. Great estates established an almost absolute sway throughout the Tavoliere, and rising land valuations and the absence of credit for the peasantry ensured that the conquest was permanent. In 1900 large holdings of over 300 hectares occupied 75 per cent of the 61,000 hectares of the commune of Cerignola, while medium properties of 50–300 hectares covered 23 per cent of the area of the township, that is to say nearly all of the remainder. Smallholdings accounted for less than 2 per cent.[12] Even the smallholdings that existed did not represent peasant proprietorship, since they were often market gardens close to the town and owned by the petite bourgeoisie. There was no room at Cerignola for the peasant smallholder.

The land was virtually monopolized by roughly a hundred powerful families who were, with a few notable exceptions, not nobles but 'new men' from the worlds of trade, banking and the professions. The Pavoncelli family was the most important and powerful of the new proprietors. Giuseppe Pavoncelli possessed one of the great fortunes in the region with net assets worth 16 million lire in 1903 and nearly 8,000 hectares in the commune, together with holdings elsewhere.[13] He served as deputy for the constituency without interruption from 1874 until his death in 1910, and was briefly Minister of Public Works. Like a southern Spanish *cacique*, he held the municipal council in his pocket, exercising a local rule known to his opponents as *Pavoncellismo*.

The family position was established by Giuseppe Pavoncelli's father Federico, the son of a Foggia silversmith. Federico Pavoncelli moved to Cerignola in the 1830s, married the daughter of a local grain merchant and took over the family business. After edging out rival Genoese merchants in Apulian markets, he made his fortune during the Crimean War, when he won the contract to supply the Allied armies with wheat. He and his son used the proceeds to speculate in land on the Tavoliere.[14] Giuseppe Pavoncelli later described himself as a 'pioneer' who tamed the 'wild'.[15]

With ownership thus heavily concentrated, Cerignola was marked by the radical contrast between the *latifondisti* and the landless citizens who worked the fields. Cerignola presented an authentic realization of Marx's misleading vision of capitalist society as a bipolar world divided between two radically unequal extremes – the narrow class of capitalists and the mass of dispossessed proletarians. Cerignola had the misfortune of being exactly such a place. With no economic activity apart from agriculture, the commune was divided between a handful of *signori* and thousands of day labourers. In the abyss between the two poles there were only the narrow strata of people who performed services for the agricultural population: builders, hucksters, artisans, lawyers, police and priests.

LANDLORDS AND FARMERS

For the Tavoliere latifundists, the risks involved in agriculture were forbidding. In good years, when rainfall was abundant, the productivity of the largely virgin soil was the highest in the South. Unfortunately, however, the climate was notoriously unpredictable, with recurrent droughts that caused crop failures on average one year in four. The great Foggia plain had no source of water in the summer months, and was famous for its late frosts, violent storms and strong winds. In such an environment, farming became a game of chance. Cultivation was based on the primitive methods of Mediterranean monocrop dry farming. Profit depended not on a calculable return on investment but on the hazards of a capricious climate.[16]

Important aspects of adaptation to this environment were absenteeism and the separation between ownership and cultivation. The interest of the proprietor was to regularize his income – a result he could achieve by letting the land instead of managing it directly, allowing the property boom following settlement to guarantee lucrative contracts. With some few exceptions, the landlords divorced themselves from agriculture and confined their activities to the negotiating of leases and the collecting of rent. Instead of living on their estates, they resided in Naples, Rome, or Paris. The concentration of wealth in the hands of the latifundists and the high risks of agriculture in the region encouraged the diversification of their financial affairs. The pluralism of economic interests drew them to the cities. The resulting divorce from the land was reinforced by the absence of cultural amenities, the ever-present danger of malaria, the disdain for physical labour and the sheer ignorance of sound farming practice. Far from investing capital in the countryside, proprietors mortgaged the land to finance urban pursuits, and passed the risks of cultivation on to an agrarian speculator – the capitalist farmer or *massaro*.[17]

The *massaro* paid a substantial rent for a short three-year contract – the length of a crop cycle – and then moved on, wealthy if the rains fell, broken if they did not. As a temporary figure in the countryside, the *massaro* adopted a productive strategy that was the antithesis of sound agricultural practice. As in Sicily during the same period, the latifundia of Foggia province were a classic example of 'modernization without development'.[18] A striking contradiction of the Apulian countryside was the combination of the class and social structures of modern capitalism with the most antiquated methods of cultivation. As the *massaro*'s concerns were exclusively short-term, he attempted to reduce investment to zero. The ground was worked with a primitive plough that barely scratched the surface. Seed was poorly selected and then broadcast. Work animals were underfed and mistreated. The soil was neither fertilized nor irrigated and weeds were permitted to flourish. Buildings decayed through neglect. The crop rotation was normally the soil-depleting three-field rotation – two years of wheat and one of fallow. Far, therefore, from sharing a community of interest with the men he employed, the farmer visibly performed a role that was pernicious for the fertility of the soil, for the welfare of the populace and for future prospects of employment.[19]

Furthermore, the combination of absenteeism on the part of the owners and of temporary residence by the farmers prevented the development of associational life. Agrarian associations, educational and cultural societies, clubs and philanthropic organizations were non-existent or languished in inactivity. The landed classes had no ideology to explain and justify latifundism and no institutions through which to propagate a common sense that rationalized the Apulian social order. Latifundism was an instrument of political as well as economic domination, but its power was not legitimated through the structures of a well-articulated civil society.

FARMERS AND WORKERS

Most decisive of all for the stability of the social order at Cerignola were the direct relations between farmers and the labourers they employed. The explosive potential of so starkly divided a society was reinforced by the economic relations between the two great classes of *cerignolani* – farmers and workers. The behaviour of the rural entrepreneur was not that of a patriarch.

The *massaro* normally split his workforce into two radically divided categories. The first consisted of a small privileged minority of salaried personnel who lived on the estates and performed the sensitive tasks that continued throughout the year. Giuseppe Pavoncelli, the greatest landlord of the commune, was exceptional in operating some of his estates under his own management. On these properties he listed the fixed personnel he retained – a chief steward, estate guards, warehousemen, carters, shepherds, surveyors, herdsmen and stable hands. These men, numbering several hundred in the whole of the township, enjoyed secure employment throughout the year, relatively favourable pay scales, bonuses for good performance, sporadic personal favours and access to plots of land to cultivate.[20]

The second and far more numerous category comprised the vast majority of the workforce and consisted of day labourers or *braccianti*. They were hired by the day, often on an anonymous basis. In his dealings with the *braccianti* the employer was well aware that, in the battle for survival in a harsh environment, the chief expense of production was the cost of labour. Pressed by the high rent he paid to the landlord and by the ever-present risk of crop failure, the *massaro* practised severe parsimony towards the workers. He was further encouraged in this direction by the desire to maintain a style of life in competition with the rest of the community. He was, moreover, unrestrained by the need to consider the long-term stability of labour relations and he established no personal relationship with the workers. In Weber's terms, his rapacity was the characteristic behaviour of a prebendal official. Unlike a salaried manager or official, he purchased his office in the manner of a tax farmer and lived by 'ruthless exploitation'.[21]

The *massaro* and the *braccianti* confronted each other in undisguised antagonism in the labour market that formed before dawn in the Piazza del Carmine, which was known locally as the 'market of human flesh'.[22] Here the farmer enjoyed overwhelmingly favourable bargaining power. After the opening of the 'frontier', Cerignola experienced a rush of settlement as new arrivals flooded the township in search of work. Peasants in neighbouring provinces – Bari and Potenza particularly – as well as from the hills of the Gargano in Foggia province itself, were driven off the land. They succumbed before a series of unrelenting pressures – the chronic overpopulation of the South, the enclosure of common land, an uncompromisingly repressive and onerous tax system, rising land prices, phylloxera and the great agricultural depression that hit Italy in the 1880s.[23] Large numbers of expropriated and impoverished peasants in search of work flooded Cerignola, which was transformed from a small town of 11,000 inhabitants in 1850 to a teeming city of 40,000 by 1900.[24]

It is vital to stress that the commune they reached possessed only one substantial economic activity. Within the dominant agricultural sector there was only one mode of access to the land for the new arrivals. Cerignola was a township with an insignificant number of peasants. The men who worked the fields all shared the same occupation, the same handful of employers and the same life chances. There was little hope of rising in the social scale or of securing a stake in society. The Cerignola *braccianti* worked exclusively as agricultural proletarians who sold their labour power. The workers cultivated no plot, owned no house, possessed no work animals and cultivated the land as individuals rather than as members of a family unit. The figures of the census of 1901 are not conclusive evidence because the returns are notoriously subject to error. On this point, however, they are highly suggestive. Of the adult male agricultural population of 9,476 at that date, 7,947 were day labourers.[25]

The terrible imbalance between supply and demand in the labour market, and the success of the *massari* in passing on the risks of cultivation, were reflected in the harsh terms struck in the darkness of the Piazza del Carmine. After the winter slack season, the workers had no resources left; there was no possibility of employment apart from the estates of the *latifondisti*; and on all sides the aspiring field-hands faced throngs of grim and hungry competitors for work.

Inevitably, wages in the commune were low. In the early years of the twentieth century, 1½ lire a day for an adult male was normal. In the abstract, such a wage for the prevailing average of 280 days of work a year was just adequate for subsistence. Such wages, however, were deceptive. Average daily wages were a fiction, combining the high season, when pay reached the heights of 3½ lire, and the long winter lay-off when labourers ran up debts and, in bad years, took to their beds in abject misery, skimping on food, light and fuel.[26] Furthermore, daily pay scales masked the reality of hourly rates, which were even less impressive, as they were reduced to a minimum by the standard practice of extending the working day to its natural maximum: from sunrise to sunset.[27] In addition, wages were universally paid partly in kind in the form of wine and meals that were adulterated to cut costs.[28] It is also important to remember that fines were arbitrarily administered for shirking or insubordination and that labour recruiters required a consideration before admitting a man to the fields.[29]

Contracts were devised to ensure that the risks of cultivation were borne by the workforce. If illness, storms, or the breakdown of machines prevented work, the *braccianti* were entitled to no compensation. Frequently work gangs set off into the dark with no agreed pay scales, waiting instead for the satisfactory performance of the task to determine how much a farmer could afford. Most intolerable of all was the practice whereby hungry and indebted labourers consented to work for meals alone. For good reason 'slavery' is a recurring term in the surviving accounts of the workers' conditions.

The greatest torment of the Cerignola *braccianti*, however, was not low pay but insecurity. Chronic underemployment and the threat of compulsory idleness were the fate of all. There was always a sizeable reserve army of the unemployed, and in the recurring droughts there was famine in the city. Hunger and malnutrition haunted even able-bodied and employable young men. Many were less fortunate. Superannuation, when a man could no longer bend double over the short-handled mattock, came early, while disability through accident or disease was frequent. In such cases a worker was obliged to labour for the same half-pay as boys or to resort to the expedients of begging and crime.

By whatever indices one chooses, hardship in the 'Red City' was a vital aspect of social relations. The records of public health in the commune, for instance, confirm that the farm labourers in Foggia province endured the worst hardships in the peninsula, with rates of death per thousand inhabitants that were double those of England and Wales, and nearly double those of the north of Italy. Cerignola, together with the surrounding Tavoliere, established national records at the turn of the century for the diseases of poverty, malnutrition and filth. Diarrhoeal illnesses, infallible indicators of deadly social conditions, were the leading cause of death in the commune, decimating the population of infants and children and accounting for one death in every three.[30]

Chronic and abject poverty, then, was an essential element in the rebellion that challenged the bases of the power of property. Poverty combined explosively with a strong sense of class identity and the clarity of the opposition of interests between the workers and the tiny elite of distant, idle and anonymous employers. Such factors bred anger and created essential preconditions for violent resistance. It was the pattern of settlement, however, that went a long way in converting potential into reality.[31]

THE CITY

The pattern of settlement characteristic of latifundism on the Tavoliere contributed powerfully to the process of severing the tenuous bonds between the classes and of creating a collective identity among the labourers. The dominant pattern in Italian agriculture as a whole was for the majority of the population to live settled on the land or scattered in hamlets and small villages. Such dispersal was a major structural foundation for Marx's description of the French peasantry in the mid-nineteenth century as a 'sack of potatoes'. According to Marx:

> The smallholding peasants form a vast mass, the members of which have a similar condition but without entering into manifold relations with one another. Their mode of production isolates them from one another. Each individual peasant is almost self-sufficient . . . and the identity of their interests begets no community, no national bond and no political organization among them. They do not form a class.[32]

The majority of peasants in most of Italy lived in such a manner. Isolation was a major component of lordly power.

Cerignola, with 40,000 inhabitants, provided a most striking contrast. The commune was the third most extensive in the kingdom, but there was not a single settlement apart from the city itself. Several hundred fixed personnel lived on the estates. Otherwise the entire population resided in the fiercely overpopulated centre.

The city itself, like the *pueblo* in Andalusia, provided new causes of discontent and created new opportunities for revolt.[33] The elegant centre of Cerignola, stretching along the Corso, the Piazza del Carmine and the Piazza

Vittorio Emanuele, belonged to the notables. Here stood the monumental stone buildings that reflected and confirmed the wealth and the domination of the *signori* – the town hall, the cathedral, the theatre and the family palaces. Behind the Piazza Vittorio Emanuele clustered the low, damp houses and narrow passages of the original workers' quarters – the 'Old City' (Terra Vecchia). With the boom of settlement, the Old City was overwhelmed and gave way to all the excesses of furious and unregulated urbanization – overcrowding, filth, high rent, disease and crime. New workers' districts, such as the Purcino quarter, known in the city as the 'pigsty', were built to absorb the influx. By the new century, fashionable Cerignola was encircled by a ring of working-class slums where the absentee landlords re-emerged as absentee slumlords.

For the workers, the combination of urban and rural poverty within sight of the opulence of the elite produced, in the words of one landlord, 'a dangerous hybridism that is the cause of so many evils'.[34] The immediate juxtaposition of social extremes sharpened tensions, particularly when the same employers who enforced such onerous conditions in the fields created new flashpoints of outrage. Landlords and farmers, speculating in urban property as well as in land, found in town new instruments of domination. Ungrateful workers were evicted from their homes to encourage the others, while losses in the fields were offset by high rents and moneylending in the city.

Furthermore, the concentration of thousands of workers sharing a single occupation and condition greatly facilitated the formation of collective solidarities. Cafés, bars, neighbourhoods and the streets themselves fostered sociability and the exchange of information. Subversive contacts took place with bricklayers, artisans and railroad navvies. Men who had emigrated to the north or to the New World, as well as conscripts who had been stationed elsewhere in the peninsula, shared their vision of alternative ways of living. Radical teachers, politicized artisans and literate labourers read newspaper articles and pamphlets aloud.[35]

If the material and moral conditions of the city made it a cauldron of discontent, the disunity of the narrow ruling elite made its position precarious. Factionalism prevented it from achieving even a semblance of moral leadership. The landlords themselves, scattered in Rome or Naples, unconcerned with their holdings and ignorant of agriculture, were incapable of uniting or of elaborating a social doctrine to justify their position. In Apulia there was no centre such as Bologna in Emilia, Florence in Tuscany, or Palermo in Sicily where they met, formed contacts and concerted their actions.

While the landlords were incapable of providing the landed interest with effective leadership, the *massari* had little incentive to do so. As temporary figures in the life of the commune, they had no concern with the long term. Furthermore, their interests clashed sharply with those of the proprietors.

Such questions as the payment of rent, the renewal of leases, the maintenance of buildings and the burden of the expenses arising from labour unrest set them at odds. Their dealings were transacted amid a torrent of litigation.

The two great subclasses of the landed interest – owners and farmers – were further divided by conflicting priorities. The minority of grape-growers and the dominant wheat-planters clashed over protectionism. Great *latifondisti* such as the Pavoncelli with large profit margins accepted the necessity of concessions to workers' demands, while smaller farmers urged uncompromising intransigence. All were divided by competition for the spoils of town hall and by rivalry for election to parliament.

Far from uniting easily in defence of their interests, the *signori* of Cerignola waged bitter struggles among themselves. Most enduring of all was the contest between the largest and most powerful landowning families in the commune – the Pavoncelli and the Larochefoucauld estates. Giuseppe Pavoncelli was the most modern and progressive of Apulian farmers. He also passed for a radical in local politics because he urged improvements in conditions in order to defuse tensions. He was adamant over the question of wages, but he pressed for reforms over hours, housing and the quality of provisions. The Duc de Larochefoucauld, by contrast, was the very symbol of productive backwardness and political intransigence. His managers reacted to the call for the eight-hour day by forcing the work gangs on his estates to work until sunset at gunpoint. The duke's plenipotentiary in Apulia, Eugène Maury, boasted that he would starve the *canaille* into submission.[36]

The factionalism and fragmentation of the landed interest had important political implications. Labour relations were severely complicated because the Cerignola Agrarian Federation, which existed chiefly on paper until after the First World War, was unable to negotiate authoritatively with the labourers. Agreements reached with one set of negotiators were then rejected by their competitors. In elections the opposing factions denounced each other and publicly questioned the legitimacy of the sitting administration in city hall.

Lacking unity, organization and a legitimating ideology, the landlords on the Apulian frontier were unable to exercise a hegemonic role. Such a negative result was confirmed by the fact that the socialization of the workforce also passed by default. The normal means of ideological control, so effective in other peasant societies, namely the school and the church, were inadequate to the task. The education of children was a statutory obligation of local government. In practice, however, child labour negated the possibility that teachers in Cerignola could impart civic virtues in the manner of the contemporary *instituteurs* of the Third Republic in France.[37] Boys normally began work in the fields from the age of 8 and were therefore beyond the reach of the schoolmaster. The town council, in any case, never seriously set itself the task of providing instruction for the working classes. The majority of the inhabitants of Cerignola were illiterate and spoke dialect rather than the national language.[38]

The church, for its part, had no substantial influence. The settlement boom, which had swamped the civic infrastructures of Cerignola, also overwhelmed the parish network. The church failed to keep pace with so radical a demographic transformation. In Italy as a whole, there was an average ratio of 1,567 inhabitants per parish church, with far more favourable proportions prevailing in such traditional areas of Catholic strength as Venetia and Tuscany.[39] In the diocese of Ascoli Sarti and Cerignola, by contrast, there were 6,225 citizens per parish. Inevitably, the priest was a remote figure and pastoral care languished.

In the mind of the populace, moreover, official religion was widely equated with oppression. With some education and a secure annual salary of 800 lire, the poorest priest seemed one of the *signori* to the residents of the Old City and the Purcino. The church and the cathedral were also located in the landlords' quarter of the city, and the labour market was conducted on the doorstep of the Chiesa del Carmine. The priest inside, moreover, was a moneylender who used his sermons to counsel resignation and the inevitability of poverty, and to threaten union members with excommunication. When the *massari* then forced the labour gangs to kneel in prayer at the end of the day's work in the fields, the estrangement of the people was complete.

Thus one of the salient aspects of life at Cerignola was the lack of religiosity among the people. The churches stood almost empty; civil weddings took precedence over religious ceremonies; and holy days were times of pagan celebration that created anxiety for public order.[40]

CRISIS

After a long and painful period of preparation, the new century witnessed the explosion of labour unrest, which found the landlords unprepared to defend their position effectively. The first major strikes between 1901 and 1904 broadened into an organized and sustained challenge to the existence of the estates and the power of property. Between 1901 and the First World War, the employers suffered a series of defeats, and were driven step by step into making major concessions – wage increases, limitations on hours, union recognition, written contracts, a ban on the hiring of outsiders, and the establishment of a labour exchange with a monopoly on the labour market. Furthermore, the extension of the franchise in 1911 opened the way for the election in 1913 of a Socialist local government with the explicit intention of using its tax powers to expropriate the owners and to furnish credit to producers' cooperatives that would lease farms directly from the proprietors, thus sweeping the *massari* aside completely.[41]

The response of landlords and farmers to such a dramatic challenge to their position was the use of force. Force, of course, was not a new departure. On the contrary, it was an integral and essential part of latifundism. Vast holdings of thousands of hectares and great concentrations of wealth in the midst of destitution required a means of enforcing order. Latifundism permanently generated social tensions that necessitated repression.

At Cerignola violence in the service of latifundism took several forms. One was the use of the armed forces of the state. Giolittian liberalism in the years between 1901 and the First World War entailed the legalization of the trade union movement and the neutrality of the state in industrial disputes. Such reformism, however, applied only to northern Italy, and was balanced by the systematic use of violence in the South. During Giolitti's premiership, Apulia, where the organization of labour was most threatening, earned a sad reputation as the 'land of chronic massacres'.[42] In major labour disputes the regular police and the *carabinieri* were reinforced by thousands of infantrymen and cavalry. During the general strike of 1904 Cerignola became the scene of a famous slaughter as the police opened fire on striking labourers. The town was placed under a state of siege as Cerignola was occupied by over 4,000 troops.[43]

State power was thus a vital element in the position of the latifundists at Cerignola. The state forces of order were supplemented by two local law enforcement agencies – the rural and the municipal guards, who were recruited, paid and commanded by the town council. Since local government was, until the extension of the electoral franchise, virtually a family affair of the propertied classes, the local guards were effectively an instrument of the employers, charged with the defence of property.

Useful for the purpose of defending public order in open confrontations and for the task of apprehending poachers and vandals, the police of all categories were nevertheless too sporadic in their attentions for the maintenance of day-to-day labour discipline. Work gangs hired anonymously by the day for little pay, with no prospect of advancement for good performance and no stake in the outcome of their labours, could not be relied upon to work diligently and well. Employers therefore depended on economic and physical sanctions. The economic means of persuasion consisted, first, of fines, eviction from the home, the threat of dismissal, and blacklisting. A labourer known for idling or subversive ideas could find neither employment or lodgings. In addition, employers used the economic weapons of the lock-out and the introduction of machines to reduce the bargaining power of the unions, known as 'peasant leagues'.

The estates also resorted to physical coercion and intimidation. Estate managers equipped the farms with overseers and guards, mounted and armed with whips and rifles. Recalcitrant workers who failed to respond to economic reason or who challenged authority overtly were threatened or flogged. Whipping is a common theme in the memories of the workers of Cerignola.[44]

Not secure in the protection of four police forces and private guards, farmers also organized unofficial vigilante squads for the spread of terror among the population. These were the infamous *mazzieri*, who were hired in the underworld of the overcrowded city, from the fixed personnel of the estates and among town hall employees. Their missions were to break strikes and to fix elections, their tools the cudgel and the revolver.[45]

The difficulties with the use of force were twofold in the long run. First, it was in some respects counterproductive. The resort to evictions, blacklisting and flogging deepened the sense of popular outrage and radicalized the farm workers' movement. The extreme intransigence of the Cerignola landlords drove the labourers' organization into revolutionary channels. On the left in Cerignola there was no space for reformist socialism, and the movement was dominated by revolutionary syndicalism. The second problem was that the traditional means of repression in Cerignola were necessarily limited. Estate guards, *carabinieri* and *mazzieri* could defeat the rebelliousness of individuals and of whole work gangs. They could delay and impede the establishment of the leagues. They could even crush such single dramatic confrontations as the general strike of 1904. What they were unable to do successfully was to contain discontent once it had become an organized mass movement. By the outbreak of the First World War, the labour movement had become the dominant force in Cerignola.

Landlords' power in the 'Red City' was now gravely in jeopardy. The traditional means of domination had been effectively challenged. Furthermore, the war itself, which acted as the greatest catalyst of all of labour militancy in the Italian countryside, deepened and inflamed the crisis. Conventional policies and politics were discarded, and the issue was resolved only in the final extremity of civil war in 1921 and 1922.[46]

NOTES

1 G. Salvemini, *Scritti sulla questione meridionale* (Turin: 1955).

2 S. Tarrow, *Peasant Communism in Southern Italy* (New Haven, Conn.: 1967), pp. 212–13. Studies of sociability and its absence in the South include E. Banfield, *The Moral Basis of a Backward Society* (Glencoe: 1958); D. Dolci, *Chi gioca solo* (Turin: 1966); and R. Miller, 'Are families amoral?', *American Ethnologist*, 1 (1974), pp. 515–35.

3 For the structures of latifundism in Sicily, see A. Blok, *The Mafia of a Sicilian Village, 1860–1960. A Study of Violent Peasant Entrepreneurs* (Oxford: 1974); J. Schneider and P. Schneider, *Culture and Political Economy in Western Sicily* (Chicago: 1979); and D. Mack Smith, 'The latifundia in modern Sicilian history', *Proceedings of the British Academy*, 51 (1965), pp. 85–124. A classic nineteenth-century report is L. Franchetti and S. Sonnino, *Inchiesta in Sicilia*, 2 vols (Florence: 1974). For Calabria, see P. Arlacchi, *Mafia, Peasants and Great Estates: Society in Traditional Calabria* (Cambridge: 1983). For Grosseto there is Biblioteca Storica Toscana, *Agricoltura e società nella maremma grossetana dell'800* (Florence: 1980). Still useful on the Mezzogiorno in general is M. Rossi-Doria, 'The land tenure system and class in Southern Italy', *American Historical Review*, 64 (1958), pp. 46–53.

4 On the history of the farm labourers' movement in Apulia in this period, see Frank M. Snowden, *Violence and Great Estates in the South of Italy: Apulia, 1900–1922* (Cambridge: 1986); F. De Felice, 'Il movimento operaio e contadino nel novecento', in G. Musca (ed.), *Storia della Puglia* (Bari: 1979), Vol. 2, pp. 251–68; and Giuliano Procacci, *La lotta di classe in Italia agli inizi del secolo XX* (Rome: 1978), pp. 145–52. A useful memoir is L. Allegato, *Socialismo e comunismo in Puglia: Ricordi di un militante* (Rome: 1971).

5 Interview with Antonio Bonito, in G. Rinaldi and P. Sobrero (eds), *La memoria che resta: vissuto quotidiano, mito e storia dei braccianti del basso Tavoliere* (Foggia: 1981), p. 105.
6 Archivio Centrale dello Stato, PS (1920), b. 85, fasc. Foggia (agitazione per uso civico di pesca), n. 215. Report of the prefect of Foggia to Ministero dell'Interno, Direzione Generale della Pubblica Sicurezza, 11 June 1920.
7 G. Angione, *La città del sole* (Foggia: 1982).
8 On patriarchal and traditional authority, see Max Weber, *Economy and Society: an Outline of Interpretative Sociology*, ed. G. Roth and C. Wittich, 3 vols (New York: 1968), pp. 212–17, 237–41, 1006–10. See also H. H. Gerth and C. Wright Mills (eds), *From Max Weber: Essays in Sociology* (London: 1948), pp. 78–9, 245–7, 295–301.
9 The history of the sheep regime of the Tavoliere is considered by the following: A. Fraccacreta, *Le forme del progresso economico in Capitanata* (Naples: 1912); C. De Cesare, *Delle condizioni economiche e morali delle classi agricole nelle tre provincie di Puglia* (Naples: 1859); M. Papa, *Valori e progressi economici della Capitanata, 1866–1936* (Foggia: 1936); G. Praitano, *Il Tavoliere di Puglia* (Bari: 1908); and V. Ricchioni, *Lavoro agricolo e trasformazione fondiaria in Terra di Bari* (Bari: 1929).
10 On the concept of the 'passive revolution', see A. Gramsci, *Quaderni del carcere*, 4 vols (Turin: 1975), esp. pp. 1220, 1228–9, 1324–5, 1766–9.
11 'Da Cerignola', *Il Foglietto*, 19 October 1902.
12 L. Giuva, 'Aspetti statistici della situazione socio-economica', in Rinaldi and Sobrero, *La memoria che resta*, p. 96.
13 Archivio Privato Pavoncelli, Cerignola [hereafter APP], fondo Giuseppe Pavoncelli fu Nicola: G. Pavoncelli, 'Illustrazione di un latifondo del Tavoliere: L'azienda Pavoncelli di Cerignola', n.d.; APP, fondo Gaetano Pavoncelli fu Giuseppe, 'Patrimonio della famiglia Pavoncelli al 31 dicembre del 1903'.
14 APP, fondo Giuseppe Pavoncelli fu Federico, 'Notizie biografiche'; a hagiographic account is G. Stasi, 'Giuseppe Pavoncelli: agricoltore e uomo politico', tesi di Laurea, University of Bari, n.d.
15 APP, fondo Giuseppe Pavoncelli fu Federico. Letter of Giuseppe Pavoncelli to Antonio Salandra, 30 August 1881.
16 The difficult climate and topography are considered in A. Pompa, *Inchiesta sul latifondo: Agro di Foggia* (Foggia: 1932), pp. 7–9; and 'Alcuni cenni statistici sulla Capitanata', *Scienza e diletto*, 11 February 1894.
17 Brief suggestions of reasons for absenteeism are made in Schneider and Schneider, *Culture and Political Economy*, pp. 46, 47n.
18 ibid., pp. 3–4.
19 On the disastrous managerial methods employed by the *massari*, see 'Concetto amministrativo dei grandi latifondi in Capitanata', *L'Agricoltore Pugliese*, 15 May 1904, pp. 129–31; and A. Jatta, 'La produzione del frumento nel barese', *Rassegna Pugliese*, 2 (1885), pp. 323–5, 355–7, and 3 (1886), pp. 67–71, 83–5.
20 On the situation of salaried personnel, see R. Pastore, 'Dopo dieci anni di lotte', *La Conquista*, 3 September 1911 and Ricchioni, *Lavoro agricolo*, p. 121.
21 For Weber's notion of prebendal organization, see Gerth and Mills, *From Max Weber*, pp. 204–9, and Weber, *Economy and Society*, pp. 965–9. In Sicily the short-term lease of the rural entrepreneur was called a *gabella*, which means 'prebend'. Schneider and Schneider, *Culture and Political Economy*, p. 69.
22 Interview with Michele Sacco, in Rinaldi and Sobrero, *La memoria che resta*, p. 135.
23 The factors which encouraged migration and emigration among the peasantry of the South are discussed by William A. Douglass, 'Migration in Italy', in M. Kenny and D. I. Kertzer (eds), *Urban Life in Mediterranean Europe* (Chicago: 1983), pp. 162–202; Robert Foerster, *The Italian Emigration of Our Time* (Cambridge, Mass.: 1919); Herbert Klein, 'The integration of Italian immigrants into the United States and Argentina: a comparative analysis', *American Historical Review*, 88 (1983), pp. 306–29; J. W. Briggs, *An Italian Passage: Immigrants to Three American Cities, 1890–1930* (New Haven, Conn.: 1978); M. Piore, *Birds of Passage: Migrant Labour and Industrial Societies* (Cambridge: 1974). An interesting analysis of the end of common land is P. Grossi, *An Alternative to Private Property: Collective Property in the Juridical Consciousness of the Nineteenth Century* (Chicago: 1981).

24 Rinaldi and Sobrero, *La memoria che resta*, pp. 105–7.

25 These details are provided by Errico Pressutti in his volume on Apulia in the report of the parliamentary commission headed by Senator Faina, *Inchiesta parlamentare sulle condizioni dei contadini nelle provincie meridionali e nella Sicilia* (Rome: 1910).

26 'Sulla breccia', *Il Randello*, 24 June 1906; 'Nelle tre Puglie', *Corriere delle Puglie*, 13 May 1903; and A. Jatta, 'Gionate e salarii nel barese', *L'Agricoltore Pugliese*, 15 August 1901.

27 Archivio di Stato di Foggia, Sottoprefettura di San Severo, fasc. 414, fasciculo 7–13 (1908). Sindaco di Torremaggiore, 'Questionario per scioperi agricoli', 27 January 1908.

28 F. Turati discussed the adulteration of food in neighbouring Candela in a speech to the Chamber of Deputies on 31 March 1903. *Atti del parlamento italiano*, Camera dei Deputati, Legislatura XII, Discussioni, Vol. 7, p. 6933.

29 The abuses of managers were the subject of discussion by the union movement in Bari province. See 'Congresso provinciale dei lavoratori della terra', *La Conquista*, 18 August 1907.

30 Ministero di Agricoltura, Industria e Commercio: Direzione Generale della Statistica, *Statistica delle cause di morte nell'anno 1903* (Rome: 1906), table V, p. 68.

31 The Faina *Inchiesta parlamentare, passim*, provides an excellent account of peasant conditions in the South during the Giolittian period.

32 Karl Marx, 'The Eighteenth Brumaire of Louis Bonaparte', in K. Marx and F. Engels, *Selected Works* (Moscow: 1962), Vol. I, p. 334.

33 A classic account of the Andalusian *pueblo* is Julian Pitt-Rivers, *The People of the Sierra* (Chicago: 1961).

34 D. Laudati, 'La politica agraria pugliese', *Corriere delle Puglie*, 6 October 1917.

35 An examination of the importance of artisans in the establishment of Sicilian socialism in the 1890s is P. Schneider, 'Rural artisans and peasant mobilization in the Socialist International: the fasci Siciliani', *Journal of Peasant Studies*, 13 (1986), pp. 63–81. Artisans also played a vital part in the spread of democratic socialism under the Second Republic in France. See M. Agulhon, *The Republic in the Village* (Cambridge: 1982).

36 APP, Carteggio Larochefoucauld-Millet. Letter of Georges Millet to Monsieur le Duc de Larochefoucauld, 30 June 1914.

37 E. Weber, *Peasants into Frenchmen: the Modernization of Rural France, 1870–1914* (London: 1979), pp. 303–39.

38 Literacy statistics for Foggia province are in Ministero di Agricoltura, Industria e Commercio: Direzione Generale di Statistica, *Movimento della popolazione secondo gli atti dello stato civile nell'anno 1903* (Rome: 1905), prospectus XIII, p. xxii; and Ministero di Agricoltura, Industria e Commercio: Direzione Generale della Statistica e del Lavoro, *Censimento della popolazione del regno d'Italia al 10 giugno 1911* (Rome: 1914), Vol. 3, table V.

39 Ministero di Agricoltura, Industria e Commercio: Direzione Generale della Statistica, *Censimento della popolazione del Regno d'Italia al 10 febbraio 1901* (Rome: 1902), table IX.

40 Discussions of anticlericalism in Apulia are G. Salvemini, 'Da un colloquio con Gaetano Salvemini', *Il Foglietto*, 15 January 1911, and G. De Falco, 'Il proletariato nel paese degli eccidi cronici', *La Conquista*, 3 September 1911. On Cerignola in particular, see 'La grandiosa dimostrazione anticlericale di Cerignola', *Il Foglietto*, 27 February 1909, 23 September 1909, and 'Clericali e anticlericali a Cerignola', *Il Foglietto*, 24 March 1910.

41 See Snowden, *Violence and Great Estates*, ch. 6.

42 G. De Falco, 'Il proletariato nel paese degli eccidi cronici', *La Conquista*, 3 September 1911. Influential accounts of the duality of Giolitti's political system are: Gramsci, *Quaderni*, esp. p. 36; and G. Salvemini, 'Fu l'Italia prefascista una democrazia?', *Il Ponte*, 8 (1952), and 'Il ministro della mala vita', in *Opere*, Vol. I (Milan: 1962).

43 A detailed account of the 1904 strike at Cerignola is 'Agitazione proletaria in Cerignola', *Il Pugliese*, 22 May 1904.

44 Considerations of the ill-treatment of workers include A. Lo Re, 'Capitanata triste', *Scienza e diletto*, 6 March 1898; and Rinaldi and Sobrero, *La memoria che resta*, pp. 119–20, 130, 132–3, 138–9.

45 The most extensive official reports on electoral abuses are to be found in the Archivio di Stato di Bari, Prefettura di Bari: Gabinetto, fasc. 260, sottofasc. 7 (Elezioni generali amministrative). Other accounts of the activities of the *mazzieri* are Salvemini, 'Fu l'Italia prefascista una democrazia?'; and 'Gli sciacalli di Cerignola', *Il Randello*, 13 September 1914.

46 On the civil war of 1921–2, see Snowden, *Violence and Great Estates*, pp. 158–202; and S. Colarizi, *Dopoguerra e fascismo in Puglia (1919–1926)* (Bari: 1971).

SPAIN

11

Land and power in Arcadia: Navarre in the early twentieth century

Martin Blinkhorn

Let us begin with a stubborn myth. The Navarrese, wrote the British historian Hugh Thomas a quarter of a century ago, were before the Spanish Civil War 'a contented group of peasant proprietors nestling in the foothills of the Pyrenees. . . .A journey to Navarre was still an expedition to the middle ages.'[1] Thomas's words present, albeit in extreme terms, a vision of Navarrese rural society which was for long accepted and indeed perpetuated by both Navarrese conservatives and anglophone historians: one of Navarre as a kind of rural Arcadia, populated by a prosperous, self-sufficient peasantry and blessed by a general and enduring social harmony.[2]

Like many persistent myths, that of a Navarrese Arcadia contains a core of truth. As Edward Malefakis has pointed out, in the nineteenth and early twentieth centuries Navarre was one of the few provinces of Spain where holdings definable as 'medium-sized' (between 10 and 100 hectares) represented a significant proportion of the land surface; small rural property certainly was widespread and large estates by no stretch of the imagination as important, in either statistical or real terms, as in southern Spain.[3] Were we to look no further we might well feel disposed to dismiss Navarre as unpromising territory for a study of the relationship between landownership and the possession and exercise of power. In reality, however, the distribution of landed property in pre-civil war Navarre, and therefore the issues of power associated with it, were less straightforward than the 'Arcadian myth' might lead us to believe. Had this not been so it would be difficult to explain how, during the 1930s, the Spanish Socialist Party could have conquered a significant part of the electorate in what was an overwhelmingly rural province, and why perhaps 3,000 Navarrese leftists, many of them peasants, should have perished in the social and political repression which accompanied the outbreak of civil war in 1936.

Before going on to examine more closely the distribution of landed property in early twentieth-century Navarre, it is necessary to make some basic points concerning the province's geography and history. First, it is important to recognize that Navarre, while possessing a clear sense of historical and territorial identity which differentiates it from most other Spanish provinces, is anything but a natural region. Geographers disagree as to the precise zonal boundaries within Navarre, but most are prepared to accept a broad division into three.[4] The 'foothills of the Pyrenees' clearly regarded by Thomas as typifying Navarre are in fact limited to slightly less than the northern half of the province. This area, the Montaña, lying north of the capital, Pamplona, is Basque Navarre: a well-watered, verdant, extensively forested region whose valleys, most though not all running north to south, are scattered with isolated family farms, small villages and, especially in the northwest, a few slightly larger centres of population. In the late nineteenth and early twentieth centuries the Montaña was devoted to mixed dairy farming, subsistence polyculture and the production of timber. Throughout most of the zone, family farms were – as they still are throughout the Spanish and French Basque country – normally passed on entire from one generation to the next via the 'single heir' system, involving the joint parental choice of one son or daughter, and not necessarily the eldest, as principal heir.[5] While this practice avoided even worse minifundism than that which actually existed, the inability of small farms to absorb an expanding population meant that in the nineteenth and early twentieth centuries the Montaña became the chief source of Navarrese emigration: overseas, to other parts of Spain, and internally within the province.

The southern third of Navarre, the Ribera, while beginning only twenty miles or so beyond the southern boundary of the Montaña, could hardly be more different. A mostly flattish, sometimes undulating zone which descends gradually southwards to end in the fertile valley of the Ebro and, at its southeastern corner, the lunar landscape of the semi-desert Bardenas Reales, the Ribera is as inescapably 'Mediterranean' in climate, topography and character as the Montaña is 'northern'. Its rural economy in the period under consideration was just as typically Mediterranean. Extensive areas were still devoted to the pasturing of sheep and goats, including transhumant flocks owned by prosperous stockbreeders from the Roncal and Salazar valleys of northeastern Navarre. From the mid-nineteenth century, however, and especially with the advent of mechanization and chemical fertilizers around the turn of the century, an increasing area of southern Navarre was turned over to the cultivation of wheat, vines, olives and, where irrigation made it possible, fruit, vegetables and sugar beet.

The population of the Ribera, in contrast to that of the Montaña, was concentrated in relatively large, 'dormitory' villages and small towns. Although the single heir system was practised in many districts of the Ribera, and in particular along its northern fringes,[6] partible inheritance was equally so and minifundism widespread. However, since partible inheritance was statutory neither in Spanish nor in Navarrese law, and since it was seldom practised by the larger landed proprietors, most of Navarre's largest estates were also to be found in this region.

Between the Montaña and the Ribera lies a central zone of varying width, displaying characteristics of the other two but more closely resembling the Montaña in the moist west and the Ribera in the much dryer east. In the whole of Spain, probably only Huesca and Lérida, Navarre's fellow sub-Pyrenean provinces, display quite such sharp internal differences. It would therefore be surprising if anything remotely resembling a uniform pattern of landholding were to emerge.

While anything but a unity in terms of physical geography, Navarre can claim a political and historical unity unique among the 52 provinces of Spain, the great majority of which were 'artificial' nineteenth-century creations. An independent medieval kingdom which was attached to the emergent Spanish state in 1512, Navarre officially enjoyed the status of a 'kingdom' until 1841, when the protracted process of Spanish 'unification', begun in the late fifteenth century, may be said to have been completed. Between the early sixteenth century and the early twentieth, Navarre enjoyed, within stable borders, not only political unity and cohesiveness but also autonomy. Although the scope of this autonomy was greatly reduced during the course of the nineteenth century, it was never completely eradicated; Navarre accordingly remained a legal and, for its people, an emotional reality.[7] Such a combination of geographical diversity and political distinctiveness offers a particularly useful basis for an examination of 'power'. This study will focus most sharply upon the early twentieth century, though in the context of developments in landownership going back over the whole of the nineteenth.

The study of landownership in pre-civil war Navarre is rendered difficult by the failure of the national cadastral survey, begun in 1906, to tackle Navarre until well after the Spanish Civil War. Although it may as a result be impossible to offer a complete, detailed and accurate account of pre-civil war landholding, the situation is not altogether desperate. In the first place, several districts of Navarre *were* systematically surveyed from around 1926 onwards by the Servicio Catastral of the Navarrese *Diputación*, most of the districts fully surveyed being those in the south where large landownership existed. Secondly, it is generally agreed that the survey finally completed in 1951 shows a situation little changed in broad terms from that which existed before the Civil War; scholars have therefore been able, with appropriate caution, to use this for statistical purposes if not, of course, for those of specific illustration. It remains the case, however, that cadastral information is largely limited to ownership, telling us little about, for example, details of tenancy and sharecropping.

Recent published calculations, based largely on detailed findings published during the 1920s and 1930s by the Navarrese agronomist Daniel Nagore, or upon extrapolations from them, suggest that in Navarre in 1930 some 73,000 persons (together, of course, with their families) out of a total population of 345,000 derived their living from agriculture, either directly or from rents. Of these something over 52 per cent – 38,000 – were proprietors, 15 per cent (around 11,000) tenants or sharecroppers (*aparceros*), and 32 per cent (around 24,000) rural labourers.[8] These figures are by no means unchallengeable (or unchallenged), but probably present a broadly accurate picture. Although adequate figures for the pre-civil war period are not available, those from the 1951 *catastro* indicate that of non-irrigated land (by far the greater portion), 78 per cent of owners possessed under 5 hectares each, 21.7 per cent between 6 and 100 hectares, and 0.3 per cent above 100 hectares. Where the much smaller, but proportionately far more valuable, amount of irrigated land was concerned the equivalent percentages were 94.3, 5.6 and 0.1.[9] While these figures demonstrate the overwhelming numerical preponderance of small-holders (a preponderance, moreover, apparent with variations throughout the province) and the significant presence by Spanish standards of middling proprietors, the full picture becomes clear only when the total *area* possessed by each group is also considered. Here we find that, taking Navarre as a whole, owners of up to 5 hectares possessed 13 per cent of all agricultural land, those of between 6 and 100 hectares 30.6 per cent, and 'large' landowners of over 100 hectares 56.4 per cent.[10] These figures, by classifying vast areas of municipally owned mountain pasture and forest as large properties, almost certainly overestimate the importance of large landowners in northern Navarre; on the other hand, by counting separately properties owned by a single owner in more than one municipality, they probably underestimate the area owned by large proprietors in the south. Whatever the shortcomings of these figures, they are certainly more than sufficient to demonstrate how far removed early twentieth-century Navarre was from being an equitable rural-agrarian society, and help us to understand the irritation of a Navarrese Socialist of the 1930s at the apparent unconcern displayed towards the province's agrarian problems by the Republican Minister of Agriculture: 'Can it be that upon [his] mind there presses the lie . . . that round here ninety per cent of us are landowners?'[11]

Large landownership was, then, a reality in early twentieth-century Navarre. Broadly speaking it took two forms: old and new landed wealth, the former exclusively noble and the latter partly noble but chiefly bourgeois. Almost 12,500 hectares of Navarre remained in the possession of grandees who had assumed outright ownership with the disentailment of seigneurial holdings in the early nineteenth century; while representing only 2.3 per cent of total grandee holdings in Spain, and scarcely comparable with the 92,956 hectares of Cáceres in Extremadura or even the 51,234 hectares of neighbouring Zaragoza, this was nevertheless a high figure for northern Spain and placed Navarre in thirteenth place among Spanish provinces.[12] Several entire Navarrese municipalities were grandee possessions based on former *señoríos* (seigneurial estates). Cadreita (2,736 hectares) and Sartaguda (1,418 hectares), both on the north bank of the Ebro, were owned respectively by the Duques de Alburquerque and Infantado; Fontellas (2,065 hectares), further downriver, was the property of the Conde de Gabarda; various members of the ducal house of Villahermosa owned the former *señoríos* of Javier and Peña (over 5,000 hectares) and Traibuenas (5,124 hectares); the Duque de Alba possessed the 2,478-hectare estate of Baigorri in the sparsely populated district of Oteiza (a mere fraction of his total landed holdings of 34,455 hectares); and the Marqués de San Adrián owned, among other Navarrese properties, most of the municipality of Monteagudo.[13] Other noble holdings of less long standing which, at anything from 500 to over 1,000 hectares, gave their owners considerable local power, existed in (for example) Castejón, Cortes, Olite and Mélida.[14]

All of these districts were in the southern half of Navarre, either in the Ribera or on its northern fringes. Noble landownership was not unknown further north, however: two of the province's highest land-tax payers in 1930, the Marqués de Vessolla and the Conde de Guendalain, derived their wealth respectively from lands adjacent to the capital, Pamplona, and to the northeast.[15] By the standards of Navarrese landholding statistics, grandee holdings are relatively easy to calculate and would appear to total perhaps 25,000 hectares by the mid-1920s. *Total* noble holdings are almost impossible to calculate, however, owing not only to the general inadequacy of the evidence but also to the sheer numbers of lesser Navarrese nobles. In common with most of the Basque country Navarre possessed an extensive though often materially modest nobility: in the census of 1797, the last to make a clear distinction, 18,753 nobles were identified out of 77,249 Navarrese to whom a specific occupation was attached, and a total population of some 220,000.[16] With the abolition of the Cortes of Navarre in 1841, the lesser local nobility lost its political privileges and by the turn of the century had become virtually indistinguishable from the emergent landholding bourgeoisie.

Much non-seigneurial land owned before the Civil War by noble families, both grandee and local, had been acquired during the course of the nineteenth and early twentieth centuries as part of a much broader process of which the chief beneficiaries were non-nobles. During the War of Independence (1808–14) many Navarrese villages sold common land in order to defray the costs of war and French occupation; during the civil wars of the 1830s, church lands were disentailed and sold off in order to bail out the Spanish state; between 1855 and the end of the century there followed a process of civil disentailment involving the alienation of mainly municipal lands; and after 1897 individuals were legally allowed to purchase outright other tracts of municipal or state land over which they had enjoyed a minimum of ten years' usufruct. Admittedly, the effects of these developments were less dramatic in Navarre than in many other parts of Spain. Notwithstanding Navarre's fervent Catholicism the church's holdings before the disentailment of the 1830s were relatively low: some 9,296 hectares or slightly under 4 per cent of the province's cultivable land; the impact of their sale was accordingly limited.[17] Civil disentailment, too, involving a total of just over 30,000 hectares, went less far than in many provinces, thanks to Navarre's continued financial autonomy and the opposition of many municipalities, especially in the Montaña, to the surrender of commons.[18] Navarre therefore entered the twentieth century with an unusually high level of common land. However, of the municipal land that was alienated, around 25,000 hectares were situated in the Ribera and the east of the central zone, where the effect was accordingly disproportionate.[19]

While various kinds of state and municipal lands were affected by disentailment and the post-1897 'privatization', the most distinctive feature of the process in Navarre was undoubtedly the *corraliza. Corralizas* were pieces of land, varying considerably in area, some privately owned and others leased by individuals from the municipality, upon which complex and often overlapping common rights of pasture, access to water-courses, fuel-gathering, and so on, nevertheless persisted. In the successive phases of noble, ecclesiastical and civil disentailment which punctuated the nineteenth century, *corralizas* throughout the Ribera were released into private hands or, where already privately owned or occupied, were brought under cultivation by their owners to the exclusion of those villagers who had previously possessed access to them. The loss of *corralizas* affected most villages of the Ribera, and combined with that of other commons bore hard upon typical *ribereño* mixed communities of small peasant proprietors, tenant farmers, sharecroppers and landless day labourers.[20] During the late nineteenth and early twentieth centuries the struggle for survival in an increasingly market-oriented economy dominated by larger producers, transporters, middlemen and processors was rendered yet more bitter by the pressure of rising population and immigration from northern Navarre.

Although some of the newly available land fell into noble hands, most appears to have been purchased on advantageous terms by better-off peasants or, more commonly, members of the Navarrese or even the non-Navarrese bourgeoisie. Indeed Navarre, a province noted in the late eighteenth century for the enterprise of its population, offers a good example of a classic nineteenth-century Mediterranean phenomenon: that of a provincial bourgeoisie diverted by the easy pickings of disentailment into the safe channels of *rentier* land-holding. Of 351 purchasers of ecclesiastical land in the 1830s, 334 were Navarrese, disproportionately from Pamplona, Tudela (the province's second city, in the deep south), and smaller towns such as Estella, Tafalla and Corella.[21] Of the land released by civil disentailment,

56 per cent of all plots were bought by local inhabitants, 18 per cent by *pamploneses*, and 20 per cent by purchasers from smaller Navarrese towns.[22] In both cases, most of the non-Navarrese buyers were residents of Madrid. The overall effect of these processes, and of the continuing alienation of *corralizas*, was undoubtedly a strengthening of Navarrese *rentiers* based in the provincial capital and a few smaller towns, together with the opening-up in many districts of a gap between a handful of better-off peasant proprietors and the great majority. By the early years of the twentieth century, certainly, several of Navarre's wealthiest landowners owed their position to the possession and exploitation of *corralizas* in the Ribera. While no firm computation has yet been possible, it seems unlikely that the area in the possession of non-noble *corraliceros* was inferior to that held by nobles.

Figures do exist of the numbers of large properties in early twentieth-century Navarre, but they need to be treated with great caution. Recent writers have used Daniel Nagore's calculations in order to claim that there existed in Navarre at that time 125 holdings of 300 hectares or more, and a further 80 of between 100 and 300 hectares.[23] Since Nagore was actually enumerating not *propiedades* but *fincas* – registered 'parcels' of land – this conclusion is strictly inexact. However, it is safe to assume that even if some of these 100+ hectare *fincas* actually formed part of still greater estates, thereby reducing the total, this would be more than cancelled out by the number of 'concealed' large properties composed of accumulations of holdings smaller than 100, let alone 300, hectares. One example, of many that could be cited, may suffice: in the southern municipality of Cortes one proprietor – in this case an absentee noble, the Duque de Miranda – owned approximately 100 separate pieces of land, none larger than 57 hectares, totalling well over 800 hectares and making him by far the richest landowner in the district.[24] Other family properties were scattered across several municipalities; some were divided by partible inheritance while continuing to be run cohesively and acting as the foundation of that family's local influence.

Large landowners in early twentieth-century Navarre thus consisted of two principal kinds: nobles possessing onetime *señoríos*, usually concentrated in a single area even if as often as not supplemented by additional holdings elsewhere; and bourgeois whose landed wealth had largely been accumulated in the course of the previous century through purchase and encroachment. In view of what is to follow, however, a third element needs to be mentioned. In Navarre, as in many parts of Spain, even in districts where truly large-scale property was unknown it was common for a few families (typically between three and ten) to exercise considerable collective power through their possession of quantities of land which, without being especially large, were well above the local average. San Adrián, Ribaforada, Miranda de Arga, Murillo el Fruto, Milagro and others were districts in which the average holding was of relatively modest size but the gap between '*caciques*' – more often a plural than a singular term – and the rest was a very real one.[25]

Perhaps the most striking feature of large landowners' power in Navarre between the late nineteenth century and the Civil War is the relative security enjoyed by the greatest noble landowners, compared with the succession of lawsuits and violent episodes, from the 1880s onwards, relating to the *corralizas* and their owners.

The power of noble owners of former *señoríos* rested upon three main foundations. The first of these was the simple legitimacy bestowed by time and continuity. Villages like Javier, Sartaguda, Cadreita, Fontellas and Monteagudo, together with their surroundings, had been in the hands of the same noble family for generations or even centuries, a situation that villagers found difficult to question – the more so when outside contacts were limited by geographical isolation, poor communications and a sluggish market economy. Where, as in Javier, the owners spent at least part of the year on the estate, actively interesting themselves in its fortunes and those of tenants and labourers, acceptance of the situation appears to have been relatively deep-rooted and deference genuine: far more so, certainly, than in Sartaguda, whose owner, the Duque de Infantado, seldom appeared and the running of which was left to a succession of unpopular managers. There, tenants' resentment exploded in 1919–20 in the shape of a rent-strike and clashes between peasants and the Civil Guard. The contrast continued down through the days of the Second Republic. Javier displaying a solid right-wing allegiance and Sartaguda veering decisively to the left.[26]

The second foundation of post-seigneurial power was, of course, the sheer economic weight of the landowner in a district where he was effectively the sole leaser of land, employer of agricultural and artisanal labour, and provider of homes. In the overpopulated south of Navarre, where a 20 per cent extension of the cultivated area between 1885 and 1931 (much of it achieved by the exploitation of *corraliza* land) attracted but failed to absorb immigration from the north, land-hunger and rural unemployment were endemic, and few alternatives accordingly available to the secure if basic livelihood which estate owners offered their tenants, sharecroppers and labourers. Protesting against low wages or the terms of tenancies and sharecropping contracts was therefore unwise and rarely indulged in. Before 1931 Sartaguda was the exception, not the rule.

Mention of 1931 is deliberate, for it was with the coming of the Second Republic in April of that year that the third foundation of noble power, the support or at least complaisance of the public authorities, began to weaken. Under the Liberal Monarchy of 1875–1931, the legal position of the great noble landowners of the Ribera was largely unchallenged. The influence of large landowners at national level, while declining relative to that of industrial and banking interests, remained great throughout this period. The grandee landowners of Navarre, most of whom were in any case absentees, thus had little or no incentive to participate in, or even seek materially to influence, politics at provincial level: beyond, perhaps, assuring themselves of the proximity of a Civil Guard post just in case habits of deference (or at any rate obedience) should, after all, break down. As for local politics, this was generally an uncomplicated expression of social and economic control, with the most reliable tenants forming the local council and, as in Monteagudo and Sartaguda in the late 1920s, the estate manager often serving as *alcalde* (mayor).[27]

While noble proprietors of former *señoríos* thus appear to have experienced little difficulty in exercising and retaining power over the local peasantry, other large Ribera landowners, and in particular *corraliceros*, encountered constant resentment and repeated challenges both litigious and physical. The fundamental reasons for this difference are not difficult to discern. Where former *señoríos* may have been legitimized in the peasant mind by custom, properties acquired as a result of disentailment, or the alienation of *corralizas*, or both, were regarded by smallholders, tenants and labourers as the fruit of greed, dishonesty, the abuse of power and downright theft. Such attitudes were encouraged by the extraordinary complexity of the customary and contractual rights attached to *corralizas*, and by the ambiguities often surrounding the terms upon which *corraliceros* had acquired them. In particular, uncertainty frequently reigned as to whether individual *corraliceros* had purchased the plots in question outright, or merely the rights of 'grazing and watering' attached to them. One group who benefited indirectly from this confusion were Navarrese lawyers, many of whom earned a steady income during the half-century before the Civil War from disputes over *corralizas*.

From the 1880s down to the 1930s the clamour of small peasants for the 'recovery of the *corralizas*', and of alienated commons in general, constituted the central and most explosive issue in Navarrese agrarian politics. Beginning in 1884 and reaching a peak between 1914 and 1923, countless cases occurred of peasants invading, occupying and 'illegally' ploughing *corralizas*, with the Civil Guard repeatedly intervening on the *corraliceros*' behalf. Four peasants were killed by the 'forces of order' in Olite in 1884 and several others in similar incidents during the years that followed; in a minority of cases, peasant protest actually succeeded in forcing *corraliceros* to surrender part of their land to the local council.[28] By no stretch of the imagination could the level of rural unrest in Navarre be said to have approached that in Andalusia or Extremadura, nevertheless the province was also a long way from being the Arcadia of legend. If, therefore, we are considering the manner in which large landowners have won and maintained acceptance of their position, then here we have a case where tradition was irrelevant, legitimacy never established and control always liable to be challenged.

Corraliceros and other large-scale owners of non-seigneurial land were thus obliged actively to defend and assert their power through the political and legal systems. In Navarre, while it is perfectly appropriate to view landownership as a route whereby the relevant sectors of the provincial bourgeoisie might come to enjoy other forms of power, it is just as profitable to see the chief attraction of political power as lying in its usefulness in defending landed wealth under threat. From the 1880s onward, in a formally representative yet only nominally democratic system, the economic and social power of *corraliceros* and other *caciques* was harnessed, as in other regions of Spain, in attempts to manage elections to the national Cortes, the provincial *Diputación*, municipal councils, municipal judgeships, and so on. In this the landowners were largely but by no means entirely successful. While no national or provincial legislation hostile to their interests was forthcoming, the relative vigour of Navarrese local government ensured that some local councils, at least, represented wider agricultural interests than merely those of the *corraliceros* and were able to mount legal challenges to the latter on the community's behalf. That some lawsuits proved successful and some *corraliceros* susceptible to local council pressure seems to suggest that there existed very real limitations on landowners' dominance of the formal structures of political and legal power. Much research needs still to be done, however, on the social base of the Navarrese political, administrative and legal elite under the Liberal Monarchy, before more can be said on this subject.[29]

That Navarre was not more troubled by rural unrest during the early twentieth century is in part due to the role played by the Catholic church. During the first decade of the century Navarre emerged as one of the principal bases in Spain for a social-Catholic movement aimed at the small farmer. Inspired and energized by socially concerned Navarrese priests like Victoriano Flamarique and Hilario Yoldi, the rapidly expanding network of *Cajas Rurales* (local savings banks), farmers' organizations and Catholic workers' syndicates was originally intended to protect the small farmer from the usury of *caciques* through the extension of credit at reasonable rates of interest; to increase his access to cheap seed, fertilizer, insurance, technical advice and legal counsel; and to encourage the development of cooperatives in both processing and marketing. Underlying these perfectly sincere motives was another, just as sincere: the desire to immunize the predominantly Catholic farming population of Navarre against the temptations of socialism.

The achievements of Navarrese social-Catholicism were undeniably considerable. In 1914 the extensive Navarrese social-Catholic network was merged into a large and powerful national organization, the Confederación Nacional Católico-Agraria (CNCA); by 1920, Navarre, with 156 Catholic farmers' syndicates, was one of the most important provinces in the CNCA. As the years passed, however, the early radicalism of Navarrese social-Catholicism declined, and figures like Flamarique were marginalized, as the movement underwent an experience similar to that noted by Colin Winston in his study of urban social-Catholicism in Catalonia: namely a muffling of any real radicalism by the ecclesiastical hierarchy and an organizational takeover by larger landowners. By the 1920s the most prominent figures within Navarrese social-Catholicism were no longer socially concerned priests but large landowners anxious to harness Catholic farmers' organizations to what they chose to label 'the agrarian interest'. Crucial to their undoubted success was the role of middling proprietors throughout the province and smallholders in the Montaña and central Navarre, where the *corralizas* issue was absent and common land still abundant. Their enrolment within social-Catholic organizations, and their acceptance of the solidaristic message issuing forth from most village pulpits, provided larger proprietors with a broad base which might otherwise have been lacking.[30]

Another distinctive element in Navarrese public life which came to play an important role in the cause of social defence for rich landowners was the dissident monarchist movement, Carlism. This was not, however, a straightforward matter. Until well into the twentieth century, Carlism, a mass cause of which Navarre became the principal base, was if anything a movement of the 'little man' and in particular of the lesser peasantry; grandees and bourgeois landowning interlopers, in Navarre as elsewhere in Spain, were usually staunch liberals. Navarrese Carlists, both priests and laity, played an important part in founding and developing Navarrese social-Catholicism: so much so that in many liberal minds the two were all but synonymous. Nevertheless, and although the process remains to be studied in detail, by the start of the 1930s the leadership of Navarrese Carlism – within which were to be found not a few large landowners – was directing the movement in a much more unambiguously conservative direction where social issues were concerned. Although some cases did occur of Carlists whose social concerns outweighed their dynastic and religious loyalties defecting to the left, the vast majority remained faithful to a cause whose claims to defend the humble against the powerful would soon look very empty.[31]

Although in the generation before 1931 the larger landowners of Navarre cannot be said to have had everything their own way, neither did they ever face a truly serious threat to their dominance over the less powerful. Local councils and provincial courts might display a sometimes unwelcome independence in confronting disputes over the *corralizas*, yet this was far from constituting a serious menace to the *corraliceros*, or to large-scale landed property, in general. And while outbursts of violence might from time to time tarnish Navarre's Arcadian image, peasant resentment of the wealthier landowners remained essentially controllable. The fall of King Alfonso XIII and the installation of the Second Republic in April 1931 promised to change all this.

In the first place, the monarchical state beneath whose protection all Spanish large landowners had previously sheltered was replaced overnight by a regime ostentatiously dedicated to a fairer, more equitable distribution of wealth and power. In particular the alliance of reforming Republicans and Socialists which governed Spain from 1931 to late 1933 was committed to agrarian reforms which the minifundists, tenant farmers, sharecroppers and day labourers of southern Navarre had reason to hope would benefit them.

Secondly, in Navarre itself the change of regime was accompanied by a rapid increase in Socialist trade union and party membership, and a vastly enhanced left-wing role in local and provincial government. At the local elections of April 1931 which precipitated the monarchy's collapse, and the partial local elections which followed in May, councils with Republican-Socialist majorities took office in something over half the local councils of southern Navarre. The Republicans and Socialists of the Ribera received further boosts, first in May when a sympathetic Comisión Gestora (Temporary Committee) was imposed from Madrid in place of the right-wing *Diputación*, and then at the June general election, when the Republican-Socialist coalition carried 35 of the Ribera's 55 electoral districts with 57 per cent of the (still all-male) southern vote. Although northern and central Navarre remained bastions of conservatism, Catholicism and Carlism, and although several southern districts continued to be dominated by the political right throughout the 'reforming' period of 1931–3, this represented a sudden and dramatic shift of political power away from landowning interests.[32]

The emergence of a significant left-wing political presence in southern Navarre was paralleled by a rapid increase in Socialist trade union membership. Between 1930 and 1933, the Navarrese Ribera shared in the general growth of the Socialist Unión General de Trabajadores (UGT), and in particular of its landworkers' section, the Federación Nacional de Trabajadores de la Tierra (FNTT). Founded only in 1930, the FNTT possessed by mid-1932 at least 3,500 affiliates in southern Navarre, comprising not only day labourers but also tenants and even small proprietors.[33] Socialism in the Ribera was nourished not only by chronic issues such as the *corralizas* but also by shorter-term factors: the effects of the general economic depression and the vicissitudes of, for example, the sugar beet and market-gardening sectors. By late 1932 the Socialist press was reporting unemployment levels equivalent to 20 per cent of the Ribera's active male population.[34] In the absence of effective financial relief, the UGT and FNTT, together with, where they existed, Socialist and Left Republican councillors, pressed for practical measures such as public works projects and the establishment, in line with government policy, of local labour offices (*bolsas de trabajo*) to apply the terms of Republican labour legislation.[35] Results were uneven but mostly negative. In some districts, such as the important town of Corella, the conservative authorities dragged their feet in actually setting up a labour office, while elsewhere employers simply went their own way and ignored the local office's existence or, as in Olite, created their own Catholic *bolsa de trabajo* in order to discriminate against UGT workers.[36]

For the Navarrese left, unemployment merely underlined the problems of the land. In a predominantly agrarian economy, the uneven distribution of landed wealth, the prevalence in many districts of minifundism and the shortage of adequate commons appeared to place tenants, sharecroppers and lesser proprietors at the mercy of richer landowners. By ending this subservience, it was believed, the redistribution of land would not only improve the lot of the small farmer but also strengthen the negotiating position of the landless labourer. From the start of the Republic, the demand was accordingly renewed for the recovery (*rescate*) or *corralizas* and alienated common land, to be carried out either by local councils backed up by the Comisión Gestora in Pamplona, or as an integral part of the Republic's agrarian reform programme. Some left-controlled councils, encouraged by the Comisión Gestora, did succeed in reaching agreements with local *corraliceros* for the cession – at a price – or *corralizas* and the creation of collective tenancies, but such cases were few and seldom took real effect before the political wind shifted in late 1933.[37]

During 1932 and 1933 the Socialists and the FNTT began to press increasingly for specific provision to be made for the Navarrese *corralizas* in the agrarian reform programme. The Navarrese Socialist trade union federation was twice assured by the Institute of Agrarian Reform that the problem would be tackled by a projected additional law on municipal rural property (*bienes rústicas municipales*),[38] but this law, like another with major implications for Navarre, the law on rural leases, was never to materialize.

Even as this legalistic approach was being attempted during 1931–2, peasants resumed the invasion of *corralizas* on a scale which, while modest, indicated that their patience was unlikely to prove boundless.[39] By the middle of 1933 the frustration of the *ribereño* peasantry with the meagre achievements of Republican legalism, and with the clear success of large landowners in resisting it, erupted in a day of demonstrations throughout the Ribera, a succession of popular assemblies sponsored by the UGT and left-wing councils, and a far more extensive outbreak of *corraliza* occupations.[40] Two years into the Republic, it was clear that not even with a reformist government in Madrid and a left-wing provincial council in Pamplona could swift and lasting success in the agrarian sphere be guaranteed. Employers and larger landowners had proved themselves able, either directly or via complaisant local councils, to delay or ignore the creation of labour offices and the applying of agreed agricultural terms of employment (*bases de trabajo*); they had successfully boycotted UGT workers and imported cheap outside labour in contravention of Republican legislation.[41] Even the most resolutely left-wing local councils had made only modest headway in persuading *corraliceros* to hand back some of their land to the community. Noble landowners, in order to stave off possible expropriation, had set about dividing their estates among offspring, 'selling' them to straw-men, or strenuously denying they had been *señoríos* in the first place.[42]

In addition, Navarrese landowners were responding to the challenge of the Republic by becoming unprecedentedly well organized in defence of their interests, and on two levels. First, to the established network of *Cajas Rurales* and farmers' syndicates – stronger in central Navarre and on the northern margins of the Ribera than in the deep south – were now added such powerful and combative landowners' pressure groups as the Asociación de Propietarios Terratenientes de Navarra and the Asociación de Patronos de Fincas Rústicas. These were in turn able to depend upon the deference of the Catholic landworkers' union, the Sindicato de Trabajadores de Campo, a much smaller force than the FNTT but influential in some conservative areas.[43]

Not only did the membership of these and kindred bodies overlap bewilderingly, but they were also linked by common membership and leadership to the principal political organizations of the Navarrese right. Landowners were now becoming more actively political. Carlism, while strongest in parts of the Montaña and especially the central zone, also possessed important strongholds by the early 1930s on the northern edge of the Ribera (Artajona, Sesma, San Martín de Unx) and in parts of the deep south (Fustiñana, Tulebras); among its leading figures it numbered several prominent landowners: for example, the Conde de Rodezno, owner of large estates in Villafranca and other southern districts; José Sánchez Marco, *corralicero* and chief *cacique* of Milagro; and the Arraiza family, holders of several southern *corralizas*: sufficient strength, in short, to nurture Carlism's claims as a rallying-point for southern anti-Republicanism should one be needed.[44] Other Catholic landowners, reluctant to throw in their lot with Carlism, opted for Unión Navarra, the regional component of the conservative-Catholic CEDA; Unión Navarra drew much of its leadership from the upper echelons of Navarrese social-Catholicism and, without challenging Carlism's overall dominance of the Navarrese right, succeeded between 1933 and 1935 in establishing itself in several southern districts where Carlism was relatively weak. So, too, did the radical right in the shape of the Falange, which appears to have had some success in recruiting the sons of southern landowners.[45] Finally it should be recorded that social conservatism was not necessarily incompatible, at least in the short term, with republican allegiance. Along the valley of the Ebro in particular, some landowners saw in the right-wing republican Radical Party a (mostly temporary) alternative to the Catholic right, and 'republican' agrarian centres soon became focuses of conservative resistance to agrarian change.[46]

The fall of the left in September 1933, followed by the election victory of the centre and right in November, returned the initiative, in Navarre as elsewhere, to the large landowners. The electoral performance of the right in the Ribera, where it carried 44 out of 55 electoral districts with a share of the poll up from 34 per cent to 64 per cent, demonstrated the continued conservatism of many Navarrese farmers and the effectiveness of rightist propaganda. Nevertheless not only did the left, while defeated, retain a substantial base of support in the Ribera, but in several districts its position actually showed some improvement since 1931.[47]

From September 1933, landowners found themselves once more in the familiar position of enjoying the backing of the state. They promptly proceeded to cut wages, victimize trade unionists, expel Socialist smallholders from the *Cajas Rurales* and in other ways reassert their dominance more nakedly than ever before.[48] In response, the provincial FNTT put aside its previous policy of respectfully requesting the authorities to take action on the *corralizas*, in favour of an increasing stress on direct action.[49] When the Navarrese FNTT joined a nationwide peasants' strike in June 1934, it was ruthlessly suppressed with the use of the Civil Guard.[50] The social and political polarization affecting most of Spain between 1933 and 1936 was as apparent in Navarre, especially the Ribera, as elsewhere. The FNTT, the much weaker anarchist CNT and the rest of the left continued to demand the reversion of *corralizas* and large estates to the community. For their part, the landowners' organizations and the right-wing parties prepared for a showdown. The Carlist 'push' into the Ribera (about which I have written elsewhere), and in particular the exploits of its paramilitary element, the Requeté, together with the parallel emergence of the Falange, can only be interpreted in terms of aggressive agrarianism and militant anti-socialism. Following the Asturias rising of October 1934 left-wing local councils were sacked, Socialist centres closed and a Carlist-dominated *Diputación* restored in Pamplona. With the number of physical clashes increasing between UGT members and 'fascists' (Carlists and Falangists), the Navarrese left in the Ribera was coming to feel itself the victim of *squadrismo*.[51]

The victory of the Popular Front in the general election of February 1936 accelerated the polarization process in Navarre as elsewhere in Spain. The election itself, while again giving victory in the Ribera as a whole to the right, demonstrated a consolidation of Socialist – as distinct from Republican – support among labourers and small cultivators in districts where the *corralizas* remained an issue.[52] The installation of the Popular Front government released in southern Navarre pressures which had been accumulating since 1933, and particularly during 1935. A fresh wave of peasant militancy brought new occupations of *corralizas* and the holding of congresses, first of local councils (Tafalla, 4 March) and then of peasants' organizations (Pamplona, 19 April) to demand swift action of the *corralizas* and the replacement of the right-wing, '*corralicero*' *Diputacíon* elected in 1935.[53] And at last, in the early summer of 1936, signs of progress on the *corralizas* were discernible. In what was to be its last issue, on 18 July 1936, the weekly of the Navarrese UGT announced that 'Parliament has begun discussion of the *ley de rescates* bill presented by the government'. On its inside pages, however, appeared early reports of a military rising that elements of the Navarrese right, among others, had been planning for months and, in some cases, dreaming of for five years.

During the early weeks of the rising there took place in Navarre a repression of left-wing militants and ordinary trade unionists which, if much exaggerated in later years and modest compared with the experiences of southern provinces, was nevertheless on a scale sufficient to demonstrate the intensity of social antagonisms in parts at least of a province often treated as if it were monolithically conservative. The most convincing calculations suggest that at least 2,700 Navarrese died in the repression, perhaps two thirds of whom were peasants or rural labourers from the Ribera.[54]

This necessarily brief survey of the conflicts unleased by the advent of the Second Republic is intended to illustrate the response of landowners faced with a sudden and dramatic challenge to their power. The distinctive features of the Navarrese situation would appear to be (a) the emergence of a class of large landowners whose 'possession' of extensive tracts of land was not only recent and contentious but also detrimental to the material interests of large numbers of peasants from small proprietors, through tenant farmers and sharecroppers, to landless day labourers; (b) the arrival of a regime which threatened the legal continuation of this situation, strengthened the position of smallholders and rural labourers and favoured the growth of organizations determined to challenge the power and even the property of large landowners; (c) the existence of an integrative ideology, Catholicism, and a 'deflecting' ideology, Carlism, capable by the 1930s of being used to secure the loyalty to pro-landowner social and political organizations of the many peasants less directly affected by these disputes; and (d) the reassertion of landowner power by the most determined means imaginable: the physical destruction not only of the organizations of the landowners' antagonists but also, in many cases, of the antagonists themselves.

NOTES

I should like to thank the British Academy and the Twenty-Seven Foundation for awarding me the grants which made possible the research on which this chapter is based.

1 H. Thomas, *The Spanish Civil War*, 3rd edn (Harmondsworth: 1977), pp. 260–5.

2 See, for example, G. Brenan, *The Spanish Labyrinth* (Cambridge: 1943), p. 97; R. Carr, *Spain 1808–1975*, 2nd edn (Oxford: 1982), p. 274; J. Harrison, *An Economic History of Modern Spain* (Manchester: 1978), pp. 6–7; and (even) M. Blinkhorn, *Carlism and Crisis in Spain, 1931–1939* (Cambridge: 1975), p. 17.

3 E. Malefakis, *Agrarian Reform and Peasant Revolution in Spain* (New Haven, Conn.: 1970), p. 15.

4 This complex issue is usefully (and concisely) explored in J. del Burgo, *Historia de Navarra. La lucha por la libertad* (Madrid: 1978), pp. 81–110.

5 Basque customs, including those of inheritance, are discussed in J. Caro Baroja, *Los vascos* (Madrid: 1971); Rodney Gallop, *A Book of the Basques* (London: 1930); and (on French Navarre) S. Ott, *The Circle of Mountains. A Basque Shepherding Community* (Oxford: 1981), esp. pp. 202–3.

6 On the use variously of the single heir system and partible inheritance on the northwestern borders of the Ribera, see V. Bielza de Ory, *Tierra Estella. Estudio Geográfico* (Pamplona: 1972), pp. 254–5.

7 R. Rodríguez Garraza, *Navarra de Reino a Provincia (1828–1941)* (Pamplona: 1968), deals with Navarre's loss of the greater part of its historic autonomy; for a brief English-language history of Navarre, see R. Bard, *Navarre. The Durable Kingdom* (Reno, Nev.: 1982).

8 E. Majuelo Gil, *La II República en Navarra. Conflictividad en la Ribera Tudelana (1931–1933)* (Pamplona: 1986), p. 81; these figures nevertheless differ somewhat from those used by the same author in his more recent *Luchas de clases en Navarra (1931–1936)* (Pamplona: 1989), p. 54.

9 Majuelo Gil, *Luchas de clases*, p. 52.

10 Majuelo Gil, *La II República en Navarra*, p. 83.

11 Jesús Boneta, in *¡¡Trabajadores!!* (Pamplona), 21 October 1932.

12 J. Maurice, *La reforma agraria en España en el siglo XX (1900–1936)* (Madrid: 1975), p. 93.

13 Diputación de Navarra, Sección de Hacienda, Servicio Catastral [hereafter DN-SC]. Legs Cadreita, Fontellas, Javier [also embracing Peña], Monteagudo, Murillo el Cuende [embracing Traibuenas], Sartaguda: exps Conservación 1927–36; DN-SC, Leg. Rentas (1933). Lists of *señoríos*, varying slightly from each other but both based on that of F. Amorena, *El problema agrario en la Ribera de Navarra* (Pamplona: 1920), are given in V. Huici, M. Sorauren and J. Ma. Jimeno Jurio, *Historia contemporánea de Navarra* (San Sebastián: 1982), p. 112 and A. García-Sanz Marcótegui, *Navarra. Conflictividad social a comienzos del siglo XX* (Pamplona: 1984), p. 74. Information concerning other noble-owned properties appears in J. J. Virto and V. M. Arbeloa, 'La cuestión agraria navarra (1900–1936) (I)', *Príncipe de Viana*, xlv, 171 (1984), pp. 121–2.

14 DN-SC, Leg. Rentas (1933): Castejón, Cortes, Mélida, Olite.

15 DN-SC, Leg. Varias: 'Relación de mayores contribuyentes de Navarra por riqueza territorial' (1930). Vessolla, thanks to holdings in and around Pamplona, came second on the list.

16 J. Andrés-Gallego, *Historia contemporánea de Navarra* (Pamplona: 1982), p. 99.

17 ibid., p. 74. Religious disentailment in Navarre is examined in detail in J. Ma. Donézar, *La desamortizacíon de Mendizábal en Navarra 1836–51* (Madrid: 1975), and J. Ma. Mutiloa Poza, *La desamortización eclesiástica en Navarra* (Pamplona: 1972).

18 R. Gómez Chaparro, *La desamortización civil en Navarra* (Pamplona: 1967), *passim*.

19 ibid., pp. 175–236.

20 To be strictly accurate, the term '*corraliza*' implied the body of rights attached to a piece of land rather than the land itself, but by the nineteenth century popular usage had transferred the meaning to the latter. Excellent brief explanations of this complex question are contained in S. Mensua Fernández, *La Navarra Media Occidental* (Zaragoza: 1960), pp. 121–3 and Andrés-Gallego, *Historia contemporánea de Navarra*, pp. 77–9. Gómez Chaparro, *Desamortización civil*, pp. 175–236 lists lands included in and excluded from the alienation process; *corralizas* are indicated, but with no details as to the areas or the precise rights involved. The most detailed study of the phenomenon remains F. Arín y Dorronsoro, *Estudio jurídico-social de las corralizas, servidumbres, montes y comunidades de Navarra* (Segovia: 1930).

21 Donézar, *Desamortización de Mendizábal en Navarra*, p. 280.

22 Andrés-Gallego, *Historia contemporánea de Navarra*, p. 77.

23 D. Nagore, *Las posibilidades agrícolas de Navarra* (Pamplona: 1932). For examples of recent use of Nagore's figures see Huici, Sorauren and Jimeno Jurio, *Historia contemporánea de Navarra*, pp. 111–12 and García-Sanz Marcótegui, *Navarra. Conflictividad social*, pp. 75–6.

24 DN-SC, Leg. Cortes, exp. Conservación (1933).

25 DN-SC, Leg. Milagro, exp. Conservacíon; Leg. Milagro III, hojas declaratorias 1927–; Leg. San Adrián, exp. Conservación and exp. 'Relación de propietarios 1927'; Leg. Rentas (1933).

26 J. J. Virto and V. M. Arbeloa, 'La cuestión agraria navarra (1900–1936) (y III)', *Príncipe de Viana*, xlv, 174 (1985), pp. 275–7.

27 *¡¡Trabajadores!!*, 4 November 1932 and 16 December 1932 (Monteagudo) and 21 April 1933 (Fontellas), provides interesting examples of the role – continuing under the Republic – of estate administrators in local government.

28 On Olite, see J. Ma. Esparza, *Un camino cortado. Tafalla 1900–1939* (Tafalla: 1985), pp. 136–9; Virto and Arbeloa, 'La cuestión agraria navarra', III, 266–8; García-Sanz Marcótegui, *Navarra. Conflictividad social*, pp. 78–84 (a list of incidents linked with *corralizas* and commons appears on pp. 79–80).

29 Of innumerable legal cases that might be cited, perhaps the most striking is that involving the municipality of Lerín and Dositeo Ochoa, a landlord from Roncal who held some 800 hectares of *corraliza* land in the district. Litigation commenced in 1923 and finally ended in 1948 when Ochoa ceded to the municipality one of his three *corralizas*. Virto and Arbeloa, 'La cuestión agraria navarra (y III)', pp. 247–50.

30 E. Majuelo Gil and A. Pascual Bonis, 'El Cooperativismo agrario católico en Navarra (1904–1939)', *Príncipe de Viana*, xlvii, 177 (1986), pp. 235–69; Virto and Arbeloa, 'La cuestión agraria navarra (I)', pp. 123–5; J. Cuesta Bustillo, *Sindicalismo católico agrario en España (1917–1919)* (Madrid: 1978), pp. 133–6; J. J. Montero, *La CEDA. El catolicismo social y político en la II República*, 2 vols (Madrid: 1877), Vol. I, p. 82. On urban social-Catholicism in Catalonia, see C. Winston, *Workers and the Right in Spain, 1900–1936* (Princeton, NJ: 1985).

31 On Carlism (and other political forces) in early twentieth-century Navarre, see Ma. C. Mina Apat, 'Elecciones y Partidos en Navarra (1891–1923)', in J. L. García Delgado (ed.), *La España de la Restauración* (Madrid: 1985), pp. 111–29 and M. Blinkhorn, 'War on two fronts: politics and society in Navarre, 1931–6', in Paul Preston (ed.), *Revolution and War in Spain 1931–1939* (London: 1984), pp. 59–84. Esparza, *Tafalla*, p. 138, refers obliquely to Catholic workers and former Carlists shifting to the left, apparently between the late 1910s and the 1930s.

32 For results of local elections see *El Pensamiento Navarro* (Pamplona) and *Diario de Navarra* (Pamplona), 13 April 1931, 2 June 1931. These elections are examined in J. J. Virto Ibáñez, *Las elecciones municipales de 1931 en Navarra* (Pamplona: 1987) (detailed results 157–214). Results in Navarre of the 1931 general election were published in *Boletín Oficial de la Provincia de Navarra* [hereafter BOPN] (Pamplona), 1 July 1931.

33 BOPN, 3 June 1932 gives a list, probably not complete, of all workers' organizations in Navarre.

34 On unemployment in the southernmost region of the Ribera see E. Majuelo Gil, 'El paro en la Merindad de Tudela en el primer Bienio Republicano', *Langaiak* (Pamplona), 4 (April 1984), pp. 56–62 and Majuelo Gil, *Luchas de clases*, pp. 164–9. Detailed figures are in *¡¡Trabajadores!!*, 4 November 1932.

35 Majuelo Gil, 'El paro en la Merindad de Tudela'.

36 *¡¡Trabajadores!!*, 3 June 1932 (Corella), 15 July 1932, 28 July 1933 (Olite).

37 Demands for action on the *corralizas* appeared in almost every issue of the UGT weekly *¡¡Trabajadores!!*. For reports of success at local level see the issues of 8 July 1932 (Mendavia) and 21 July 1932 (Tafalla).

38 *¡¡Trabajadores!!*, 2 December 1932, 10 March 1933.

39 Archivo Histórico Nacional (Madrid) [hereafter AHN], Gobernación Leg. 7A, exp. 6, 'Cuestiones sociales, 1931: Navarra', Civil Governor to Ministerio de Gobernación, 23 October 1931 (Mendavia), 24 December 1931 (Los Arcos, Mendavia); Leg. 16A, exp. 16 'Desórdenes públicas: circulares y provincias: Alava-Navarra, 1931', Civil Governor to Ministerio de Gobernación, 11 November 1931 (Cáseda).

40 *¡¡Trabajadores!!*, 7 and 31 March 1933, 23 June 1933, 20 October 1933.

41 Individual cases of such employer and landowner resistance, reported in *¡¡Trabajadores!!*, are too numerous for there to be much point in singling any out. Even allowing for the UGT weekly's unashamed partiality, the evidence – rarely countered in the right-wing press – is overwhelming.

42 DN-SC, Leg. Javier-Peña, exps. Conservación (1933, 1934); *¡¡Trabajadores!!*, 4 November 1932, 16 June 1933 (Monteagudo).

43 *El Siglo Futuro* (Madrid), 8 August 1932; *Revista Social y Agraria* (Madrid), 30 September 1933; Majuelo Gil and Pascual Bonis, 'El Cooperativismo agrario', pp. 256–9; *¡¡Trabajadores!!*, 6 December 1932, 15 December 1934. For a list of such organizations in 1935 see the *Censo* of professional and social organizations published in BOPN, 1 July 1935.

44 On Navarrese Carlism during the Republic see Blinkhorn, 'War on two fronts', *passim*.

45 J. R. Montero, *La CEDA*, Vol. I, p. 408, gives 7,000 as the membership of Union Navarra in 1934. Information on the Navarrese Falange is sketchy, but see the details scattered through ALTAFFAYLLA KULTUR TALDEA, *Navarra 1936. De la esperanza al terror*, 2 vols (Estella: 1986), *passim*.

46 O. Ruiz Manjón, *El Partido Republicano Radical 1908–1936* (Madrid: 1976), pp. 612–13 notes a surge (it would appear shortlived) in Radical strength in Navarre during 1934, when 27 local committees were recorded as existing in the province. This figure is confirmed by J. J. Virto Ibáñez, *Partidos republicanos de Navarra* (Pamplona: 1986), pp. 36–40, who actually lists local organizations, the great majority of which were in the Ribera or along its northern boundaries. See also *¡¡Trabajadores!!*, 17 March 1933, 27 August, 1933, 24 November 1933 for reports of Radical Party activity in the Ebro Valley.

47 The discussion of election results is based upon detailed analysis of the figures published in BOPN, 22 November 1933.

48 *¡¡Trabajadores!!*, 6 October 1933; *El Socialista* (Madrid), 10 October 1933.

49 *¡¡Trabajadores!!*, 6 October 1933, 9 February 1934, 29 June 1934.

50 AHN, Gobernación, Leg. 50A, exps 10–17, 'Huelga de campesinos: Navarra'; *¡¡Trabajadores!!* was censored, for the first time in its existence, before, during and immediately after the strike (i.e. the issues of 1 and 8 June 1934). Guarded reports appeared in the issues of 29 June 1934, 13 July 1934 and 3 and 24 August 1934, with the villages of Cortes, Funes and Monteagudo receiving particular prominence. A useful brief analysis is J. J. Virto, 'Junio de 1934; las huelgas de campesinos en Navarra', *Príncipe de Viana*, xlix, Anejo 10 (1988), pp. 465–72.

51 Blinkhorn, 'War on two fronts', pp. 76–80. For reports of rightist aggression (about which, not surprisingly, the right-wing press was silent), see *¡¡Trabajadores!!*, 20 April 1935 (Berbinzana), 28 April 1935 (Mendavia), 18 January 1936 (Cáseda).

52 Detailed results of the general election of February 1936 in Navarre appear in BOPN, 19 February 1936; see also A. Pascual, 'Navarra ante las elecciones del Frente Popular', *Langaiak*, 5 (April 1984), pp. 63–83. A further strengthening of the left's position was apparent at the election in April for presidential electors (*compromisarios*), the detailed results of which were published in BOPN, 29 April 1936. On these last Republican elections, see J. L. Manas and J. P. Urabayen, 'Las últimas elecciones de la II República en Navarra (elecciones a compromisarios para la elección de Presidente de la República, 26-IV-36', *Príncipe de Viana*, xix, Anejo 10 (1988), pp. 243–64.

53 *¡¡Trabajadores!!*, 21 March 1936 (Tafalla assembly), 28 March 1936, 11 and 25 April 1936 (Pamplona assembly), 16 May 1936.

54 On the repression of the Navarrese left, see R. Salas Larrazábal, *Los fusilados en Navarra en la guerra de 1936* (Madrid: 1983), where a figure of 1,100 is accepted; this has been vigorously contested by Colectivo Afán, *¡¡No. General!! fueron más de tres mil los asésinados* (Pamplona: 1984) where, as the title indicates, one of over 3,000 is suggested and the minimum of 2,789 convincingly established. See also the village-by-village account in ALTAFFAYLLA KULTUR TALDEA, *Navarra 1936. De la esperanza al terror*.

12

Agrarian power and crisis in southern Spain: the province of Badajoz, 1875–1936

Tim Rees

Proof that the Spanish Civil War of 1936–9 had important roots in the agrarian conflicts of southern Spain came with the westward advance of insurgent forces from Seville following the rising of 18 July 1936. Although militarily speaking a brief, opening phase to the agonizing struggle that followed, this campaign ruthlessly eliminated southern rural society as an area of support for the democratic Second Republic established in 1931. Caught in the path of the advance, the province of Badajoz, in the southwestern region of Extremadura, provided the first evidence for the outside world of the brutality of the war when a fierce repression by the victorious forces, including massacres in town cemeteries and bullrings, came to light. Though initially justified as a wartime necessity, the involvement of civilians in systematic and continuing violence to eliminate social and political enemies suggested that far more than military pacification was at stake.[1] Rather, the war interrupted a bitter power struggle, which reached crisis proportions during the Republic, in a province dominated for centuries by agrarian elites that constituted a rural ruling class well into the twentieth century.

Agrarian power in the modern period in Badajoz lay in a pattern of landownership that was strongly influenced by the sale of rural property resulting from a series of liberalization measures introduced by governments from the 1830s onwards. These encouraged land speculation by allowing a fully free market and disentailing church and municipal holdings. This commerce exacerbated an existing inequality in the distribution of land while shifting the concentration of ownership into new hands.[2] More exact information about the narrow stratum of large landowners is available for the twentieth century from the cadastral survey begun in 1906 and completed, as far as southern Spain was concerned, by 1930. The picture was one in which just 1.74 per cent of all those who owned rural property – some 1,576 persons – possessed 61.94 per cent of total available land. Within the ranks of major landowners, nobles continued to account for between a sixth and an eighth of the total, retaining many of the largest individual ownerships in the province. But the overwhelming beneficiaries of land transfers were persons of bourgeois origins, many of whom were attracted into ownership for the first time by the prestige and rising material value attached to land.[3]

Latifundios – estates defined as consolidated holdings of over 250 hectares – were the most important possessions of these great owners or *latifundistas*. Of the 1,368 *latifundios* counted in the cadastral survey, most were of 1,000 hectares or less, but a number were larger than 1,000 hectares with at least five reaching an area of 5,000 hectares. Covering 34.06 per cent of the total area of the province, large estates coexisted alongside 16,083 small to medium holdings of between 10 and 250 hectares. Within this category the larger holdings seem to have been municipal lands that passed wholesale into the hands of large owners, who also gained control of a considerable portion of the remainder that seem to have arrived on the market owing to the accumulation of debt on the part of their original owners. Even so, some 12,375 families survived to be reported in the cadastral survey as owners of individual smallholdings.[4] Large landowners were unable to consolidate small to medium holdings because of the dense field pattern that prevailed in Badajoz. Centred on defensive medieval village sites, fields of similar size clustered in rings radiating out from numerous minute gardens around the boundary to estates in the open countryside. It was correspondingly highly unlikely that different holdings belonging to the same person would share the same borders.[5]

Chronic absenteeism encouraged the existence of a stratum of non-landed intermediaries that formed an important component of the provincial agrarian elite. A rising rentable value for estates in the nineteenth century encouraged the more aristocratic and most landed of owners, 36.5 per cent of the total according to the cadastral survey, to live on *rentier* incomes in Seville, Madrid, or even abroad. They passed on the actual costs and risks of production to substantial tenants, known as *labradores*, who rented entire estates on long leases. Although the numbers of such persons are impossible to calculate, the 142,000 hectares of estate land reported as permanently leased by the cadastral survey indicates that they were a considerable force.[6] A further addition to the ranks of the elite included estate managers, more typically appointed by resident owners with multiple estate holdings than acting as the agents of absentees. As Richard Herr has pointed out, the justification for the inclusion of managers and *labradores* in the agrarian elite was that practical control of the majority of land in a rural economy gave enormous opportunities to exercise power over a provincial populace that was overwhelmingly dependent on the soil for a living.[7] By the later nineteenth century this produced in Badajoz a thoroughly commercialized latifundist economy based on a rigid division between the agrarian elite and the rural lower orders. Nevertheless, adaptation to differing natural conditions allowed considerable variety in rural production and economic organization.[8]

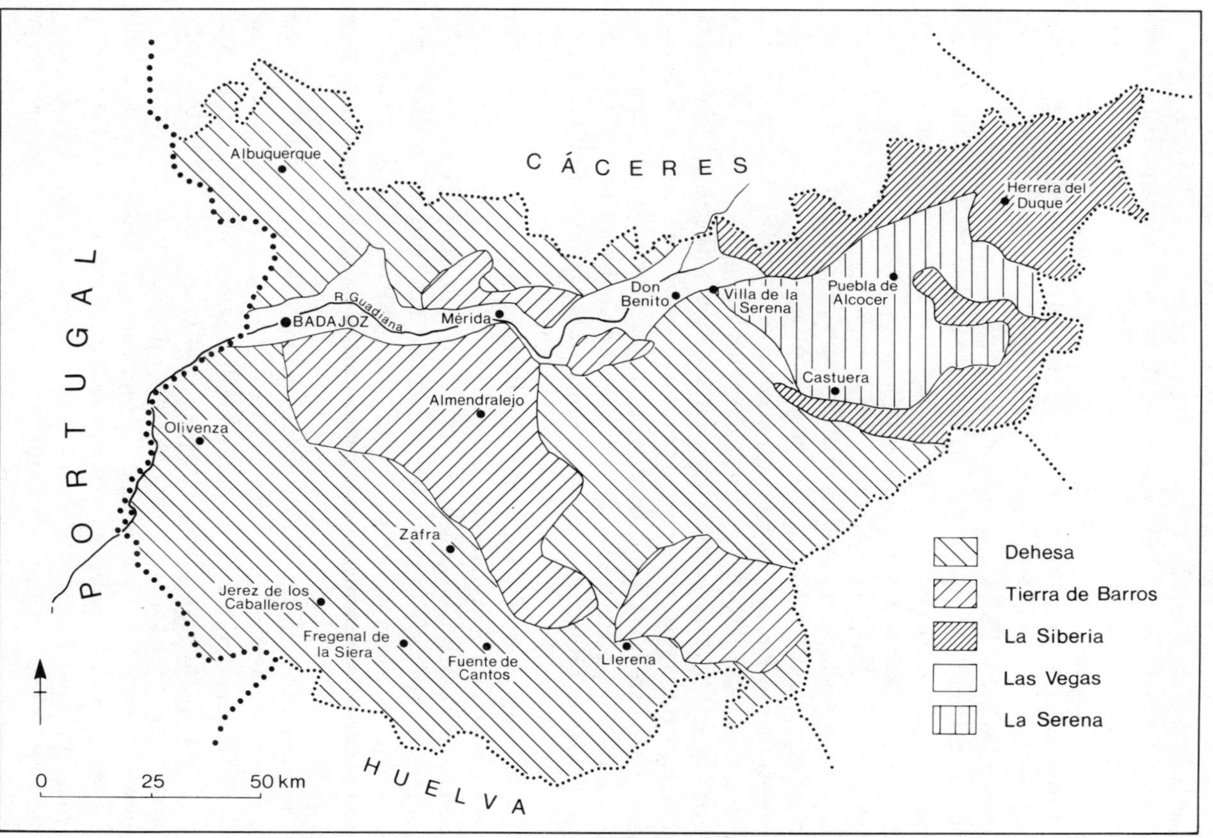

Map 12.1 The province of Badajoz: agricultural regions

Estates in the periphery were tracts of open land, mainly covered by a parkland *dehesa* of pasture and acorn-bearing holm oaks. This gave way to less regular tree coverage and scrub pastures, as soils became poorer towards the eastern highlands of the aptly named La Siberia and La Serena regions. Although frequently mistaken for barren wastes, these landscapes were actually carefully maintained to support the sedentary herds of pigs, sheep and goats that were its staple product, employing some 15,000 shepherds and foresters in the 1930s.[9] Organized around regional animal markets (*rodeos*), this pastoral economy developed following the final destruction of the famous *Mesta* in 1839, which prevented the herd of transhumant merinos belonging to the organization from using Badajoz as a sheep walk under crown protection.[10] With the exception of specialist cork growing around Albuquerque which required direct labour, agrarians integrated an extensive, mixed agriculture – subsistence in the case of La Siberia – with their animal interests largely through indirect exploitation that passed on the major risks of production to family producers engaged on sharecropping agreements of two broad types.[11] *Aparcería*, covering some 12,000 households in the cadastral survey, involved smallholdings and portions of estates split into 30–50 hectare parcels with tenancies which lasted a number of years. Though terms varied considerably, agreements usually strongly favoured the landlord, involving obligations to provide free labour services, make improvements and grow directed crops. The 20,000 families engaged as *yunteros* – a peculiarity of Extremadura – had less autonomy and security than the *aparceros*, being assigned land on short tenancies of only a year. They relied for part of their income on work as ploughmen, using a pair of draught animals, a *yunta*, that comprised their only capital. The semi-independence of family production was balanced against the constraints of a cycle of poverty and indebtedness for seed and tools, which tied sharecroppers to landlords for whom the needs of animals always came first.[12]

In contrast to this pastoral-agricultural mix, the highly fertile central regions of the province formed by Las Vegas (the meadows) and the Tierra de Barros (land of clay) had been transformed by entrepreneurial agrarians into a zone of intensive agriculture by the last quarter of the nineteenth century. Here estates were compact farms (*cortijos*), producing mainly cereals, with some wine and olives, for national and international markets. Tensions with pastoralists, who had previously dominated land use in the region, and the late arrival of railway communication had delayed the process of cerealization common to the south.[13] Profitability rested, not on expensive capital investment in irrigation, fertilizers and machinery, but on the instrumentalization of a rural proletariat and a repressive system of labour relations that kept wage costs low and extracted a high quantum of seasonal manual work. As a result, the workforce of estates was divided into a minority of permanent hands (*fijos*) who carried out skilled work and closely supervised the hiring and employment of day labourers (*jornaleros*) during the digging, sowing and harvesting seasons. With a rural population rising particularly rapidly in the cereal zone, no possibility of emigration, and the reduction of alternative sources of employment that was implicit in cerealization, competition for scarce work in town labour markets was fierce and the constant menace of unemployment a great terror. Consequently, agrarians were able to keep wages low, easily discard workers during economic downturns or harvest failure and impose harsh conditions and long hours of work on the gangs of labourers who worked the fields. When temporary local labour shortages arose at harvest times, and women and children were drafted into the gangs, agrarians avoided any reversal of the economic circumstances that favoured their domination of labour by bringing in migrant workers from Portugal. Not surprisingly, contemporary descriptions of cereal estates often used military metaphors, with agrarians as officers, *fijos* as NCOs and labourers as the cannon fodder. However, even such analogies underplayed the brutalities of a system of labour relations run by fear of the sanctions of dismissal, victimization, and fines and punishments inflicted by foremen.[14]

Latifundism promoted localized autocracies that extended agrarian power into the concentrated villages and towns (*pueblos*) which formed the residential and administrative centres of the province. Except in the largest towns, Badajoz (the provincial capital which gave its name to the province) and Mérida, trades such as manufacturing, retailing and construction were small-scale and peripheral, and usually served the needs of the rural economy.[15] Moreover the property interests of agrarians continued in the *pueblo* environment through the activities of landlordship and moneylending. Consequently, the way was clear for agrarians, as the major providers of work, land and credit, to act as the arbiters of urban life and public affairs. Indeed, the stability of a rural regime dominated by an agrarian elite required effective control over law and order, and the functioning of civil and judicial administration. In this respect the agrarians consolidated their position with the creation in 1875 of the Restoration state, which ensured its own stability by delegating authority to the rural elites and provided subsidy and protection for agriculture.[16] Often the complex and competing hierarchies of bosses (*caciques*) who actually filled municipal offices or sat as provincial party deputies for the Liberal and Conservative monarchist parties, were not agrarians themselves but professionals (lawyers, doctors, pharmacists), shopkeepers and officials, who effectively acted on the agrarians' behalf.[17] Alongside the enormous patronage of agrarians, *caciquismo* effectively protected the privileges of rural property and reinforced the social divisions of the province. Freedom to act with only self-restraint as a guide had important material implications for agrarians, not just as a licence in the straightforward pursuit of profit, but also by excluding any possible measures – taxation of land, controls on the labour market and conditions of work, regulation of rents and tenancies – that would have disrupted the basis of latifundism.

Very little existed to bridge a prevailing social distance in Badajoz between the agrarians and the rural lower orders that became a vast gulf in the case of *jornaleros*. The arrangement of housing, local services and sociability in the *pueblos* largely reproduced the divisions found on the land, making obvious the relative wealth and comfort of even the most minor agrarian. For the rest of society, poor incomes from rural work precluded any systematic means to foster any deep sense of community or cultural identification.[18] On occasion individual agrarians did win reputations for paternalism towards the poor. This did not extend beyond giving work on ditch-digging or road-mending (*alojamiento*) during periods of forced employment and precluded any public policy of relief or welfare to improve housing, food supplies, hygiene and education that would have raised local taxes.[19]

Nor did Catholicism and the charity of the church produce any real cement to bind society together. Rates of religious practice had probably always been low, and certainly the image of the church as the servant of the privileged did nothing to alter this situation. Local priests were seen as the allies of agrarians and as agents of social control through their role in charity. Labouring families particularly dreaded being forced to accept the aid of the church because of the need to prove their piety and moral worthiness.[20] The message passed on by a church largely absent from the everyday lives of the majority was one of passive acceptance of the established order and obedience to authority – views that exactly reproduced those of agrarians. Such a starkly unmediated pattern of divisions gave correspondingly scant basis for any form of unquestioned traditional authority for the upholding of autocracy.

Even during the seemingly effortless supremacy that stretched for the majority of the elite until the First World War, agrarian rule achieved at best only limited legitimacy. In so far as they possessed an ideology, agrarians maintained a commitment to the exercise of virtually absolute property rights over a deferential rural majority. Such an apparent archaism actually fitted perfectly the conditions of social and economic subordination required by cereal and animal latifundism. It was also consistent with the autocratic ethics of individualism and robust self-reliance of an elite that lacked cohesion. No shared field sports or country house weekends tied together agrarians divided by economic interests, local competition and status – this last illustrated when landowners refused membership of town clubs (*casinos*) to *labradores*. Consequently, no agrarian organization developed in Badajoz to defend the elite as a whole, nor did it seem a serious necessity. The disruptive effects of social and economic change, the relative isolation of the province and populace, and a lack of political resources, meant that during the nineteenth century no serious challenge developed among the rural lower orders of Badajoz to the province's modern agrarian elite or rural order.

The surface tranquillity of Badajoz nevertheless covered a smouldering subterranean discontent among the labouring poor that found an outlet, even amid tight agrarian control, in a variety of desperate acts of survival and revenge. Smuggling, poaching and rural theft were rife, while resentment at work discipline and wages led to nocturnal incendiarist attacks on crops and hayricks, and similar furtive mutilation of trees, olive plants and animals. Unemployment and food shortages sparked off occasional outbursts of serious local unrest, like those of the 1890s when crises in cork and cereal prices produced riotous crowds demanding relief and work in the Albuquerque and Badajoz districts. In the absence of any other means, agrarians dealt with even the most minor of these symptoms of disaffection by resorting to a ruthless naked force designed to punish and dissuade. The local state, in the form of the paramilitary Civil Guard, stood ready to defend property and public order, often with great violence and brutality. At the same time agrarians administered summary punishments using their estate guards and foremen.[21] Although persistent, such spontaneous and sporadic conflicts could never pose a fundamental threat to the power of the elite. Agrarians accordingly failed to recognize that the rural order in Badajoz was certainly not immune to pressures for change from below such as those which had already produced anarchist movements in western Andalusia.[22]

The characteristic reaction of agrarians to the unanticipated beginnings of organized resistance in the countryside was to meet it with all the means of force at their command. A bitter syndical and political struggle was first joined on the *cortijos* and in the larger towns of the cereal zone, where conditions most favoured collective action and where elite supervision of urban life was at its weakest. The handful of *sociedades obreras* (workers' societies) formed here by labourers and artisans between 1901 and 1914 had an uncertain ideological inspiration that blended elements of anarchism, socialism and republicanism, but provided a model of far-reaching goals and clear methods firmly rooted in rural sociology. Taken together, demands for improvements in wages and working conditions, regulated employment and public welfare, hit at the whole basis of latifundism and the elite social order. Similarly, the harvest-time general strike to paralyse the labour market and political mobilization to capture control of the town hall recognized the realities of agrarian power. The agrarians affected evolved a severely inflexible range of responses to *sociedades* that increasingly adopted the banners of the Socialist trade union, the Unión General de Trabajadores (UGT), and party, the Partido Socialista Obrero Español (PSOE).[23] Although many agrarians, confused when first faced by disciplined strike activity, initially gave way to workers' demands, reliance on increased intimidation and force to break the solidarity and endurance of strikers became the norm. Negotiation and conciliation were rare, as agrarians feared for profitability and were strongly resistant to discussing management decisions with their inferiors. *Labradores*, with the smallest margins on the basis of which to grant improvements or wage increases, proved particularly intransigent in the use of lock-outs, evictions and blacklisting, the arrest and beating of ringleaders, the employment of *fijos* and Portuguese labour under guard to work fields, and the meeting of demonstrations and deputations with violence. Meanwhile, to meet the challenge of worker candidates in local elections, agrarians promoted a turn towards the electoral falsification, bribery and menace that became the hallmarks of *caciquismo* under pressure.[24] The undoubted success of these measures, which isolated protest to very few areas and led to only fleeting gains for the *sociedades*, justified autocracy despite the fragmentation of the provincial elite that was also evident. While violence remained functional, even temporary local alliances were rare among the small minority of agrarians actually engaged in these disputes, and no measures for collective, permanent defence were taken – or needed.

Dramatic proof of the vulnerability of agrarian power in Badajoz was provided by the effects of the First World War. Spanish neutrality led to a cereals boom stimulated by demand from the Allied powers. High prices allowed agrarians in Badajoz to place more marginal land profitably under the plough, which in turn created demand for more labour. The easiest way to raise labour productivity on the *cortijos* and avoid disputes was to increase wages, stimulating rising expectations in the process. However, when cereal prices collapsed with the coming of peace, agrarians reacted to overproduction by returning land to fallow, reducing their use of labour and forcing wage cuts. The subsequent frustration felt by *jornaleros* during the summer of 1918 at a return to poverty-level incomes, unemployment and increased labour discipline, was exacerbated by a cost of living for basic foodstuffs which doubled nationally between 1914 and 1920.[25] The three years of agitation that followed formed part of the so-called Bolshevik Years that swept the whole of southern Spain. A wave of harvest strikes, organized by new *sociedades obreras*, spread across the entire central zone of Badajoz, destroying any remaining complacency or sense of paternalism among cereal-producing agrarians. Frightened at this explosion of protest, rural employers again frequently gave way initially to workers' demands, only to return as soon as possible to forceful means of breaking strikes where latifundism and local political control enabled them to do so. Violence occurred when armed *fijos* and Civil Guards opened fire on crowds, in pitched battles between strikers and strikebreakers, and when local strikes degenerated into attacks on the property, and even persons, of agrarians. Nevertheless agrarians now found their private means and disorganized local actions, even when supported by the Civil Guard and local courts, insufficient to cow the workforce. The desperate situation was only finally resolved in the summer of 1920, when the Civil Governor of the province called on the central government for troops and Civil Guard reinforcements. Under a state of emergency, the workers' centres (*casas del pueblo*) were closed down and the countryside placed under virtual occupation. Although afterwards the *sociedades* mostly collapsed under repression and exhaustion, the bitterness of the truce that followed only encouraged agrarian acceptance of the Primo de Rivera dictatorship, established in 1923, as a strong regime that promised to guarantee their continued supremacy.[26]

Within Badajoz the sense of an opportunity lost under Primo de Rivera was felt particularly keenly by the leading figures of the Cámara Agrícola (Chamber of Agriculture). Formed in 1908 to promote agricultural improvement, the Cámara Agrícola gradually brought together landowners interested in scientific agriculture, professional agronomists, surveyors and engineers, and 'social' Catholics concerned with religious recovery. While all those involved were staunch defenders of private property, they pointed to the contrast between the product of economic change in Badajoz, namely, a multiplying rural proletariat which represented a permanent threat of revolt, and the supposed conservative Catholic and family virtues of peasants in harmonious Castile.[27] According to this view, peace and property could best be preserved by turning the cereal estates over to sharecropping while improving tenancies throughout the province, thus creating true 'partnerships' on the land between agrarians and a substantial stratum of stable family producers. Shortage of land could be overcome by extensive irrigation and technical improvement that would dramatically raise yields and incomes.

Until 1918 this vision commanded the acceptance of only a farsighted minority of the elite, prepared to become involved in the activities of the Cámara Agrícola or participate in local initiatives to form Catholic syndicates and rural banks that encouraged settlement of labourers and provided agricultural education and credit.[28] Following the postwar disturbances, an upsurge of agrarian interest in the Catholic syndicates and employers' organization encouraged high expectations that a rational restructuring of the rural economy and society might now prove possible. Gradually, however, these hopes turned to disillusionment. As the immediate fear of renewed protest receded, the Cámara Agrícola and the newly created Federación Provincial de Sindicatos Católicos Agrícolas found their strenuous efforts to promote their reform policies and create a permanent agrarian organization to support them largely ignored by agrarians.[29] For the majority these schemes involved unacceptable modifications to latifundism and hence to the whole social order. Moreover the condemnations of absenteeism, as encouraging poor attitudes to rural property, which accompanied these plans directly threatened both the interests of absentees and the existence of the *labradores* who rented their lands. The continued identification of rural property rights with autocracy was clearly at odds with any serious attempt to promote unity of purpose among agrarians while force sufficed.

The accusations of apathy and shortsightedness made against agrarians, however plausible, ignored the corrosive effects of the accelerating deterioration of latifundism. The main cause was a catastrophic crisis in animal prices and production that began during the First World War, leading to the loss of over half a million head of livestock between 1917 and 1921 alone. In 1919 this did inspire the formation of an agrarian association, the Junta Provincial de

Ganaderos, which was concerned purely with sectional campaigns on behalf of stockbreeders rather than acting as a fully fledged patronal organization. Moreover, while calling for aid to protect animal prices and modernize production, the Junta attacked the Cámara Agrícola as too closely identified with favoured cereal interests.[30] Yet beneath this clash of interests, pastoral agrarians reacted to the crisis by furthering the extension of cerealization into the *dehesa* to the detriment of sharecroppers. Beginning with the wartime boom and continuing with the recovery of agricultural prices in the mid-1920s, *aparceros* came under increasing pressure from landlords who altered tenancies to force the exclusive production of cereals as a cash crop and began charging higher rents. Simultaneously, agrarians increasingly used *yunteros* merely to clear areas of parkland preparatory to soil-depleting direct cultivation by labourers, themselves often unemployed herdsmen and foresters. This virtual proletarianization of *yunteros* was compounded by the beginnings of mechanization on the *cortijos*, which threatened their livelihood and their skilled status as ploughmen.[31] As a result of these changes, the always precarious balance in relations between agrarians and sharecroppers which had helped keep the *dehesa* largely immune from the events of 1918–20 was destroyed.

Elite division, lack of proper organization, and complete alienation from rural society made unavoidable the full crisis of agrarian power that accompanied the transition to the Republic in Badajoz.[32] Landed interests actually dealt a blow to the Primo de Rivera dictatorship when the Confederación Nacional Católico-Agraria (CNCA), strongly supported in Badajoz by the Cámara Agrícola, objected to the proposed creation of rural arbitration committees (*comités paritarios*) to decide wages and working conditions as an unacceptable invasion of rural property rights.[33] Bereft of government support, from the winter of 1929–30 latifundism was caught in a social and economic crisis that fuelled what appeared to be a growing revolutionary threat to the entire rural regime. *Sociedades obreras* began reforming and affiliating themselves to the Socialist landworkers' union, the Federación Nacional de Trabajadores de la Tierra (FNTT). With the support of both labourers and radicalized *yunteros*, labour organization now spread rapidly to cover the entire province by the summer of 1931. Renewed demands then followed for labour contracts to improve wages, conditions and availability of work, the impact of which was strengthened by falling animal and cereal prices caused by depression and overproduction. In particular, world cereal prices fell from a base of 100 in 1929 to a level of 43 in 1933, without the enactment of any corresponding measures to protect the internal market. Agrarians tried to respond by putting more land into fallow, accelerating the substitution of direct labour for sharecropping, and lowering wages. A rising tide of strikes and land invasions by *yunteros* followed as rural workers resisted the decisions of agrarians.[34] While the elite rediscovered that individual and localized action, however forceful, was insufficient in itself to hold the syndical challenge in check, the climate of the early Republic (1931–3) deprived them of the final resort of an appeal for state intervention to redeem the situation.

Political weakness crucially completed the eclipse of agrarian power. With its mechanisms already undermined by the dictatorship, years of open corruption and the break-up of the two oligarchical parties of the Restoration, *caciquismo* finally proved itself to be more a system of patronage and social control than a developed political system. During the decisive municipal elections of 12 April 1931 the *caciques* were powerless in the face of well-prepared campaigns by Socialist and Republican candidates in what was essentially a free vote. In most areas local rivalries hampered any concerted response by agrarians, leading to a variety of monarchist candidates, representing different Liberal and Conservative factions, being put forward.[35] When, following the collapse of the monarchy and the proclamation of the Second Republic, Socialist mayors took control of town councils they immediately set to work at raising local taxes in order to subsidize public works and welfare, supporting striking workers, controlling the Civil Guard and setting up commissions to adjudicate conditions of pay and employment. To the further horror of agrarians, a symbolic destruction of the old order also took place, with red banners and Republican flags unfurled over town halls, and street demonstrations welcoming the new provisional government.

The new regime completed the catastrophe now overtaking agrarians by introducing decrees that undermined their freedom of economic decision-making and offered reinforcement to rural labour. *Laboreo forzoso* (obligatory cultivation) prevented agrarians from taking land out of cultivation and enforcing a lock-out. The *términos municipales* (Municipal Boundaries) decree prohibited the use of labour from outside village boundaries before all that was locally available had been employed, effectively handing control of the labour market to the *sociedades obreras*. The most important measure was that setting up *jurados mixtos* (mixed juries or arbitration committees) which extended compulsory collective bargaining, promoted fair rent agreements and applied social legislation to the countryside for the first time. Taken together these measures effectively undermined the bases of agrarian autocracy in the countryside and instead introduced a corporatist framework of rural social and economic relations that institutionalized the interests of the *sociedades obreras*.[36]

The reverses suffered by beleaguered agrarians were sudden and considerable, but not complete. Though the balance of power had been shifted dramatically in rural society, the actual structures and institutions of latifundism were not destroyed. Similarly, agrarians were still free within the Republic to undertake the tasks of united organization and campaigning on class lines which now, *in extremis*, became vital necessities rather than the luxuries that they had previously seemed to many of the elite. Circumstances naturally placed the Cámara Agrícola and its allies in the Catholic syndicates at the forefront of agrarian defence. At the June 1931 election to the Republican Constituent Cortes, the Cámara leaders' strategy of attaching themselves to the hastily prepared rightist party, Acción Nacional, proved a failure. They thereupon moved quickly to create a grass-roots patronal organization as the first step towards rebuilding agrarian power.[37] On 6 July 1931 the Federación de Propietarios de Fincas Rústicas de Badajoz was launched to coordinate the activities of all rural employers in the struggle against the provincial Socialist movement and the reforming government, in an alliance with similar bodies across southern Spain. Over the next two years the Federación de Propietarios achieved remarkable success in gaining agrarian membership and frustrating the advance of the *sociedades obreras*. Its tactics in this struggle were to engineer the withdrawal of work and the virtual cessation of cultivation on the estates to nullify the decrees and labour agreements, while protesting at unjust attacks on property rights when the *jurados mixtos* and local Socialist councils tried to impose fines and enforce *laboreo forzoso*. As social and political polarization in the countryside worsened under pressure from increasing levels of strikes, land invasions by *yunteros* and clashes with the Civil Guard, the Federación de Propietarios became the principal sponsor behind the formation of an agrarian Catholic party that aimed to seize the political initiative in Badajoz for the elite.[38]

Launched in January 1933, Acción Popular Agraria (APA) was affiliated to the national right through the Confederación Española de Derechas Autónomas (CEDA: Spanish Confederation of Autonomous Right-Wing Organizations), whose virulent anti-socialism and commitment to the defence of religion and property it shared. Given the nature of rural society in Badajoz, the basis of support for such ideals was inevitably narrow. Even so, APA rapidly created branches in every town and village of the province. Its recruitment drive was immensely aided by the Agrarian Reform Law eventually passed by the Cortes in September 1932, which, although totally ineffectual in its avowed aim of redistributing the great estates, could plausibly be represented as a menace to all rural property holders. When combined with denunciations of a 'Socialist dictatorship' such propaganda had the effect of rallying smallholders to APA, turning the areas of Mérida and Almendralejo where they were particularly concentrated into major rightist centres.[39] Still numerically weak in the face of the Socialist movement, APA, in order to fight a new general election in November 1933, was forced into an 'anti-Marxist alliance' with the provincial Radical Party, a Republican organization which had attracted a considerable following among professionals, shopkeepers and small businessmen who rejected the monarchy but were still strongly conservative.[40] Voting took place in a province effectively paralysed by a concerted campaign on the part of the Federación de Propietarios to ignore the rulings of the *jurados mixtos* and the Agrarian Reform Commission. Against this background APA offered its reactionary political alternative: the dismemberment of socialism and the creation of a 'just Catholic social order', which returned to the idea of a social barrier of family producers as the antidote to the rural class struggle. Narrow victory alongside its uncertain Radical allies both contributed to a rightward shift in national government and ensured in the Badajoz countryside a direct confrontation with a still powerful, though now defensive, rural workers' movement.[41]

With all elements of rural corporatism and the Republic's social legislation suspended, and the Radicals in control of provincial administration, the Federación de Propietarios intensified an offensive against organized labour that had begun even before the general election. Unrestrained, agrarians tightened their boycott by giving work only to those of proven loyalty, importing labour from Portugal, increasing the use of machinery and evicting *yunteros* from the land. The result was a huge rise in 'forced' unemployment. A further strengthening of political support for rural property and a return to latifundist practice was achieved when Salazar Alonso, the conservative Minister of the Interior and a Radical deputy for Badajoz, launched a campaign which removed Socialist-controlled municipal councils from office.[42] When the FNTT called a national harvest strike in the early summer of 1934 to protest at worsening conditions in the countryside, Salazar Alonso declared a national emergency and authorized provincial civil governors to use all means possible to break the strike. In view of the level of unemployment and the state of preparedness of the authorities and agrarians in Badajoz, the strike was not surprisingly a failure despite being well supported. In a rerun of the situation in 1920, the *sociedades obreras* were suppressed, with *casas del pueblo* closed down and local labour leaders arrested, victimized and kept under close surveillance by the Civil Guard.[43] Though the organization of rural socialism in Badajoz appeared completely destroyed, agrarians maintained cultivation at a low level and strengthened the boycott again during the next agricultural cycle in a collective punishment of the workforce. There was also violence, when *fijos* and Civil Guards patrolling the estates opened fire on poachers and acorn-stealers desperate for food. Indeed, the pressure of hunger on labouring and sharecropping families was the chief means used by agrarians to take revenge and drive the rural workforce into submission.

Success in regaining the advantage in the political and syndical struggle with rural labour was not translated into permanent changes that could have entrenched the power of the elite into the social and economic fabric of the province. The limits to consensus in agrarian ranks and the contradictions of social-Catholic doctrines proved the main causes of this failure. During 1934–5 Catholic syndicates appeared in virtually every village as labourers and *yunteros* were dragooned into membership by unemployment and hunger.[44] However, agrarian satisfaction at this regimentation of the workforce was not accompanied by a general willingness to make the sacrifices necessary to realize the aim of converting latifundism into a stable sharecropping regime. Local efforts to encourage the voluntary distribution of land in secure sharecropping tenancies were bitterly resisted as an invitation to the self-destruction of the status and livelihood of agrarians. *Labradores* in particular saw the parcelling up of the estates into semi-independent plots as inevitably leading to their abolition, since landowners would have less incentive to use them as middlemen in a landlord and tenant system. Although there were agrarians who did pass over land at well-publicized ceremonies, in general the policy was a non-starter without the force of legislation behind it. However, when Giménez Fernández, the social-Catholic Minister of Agriculture, proposed measures to improve rural tenancies and to give security of tenure to *yunteros*, APA and the Federación de Propietarios were pushed by their memberships into resisting the measures and rejecting their own provincial deputy.[45]

Meanwhile, reliance on pure force as the only means to maintain agrarian power faltered in the face of disagreements with the Radicals. Alarmed at ever worsening social conditions in the countryside and threatened by the agrarians' naked ambition to complete their resurgence following the suppression of the Socialist movement, Radical mayors, some parliamentary deputies and the Civil Governor opposed any further drift towards total authoritarianism. When a new general election was suddenly called for February 1936, following the break-up of the Radicals as a national party and the removal of the CEDA from office, no effective conservative coalition was possible in Badajoz. Moreover, with the relaxation of repressive policies, agrarian organizations were faced with yet another revival of the *sociedades obreras* and the Socialist movement, which now constituted the major force in a provincial Popular Front committed to the final dissolution of the rural regime as rapidly as possible.

Following the victory of the Popular Front, agrarians abandoned their own organizations and looked entirely to outside intervention, principally from the army, for the destruction of all that the Republic had allowed on the land. Attempts to influence the vote in Badajoz by intimidation and bribery had proved futile. With access to political and syndical organization once again, rural labour immediately moved to take advantage of the shift in provincial and national administration that followed the election. As all the legislation of 1931–3 was reintroduced, labourers launched a wave of strikes across the province. Meanwhile, *yunteros* began physically to occupy estates of local agrarians, culminating in a mass land invasion that was later legalized by the new government.[46] Having previously faced the loss of effective control of the land, agrarians now contemplated the actual loss of the land itself, in what was effectively agrarian reform by direct action. APA disbanded and its leadership called for its supporters to put their faith in the conspiracies being prepared elsewhere against the regime. By July 1936 many had fled the countryside to the relative safety of Almendralejo, Mérida and Seville to await developments.

The Civil War brought a permanent settling of accounts in the countryside across the whole of the latifundist south. In the case of Badajoz the initial military rising of 18 July 1936 failed when the garrison in the provincial capital refused to act in support. Virtually without direction from Madrid or the provincial administration, real power effectively passed to local mayors and Popular Front committees that immediately acted to secure their areas for the Republic and seized the opportunity to make lasting changes. Supporters of the right, priests and Civil Guards, suspected of sympathy for the rising, were imprisoned and indeed in a few cases executed. Meanwhile, the estates, and in some cases smallholdings, of rightists, were expropriated and turned over to the *sociedades obreras*.[47] However, the local militias hastily improvised for defence proved no match for the Army of Africa that rapidly swept through Badajoz during August 1936 to link up with Nationalist forces already established in the province of Cáceres to the north.

Not surprisingly, agrarians and local rightists welcomed the advancing rebel troops as liberators from the collectivist rural order that was in the process of emerging, and acted alongside those returning from self-imposed exile to direct the fierce repression that immediately followed. Backed by the army, agrarian power was finally re-established, once again through the use of force but this time by the apocalyptical means of a white terror that physically eliminated the opposition at a grassroots level. Summary executions in the aftermath of conquest gave way to the more organized methods of the death squads operated by the rapidly expanding fascist Falange, and of the concentration camps established at Castuera and Mérida. Tens of thousands were killed and many more were imprisoned and sentenced to hard labour, in an act of massive vengeance that lasted into the postwar era.[48] In the process the agrarian elite became unconditional supporters of the new, strong Francoist state. In return the dictatorship provided an economic and political framework in the countryside which, in a manner analogous to Italian fascism, guaranteed agrarian incomes no matter what the cost and subordinated rural labour, giving twenty extra years of untroubled life to the estates and to an autocratic rural order.[49]

NOTES

1 A modern study is J. Vila Izquierdo, *Extremadura: la Guerra Civil* (Badajoz: 1983). P. Preston, 'The agrarian war in the south', in P. Preston (ed.), *Revolution and War in Spain 1931–1939* (London: 1984), pp. 159–81; M. Tuñón de Lara, *Tres claves de la Segunda República* (Madrid: 1985), pp. 21–212 gives recent surveys of the rural contribution to the origins of the war.

2 For this process see J. P. Merino Navarro, *La desamortización en Extremadura* (Madrid: 1976), esp. pp. 62–79 for figures; T. Martín Martín, *Notas sobre la desamortización en Extremadura* (Badajoz: 1975); I. F. Bohoyo Velásquez, *Situación socio-económica y condiciones de vida en la provincia de Badajoz 1880–1902* (Badajoz: 1984), pp. 11–22. Useful accounts of the previous pattern are F. Rey Velasco, *Historia económica y social de Extremadura a finales del antiguo régimen* (Badajoz: 1983); R. Herr, *The Eighteenth Century Revolution in Spain* (Princeton, NJ: 1958), pp. 90–119.

3 P. Carrión, *Los latifundios en España* (Madrid: 1932), table pp. 70–1 gives results. The survey defined as a large owner anyone possessing more than a total of 250 hectares of land. E. Malefakis, *Agrarian Reform and Peasant Revolution in Spain* (New Haven, Conn.: 1970), pp. 75–6, using the register of expropriable property drawn up under the Republic, identifies a further group of only 400 persons, many of whom were linked by family ties, that owned 26.6 per cent of the surface area of the province and 32.5 per cent of the cultivated area. See Merino Navarro, *Desamortización*, pp. 73–7 for the backgrounds of buyers.

4 Figures from Carrión, *Los latifundios*, tables pp. 50–1, 54–5, 160–80. Also E. Cerro, 'Algunos datos sobre la vida en la provincia', *Revista del Centro de Estudios Extremeños*, 2 (1927), p. 149. J. G. Carapeto, 'El siglo XIX en Extremadura: los grandes cambios', *Revista Alminar*, 12 (1980); J. Naredo, 'Antecedentes y características de una sociedad jerárquica', in M. Gaviría (ed.), *Extremadura saqueada* (Paris: 1978), pp. 13–17; A. Merino de Torres, *El obrero del campo*, 2nd edn (Badajoz: 1920), pp. 25–30, 49–51; J. Polo Benito, *El problema social del campo en Extremadura* (Salamanca: 1919), p. 62.

5 On field systems see J. Martín Galindo, *La dehesa extremeña como tipo de explotación agraria* (Valladolid: 1965), pp. 2–5.

6 Malefakis, *Agrarian Reform and Peasant Revolution*, p. 86; Cerro, 'Algunos datos sobre la vida en la provincia', pp. 149–50; Martín Galindo, *La dehesa extremeña*, pp. 13–14; J. Martínez Alier, *Labourers and Landowners in Southern Spain* (London: 1971), p. 28.

7 R. Herr, 'Spain', in D. Spring (ed.), *European Landed Elites in the Nineteenth Century* (Baltimore, Md: 1977), pp. 98–105. From this point the term 'agrarian' embraces landowners, *labradores* and managers.

8 On latifundism see Martínez Alier, *Labourers and Landowners*, pp. 20–2 and *passim*; M. Artola, *El latifundio* (Madrid: 1978), *passim*; Martín Galindo, *La dehesa extremeña*, pp. 2–4. For provincial geography and natural divisions see Instituto Nacional de Estadística, *Reseña estadística de la provincia de Badajoz* (Madrid: 1954), pp. 191–5; F. Hernández Pacheco, 'Bosquejo preliminar de las comarcas geográficas de Extremadura', *Boletín del Instituto de Reforma Agraria*, 16 (1933); Carrión, *Los latifundios*, table pp. 328–9.

9 Typical pictures of neglect are given in Carrión, *Los latifundios*, pp. 359–61; L. Marichalar, *La reforma agraria en España* (Madrid: 1931), pp. 56–7. For general descriptions of the animal economy see Naval Intelligence Division, *Spain and Portugal* (London: 1943), Vol. 3, p. 246; Martín Galindo, *La dehesa extremeña*, p. 2; Ministerio de Fomento, *Estudio de la Ganadería en España de 1917* (Madrid: 1920), Vol. I, p. 333; Polo Benito, *El problema social*, p. 24. *Censo de la Población: región de Badajoz 1930* gives figures for shepherds and foresters.

10 On the *Mesta* and its decline see J. Klein, *The Mesta* (Cambridge: 1920), pp. 99, 356 and *passim*; A. García Sanz, 'La agonía de la Mesta', in A. García Sanz and R. Garrabou (eds), *Historia agraria de la España contemporánea* (Barcelona: 1985), pp. 174–219; Naval Intelligence Division, *Spain and Portugal*, Vol. 3, p. 186.

11 J. J. Parsons, 'The cork oak forests and the evolution of the cork industry in southern Spain and Portugal', *Economic Geography*, 38 (July 1962), pp. 195–214. For an overview of agriculture and its limitations in these regions see Naval Intelligence Division, *Spain and Portugal*, Vol. 3, p. 184, and M. Gaviría (ed.), *El modelo extremeño: ecodesarrollo de La Serena y La Siberia* (Madrid: 1980), *passim*.

12 Malefakis, *Agrarian Reform and Peasant Revolution*, pp. 77–9, 117–18; Martínez Alier, *Labourers and Landowners*, pp. 20, 269; 'Share tenancy in Spain', *International Review of Agricultural Economics*, 1 (1923), pp. 19–36; Cerro, 'Algunos datos', pp. 153–5; Polo Benito, *El problema social*, pp. 60–2; Merino de Torres, *El obrero del campo*, pp. 16–23, 31–2.

13 J. Muñoz, 'La inserción de Extremadura en el mercado', in Gaviría, *Extremadura saqueada*, pp. 29–33; Naval Intelligence Division, *Spain and Portugal*, Vol. 3, pp. 184–6; G. Tortella, 'Agriculture: a slow moving sector, 1830–1935', in N. Sánchez Albornoz (ed.), *The Economic Modernization of Spain* (New York: 1987), pp. 47–54 gives a useful overview of cerealization.

14 Surveys gave figures for the number of *jornaleros* as 61,461 men and 9,176 women in 1921 and 88,032 in total for 1933. Consejo Provincial de Fomento de Badajoz, *Estadística Social Agraria* (Badajoz: 1921); report on provinces of Badajoz and Cáceres, in 'Actas del Comité Ejecutivo del Instituto de Reformas Agrarias' (May 1933), Archivo de la Guerra Civil

(Salamanca) [hereafter AGCS], sección de Madrid, legajo 662. On the organization and conditions of work see *Informe de la Comisión de Reformas Sociales* (Madrid: 1884); Instituto de Reformas Sociales, *Resúmen de la información acerca de los obreros agrícolas en las provincias de Andalucía y Badajoz* (Madrid: 1905); Polo Benito, *El problema social*, pp. 41–50; Merino de Torres, *El obrero del campo, passim*; J. C. Molano Gragera, *Introducción a la historia del movimiento obrero en Montijo* (Montijo: 1982), pp. 12–15.

15 *Censo de la población de España de 1930: región de Extremadura* gives a breakdown of urban occupations. Molano Gragera, *Movimiento obrero en Montijo*, p. 14 and J. Simeón Vidarte, *No queríamos al Rey* (Barcelona: 1977), pp. 19–20 give descriptions of shopkeepers and craftsmen in towns.

16 See A. M. Bernal, *La lucha por la tierra en la crisis del antiguo régimen* (Madrid: 1979), pp. 97–108; R. Carr, *Spain 1808–1975* (Oxford: 1982), pp. 402–3.

17 The provincial situation is described in Vidarte, *No queríamos al Rey*, pp. 50–1; J. Raya, 'Anatomía del caciquismo extremeño', *Revista de Estudios Extremeños* (1980), pp. 45–58; Merino de Torres, *El obrero del campo*, pp. 49–52; Bohoyo Velásquez, *Situación socio-económica*, pp. 53–9. On the continuing controversy concerning the nature of *caciquismo* see Herr, 'Spain', in Spring, *European Landed Elites*, pp. 111–19.

18 N. Pérez y Giménez, *Estudio físico, médico y social de la comarca de la Serena y la de Cabeza del Buey en particular* (Badajoz: 1888) gives a fascinating picture of one town. Bohoyo Velásquez, *Situación socio-económica*, pp. 24–6; Merino de Torres, *El obrero del campo*, pp. 9–10, 101–2; and Polo Benito, *El problema social*, pp. 30–5 contrast the conditions of different sections of society.

19 See Merino de Torres, *El obrero del campo*, pp. 61, 84–8 and Molano Gragera, *Movimiento obrero en Montijo*, p. 13 on elite paternalism.

20 On attitudes to religious practice and charity see W. J. Callahan, *Church, Politics and Society in Spain 1750–1874* (Cambridge, Mass.: 1984), pp. 242–4, 276; F. Lannon, *Privilege, Persecution and Prophecy: The Catholic Church in Spain 1875–1975* (Oxford: 1987), pp. 13–16, 75–7; and Merino de Torres, *El obrero del campo*, p. 100.

21 Bohoyo Velásquez, *Situación socio-económica*, pp. 89–109; J. Raya Tellez, 'El movimiento obrero en Badajoz: aproximaciones a sus orígenes', *Revista Alminar* (1979); Molano Gragera, *Movimiento obrero en Montijo*, pp. 15–17.

22 On the development of anarchism see J. Díaz del Moral, *Historia de las agitaciones campesinas andaluzas* (Madrid: 1973); T. Kaplan, *Anarchists of Andalusia 1868–1903* (Princeton, NJ: 1977); C. E. Lida, 'Agrarian anarchism in Andalusia', *International Review of Social History*, 3 (1969), pp. 315–52.

23 For the evolution of *sociedades*, their aims and early activities see Bohoyo Velásquez, *Situación socio-económica*, pp. 121–34; Molano Gragera, *Movimiento obrero en Montijo*, pp. 34–43; Merino de Torres, *El obrero del campo*, pp. 39, 90; Polo Benito, *El problema social*, pp. 15–16; P. Biglino, *El socialismo español y la cuestión agraria 1890–1936* (Madrid: 1986), p. 100.

24 See Merino de Torres, *El obrero del campo*, pp. 36, 90–1; Molano Gragera, *Movimiento obrero en Montijo*, pp. 24–5, 37; Bohoyo Velásquez, *Situación socio-económica*, p. 128 on agrarian reactions and tactics.

25 J. Harrison, *The Spanish Economy in the Twentieth Century* (Beckenham: 1985), p. 46. In fact food prices in Badajoz seem to have run ahead of national inflation, with constant complaints of local speculation by shopkeepers. Molano Gragera, *Movimiento obrero en Montijo*, p. 45 gives figures for rises in the prices of potatoes (218 per cent), sugar (153 per cent) and eggs (211 per cent) for 1914–16 alone.

26 Federación Provincial Socialista de Badajoz, *El fascismo sobre Extremadura* (Madrid: 1938), pp. 9–10; Polo Benito, *El problema social*, pp. 12–16; Vidarte, *No queríamos al Rey*, pp. 47–66; Molano Gragera, *Movimiento obrero en Montijo*, pp. 47–8; Biglino, *El socialismo español y la cuestión agraria*, pp. 195–8, 523.

27 E. Fernández Santana, *La cuestión social en Extremadura* (Los Santos: 1935), *passim*; Merino de Torres, *El obrero del campo*, pp. 5, 41; Polo Benito, *El problema social*, p. 8; Consejo Provincial de Fomento, *Cartilla redactada para dar a conocer los trabajos que se realizan en la Granja Escela* (Badajoz: 1913); A. Guerra, *Bosquejo histórico de la economía agraria en Badajoz y su término* (Badajoz: 1979), pp. 9–14.

28 For rehearsals of these proposals see Polo Benito, *El problema social*, pp. 50–5, 60–2; Merino de Torres, *El obrero del campo*, pp. 43–7; Consejo Provincial de Fomento, *Folleto de las conferencias dadas durante la semana agrícola 12–16 nov. 1912* (Badajoz: 1913); A. Cruz Valero, *Para los propietarios extremeños* (Badajoz: 1936); N. Ortega, 'Política hidráulica', pp. 112–15. See also G. Blanco Nieto, 'Escuelas y sindicatos: la obra social de Ezequiel Fernández Santana', *Revista Alminar* (1982). In 1910 some 42 banks and syndicates were reported in the province, though their effectiveness seems to have been minimal: see Instituto de Reformas Sociales, *Estadística de Asociaciones* (Madrid: 1917), pp. 8–9. During the war these merged into the Confederación Nacional Católico-Agraria (CNCA): J. J. Castillo, *Propietarios muy pobres. Sobre la subordinación política del pequeño campesino* (Madrid: 1979), p. 75–81 and *passim*.

29 See the social-Catholic magazine *Ara y Canta*, 31 August 1927, 5 July 1928; Unión Patriótica, *Barógrafo de un lustro: memoria demonstrativa del avance dada por la provincia de Badajoz desde el 13 de septiembre de 1923 a igual fecha del 1928* (Madrid: 1929), pp. 91–2, 124–7; Molano Gragera, *Movimiento obrero en Montijo*, pp. 49–50; S. Ben-Ami, *Fascism from Above. The Dictatorship of Primo de Rivera in Spain 1923–1930* (Oxford: 1983), pp. 128, 136–42.

30 Ministerio de Fomento, *Estudio de la ganadería*; Consejo Provincial de Fomento de Badajoz, *Estadística social*, gives figures of 1,783,744 down to 1,251,456 of all animal types. Unión Patriótica, *Barógrafo de un lustro*, pp. 153–60 gives details of organization. *Ara y Canta*, 5 June 1927, 31 August 1927 have articles containing attacks.

31 International Labour Organization, 'Agrarian conditions in Spain', *Reports 2, series K* (1928), pp. 4–5; *Ara y Canta*, 20 March 1930; Malefakis, *Agrarian Reform and Peasant Revolution*, pp. 77–9; Merino de Torres, *El obrero del campo*, pp. 17–18.

32 For a detailed examination of Badajoz under the Republic see T. Rees, 'Agrarian society and politics in the province of Badajoz under the Second Spanish Republic, 1931–36', DPhil thesis, University of Oxford, 1990.

33 *Ara y Canta*, 25 June 1928; Ben-Ami, *Fascism from Above*, pp. 301–2.

34 M. Pidal, *La farsa del llamado problema de yunteros en Extremadura* (Madrid: 1934), *passim*; 'Cuestiones agrarias', *El Correo Extremeño* (Badajoz), 28 February 1931; J. Hernández Andreu, *España y la crisis de 29* (Madrid: 1986), pp. 31, 69–90.

35 See local press reports in *El Correo Extremeño*, 8–14 April 1931; *La Libertad de Badajoz* (Badajoz), 10–14 April 1931; *La Vanguardia de Badajoz* (Badajoz), 14 April 1931.

36 *El Correo Extremeño*, 8 May 1931; *La Voz Extremeña*, 9 May 1931; *Anuario Español de Política-Social* (Madrid: 1935), pp. 186–99, 419–22; *El Socialista*, 10 October 1932; FNTT, *Memoria: II congreso* (Madrid: 1932), pp. 40–6.

37 On these efforts, undermined by agrarian disunity and too close an identification with the unpopular monarch, see *El Correo Extremeño*, 10–26 June 1931; *La Voz Extremeña* and *La Libertad de Badajoz*, 1–25 June 1931.

38 *La Libertad de Badajoz* and *El Correo Extremeño*, 6 July 1931; M. Cabrera, *La patronal ante la II República* (Madrid: 1983), pp. 66–71.

39 *Hoy* (Badajoz), 14 January, 17 January, 9 March, 30 May 1933; *La Libertad de Badajoz*, 9 March 1933; J. R. Montero, *La CEDA. El Catolicismo social y político en la II República*, 2 vols (Madrid: 1977), Vol. I, pp. 394–5, 436; F. Rosique Navarro, *La reforma agraria en Badajoz durante la II República* (Badajoz: 1988).

40 On Radicals and alliance see *Hoy*, 19 April 1933; *La Libertad de Badajoz*, 20 April 1933; R. Salazar Alonso, *Bajo el signo de la revolución* (Madrid: 1935), pp. 24–5; J. Simeón Vidarte, *El bienio negro* (Barcelona: 1978), pp. 30–3.

41 For the campaign and APA programme see *Hoy*, 20 October to 19 November 1933; *La Libertad de Badajoz*, 2–19 November 1933. On conditions in the province see *El Obrero de la Tierra* (Madrid), 3 June 1933; *Boletín del Instituto de Reforma Agraria*, May and July 1933.

42 *El Obrero de la Tierra*, 6 January, 13 January, 20 January 1934; Salazar Alonso, *Bajo el signo de la revolución*, pp. 115–29; *Hoy*, 9 March to 22 May 1934.

43 *Hoy*, 30 May to 20 June 1934; *El Socialista*, 27–30 June 1934; Molano Gragera, *Movimiento obrero en Montijo*, pp. 64–5; Federación Provincial Socialista, *El fascismo*, p. 5.

44 *Hoy*, 21 January 1936 gives figures of 28 and 91 for the rise in the numbers of syndicates between 1934 and 1935. See also Castillo, *Propietarios muy pobres*, p. 289.

45 Malefakis, *Agrarian Reform and Peasant Revolution*, pp. 347–55.
46 *El Obrero de la Tierra*, 4 April 1936; Federación Provincial Socialista, *El fascismo*, p. 13.
47 Vila Izquierdo, *Extremadura: la Guerra Civil*, pp. 27–32; Molano Gragera, *Movimiento obrero en Montijo*, pp. 69–71. Reports on 63 towns and villages compiled by the Falange soon after the capture of the province show the relatively few executions of rightists, in contrast to Nationalist propaganda at the time. Noticeably, it was major rightist centres such as Almendralejo where numbers were greatest. AGCS, sección de Extremadura, legajo 24.
48 On the campaign and terror see the accounts of Vila Izquierdo, *Extremadura: la Guerra Civil*, pp. 32–3, 37–94, 157–66; Molano Gragera, *Movimiento obrero en Montijo*, pp. 77–80. For contemporary views, see Federación Provincial Socialista, *El fascismo*, pp. 17–32; *El Obrero de la Tierra*, 10 October 1936. Calculations of the number of victims, impossible to verify, range up to 40,000.
49 E. Sevilla Guzmán, *La evolución del campesinado en España* (Barcelona: 1979), pp. 125–73 details Francoist policy.

List of contributors

Ralph Gibson is Lecturer in French History in the Departments of History and Modern Languages at Lancaster University. He is the author of *A Social History of French Catholicism, 1789–1914* and of articles on religion, society and culture in France between the Revolution and the First World War.

Martin Blinkhorn is Professor of Modern European History at Lancaster University. His publications include *Carlism and Crisis in Spain 1931–1939*, the edited volumes *Spain in Conflict 1931–1939. Democracy and its Enemies* and *Fascists and Conservatives. The Radical Right and the Establishment in Twentieth-Century Europe*, and numerous articles and essays on the history of modern Spain.

Anthony L. Cardoza is Professor of History at Loyola University, Chicago, and the author of *Agrarian Elites and Italian Fascism: The Province of Bologna, 1901–1926.*

Eric J. Evans is Professor of Social History and Director of the Centre for Social History at Lancaster University. He is the author of *The Contentious Tithe: the Tithe Problem and English Agriculture, 1750–1850* and *The Forging of the Modern State: Early Industrial Britain, 1783–1870.*

K. Theodore Hoppen is Reader in History at the University of Hull. Among his numerous publications on the history of Ireland are *Elections, Politics and Society in Ireland 1832–1885* and *Ireland since 1800: Conflict and Conformity.*

Pierre Lévêque is Professor of History at the University of Burgundy, Dijon. His state doctorate has been published in two volumes: *Une société provinciale: la Bourgogne sous la Monarchie de Juillet* and *Une société en crise: la Bourgogne au milieu du XIXe siècle.*

Jonathan Osmond is Lecturer in History at the University of Leicester, the author of several articles on modern German history and a contributor to R. G. Moeller (ed.), *Peasants and Lords in Modern Germany: Recent Studies in Agricultural History.* His book, *Rural Protest in the Weimar Republic: the Free Peasantry in the Rhineland and Bavaria*, is forthcoming.

Gregory W. Pedlow directs NATO's historical programme in Europe, as Chief of the Historical Section at Supreme Headquarters Allied Powers Europe (SHAPE), Belgium. He is the author of *The Survival of the Hessian Nobility, 1770–1870* and two classified official histories, *The CIA and Overhead Reconnaissance 1954–1974* and *LIVE OAK and the Preservation of Allied Access to West Berlin 1959–1990.*

Tim Rees is Lecturer in History at the University of Exeter. He is the author of a University of Oxford DPhil thesis, 'Agrarian society and politics in the province of Badajoz under the Spanish Second Republic, 1931–1936'.

Hanna Schissler is Senior Research Fellow at the German Historical Institute, Washington, DC, and a Research Associate at the Georg-Eckert-Institut für internationale Schulbuchforschung, Braunschweig. Among her publications are *Preussische Agrargesellschaft im Wandel. Wirtschaftliche, gesellschaftliche und politische Transformationsprozesse von 1763–1847*, *Preussische Finanzpolitik* and, with Volker Berghahn, *National Identity and Perceptions of the Past.*

Frank M. Snowden is Professor of History at Yale University. He is the author of two major books, *Violence and Great Estates in the South of Italy: Apulia, 1900–1922* and *The Fascist Revolution in Tuscany, 1919–1922.*

Donald Sutherland is Professor of History at the University of Maryland and author of *The Chouans: the Social Origins of Popular Counterrevolution in Upper Brittany* and *France 1789–1815. Revolution and Counterrevolution.*

Index